Bruce A. Scholten is Honorary Research Fellow in the Department of Geography, Durham University. He has written on agricultural policy for a variety of international publications and his current research focus is the political economy of food. He grew up on a dairy farm near Lynden, Washington, USA.

This is an extremely well-documented and innovative analysis of the dairy cooperative initiative in India and its impact on small producers. Bruce A. Scholten provides a critical understanding of the role of global-local interaction in the growth and development of this sector and the resultant contradictions. An essential reading for researchers working on India's contemporary development scenario.

Swapna Banerjee-Guha, Tata Institute of Social Science Mumbai, and author of *Spatial Dynamics of International Capital*

This is a fascinating and important book. Its account of Operation Flood and subsequent developments provides an important basis for understanding the modernisation of Indian agriculture - still a vital part of the country's ever-growing economy - and yields insights into India's relationships with its former aid donors and now trading partners. Bruce A. Scholten's analysis of the politics of dairying in India also tells us a great deal about centre vs. state politics and the problems of steering such a vast and diverse economy into the global era of the twenty-first century.

Peter J. Atkins, Professor of Geography, Durham University, and co-author of *Food in Society*

This book is worth a serious look. Most publications on Operation Flood focus on minutiae, but *India's White Revolution* takes long-term data to show the national-scale success of cooperative dairying in India. After finishing his initial academic research on Operation Flood, Bruce A. Scholten visited Anand. He understood that European dairy gifts could have been a Trojan Horse to neo-colonial dependence. This book shows how farmers in the Anand Pattern monetised EEC commodities to improve India's food security. Now that the World Bank plans to replicate India's success in Africa, the world should understand how and why it worked. The book recounts the Jha Committee Report of 1984, which stressed the importance of price incentives to stimulate village milk production to multiply consumption in a growing population. I dreamed of a country where city people enjoy affordable dairy products, while farm families earn income, education and health benefits by producing that milk. Part of the dream has been fulfilled and the dairy revolution could be fully won, wherever the principles of cooperative farming are applied.

Verghese Kurien, Chair (retd) National Dairy Development Board, winner 1989 World Food Prize, and author of *I Too Had a Dream*

INDIA'S WHITE REVOLUTION

Operation Flood, Food Aid and Development

Bruce A. Scholten

TAURIS ACADEMIC STUDIES
an imprint of

I.B.Tauris Publishers
LONDON • NEW YORK

Published in 2010 by Tauris Academic Studies
An imprint of I.B. Tauris & Co Ltd
6 Salem Road, London W2 4BU
175 Fifth Avenue, New York NY 10010
www.ibtauris.com

Distributed in the United States and Canada exclusively by Palgrave Macmillan, 175 Fifth Avenue, New York NY 10010

Library of Development Studies 1

ISBN 978 1 84885 176 4

A full CIP record for this book is available from the British Library
A full CIP record for this book is available from the Library of Congress
Library of Congress catalog card: available

Printed and bound in India by Thomson Press
Camera-ready copy edited and supplied by the author.

CONTENTS

LIST OF ILLUSTRATIONS

Charts

Maps

Tables

Photos

GLOSSARY & ABBREVIATIONS

Additionality: use of food aid to provide additional consumption for people whose 'incomes are too low for them to buy sufficient food'.[1]

AI: artificial insemination of dairy cows or other animals.

BO: butter oil; accompanied SMP as dairy aid from the EEC to India.

BST: (bovine somatotropin) natural hormone stimulating milk production; genetically engineered as rBST or rBGH (bovine growth hormone).

Bt: biotechnology.

CAP: Common Agricultural Policy (of the EU *aka* EC or EEC or Common Market).

CFA: Committee on Food Aid Policies and Programmes; oversees WFP.

CUP: Cambrigge University Press.

DC: developed country. This book alternates the older acronym IC (industrialised country) with DC to denote rich countries with advanced service sectors.

Dairist: person engaged in dairying.

Dudhia: petty dairy marketeer or milk vendor.

EEC: European Economic Community. This book alternates EEC with the European Communities (EC) est. in 1957 Treaty of Rome; called European Union (EU) in 1992 Maastricht Treaty.

FAO: Food and Agriculture Organisation of the UN.

FFW: food-for-work, i.e. food aid as partial payment, e.g. in road-building.

GATT: General Agreement on Tariffs & Trade; followed by WTO 1995.

GCMMF: Gujarat Cooperative Milk Marketing Federation.

GE/GM: genetically engineered/genetically modified.

GOI: Government of India.

IC: industrialised or developed country (DC). ICs comprise 'The North'.

IDC: Indian Dairy Corporation.

IFAD: International Fund for Agricultural Development (UN).

IMF: International Monetary Fund.

IFPRI: International Food Policy Research Institute.

ISO 9000 series: benchmark standards est. with Codex Alimentarius.

LDC: unless specified, used collectively in here for poor countries, including less developed countries (LDCs), low-income-food-deficit countries (LIFD), and what formerly were termed least-developed countries (LLDCs). LDCs are sometimes called the Third World or the Global South. (In 1991 the UN redefined 'least developed countries' or LDCs as 'low-income countries that are suffering from long-term handicaps to growth, in particular low levels of human resource development and/or severe structural weakness.'[1] Previously, LDCs were often defined as 'less developed countries' and LLDCs as 'least developed.') The World Bank Development Report (1996) estimates the poverty line (GNP per capita in weighted $US) at $380w in low-income countries including China and India, and at $360w for other low-income countries.[2]

lpd/lmpd: litres per day; litres of milk per day, etc.

MAFF: Ministry of Agriculture, Fisheries and Food (United Kingdom).

Metric/US measures: 1.016 metric tonnes/US long ton. 0.454 kilograms = US lb. Metric tonne = 2204.6 US pounds.[3] 3.785 litres = US gallon. (0.454 kg./US lb.) Milk weighs ca. 1.03 kg./litre = 0.975 kg./US quart = 8.6 US pounds per gallon.

NFU: National Farmers Union (Great Britain).

NDDB: National Dairy Development Board; later merged with IDC.

NGO: non-governmental organisation; e.g. Christian Aid or Oxfam.

NMGS: National Milk Grid System; milk transport infrastructure in India.

NTB: nontariff barriers, e.g. quotas or voluntary export restraints (VERs).

NY: New York. (*NYC*: New York City).

OF: Operation Flood, world's largest food aid project in India.

OUP: Oxford University Press.

PL 480: Public Law 480, basis for US food aid operations since 1954.

PM: Prime Minister.

Reciprocity: 'symmetric rights and obligations of member states'.[4]

SAPs: structural adjustment programmes, as mandated on debtor countries by the IMF.

SMP: skimmed milk powder; nonfat dry milk powder (NDMP) in US.

Tariffication: clarifying hidden tariffs or protection against imports.

Third World: connoting LDCs or the South, compared to the Western First World (*aka* ICs, DCs, the North), or ex-socialist Second World.

Triangular operations: food bought in one LDC, sent as food aid to another.

UHT: ultra high temperature processing of milk.

USDA: United States Department of Agriculture.

URAA: Uruguay Round Agricultural Agreement.

VER: voluntary export restraint/restriction. A form of nontariff barrier.

WFP: World Food Programme.

WTO: World Trade Organisation; superseded most GATT roles, 1995.

zebus: non-descript Indian cattle.

ACKNOWLEDGEMENTS

Colleagues from farms to universities around the world deserve gratitude. A shortlist begins with Steve Larson at *Hoard's Dairyman* for helping me grow as a writer, and Michael Griffin and Barbara Senfter at FAO-Rome Dairy Outlook for hosting debates online. Thanks to those who read manuscript drafts including Peter J. Atkins at Durham University, and P.R. Gupta of *Dairy India Yearbook*. Thanks to sources at AMUL, GCMMF, IRMA, NDDB and elsewhere in India for interviews and information. Plaudits to I.B.Tauris editors David Stonestreet and Joanna Godfrey, and also to Randall Pederson, Rola Naeb and Lucy Smout. Thanks to family and friends for keeping me true. Love to Martha Clemewell Young-Scholten who captured pictures in this book and much more. Errors are my responsibility, and your comments are welcome.

1. Old & young cows & herders on Anand-Ahmedabad road.

The cow is the foster mother of the human race. From the time of the ancient Hindoo to this time have the thoughts of men turned to this kindly and beneficent creature as one of the chief sustaining forces of human life. - W.D. Hoard, 1885

PREFACE

A need to understand the role of family farming in the world economy motivated this book. My boyhood community around Lynden in Washington State was dominated by Dutch immigrants to American pastures, cleared from forest previously occupied by Native Americans in the Nooksack River Valley. As 10-year-old schoolchildren, teachers startled us with predictions that economic prospects made it unlikely many of us would be dairy farmers. A decade later, our farmers' dairy cooperative, which formerly supplied the region with speciality cheeses, ice cream and other products, refocused on supplying dry milk powder to the world market when President Richard Nixon and agricultural secretary Earl Butz claimed the USA must feed the world. The policy was actually promulgated to feed the Treasury, emptied by inflationary spending in the Vietnam War. For awhile our coop prospered, paying dividends to farmers.

Each year we heard that cheaper foreign competitors threatened our market niche. This was puzzling, as my schoolmates and I assumed our geographic factors of rich soil, plentiful rain, and intensive breeding and production technology, coupled with cheap petroleum and hydro-electric power, made our region's dairy export position unassailable. Our suspicion was that foreign export successes were based on unfair advantage or government subsidies, and so our local sentiments were expressed as a desire for 'a level playing field' on the world market. At the same time, the push-pull factors of US farming meant that real farm-gate prices decreased gradually, and greater production was required to earn the same income. As an uncle expressed it, 'In the 1950s a farmer could succeed with 20 cows. Now you can hardly make it with 200.'

Although seldom eager to rise for morning milking, I have burned the midnight oil trying to determine whether or not small farms everywhere are doomed. This book is an outcome of those studies and focuses on Operation Flood in India's White Revolution because so much can be illuminated by it. It is a case relevant to the Group of 8 major industrialized countries' agreement of 2009 to replace food aid with sustainable agriculture in Africa.

Hindsight shows that the success of the Marshall Plan in rebuilding post-war Europe inadvertently boosted Western hubris. Inept attempts at poverty alleviation in poor countries and the non-aligned world masked Cold War rivalry; there was too little understanding of colonialism and the disruption that lingered after independence. There were successes: Norway and The Netherlands won reputations as honest development partners, and the USA facilitated land reforms in some Asian countries. However, Western policy makers too often touted solutions with little distinction for technology appropriate to conditions abroad; they credited Western dairy productivity to high-technology but overlooked the subsidies in which their own industries were embedded. Food aid was often the smiley face of surplus disposal, benefiting special interests in donor countries and disrupting farming in recipient countries.

So, it was with suspicion that I studied Operation Flood (OF, or Flood), the world's largest dairy and food development programme assisted by the World Food Programme, World Bank, and non-government organisations such as Oxfam. Obviously, the European Economic Community - then the EEC, now the European Union or EU - sought to: maintain its farm policy status quo, dispose of its Butter Mountain, and earn political cachet such as the USA enjoyed via cereal food aid. But critics warned that Europe's dairy commodity aid could be a 'Trojan Horse' to dairy dependence, ensuring economic exclusion for India's village farmers.

After nurturing by Prime Minister Lal Shastri in the 1960s, the parastatal National Dairy Development Board (NDDB) was established in the small town of Anand, Gujarat, where it led replication of its Amul cooperative pattern in much of the country. This tale examines the official span of Operation Flood, 1970-96, in which EEC dairy commodities were monetised to fund national processing and transport infrastructure.

There was much controversy. Western experts advised India's dairists to switch from Buffalo to Holstein-Friesian cattle, partly because it was supposedly 'impossible' to make milk powder from buffalo milk. This was bad advice, which coop leaders including Tribhuvandas Patel and Verghese Kurien soon proved wrong. But that did not stop detractors from dubbing the White Revolution a 'black lie'. Claims that dairying could benefit women and minorities attracted funding, but critics accused OF of unmet goals. Worse, warned detractors, Europe's lactic largess imperilled the labour and environmental advantages of India's low-input/low-output buffalo-based dairying. OF officials replied that they were simply accomplishing their mission to improve the national milk marketing system. Yet, proper pricing ensured that aid did not disincentivise farmers and, once production was stimulated, EEC dairy aid ceased. Operation Flood is the exception to the rule that food aid does more harm than good.

Eventually, my doubts on Operation Flood were dispelled by data from the Food and Agricultural Organisation of the United Nations (FAO-UN) on which most illustrations in this book are based. *Dairy India 2007* reports that India tripled dairy production and nearly doubled per capita availability during Flood as population soared. In 1998 the World Bank reported positive 'poverty effects' attributed to OF including more reliable incomes, primary education for girls and boys, and encouragement of ancillary rural enterprises. As the overall farm sector declined, researchers from the Government of India's Central Statistical Organisation, the International Food Policy Research Institute, and the FAO found that dairying thrived at about 5.5 per cent of national GDP, bringing income to 70 million families – about 10 million of which participated in the cooperative Anand Pattern (CSO 2001; IFPRI-FAO 2002). As comparator countries declined, India rose from its dairy stagnation of the 1960s, and in the late-1990s bypassed the USA as the world's largest milk producer. Coop dairying readied India for a small but growing role as a low-cost exporter, meeting ISO 9000 standards in the WTO era. Despite reduced EU and US surpluses in the new century, dairy aid remains appropriate in emergency aid, and in structural adjustment in some countries suffering food insecurity.

In the 1990s dairy development fell from academic discourse – a lapse that coincided with release of FAO data showing strong improvement in India's dairy fortunes. In subsequent years, I noticed that students asking about Operation Flood were familiar only with books criticising it. This was regrettable because millions more people could benefit from coop dairying inside and outside India.

Interest returned in 2008 when the World Bank underlined its regard for India's low-input/low-output Anand Pattern, and announced plans to replicate it in Africa. Meanwhile EU and US foundations plan another Green Revolution in Africa. Some experts urge large-scale use of genetically-modified technologies to solve food crises in Africa. But the case of Operation Flood suggests that we ask exactly whom such fixes benefit and consider whether political-economic reform and public agricultural research could assure people's entitlements to food better than big commercial ventures.

Analysis of the rhetoric and outcomes of aid and trade negotiations reveals that, just as farm families in poor countries can suffer at the whims of rich countries, family farmers in rich countries can also be sacrificed to the benefit of powerful actors in their own economies. Adam Smith might agree that India's White Revolution has been successful due to the cooperative efforts of its small farmers, akin to those of coop farmers fighting for survival in my home community.

- Bruce A. Scholten

'All for ourselves and nothing for other people seems, in every age of the world, to have been the vile maxim of the masters of mankind.'
- Adam Smith (1776 *The Wealth of Nations*)

Chapter 1

After the Deluge

Why Operation Flood requires a summing up

Whither the Butter Mountain, the Milk Lake? Massive flows of European dairy commodity aid made India the world's ultimate battleground in the White Revolution. Called Operation Flood, its scope exceeded by most counts even major campaigns in the Green Revolution in cereals. Today milk represents more economic output in India than rice, oilseeds or wheat, and despite decades of doom-saying by pessimists, the country has surpassed the United States as the world's top dairy producer.

Launched in July 1970 and wound down a quarter-century later in 1996 Operation Flood was indeed an enormous experiment. Its origins were a small but portentous farmers' revolt, 50 years earlier in the Charotar area of Kaira district in the present state of Gujarat. The early story is well told elsewhere, by writers such as Ruth Heredia, but some points bear repeating here.

An important moment in decades of campaigning to *get the prices right* - pricing is a recurring theme in this book - came when farmers heeded advice from nationalist leader Sardar Vallabhbhai Patel to boycott milk deliveries to Polson Ltd., the private monopoly supplier to Bombay (Mumbai), 400 kilometers to the south. After a 15 day strike led by Shri Morarji Desai, who was destined to be Indian Finance Minister a decade later, and Tribhuvandas Kishibhai Patel - Anand born, Tribhuvandas had pamphleteerd for such action from 1920 - the farmers won control of their milk supply. The milk commissioner of Bombay agreed to bypass the middleman, Polson Model Dairy, and buy milk directly from the farmers' cooperative.

So began the Kaira District Cooperative Milk Producers Union Ltd. (KDCMPU), led by Tribhuvandas Patel, on December 14, 1946. Initially, coops from the villages of Kaira supplied barely 250 litres per day (lpd) of milk to the union, and its detractors said coop members had won just enough freedom to embarrass themselves. But despite the deplorable state of the equipment, the farmers and a few hired technocrats gradually raised output to 5000 lpd, while they planned a major increase to the 'value-added' of their production with construction of a modern plant. Investment in this infrastructure transformed surplus milk from the flush season into milk powder and butter to be sold in the hot, lean summer months, raising total annual coop sales, and moderating fluctuations in earnings.

But such business-speak masks the benefits this infrastructure meant to farm families. Most were small-holders, marginal and landless households whose menfolk depended on seasonal labour on larger arable estates for cash income, while women and children tended one or two cows or buffalo around the family home. In such circumstances, increasing reliable cash-flow by a few rupees means a great deal.

With financial assistance from UNICEF and the Government of New Zealand, and technical assistance from the FAO, the Rs. 5 million dairy factory was inaugurated by Prime Minister Jawaharlal Nehru on October 31, 1955. In later years, detractors of the White Revolution claimed that coop successes, if any, were due to Government favouritism. From the vantage point of the twenty-first century, it seems obvious that while foreign and domestic governments lent assistance, their often haphazard extension of dairy aid could just as easily have wrecked indigenous farmers' milk markets in India. In the end, the fact that farmers - and the professional administrators they employed - responded adroitly to powerful political and economic forces was the secret of their success. Reasonable decisions, made cooperatively in response to successive challenges (from unfair monopoly by Polson to later bullying by international institutions) ensured farmers' survival, long-term supply to consumers and ultimately, India's dairy autonomy.

In 1955, Kaira Union became parent to Anand Milk Union Ltd., known as Amul - an acronym meaning 'priceless' or 'happiness' in Sanskrit. In his lively biography of Verghese Kurien, the man who after Tribhuvandas Patel came to personify Amul, M.V. Kamath[1] writes:

> To appreciate what Anand has done, one must imagine India without Anand, where the market was open to multinationals fully to exploit. Till Amul came on the scene the only packaged butter known to the consumer was Polson's and Anchor Brand. The only cheese with which people were familiar was Kraft's. The only baby food was Cow and Gate. In the whole area of milk and milk products Amul has pushed back the multinationals.

Today Amul brand holds predominant market share against the doughty multinational corporations (MNCs) mentioned by Kamath, and other giants such as Glaxo and Nestlé. Kamath found it ironic that 'ignorant writers' had accused Kurien of opening India to MNCs. On the touchy issue of food aid (typified by US Public Law 480 which, with mixed success, scattered mostly surplus grain worldwide after World War II) Kamath maintains: 'Kurien never used the gift of milk powder and butter oil to achieve self-reliance by selling the gift at a price below that of the domestic producers. It is the reverse of the case of PL 480 wheat.'

Adherents to the 'great man' theory of history might argue that the Kaira Union would never have flourished without the almost accidental hiring of Verghese Kurien, who was engaged by Tribhuvandas Patel in 1949.[2]

Be that as it may, Kurien had earned an MSc in metallurgy at Michigan State University before returning to work off his scholarship debt to the Government of India (GOI) in the Gujarati cow town of Anand. His *alma mater* was eventually to award Kurien an honorary doctorate, after his career took a slightly unexpected turn. Although Kurien had minored in dairy engineering, this expertise was secondary to another characteristic Tribhuvandas sought to harness - Kurien's bent for independence. A maverick who delights in being called a 'monster' by the opponents of farmers' cooperatives, Kurien provides further clues to his complex strengths and loyalties by describing himself as: 'A meat-eating atheist - until someone criticises Indian Christians! Then I'm a Christian from Kerala.'

Family connections in the steel industry, a heavily-subsidised pet of Nehruvian socialism, could have found Kurien a sinecure. But, fleeing the taint of nepotism, Kurien was finally persuaded by Tribhuvandas to remain at his job in Anand. Before long he was chief strategist in what became India's dairy revolution.

By the mid-1960s the farmers' cooperative union, by then known interchangeably as Amul or Anand, was distinguished by its prosperity, self-reliance - and its leadership accountable to votes by the farmers themselves. Anand's assistance in organising similarly successful dairy coops in neighbouring Mehsana, Surat and other districts, was appreciated by powerful figures in Delhi. In 1965, PM Lal Shastri ordered establishment of a National Dairy Development Board (NDDB) whose purpose was to replicate 'Anand Pattern' dairy coops across India. Kurien and colleagues drew up plans for the optimistically-titled operation to flood a country parched by milk famines.

Operation Flood was one of the most controversial development schemes of the Cold War period, and it was played out against a backdrop of global conflict on several levels. The victors of World War II, fronted by the USA and the USSR, fought for the hearts and minds of the non-aligned or so-called Third World of developing countries, in a bi-polar struggle between capitalism and communism. The exponents of these rival ideologies deployed all the carrots and sticks at their disposal, e.g. financial, technical and food aid, propaganda, military alliances and adventures. As this East-West struggle continued the food production and distribution facilities of - primarily - the West which had boomed during World War II, began to erode the terms-of-trade of agricultural exporters in the Third World. Economists such as Jagdish Bhagwati, Anderson & Tyers, as well as Hoekman & Kostecki have detailed how this erosion was exacerbated by GATT rules on import tariffs and export subsidies which blocked poor country food exports after 1947.

The worst culprit was Western Europe, especially after the establishment of the European Economic Community (EEC) in 1957, whose farm exports, subsidised by the Common Agricultural Policy (CAP), further weakened poor countries' export potential. Talk of a 'North-South' divide began to replace rhetoric about the East-West conflict. Economic development among the 'Asian Tigers' such as Japan and Taiwan was sceptically ascribed to their status as clients of the Western capitalist alliance (if not the authoritarian nature of their regimes, which could manage their export-led economies more by *fiat* than relatively democratic India). Meanwhile, to the extent that developing countries emulated the bureaucracy and price regulation of centrally-planned Eastbloc economies, they often sabotaged their own development.

It was an ideological conflagration worthy of the Apocalypse - or the Bhagavad-Gita - and its denouement was in doubt until (at least) the fall of the Berlin Wall in 1989. It was around that same time that evidence for the success of Operation Flood became undeniable. As the Cold War ground to a halt, it was superseded by debate over the Uruguay Round Agricultural Agreement (URAA) in negotiations on the General Agreement on Tariffs and Trade (almighty GATT), which for the first time began to liberalise world farm trade. Without hoping to do these disparate themes justice, this book touches on them insofar as they impacted the White Revolution.

Perhaps Francis Fukuyama, whose book *The End of History* was part of post-Wall *Zeitgeist*, was correct in suggesting the debate between capitalism and socialism was settled. It certainly seemed plain that although Paul Kennedy had not predicted the disintegration of the USSR (neither did the CIA) in *The Rise and Fall of the Great Powers* his warnings on national or imperial overstretch were apt for the spent hulk of the Soviet bear. Most important was the vindication of Kennedy's thesis that long-term political power rested less on military prowess than strong economic underpinnings.

With the dissolution of the Soviet Union and China's acceptance of some free market realities behind its socialist facade the USA was described as the lone remaining political, economic and military superpower. The present danger, say those wary of multi- or transnational capitalism, was that rich countries could manipulate the World Trade Organisation (WTO) set up under the GATT-1994 agreement to exact more profits from poor countries, stifling their progress. Please note that the WTO has in many respects superseded what was known as the GATT apparatus for trade negotiations and dispute adjudication. However, GATT does maintain some functions within the WTO, and since GATT has for decades been so well known, the abbreviation GATT/WTO-1994 of the Uruguay round is used occasionally to indicate the agreements and institutions that monitor world trade until the completion of the current Doha development round which began at the turn of the century. Previous rounds have sometimes taken over a decade for resolution, so the odds are that the Doha negotiations will eventually be concluded.

Critics find corollary evidence for the insidious profit-extracting nature of neo-liberal free trade in Africa. Besides military conflict and serious drought in the 1980s-1990s, Sub-Saharan Africa (SSA) also suffered from net disinvestment due to large debt repayments to international lending institutions and repatriation of profits to multinational corporations (MNCs) in the same period. Even if Soviet-style communism is history, who can doubt that the struggle for economic development goes on.

View from Anand

In April, 1998, Dr. Verghese Kurien traced a thumbnail sketch of India's dairy saga. While this author, an American writing in Britain, has often viewed the GATT/WTO process as a basically neutral economic forum, the danger exists that rich country interests can damage poor countries, in sins of omission or commission. Under sheep's clothing of free trade, the wolf of *laissez-faire* capitalism might plunder the developing world. But predators do not go unchallenged. Kurien[3] vows: 'If some fool in Delhi signs an unfair agreement with the GATT or World Bank, that doesn't mean Kurien or the NDDB has to abide by it!'

While Kurien has won enough battles to say what he thinks, he can also joke about himself. Barbed comments on rivals are apt to lapse into, for instance, a comment about a photograph mural in his office in Anand. Pointing to a man listening to a speech by then PM Indira Gandhi, he says: That's the best picture of myself - back of my head!'

Kurien, born in 1921, was *primus inter pares* of Indian dairy development for five long decades, and his influence persisted even after he welcomed his favoured successor, Dr. Amrita Patel to the chair of the NDDB in 1998.

His resilience is remarkable, in the wake of the economic liberalisations of 1991, and the demise of the Congress Party which was powerbase to some of his mentors. Perhaps his staying power depends less on political patronage than populist regard. Kurien is lengthily listed in *Who's Who*. But most significant is the popular perception of the White Revolution, with which he is identified. If one asks ten Indian citizens at random whether Operation Flood was successful, most answer affirmatively, implying the question was naive.

However, many politicians and academics - within and without India - predicted that bringing European/EEC dairy commodity aid into India would be disastrous. Particularly influential were researchers from scholars known as 'the Dutch School' or 'the Hague School', including Martin Doornbos and Shanti George. In her 1985 book *Operation Flood*, George critically evaluated 'the policy design' of the programme as her 'main task' while making 'subsidiary reference...to execution and attainments.' In the fifteenth year of what became a 26 year programme, George[4] wrote:

> It is in the context of food aid as trap that India has been warned to look EEC gift horses long and hard in the mouth, as they may well turn out to be Trojan horses. The Greeks are not the only ones who should be most feared when bearing gifts; EEC donations, accepted with cries of gratitude and euphoria, can destroy India's already precarious dairy economy from within and render it forever dependent on imports.

George also decried the rash introduction of North European bovine gene plasm into a country better suited to buffalo, and cast doubt on wholesale replication of the 'Anand Pattern' over the sub-continent. But George's worst fear, supported at that time by some disturbing evidence, was the prospect of permanent import dependence.

Certainly development literature is abundant with horror stories in which food aid sabotaged a country's agricultural fabric - and reasons why Operation Flood (OF) would prove no different. What was the upshot? Building upon previous work by Dr. Peter J. Atkins, I undertook postgraduate research at Durham University in England, and turned the Agrostat-FAO computer database into charts, maps and tables. These showed that, as comparable countries declined, Indian per capita intake of 'butter & ghee' rose 20 per cent from 1.0 kg. in 1961 to 1.2 kg. in 1992; per capita intake of 'milk excluding butter' rose 40 per cent from 39 kg. in 1961 to 54 kg. in 1989. They revealed a reversal of India's dairy fortunes since the 1960s, when urban consumers routinely queued for milk, clutching ration cards. Meanwhile, dairy aid was cut. Fears of dependence were not borne out. Subsequent data continue to affirm the positive effects of OF or 'Flood'.

Kurien seems quietly proud of his role in these achievements. Nobel laureate and Green Revolution leader Norman Borlaug has called him 'one of the great agricultural leaders of this century'. But in conversation Kurien reiterates his conviction that Operation Flood was successful because it was controlled by officials like himself *who were accountable to farmers*, rather than to Government ministers who might have manipulated food aid to build their political careers. Kurien also frequently expresses his gratitude to Tribhuvandas Patel, who harnessed his talents at an age when he was more inclined to take a better-paid job at Union Carbide in Calcutta, than to work as a dairy engineer in dusty Anand. Heredia writes that without the influence of Tribhuvandas, it is unlikely the ambitious Kurien ever would have developed loyalty to the dairy industry - or to farmers.

Kurien also credits a colourful cast of characters, including an Inspector of Police in Gujarat who acted as intermediary with the GOI Home Secretary; a German count who coached him before negotiations in Brussels; and a Harvard researcher who waxed eloquent in grant applications to mighty international institutions. These are just a few fellow travellers who assisted at critical junctures on the road to India's dairy success - success so profound there are kudos enough to go around.

As a vigorous septugenarian, Kurien continued to monitor dairy development. Are there irregularities in a cooperative election in Rajasthan? The matter lands on his desk. International cooperation has already been initiated, or is pending, with China, Kyrghyzstan, Nepal, Sri Lanka, Thailand, Vietnam and perhaps - despite a spate of tit-for-tat nuclear tests in 1998 - even Pakistan. Future prospects on the world stage beckon, but he readily discusses the past: 'Operation Flood was a big solution for a big problem. It was the world's largest food aid programme - dairy or cereal. If we failed, all would know, the world over.'

The biggest inducement to failure was, ironically, dairy aid itself. By the late-1960s, the EEC budget was awash in the Milk Lake and shadowed by the Butter Mountain.[5] Growing surpluses threatened market stability and the budget of the Common Agricultural Policy (CAP) whose price supports fostered overproduction. A 'pure' economic solution would have been simply to destroy Europe's surplus food commodities. But Europe had only recently regained food self-sufficiency in the late-1960s, and memories of World War II era hunger were so vivid that popular opinion would not permit destruction of stored food. Kurien says:

> Europeans wouldn't allow their governments to destroy food. The only solution for the EEC was to give it away. Not to a small country.

> Not to China, where they don't drink much milk. They had to give it to us, because India has a cultural tradition and religions suitable for milk...

There were also logistical reasons to send dairy aid to India. It generally costs a donor less to ship a given quantity of commodity aid to one country than to two or more recipients. Despite popular misconceptions, food aid is not free. Transport to remote recipients can easily cost as much as the market value of the food at its source. In previous Green Revolution programmes, India had proven its ability to absorb large quantities of cereal aid with a minimum of fuss, i.e. transport and administration costs. This administrative efficiency probably owed something to the competence and general incorruptibility of the Indian Civil Service (ICS). Kurien notes that India was in a good position to negotiate for the best terms, for a broached 100,000 tonnes of skimmed milk powder and 30,000 tonnes of butter oil. Refrigerated storage of dairy commodities was costly to European taxpayers and a nuisance for EEC bureaucrats. 'They wanted to get rid of the damn stuff,' says Kurien, 'and I wanted the commodities.' With a smile Kurien added, 'Would the EEC bear the cost of freight? Yes, they would.'

Adding moral weight to its prospects was India's relatively better record of food aid utilisation than many countries, where it acted as a major disincentive to farmers. Dairy consultant John Empson[6] observed: '...India would seem to have handled her dairy development rather well.... However, in many developing countries, donations ruined the economics for domestic milk production.' Kurien agrees full-heartedly, offering examples from the 1980s: 'Food aid is a two-edged sword that can cut your own throat - in the Sahel and Horn of Africa, it turned into permanent dependence on food aid...' The NDDB leadership of the late-1960s saw the danger that cheap EEC dairy aid could break the fragile supply chain between rural farmers and urban consumers. Kurien says:

> There were Government ministers who wanted to distribute free EEC milk to poor kids in Delhi and make big names for themselves. At the NDDB we proposed to Delhi how to turn this threat into an opportunity. So I went to Rome, to discuss with the FAO and WFP how to distribute this enormous surplus.

Assisted in writing the programme proposal by Harvard researcher Michael Halse, Kurien and the NDDB detailed a plan to 'take over' what World Food Programme officials had tagged WFP 348. Sensing the acronym WFP 348 was, if possible, less-poetic than the United States' ubiquitous PL 480, Kurien says they dubbed their big solution 'Operation Flood'. Under OF, 'four Mother Dairies' in the metropoles of Bombay, Calcutta, Delhi and Madras would recombine milk from, initially, 1 million rural Indian farmers with EEC milk powder and butter oil, and sell it to urban consumers, while upwards of 18 cooperative dairy milksheds were developed in 10 Indian states.[7] The profits from the 'monetised' dairy aid, sold in reconstituted (*aka* 'toned') milk in the cities, would be reinvested in the country's dairy infrastructure, encompassing cooperative ventures in cities and the milksheds. Such a virtuous circle was calculated to increase incentives and productivity in domestic dairying and strengthen - rather than demolish - links between town and country. By and by, it would make the country less dependent on imports. In other words, Kurien and the NDDB would invest food aid - which domestic and foreign *Realpolitik* were thrusting upon them anyway - to increase India's dairy autonomy. They would fight fire with fire. Milk with milk. Since World War II, 'food aid' too often was a polite phrase for 'surplus disposal' of mouldy or otherwise sub-standard grain or dairy commodities. Kurien knew how easily OF could fall foul of donor complaisance or misguided sentiment:

> That is why if Germany gives me green milk powder, we'll abuse them. We were not in the business of giving milk away to starving children, we were selling it to urban office workers. If I exploit them, I do it gently!

Behind this blunt humour is the discipline that prevented the onslaught of WFP commodities from worsening India's precarious food situation in the late-1960s. The country was experiencing growing population, milk rationing and even famine in drought-stricken Rajasthan. Kurien's remarks illustrate the dilemma of food aid: Although sharing surplus food is normal human behaviour, the danger is that such altruism addresses only the symptoms of consumers' hunger, while exacerbating the root economic causes of why farmers failed to produce food in the first place. But the Kaira Cooperatives Union and NDDB had been inspired by the hard-headed rural vision of Sardar Patel. Like many Indians of his era, Patel was wary of capitalism. At the same time he was opposed to communism, doubtful of Nehruvian socialism and - having a deeper understanding of Indian village agriculture than many national leaders - less sanguine than his mentor Mohandas Gandhi had been on the self-sufficiency of rural agricultural communities. Ruth Heredia writes that the 'three harmonious elements' of Patel's rural strategy were technology, education and 'organisation of producers' cooperative marketing institutions'. Like Sardar Patel, Kurien had little use for fantasy. Kurien knew the best way to help the 'starving children' patronised by cynical politicians was to unleash the productive power of farmers.

For the milk cooperatives, this began with the 1946 milk strike, cutting out the middle-man, Polsons, in the supply chain to Bombay. Gradually they took more control over all aspects of production, processing and marketing of milk. While some progress was undoubtedly achieved via materiel and technical cooperation with MNCs and marketing bodies from other countries, Indian dairy coops encountered plenty of bad advice on en route to status as number one world milk producer around 1998. Dissembling - verging on outright lies - can charitably describe some behaviour of multinational corporations in India, and it is why Kurien says flatly: 'MNCs lack the morality of cooperatives.'

In other words, without self-reliance and careful scrutiny of advice and tenders for dairy technology, the Kaira Cooperative would never have produced its sweeping Amul range of dairy products independently. M.V. Kamath and more recently Ruth Heredia[8] detail one of Anand's earliest and greatest victories, i.e. the manufacture of skim milk powder from buffalo milk. Now it is being forgotten, but Western experts once airily recommended that India switch from buffalo to cows because it was thought impossible to make powder from richer buffalo milk, with its higher lactose and solids-not-fat (SNF) content. In 1953, against the advice of 'experts' from the Bombay Milk Commission, UNICEF, Britain, New Zealand, and various MNC manufacturers, Kurien and fellow engineer Harichand Meghaa Dalaya (working in tandem under Tribhuvandas) did just that. Not for the first time they realised that - whether or not advice was offered in good faith - it could be wrong.

Abandon buffaloes for northern breeds of cows? Nonsense, reasoned Anand. Since they wanted to balance out the lean/flush procurement patterns of the hot weather/monsoon seasons and buffalo are better suited to Indian conditions than European breeds, and because Indian buffalo produce more and richer milk than cows which are traditionally held to produce bullocks for traction power (cow milk being just an ancillary benefit of their chief roles in transport) Kurien and Dalaya were determined to make powder from surplus buffalo milk. Because the newest spraying technology from Denmark could accomplish the task, they insisted on it - against an older design from The Netherlands strongly recommended by UNICEF. Heredia notes: 'It was the first plant in India to make spray dried milk powder, and probably the first anywhere in the world to make it out of buffalo milk.'

The Anand team went on to produce a full range of 'the most unlikely products' from buffalo milk says Heredia, including 'baby food, cheese, condensed milk and chocolates.' FAO statistics show that by 1995, buffalo accounted for more milk procurement in India than cows. The pro-buffalo policy was promoted by critics of Flood including Shanti George who feared foreign interests would make Indian dairying a poor carbon-copy of European dairying whose high-input/high-output Guernsey, Jersey and Holstein-Friesian breeds were wrong for the low input/low-output Anand Pattern. (There is linked evidence that petroleum-based, intensive dairying adds to climate change, the object of the 2009 Copenhagen summit.)

Kurien and George - apparently at loggerheads - were revealed over time to share the same goal: India's dairy autonomy.

Today the NDDB utilises sufficient stored domestic powder to keep milk flowing from ruralities to cities, meeting effective demand despite seasonal fluctuations.

Since 1970, per capita consumption of milk in India has nearly doubled (from 110 to about 208 grams/day). Three decades later dairy production had tripled and was rising about 4 per cent a year. Most telling to India's dairy success, P.R. Gupta, editor of *Dairy India Yearbook*[9] noted: 'India is projected to be the world's number one milk producer in 1998 with output of about 74 million tonnes, ahead of the previous leader USA at about 72 million tonnes.' For a country accustomed to milk rationing before Operation Flood, these are spectacular statistics. But they would mean little, if not for the fact that India gradually weaned itself from dairy aid, and become autonomous in milk production and marketing.

Beware of Gifts?

Critics of Operation Flood protested - vociferously - that India's dairy autonomy was in jeopardy. In just its initial 11-year period, 1970-81, write food aid experts John Shaw and Edward Clay, the World Food Programme (WFP) committed 126,000 tonnes of dried skim milk powder and 42,000 tonnes of butter oil to Operation Flood, worth ca. US$166 million.[10] This was an astounding quantity, and detractors sniggered that if India's own dairy cooperatives failed to flood the country with milk, the EEC's Butter Mountain and Milk Lake already were doing so.

Advocates claim OF was *designed* from the beginning to avoid the pitfalls of food aid. Lessons had been learned by failures in the initial post-war 'surplus disposal' period of the United States food aid programme. By the mid-1960s it was widely understood, and noted by experts such as John W. Mellor, that food aid often hampered not only indigenous agriculture, but also a country's overall economic development, unless food aid concomitantly increased the productivity of the target country's farmers. Therefore, in the 'monetised aid' plan devised by Kurien and his colleagues, it was important that surplus European (EEC) milk powder and butter oil were recombined *with indigenous milk* before sale to urban consumers. This strengthened supply chains between village and metropole. When local milk supplies were ignored by metropolitan processors (because commodity imports were priced more cheaply), critics such as Shanti George, Claude Alvares, Martin Doornbos and others naturally and rightly deplored the disincentive effects on Indian farmers. George, for instance, brandished 1981 WFP and FAO statistics of what she suspected was a faulty emphasis on procurement (24.6 per cent of budget), processing (40 per cent), and distribution (23 per cent) to the detriment of production (just 5.7 per cent). George also quoted WFP remarks that 'giving dairy processing and marketing… higher priority over dairy production technology' was an 'unorthodox approach'.[11]

Yet, the unorthodox approach of Operation Flood was not just appropriate, but a wise measure taken in order to improve the logistics of milk marketing within India so that it could absorb the massive dairy flows that European political-economic realities were unleashing on the country. If EEC dairy aid was not to rot on the docks, or totally supplant milk production in the vicinity of main harbours (because it was difficult to ship commodities where they could be used elsewhere) India needed more sophisticated processing and distribution technology than it had before dairy aid arrived. Martin Doornbos and colleagues were not alone in pointing out occasions when processing plants utilised a disproportionate ratio of commodity aid to domestic milk, as well as the continuance of food aid flows past previously-announced cut-off dates. Behind such criticism was the suspicion that, having secured entrée to India's food systems - not unlike that fabled horse within the gates of Troy - European exporters conspired to export their dairy surpluses *ad infinitum*.

More alarming was the fear that GOI and NDDB authorities were acting as compradores in this neo-colonialist ploy. The intention of the Anand authorities to incorporate modern transport, processing and other technology into Indian dairying was opposed by pastoralists who resisted technology, and mistrusted by others who feared farmers and consumers would benefit from capital-intensive investments less than the brokers and careerists who managed their sales and construction.

Nevertheless, in OF the profits from urban sales (along with various monies from foreign donors, and lenders such as UNICEF which, noted Kurien, drove a bargain as hard as any commercial bank) were carefully invested in a National Milk Grid System of processing plants, insulated trucks and railcars. The national dairy herd was to be enhanced via improvements to feeding and breeding of cows and buffalo. Milk gathering, testing and payment would be controlled by democratic village cooperatives modelled after the original Anand Pattern coop guided by the NDDB. Membership cut caste, gender and religious lines. So described, it might be thought that little of this programme would spawn argument now or three decades ago. But there were reasons why critics opposed aspects of the modernisation policy, or suspected that OF would be corrupted or go awry through faulty planning.

Micro-/Macro- and Top-/Bottom- critiques

In a micro-/macroeconomic critique, the huge investments in the four 'Mother Dairies' in Bombay, Calcutta, Delhi and Madras were deemed wasteful White Elephants. Just as Nehru's macroeconomic obsession with centralised 'top-down' planning for steel and other heavy industries had sapped GOI budgets (with little to show in improved living standards for the average citizen) detractors said money spent on the 'stainless steel temples' of dairy processing plants could better be spent on 'bottom-up' microeconomic inputs such as fertiliser, fodder, loans and education for small farmers.

There was some substance to this point of view, and in fact 'bottom-up' aspects of Operation Flood did increase inputs to farmers on the microeconomic level. But, OF's 'top-down' investment represented by the Mother Dairies and National Milk Grid System paid off.

Neo-colonialist corruption

There was always the worry that big capital investments would be corrupting - as they sometimes proved in development programmes around the world. Greed might manifest itself as outright kickbacks to officials, in sales involving dairy equipment manufactured overseas. Or more insidiously, the Mother Dairies might serve as Trojan Horses, from which foreign suppliers could gradually exert greater control over India's food systems.

Thus, the colonial era would be succeeded by a neo-colonial era of capitalist exploitation of developing countries by the West (or North, depending on one's perspective). Gunilla Andræ & Björn Beckmann had found precedence for this dour fantasy in Nigeria. Just as Western grain companies had established flour milling plants in Nigeria's ports and cities as prelude to altering that country's consumption patterns to favour imported wheat over indigenous grains (to the detriment of Nigeria's arable farmers), so might the adoption of high-tech processing plants be a prelude to losing India's dairy autonomy. However, although India's modern dairy processing plants continue to source some of the finest technology from New Zealand, Scandinavia, etc., M.V. Kamath claims that the country has manufactured most such equipment for decades.

Feminist critique

It was feared that large-scale investments such as the Mother Dairies and subsidiary feeder plants constituted inappropriate technology that might usurp the traditional roles of women in village ghee-making. After all, the transformation of milk into products such as ghee had been the traditional method of preserving it - until the advent of sprayed milk powder. Not only was stainless steel high-tech equipment 'inappropriate technology ' by this estimate, but by the placement of men into most of the jobs created in these new processing and transport initiatives, Operation Flood became vulnerable to charges of discrimination in employment. Some said OF was skewing gender roles: women were deprived of traditional cash-making employment in ghee-making while men went off to well-paid jobs in their high-tech dairy temples.

Meanwhile, pressure by cooperatives for households to take on additional milk cows only added to a woman's already onerous workload. However uncomfortably close to the truth that the feminist critique came on points about gender discrimination in new jobs, it often ignored the fact that cash from daily milk collections in village cooperatives normally went home clutched in the hands of women. Furthermore, the fact that the NDDB's managing director, Amrita Patel, is female demonstrates that the employment of women is taken seriously at all levels of dairying - from milking to management. For example, of a cohort of 40 students enrolled at Vidya Student dairy at Anand in 1998, 10 per cent are women. Male and female students alike learn financial accountability, auditing, technical aspects of refrigeration, energy conservation and sanitation. Adopting such world class manufacturing practices for butter, cheese, ghee, paneer, ice cream, etc. can maintain Indian cooperative farmers' role in supplying metropolitan consumers - and increases the country's potential as a competitor on world dairy exports markets.

NDDB officials vehemently discount the well-intentioned but counter-productive portrayals by some advocates of dairy development as a panacea for all the woes of rural societies. They say Operation Flood was *not* an anti-poverty programme, but a means to enhance incomes of rural small-holders by reducing the role of middlemen, easing fluctuations in seasonal demand, and adding value to their milk through farmer-owned processing, marketing and distribution facilities. Likewise, the NDDB downplayed hyperbolic claims that scientific approaches to the health, nutrition and reproduction of milk animals would be reflected in welfare gains to the women and children who tend them. However, after mounting evidence of just such improvements, disclaimers are gradually being replaced in NDDB literature[12] by suggestions such as: 'Does not their knowledge of conception in animals help them to better understand their own lives and to begin to control what once was simply assumed as a matter of fate?'

Cultural and ethical concern

Pragmatic, carnivorous, human-focused Western practices such as the eating of meat, and the culling of unproductive milk cows are anathema to large portions of the Indian population. Civil unrest and rioting not infrequently follow rumours of surreptitious slaughter of unproductive cattle who, by popular consensus, should be allowed to wander India's villages and cities freely. The sight of cattle sharing the roads with cars and trucks, or lolling on city roundabouts has sent many a Western taxicab passenger into culture shock. Conversely, many Indians are revolted by the thought of large animal concentrations in rich countries, where cattle seldom if ever graze outside feedlots and face slaughter after as few as two lactations.

Thus, it is unsurprising that the some feared the introduction of high-tech hardware from rich, meat-eating countries would in turn encourage the exploitation of cattle. Resistance to non-traditional practices included artificial insemination (AI), which some regarded as an infringement of the animal's natural rights. When AI met resistance on its introduction to India some decades ago, Western dairists[13] deplored what they regarded as sentimental concern for animals' sexual rights. Today the dairy industry in rich countries is beset by a backlash of concern for animal welfare among consumers, and many university libraries list Peter Singer's 1975 book *Animal Liberation*.[14] One wonders if the 'live and let live' inter-species ethos prevalent in India could eventually prevail in rich countries.

One argument that the Anand authorities used in behalf of their development plans was that improving India's dairy independence would be not only a boon to national pride, but could also ameliorate the country's balance of payments, and repatriate profits from recombination sales to needy rural farmers instead of foreign investors. But when Kurien, Dalaya and colleagues managed to produce baby food and milk replacer, Amul was attacked on the grounds that baby food was affordable only by rich elites. This purist indictment conveniently overlooked the fact that Nestlé and Glaxo had sold such products in India for years.

In the 1970s, as worldwide criticism befell Nestlé, the multinational accused of unscrupulous tactics in marketing its milk replacer in poor countries where mothers could ill afford it (and whose babies might suffer immuno-deficiency if deprived of mothers' milk), Anand also suffered some undeserved guilt-by-association.

Anand prevails

Amidst all this contention Operation Flood proceeded inexorably. Yet with such large quantities of dairy aid commodities, money and prestige involved, there were many attempts by state and national ministers to usurp leadership of the programme from the NDDB. Bureaucrats in states such as Karnataka and Kerala which had previously-established, if not stellar, dairy development projects, were unsurprisingly resistant to assimilation by Anand. In such circumstances, the imposition of authority from officials situated in the state of Gujarat definitely felt 'top-down', whatever the 'bottom-up' tenets of the Anand cooperatives.

Kurien enjoys storytelling and cites several tales of brinkmanship, first (after all the negotiations with the FAO, WFP and EEC in the 1965-70 run-up to the programme) in getting OF approved against obstruction by the minister for agriculture in Delhi, who wanted control of Europe's lactic largess for himself. 'He was a megalomaniac,' Kurien says recalling the unwillingness of the official to assist Anand: 'There was laughter in the ministry of agriculture. Nothing happened. I said to hell with it, this damn country can't be salvaged.' The impasse was finally broken when the Inspector-General of the Gujarat State Police telephoned Kurien, claiming he was in trouble, because his 'big boss' from Delhi was coming on an official two-day visit, but only one and one-half days of activities were arranged for him. Pray, could Dr. Kurien oblige by hosting this bigwig at Anand? Kurien in fact could. Happily - since the official's report could serve as a deft end run, round the minister of agriculture to the PM. When GOI Home Minister L.P. Singh did visit Anand, he indicated that he was one of many before - and after - himself who got religion once there. That Anand was a showpiece, the groomed, irrigated, modern face of Indian dairy potential was undoubtedly apparent to Singh. But the fact that it had to a great extent been achieved by farmers working cooperatively suggested it could serve as a national model. Singh told Kurien: 'I've never seen anything like this dairy run by farmers. You see Dr. Kurien, the true development is of people, not cows. To teach people responsibility in such a 'bottom-up' programme is fantastic.'

Kurien could play hard to get. He said, 'The British may have gone, but the same mentality remains, maybe worse.' The only good had to come top-down from Delhi. 'More Anands? The GOI can't write one letter costing one rupee to get it approved!' he stormed. Soon the Home Minister asked Kurien for a letter outlining his needs to take back to Delhi. Kurien recalls:

> In four days he discussed the plans with all the ministers, including finance, saying they were all for it [OF]. 'Please come to Delhi!' he

> asked me. But I had no plans to go to Delhi. I had recently been there. I told him. 'I'll tell you when…'

Several times in his career Kurien has used the tactic of delay with good effect. In the due course of time, he did indeed have business in Delhi and thereupon informed Singh of that this might be an opportunity for them to meet as well. On arrival Kurien was told, 'Sir, the Home Secretary is waiting for you.' Kurien was met by the minister in his car, proffering a cut glass tumbler, asking, 'Dr. Kurien, how do you like your whiskey?' As revenge is best imbibed cold, ice was presumably at hand. His rival, the agriculture minister had been cut out of the loop. Kurien remembers that his victorious meeting with top officials of the ICS lasted over three hours. Some 'soul searching ensued' and he berated them:

> No politicians were involved, it was all done by the civil service. The mountain came to Mohammed…. I asked, 'What kind of a civil service is it, if a project that costs nothing and benefits 1 million farmers isn't even considered?'

Singh, Kurien's friend in the cabinet, finally bid him *Pace!* Forthwith, the long-delayed letter on GOI stationery was sent to the WFP and FAO in Rome. Kurien was invited to appear before a 24-member executive session for these organisations: 'I was in good form. Some came to shoot us down - but they couldn't.' Although Kurien travelled the world tirelessly on behalf of the NDDB in the planning stages of Operation Flood, and in the three phases of its duration, it is remarkable how often the mountain did come to Mohammed. He recalls:

> About year four of Phase I, Indian milk production and farmer income were up, and a gentleman from Washington, DC came to me at Anand - Robert McNamara, President of the World Bank said, we fund dams and other expensive projects, but not work with small and landless farmers. Dr. Kurien, I have dollars. Will you let me fund this project?

Thus, in the 1970s, additional finance became available for construction of modern infrastructure in the National Milk Grid System. Increased funding had the likely effect of prolonging OF past earlier, mooted cut-off dates. It also upped the ante, in the credibility stakes with the detractors of Operation Flood. For example, the newly-constructed processing plants would indeed be uneconomic White Elephants if they were not operated near capacity. One of the chronic and more reasonable complaints levelled against OF was that stainless steel dairy temples, costing millions of rupees, were under-utilised. The imperative to keep plants busy increased the inclination of plant managers - and NDDB officials - to accept dairy aid. Critics watched and wept at what they saw as a vicious circle of inappropriately high-tech Mother Dairies fuelled by the burgeoning Butter Mountains and Milk Lakes of Europe - while in some documented cases, the products of Indian farmers were ignored. Would dairy aid continue forever? Indian nationalists and leftists in the European Parliament raised the neo-colonialist spectre of Europe's subsidised dairy farmers supplanting the proper role of Indian farmers in that nation's nutrition.

Fortunately, the overall implementation of Operation Flood was being managed better than its detractors feared. The frequently changed schedule of its execution, however, turned some sceptics into cynics. For instance, although the GOI and NDDB[15] began planning Operation Flood in the mid-1960s, involvement by the World Food Programme dairy aid was initially approved by the WFP and GOI in 1969 for a period of 5 years.[16] Martin Doornbos *et al.* explain that delays in plant expansion in India along with 'a world crisis in dairy commodities' that 'severely curtailed WFP shipments to the projects' prolonged implementation.

But before long Europe (EEC) and the NDDB found that dairy aid flows could, indeed, be as mutually advantageous as food aid champions such as Hans W. Singer and John W. Mellor suggested: the NDDB from aid's monetisation into infrastructure (not to mention relief of severe milk shortages that sometimes left hospitals dangerously short of milk), and the EEC to placate taxpayers and farmers, by reducing Milk Mountains. However, suspicious observers found it risible that after the 5 years originally projected for WFP dairy aid, it was still pouring in. As Shanti George[17] expressed it: 'An extended time frame, enhanced funding, ambitious targets fallen short in some cases and exceeded in others…thus the first phase of the flood washed into the second.'

In the way of government programmes around the world, delays and extensions were numerous. As this was probably the largest development programme in the world - ever - it is no wonder that over-lapping national, international (bilateral and multilateral) funding, commodity and technical aid make its delineation into distinct phases somewhat artificial. It explains why, depending on the date of writing, authors give slightly different dates for what, by its eventual end in 1996, became the 3 phases of Operation Flood. (Cut-off dates of 1990 and 1994 were previously mooted in OF-III.) The NDDB, which as victor in this dairy war can write its own history, offers the following dates:[18]

Phase I 1970-8: Financed by sale in India of skimmed milk powder and butter oil from the EEC *via* the WFP. Plans and terms negotiated by Dr. Verghese Kurien as 'founder-chairman' of the NDDB, and also as 'founder-chairman of the erstwhile Indian dairy Corporation, the project authority' for OF, which was later absorbed by the NDDB. Original plans for OF-I 'aimed at linking India's 18 best milksheds' with metropolitan Bombay, Calcutta, Delhi and Madras. Later NDDB histories[19] say this was 27 milksheds in 10 states, but the thrust is the same. Much of the early phases of OF was undertaken in the states of Rajasthan, Madhya Pradesh and Karnataka. NDDB documents from 1985 noted that about 1.5 million farm families took part in OF-I, and rural procurement rose from 'a pre-project level of 0.46 million litres daily' to 2.2m lpd nationally.

Phase II 1981-85: About 136 milksheds were linked to over 290 urban markets. Although Kurien dealt more directly with the EEC and the World Bank, the WFP stamp remained on OF-II. Seed capital raised through sale of WFP/EEC gifts and a World Bank loan created what the NDDB called 'a self-sustaining system of 43,000 village cooperatives covering 4.25 million milk producers' and 'Direct marketing of milk by producers' cooperatives - resulting in the transfer of profits from milk contracts - increased by several million litres a day.' Milk powder production rose from 20,000 tonnes in the pre-project year to 1,40,000 [crores/lakhs] tonnes in 1989.' While it likely took until the mid-1990s for the NDDB coops' share of national milk output to exceed 10 per cent, one begins to understand the leveraged effect that reinvesting some of these profits into productive infrastructure had.

Phase III 1985-96: OF-III was basically a consolidation of gains made in OF-II and extension of what the NDDB calls its ability 'to procure and market more and more milk daily.' Increased emphasis was put on veterinary care, feeding (symbiotic with the NDDB oilseeds project), and breeding of non-descript cattle. From daily collections of 500 litres per day in Anand in 1948, the organisation that grew there, the NDDB, claimed to gather 1 million lpd at Anand by early 1990. The NDDB maintained also that by eliminating middlemen it increased 'an assured source of income' to nearly 10 million farm families, helping to sustain them during droughts. From NDDB claims that, 'Migrating population is settling down,' can be inferred the conclusion that educating children of former nomads will be easier than in the past. Current NDDB literature says that in OF-III about 75,000 village cooperatives were linked 'to 170 district level cooperatives' in a 'federal cooperative marketing structure' in each state in India. The NDDB says coop products compete 'in the open market' with other coops as well as the 'private dairy sector that runs side by side'. But most germane to any evaluation of Operation Flood is this statement: 'The industry as a whole produces enough milk and milk products to ensure that the country imports virtually no dairy products.'

To illustrate how dire were India's dairy fortunes outside the enclaves of Anand-style coops in Gujarat before Operation Flood, please note that national total milk production of 20.8 million tonnes was hardly greater in 1970 than the 20.375 million tonnes noted by Agrostat/FAO in 1961! Dairy doldrums indeed. But from the abysmal 1961-1970 stasis of 20 million tonnes, India managed to exceed 70 million tonnes toward the end of OF-III in the mid-1990s, as the country challenged the USA for production supremacy.

There is the possibility that without sceptical monitoring, OF might have become a Trojan Horse to permanent dependence. Perhaps the critics are due an olive branch. After all, it is a principle of democratic government - and of modern business practice - that all enterprises, including development, generally benefit from scrutiny and assessment. But a review of development literature in the early-1990s shows it did little to instil the notion that OF was a worthwhile initiative. On the contrary. The microeconomic jots and tittles of this sweeping programme were investigated by sundry researchers, but few seemed bold enough to make a macroeconomic assessment of Operation Flood as a whole. One academic presentation illustrates how often investigators 'missed the forest for the trees': a PhD researcher studying agrarian change and division of labour lived months in Indian villages, quantifying the effects of participation in coop dairying on women's household responsibilities. The conclusion was that, yes, the woman's workload was somewhat increased. The connotation was that this was unfortunate - while side-stepping the likelihood that dairying not only increased reliable household cash flow but also enhanced women's control of it, while increasing the economic options available to her and her family. Little credence was given to the woman's ability as a rational economic actor to choose between options, or to substitute one activity or product for another if it appeared more profitable. When this writer asked whether or not OF had been an aggregate benefit or detriment to village families, or to the country on the macroeconomic level, the visiting lecturer was nonplussed. There were criticisms of minutiae aplenty, but no cost/benefit judgement was made on the marginal (non-) success of Operation Flood.

But even venerable food aid practitioners were equivocal on the overall merit of Operation Flood. As late as 1991[20], Edward Clay and Olav Stokke, who relied largely on the work of Martin Doornbos, Liana Gertsch and Piet Terhal from the Institute of Social Studies (ISS) at the Hague, 'which probably represents the most substantial attempt to fill the gap in our knowledge ', were mixed in their assessment. Clay & Stokke said massive research by Doornbos and others 'had not ended controversy ' over Operation Flood 'in part because views of protagonists are only partially based on the record of performance and impact.' These comments attest to the inherent integrity of research by Martin Doornbos *et al.*, and why this present book will cite ISS research so frequently. This is so even though my examination of longitudinal production and consumption data (which implies OF's performance and overall impact on India) from the FAO since 1960 leads me to conclude that by the mid-1990s OF was an extraordinary success.

About India's White Revolution Clay & Stokke wrote that, 'Unlike the Green Revolution innovations, technical change has played a minimal role in the growth process.' This may run counter to complaints by detractors alleging over-reliance upon high-tech processing plants. But it more easily corresponds to Clay & Stokke's view that, 'the effort to increase milk yields through cross-bred animals has been a failure.' It is true that by the early 1990s, the *general* superiority of indigenous buffalo to imported cattle breeds was generally recognised. (And today shown by the fact that buffalo, although just 40 per cent of milk livestock, contribute slightly more than cows to national milk production.) Ill-thought-out genetic programmes were abandoned. India's national milk herd was not corrupted by Trojan Cows. But (not to belabour a point which will be elaborated below) as India's dairy expertise continues to pioneer the use of artificial insemination (AI) and embryo transfer (ET) even in rustic settings, it is becoming clear that improved genetics in both buffalo and cows - with some 'Northern ' genetic input - will play an increasing role.

Some researchers attacked OF on grounds that by putting milk on a more economic base (than in the milk rationing of the 1960s) consumption patterns might be skewed, and vulnerable groups would suffer. However, Clay & Stokke found there had been: 'no dramatic nutritional impact, either negative, in the producing communities, or positive, in the consuming urban areas.' But they concluded that, like other rural development schemes, the income benefits from OF were 'distributed inequitably' across India. That is unsurprising, in such a huge, variegated country. Further, Clay & Stokke said 'none of the evaluations of Operation Flood from a donor perspective' showed 'that the benefits have justified' transfers from European taxpayers through EEC aid programmes. But this begs the question of how Brussels would have managed EEC Milk Mountains *without* its enlightened form of surplus disposal in India. In the late-1960s planning stages of Operation Flood, that was simply unlikely (if not impossible) for a variety of social, political-economic and other considerations that were all part and parcel of Western strategy to defeat the socialist Eastbloc in the Cold War. This book will deploy analysis from the EC milk quotas begun in 1984 to bolster that argument. Moreover, I argue, influenced by Jagdish Bhagwati and other free traders, that insofar as European aid gradually helped improve the terms-of-trade for India (to the extent that India had the political will to sign the GATT/WTO-1994 accords) the long-term gains from increased trade with a more prosperous India will recompense every penny spent on Flood by European taxpayers - whether or not EEC Milk Mountains would have been manageable without it!

More recently the World Bank which, besides funding portions of OF, sometimes criticised aspects of its execution, has come on board. In a final report (ca. 1997) the Bank lavished praise on OF, calling it one of the most successful development programmes of all time, and estimating that investments in OF are now paying off at an astonishing rate.[21] Although the earlier passion of the World Bank and the International Monetary Fund's (IMF) for 'Integrated Rural Development' has been eclipsed in the 1980-90s by zeal for new paradigms called 'Structural Adjustment' and 'Good Governance', the Bank's praise indicates that the WFP/FAO's 'Operation Flood' in India was one example of truly integrated rural development, whatever its label.

This book was written because, by the early-1990s when sufficient data became available to show conclusively that Operation Flood was a success, research journal articles about it dwindled - before trumpeting its achievements. That is a gross disservice to the efforts of development practitioners, farmers and others who earned this success. Worse, ignoring the success of OF can result in foregoing other opportunities, in situations wherein other countries might conceivably deploy dairy aid as effectively as did India. Nothing on the scale of Flood is in the offing. But where surpluses exist and use can be made of them, politicians ought to practice their art of achieving the possible.

Certainly more empirical data (e.g. the FAO Agrostat/1990/94 computer database) was at hand for this book than was available to most previous writers. The productive infrastructure financed by monetised aid, and improvements to milk animals have come on stream. Agrostat and other FAO data show that imported dairy aid evaporated, while Indian production - and per capita availability - soared. In sum, the data stand to the credit first of all to farmers, and then to an alphabet soup of organisations, including the NDDB, the GOI, DANIDA (development arm of Denmark), the Swiss Government, the EEC (now EU), the FAO of the UN, the World Bank, the WFP, food aid efforts of US PL 480 and other developmental entities including NGOs such as Oxfam. Together the individuals encompassed by these organisations ensured that instead of subverting India's dairy autonomy with food aid, Operation Flood actually increased it.

No topic is more serious than the war on hunger. But the pain of human struggle is relieved, however momentarily, by the balm of victory. It can be instructive as well as satisfying to savour these victories. The role of Operation Flood (OF) in the White Revolution is an exhilarating story, with India dodging the slings and arrows of the Cold War - and seductions of MNCs - to emerge at the turn of the millennium as the world's number one dairy producer. A political-economy tale with a happy ending.

But its happy ending might have been jeopardised without dissonant Cassandras in the press, parliaments and ivory towers of India and Europe, calling attention to anomalies in the programme. Although cynics such as Claude Alvares, author of *White Lie*, irritated Kurien enough for him to pen a rejoinder titled *Black Lie*, it is possible that price reforms crucial to the success of Operation Flood (called for in the 1984 *Jha Commission Report*) would not have been made without the furore sparked by domestic and European critics. This is an important point. The uproar over the continuation of European dairy aid in the late 1980s, *past previously published cut-off dates*, prompted the GOI to reform pricing policies to ensure it was cheaper for plants to obtain domestic supplies than imported milk powder and butter oil donations from Europe. For example, a 1978 GOI report found that plants in the state of Bihar paid farmers too little for their milk. After the *Jha Report* was publicised the GOI increased Anand's authority nationally, bringing rogue managers into line with more sensible pricing policies. And the national and international debate no doubt intensified the efforts of NDDB leaders to wean dairy development from aid dependence.

This has been accomplished. As European milk quotas, instituted in 1984, gradually reduced the dairy mountains, India correspondingly reduced its commodity aid imports. Although a balance-of-payments crisis linked to oil price rises in the 1991 Gulf War sparked a temporary resurgence in dairy and other commodity aid (e.g. vegetable oil), dairy commodity aid has dwindled to nothing. Because cooperatives return, according to Dr. Kurien, up to '80 per cent of the sale price of milk' to their farmers (far more than middleman Polson Ltd. had before the milk strike in 1946), they succeeded in stimulating a flood of rural milk to the cities. By transforming flush season surpluses into baby food, cheese, condensed milk, chocolates, ice cream, etc., which once were imported from abroad, or manufactured by MNCs in India, coops made the country self-sufficient in the range of dairy products desired by urban consumers, and improved its balance-of-payments accounts. Three of the five biggest businesses in Indian dairying are now, according to the NDDB, in the cooperative sector'. Today NDDB promotional literature[22] can truthfully claim: 'The dependence on commercial imports of milk solids is done away with.'

What is most heartening about the Operation Flood saga is that, after decades of disappointment and recrimination over declining food security in the South, India (which even Kurien was nearly tempted to write off as a basket case) has shown the way forward to food security, rising incomes for private farm families and pluralistic institutions. In the context of the economic recession that struck 'Asian tigers' such as Indonesia, Malaysia, Singapore and South Korea around 1997, India's performance stands in contrast. According to 'Asian values' (a term perhaps coined by the *Economist* in 1980[23]) politicians such as Singaporean leader Lee Kuan Yew, had for years espoused the thesis that in the social and cultural context of Asia, authoritarian government was a better route to prosperity than democracy - with the latter's supposed over-emphasis on multi-party politics, and freedom of speech. But pluralist India has shown that a *democratic* country, whose private farmers benefit from professional leadership, accountable to them in a democratic cooperative marketing organisation, can negotiate the pitfalls of international agricultural aid and trade to its own advantage.

Ironically, decades of breast-beating by dependency theorists has propagated the reactionary view that 'the poor shall be with you always'. Few Europeans, and even fewer Americans, have noticed that although India remains relatively underdeveloped (e.g. illiteracy among girls and women is higher than in China), progress *is* being made in education, nutrition, sanitation, health services, population control and employment at home, while India plays an increasingly competitive role in world food, textiles and services trade. Australians and New Zealanders will have been marginally more observant, because India has developed competitive potential for a world market they tend to dominate - dairy.

Overall, India provides reassuring evidence for neo-classical economists who insist that in a liberalising world trade system, David Ricardo's theory of comparative advantage still applies. In other words, even the poorest countries can approach what Walt W. Rostow called economic 'take-off'. Those who scoffed that 'pigs will fly' before India fed itself are beginning to see that at least 'cows will fly'. This not a specious argument. India is not only self-sufficient in effective demand for milk domestically, but the country has begun to compete as a low-cost producer on world markets.

Of course, domestic gains are paramount. The NDDB states (1998) that with a rise from 20 million tonnes in milk production to more than 70 million tonnes over the quarter century of Operation Flood, 1970~1996: 'something like Rs 50,000 crores more ($125 billion) is today flowing back into the rural economy each year to directly benefit the poorest of India's farmers than it did in 1970.'

Basing their claims on US$250 per tonne of milk, these NDDB claims may or may not be slightly exaggerated. On the other hand, John Shaw and Edward Clay[24] (1993) may be underestimating income returns to coop farmers, writing that in the first two decades of OF, when '6 million dairy farmers' (40 per cent fewer than the nearly 10m members of OF-affiliated coops in 1998) in '60,000' coops: 'earned more than US$1 billion a year, and now own some of the most successful businesses in the country.'

Doubters of the Anand-led revolution, who assume dairy production somehow would have kept pace with population growth, overlook the fact that before the NDDB began to replicate Anand's democratic cooperative model outside Gujarat, the country's dairying was by all accounts moribund. FAO data show that, partly due to drought and famine after the mid-1960s, per capita intake of milk and ghee plunged, until it began to rise in the early 1970s, a couple years after OF came on stream. (N.B. Without a National Milk Grid System, it was difficult to mobilise surpluses to drought-ridden areas.) By the mid-1990s, dairying was growing by approximately 5 per cent annually, and has even been maintaining a 4 per cent growth rate during an El Niño-related drought so far in 1998. These are some of the reasons why (apparently referring to farm families, not individual memberships) the NDDB[25] claims:

> This clearly makes India's dairy effort one of the best attempts in economic development anywhere in the world generating employment for some 18 million farmers spread over 22 states of the country. And most important of all, it is completely voluntary.

The Anand Pattern had been debated for decades, but in time a national consensus - in government and among the populace - acknowledged its merits. In 1979 Anand inspired the national launch of oilseeds grower cooperatives. There is a natural symbiosis between dairying and oilseeds, as the seeds are used in animal fodder as well as human food. Like Operation Flood in dairying, the oilseeds cooperative programme was established to circumvent middlemen in a direct link between producers and consumers. In less than 5 years, Dhara brand edible oil products won status as national market leader, like Amul in milk before it.

Farmers benefited from higher returns, and consumers benefited from an end to adulteration of cooking oil, an endemic problem that occasionally resulted in fatalities when oils were adulterated with toxic liquids. Just as it had in urban sales of milk and fruit juice, the NDDB utilised the 'Tetra-Pak' packing system to ensure product purity. This modern technology, once deplored by sentimental purists as inappropriate to India, had also proven its worth. Even ardent environmentalists admit the paper-based Tetra-Pak cartons not only curtail adulteration, but can also be recycled. In 1989 the GOI named Dr. Kurien head of the Market Intervention Agency for edible oils, and by the late-1990s, according to the NDDB, the project linked nearly one million farmers in eight states in over 6000 oilseeds growers' coops.

After some previous, scandalous failures of agricultural cooperatives, e.g. in sugar cane, which betrayed the public trust, Operation Flood has rehabilitated the reputation of farmers' coops in several ways. Now that the NDDB's record in improving the incomes of so many farmers in India has been established, Dr. Kurien, Dr. Amrita Patel and other NDDB officials are being consulted by counterparts in Sri Lanka, China, Nepal and even Pakistan. This is a fresh countervailing wind to the ominous political fall-out (e.g. international consternation, economic sanctions by Japan and the USA) from the aforementioned round of nuclear tests by Pakistan and India in mid-1998. Fortunately, insiders predict that following a spate of militaristic chest-thumping, the two countries may focus on what Paul Kennedy has shown is the strongest long-term source of national security: economic power.

India is now routinely described as an 'emerging economy' boasting international leadership in important niches in computer software, financial and travel services, as well as earning significant remittances from companies working abroad in heavy construction, etc. In the context of such economic growth, India's dairy performance is even more dramatic: from about 5.6 per cent GDP in 1980-81, the dairy sector's share of national output rose to nearly 6 per cent in 1994-95. Dairying actually grew as: (1) agriculture *in toto* dropped in share of national output; while (2) industry and services growth in the period 1980-95 gave India status as an emerging economy. About 250 million Indians now lead middle-class life styles comparable to citizens of Europe. Just as the Green Revolution increased cereals availability, the White Revolution nearly doubled per capita availability of milk from 107 grams/day in 1970 to about 208 grams/day in 1995. Improved food security benefits all Indians and farm families benefit from increased earnings reliability and a gradual increase in employment options as dairying encourages a number of ancillary businesses in the rural economy.

1990s liberalisations

Dairy cooperatives went into the crucible in the early 1990s. Anand's political clout in Delhi may have been weakened in the wake of the assassinations of prime ministers Indira and Rajiv Gandhi and attendant diminution of Congress Party authority. But the oil price rises resulting from embargoes in the 1991 Gulf War strained India's balance-of-payments accounts until 'Nehruvian socialism', with its Gordian knot of price regulation and subsidies, was essentially abandoned. The GOI set the country on a free trade course and with some trepidation (e.g. over intellectual property provisions on biotechnological products sold in agriculture) it signed the 1994 Uruguay GATT agreement. Most observers now acknowledge that what are routinely called 'the 1991 reforms' were a significant shift in the country's economic course toward freer trade, and that they can be sustained if the country continues its performance as 'an emerging economy'.

GATT/WTO-1994 opened India's dairy markets to multinational and private sector investment. MNCs were allowed equity holdings up to 51 per cent, and restrictions on repatriation of profits were somewhat eased. R.P. Aneja & B.P.S. Puri noted in *Dairy India 1997*[26] that a year after delicensing, 'over 100 new dairy plants were established around the country'. That most of these were constructed to produce high-value-added products for upper-income consumers probably explains why some investors wagered that they could afford to lure coop farmers with, as it proved, unrealistically inflated farmgate prices. Some ambitious entrepreneurs expected the marketing hegemony of the NDDB to unravel. Soon NDDB officials accused private and MNC competitors of 'poaching' milk suppliers and selling adulterated or contaminated milk - an abomination that Operation Flood had been designed to eradicate. Some of these charges of adulteration, e.g. inappropriate use of chemical preservatives in unrefrigerated milk, involved local agents for major international companies which would have been scandalised, had the charges been proven in court. The commercial upstarts responded by accusing the coops of seeking unfair protection.

Meanwhile, the Government was concerned about over-capacity in dairy processing - a bugbear of the early phases of Operation Flood, when under-utilised Mother Dairies were mocked as White Elephants. Legislation titled the Milk and Milk Products Order of 1992 was duly passed. Chief stipulations were that plants up to 75,000 litres per day capacity were to be registered (and presumably inspected) by state governments, and larger ones by the GOI. By September 27, 1996, notes *Dairy India 1997*[27], 319 of 734 applications for new plant registrations were granted, 'but only after ascertaining the availability of marketable milk' in the locality.

Although Dr. Kurien is often portrayed as a maverick bucking the tide of bureaucracy, critics say he showed his own penchant for protection in decrying disruption to 'the orderly development of Indian dairying' after the 1991 liberalisations. They argue that even if some entrepreneurs were guilty of contamination and shortcuts, it is likely that competition spurred the

NDDB to additional efficiencies benefiting farmers and consumers - which was after all the intended effect of the 1991 reforms. Yet, Kurien argues that commercial processors were woefully under-regulated until 1992. He stresses also that despite a growing middle class, most Indians remain poor and the rural employment of millions is vulnerable to: 'the risk that big business will transform the dairy industry from one based on crop residues and small farmers to one that competes with man for scarce land...'

Nevertheless, by 1996 it was apparent that despite inroads by new commercial enterprises the Anand pattern coops would prevail. True, the 1991 reforms triggered a house-cleaning: by 1998 the NDDB had cut a few marginal coops from NDDB membership, while investing in others. Kurien says the cooperative system keeps the loyalty of about 10 million farm family members by paying more for their milk, year after year, than competitors - and ploughing some profits back into village roads, wells and schools. The NDDB continues to strengthen links between rural farmers and urban consumers with creative, humorous billboards and state-of-the art advertising and packaging for its expanding range of Amul products. In Ahmedabad, a typically cheerful billboard touting Amul ice cream and other treats shows cricket bat-toting cartoon figures over the slogan: *'See many colas. Drink many colas. Eat only Amul.'* One begins to suspect that Anand has withstood increased competition in the 1990s simply because the NDDB manages the marketing links between producers, processors and consumers better than its competitors.

The 1991 reforms and the GATT/WTO-1994 agreement amount to a two-edged sword. Besides the shock of what Charles De Gaulle dubbed the 'cold shower' of foreign competition, liberalised trade offers the opportunity for increased exports. Dairy publications such as *Dairy India Yearbook* reflect India's openness to joint ventures with foreign firms and dispel the myth that warm climates such as India's are always at a cost disadvantage to temperate climates. (Agri-economists estimate countries such as India have a dairy factorial advantage in 30-40 per cent lower labour costs compared to Europe or North America.) Current literature and conversations with NDDB officials also reflect India's determination to meet ISO 9000 hygiene standards - and readiness to fight in the WTO if cheese export rules are prejudiced against buffalo milk.

Ironically, for the man who personifies Operation Flood, a programme pilloried as a Trojan Horse to foreign subversion, Dr. Kurien is suspicious that the GATT/WTO/FAO nexus could be a subterfuge by rich countries for 'penetration of Indian markets'. He hints a move is afoot to write rules in the sanitary and phyto-sanitary committee of the WTO to effectively outlaw milk exports from poor countries. (Rumoured are absurd rules requiring that exportable milk must be produced by sanitised robot milking machines - clearly beyond the capital means of poor countries!) Kurien vows: 'I don't even know or care who is in the WTO. We will make policy in favour of India.' He happily admits the export of 8200 tons of milk powder and 631 tons of ghee to neighbouring countries such as Bangladesh and the Mid-East in 1995 was a milestone. But, partly due to a combination of factors including drought and internal demand, exports have settled to about 2000 tonnes annually. Kurien warns: 'It'll be quite an achievement if we can continue to export a bit. It will take a long time to satisfy India's demand for milk.'

Kurien's point on the country's ability to absorb future production increases is backed up by the summer 1998 *World Outlook* from the FAO in Rome.[28] The report states that Indian production growth has been: 'sustained by an expansion in internal demand, although per capita consumption is still a relatively modest 65 kg of milk equivalent per year, less than that of, for example, Japan.'

If Japan, a nation synonymous with 'lactose-intolerance' still consumes more milk per capita than India, known as 'a nation of milk lovers', Indian farmers have clearly not yet exhausted internal market potential. And although India's milk exports may grow gradually, it is likely that in the foreseeable future India will make its mark on world dairying by exporting its expertise. The NDDB is working with Kirya Milk Industries of Sri Lanka, to make that island nation independent of milk imports in the next 10 years. Kurien says he told the Sri Lankan PM: 'Madame, I'm committed to doing it in 10 years. Don't be surprised if I do it in five.' As security in Colombo was uncomfortably tight, Kurien protested that protecting him against guerillas was unnecessary as, 'I doubt the Tamil Tigers are interested' in harming someone trying to bring Operation Flood to Sri Lanka. Kurien says MNCs and even the World Bank have warned Sri Lanka not to allow 'that monster Kurien' to influence their dairy plans, and that is why the PM coolly responded: 'Dr. Kurien, it's not the Tamil Tigers I am worried about. It's your enemies among the multinationals.'

As mentioned above, Asian countries such as China, Nepal, Sri Lanka, Thailand, and Vietnam are consulting Anand. The former Soviet Republic of Kyrghyzstan has had a dairy set up for it by the NDDB. Most intriguing is potential for cooperation with the Pakistan Dairy Association, which sent a delegation to Anand in 1997. Its executive director Mian Asif Said wrote Dr. Kurien suggesting: 'innumerable opportunities for mutually beneficial cooperation for both countries.' Now that India and Pakistan have headlined their elite nuclear club membership in newspapers worldwide, perhaps both can now return to the quieter, more profitable activity for which their cultures are traditionally renowned: livestock farming.

Operation Flood's critics retreat

Shrill warnings that European dairy gifts would subvert Indian dairying have proven false. In 1998, Kurien said: 'Shanti George and some of her colleagues came to a conference at Anand last year to apologise. Their thesis was very simple: Food aid is bad; Operation Flood, the largest food aid programme in the world, is therefore very bad!'

If subsequent data have proven the pessimistic predictions of 'the Hague school' wrong, the body of ISS work contains data of great value to development practitioners seeking to seek to spread Flood's lessons to Africa and other continents in the twenty-first century. Former targets of their taunts say the reputations of these researchers are enhanced by their honesty in admitting errors. Someone has to be wrong on the tough questions. Great researchers learn from mistakes and alter course.

In retrospect Anand's victory looks a foregone conclusion. But on the murky post-colonial landscape after World War II - the conflict which hastened global decolonisation - the road to self-sufficiency was not clear. Impressive achievements by state planners in the Soviet Union and Nazi Germany and the rapid reconstruction of post-World War II Europe with Marshall Plan aid all suggested that 'top-down' (i.e. highly-centralised) industrial planning was key to economic growth. Many countries still clung to the mercantilist tenet that international trade was a 'zero-sum' game. Chinese policies, after the 1949 communist revolution, suggested import-substitution (if not autarky) was preferable to the liberal Bretton Woods free trade regime established under US leadership in 1944. All this uncertainty about the GATT - along with unsavoury bi-polar competition in the Cold War - inspired PM Jawaharlal Nehru's promotion of the non-aligned Third World movement at the Bandung Conference in 1955. Much can be learned from investigating the background to Operation Flood, and in succeeding pages we will do so.

After 1947 in post-independence India, farmers seemed just as likely to be hindered as helped by the agents of national and international dairying - whether from Delhi, Brussels, Washington or Rome. Even a friend can step on your foot. Some of these so-called friends (or the constituencies they acted for) were perfectly willing to set up recombination plants in Indian cities, and supply them endlessly with surplus from Europe's Milk Mountains. Such a scenario (similar to the *The Wheat Trap*[29] Gunilla & Beckmann described in Nigeria) would have perfectly suited many MNCs, foreign farmers and politicians - if not taxpayers. But that did not happen, largely due to the discerning sense of Indian farmers and the professional leadership accountable to them.

The economies-of-scale achieved by India's cooperative movement are worth noting by farmers wherever they are subject to 'push-pull' economic forces, i.e. lower prices paid for produce while input costs keep rising. Dairy farmers in rich countries like the USA and Britain are loath to commit a fraction of one per cent of their milk cheques toward advertising, while heavily-advertised colas and other soft drinks gradually erode dairy's market share. As the effects of GATT/WTO-1994 take hold, and supports for US and EU farmers disappear, more rich country farmers are tempted to abandon coops and 'go it alone' with 1000 cow mega-dairies and exclusive contracts to supply supermarkets. Take a lesson from Anand, whose farmers knew before the 1946 milk strike that they must 'hang together or they would hang separately'. Today, lively Amul adverts help cooperative dairists hold predominant market share against multinational giants, while enhancing the livelihoods of 11 to 13 million families.

The sum of India's experience also offers lessons to developing countries wary of liberalised agricultural trade in the GATT/WTO-1994 era. The GOI encouraged rural development *via* Anand-modelled dairy cooperatives as a better, middle option between lethargic centrally-planned or state government-led dairy projects on one hand and frenetic *laissez-faire* capitalism on the other. Kurien, his mentor Tribhuvandas and colleagues such as Dalaya adapted technology to make powder and a full range of high-value products from indigenous *buffalo* milk, transformed the problematic gift of European/EEC dairy aid into productive infrastructure, and strengthened the marketing network between rural farmers and urban consumers in a National Milk Grid System. India eventually weaned itself from commodity aid, and in stark contrast to the milk rationing of the 1960s, now leads the world in milk production. The country transformed a potentially-devastating deluge of foreign dairy aid into a resilient national milk marketing system with world-class potential.

Asked in his Anand office at the NDDB in April 1998 how dairy aid increased food security instead of dependence, Dr. Verghese Kurien said: 'Operation Flood was the first time aid was put in the hands of someone answerable to farmers.' That is why, when all is said and done, Operation Flood was no Trojan Horse - not even a Trojan Cow.

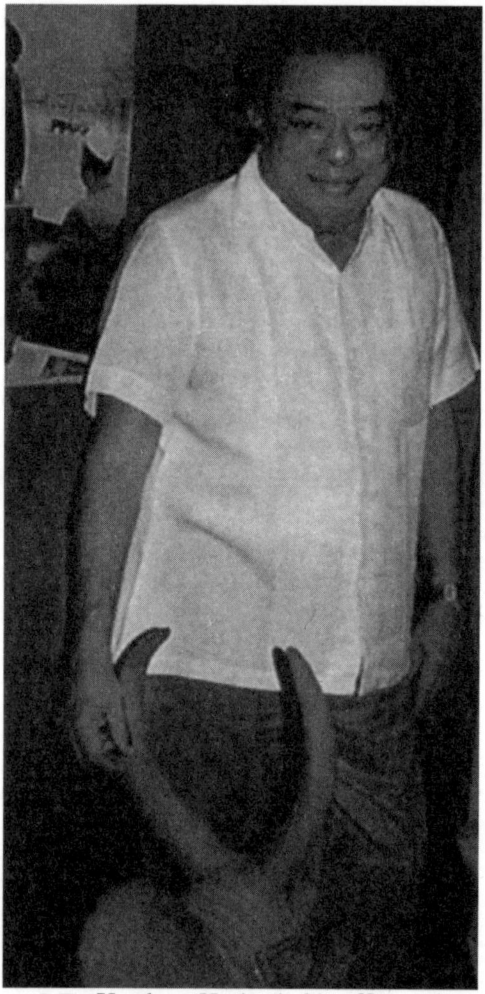

Photo 2: Dr. Verghese Kurien in his office at Anand.

Chapter 2

Recurring Depression?

Free trade in goods, services and *capital* too?

What a difference a day makes. For the dozen or so millennia since our ancestors turned from hunting-gathering to agriculture approximate a day in the life of humans on earth. Farming wrought enormous changes in human existence. The wolf of hunger was partially domesticated, if not completely tamed. The establishment of permanent settlements contributed to specialisation of labour, fostering art and culture along with the advance of technology. Agriculture made global civilisation and urbanisation possible.

Change quickened. Agricultural transformation and trade have accelerated in the last few centuries. But just as there is no free lunch, no change is unencumbered by cost/benefit considerations. Today people wonder if gains from trade outweigh the pain of economic adjustment. In the past, cultivation of crops and domestication of animals enabled the establishment of cities and division of labour, but burgeoning populations strained the capacity of surrounding fields, making them vulnerable to crop failure and drought. Not to mention the pestilence that - if it was not borne by travelling traders or warriors - crept from the squalor of permanent dwellings that were less hygienic than the airy tents of nomads.

But it wasn't all plague and famine. Or why would our ancestors keep building towns and cities? Improvements in transport fostered trade and staved off hunger in lean times (A tip of the hat to ancient bullocks is due.). If bands of marauders threatened settlements, these could be defended by citizen-soldiers, even small standing armies.

City-states and regional authorities made structural innovations of a political-economic nature; in times of political stability, coins and other specie replaced awkward, time-consuming barter. There is archaeological evidence from ancient cities not only of daily transactions recorded on clay tablets, but of surprisingly sophisticated futures markets for food commodities to be delivered on specified dates.

Economic shocks' relation to dairy development

Unfortunately, the August 1998 fall of the Russian rouble and other economic woes in the ex-USSR illustrate how quickly an economy can backslide from a modern banking system into raw barter. In such circumstances the sophistication of twentieth century commerce is revealed as a precariously thin veneer atop a shifting bedrock of problems that have troubled mankind for aeons.

Although post-Soviet Russia is geographically far from the epicentres of Asian economic tremors in Thailand, Malaysia, Indonesia, etc., comparisons are fruitful. In the 1990s (a decade in which signing of the Uruguay Accords marked a worldwide trend toward free markets) they shared an economic boom that threatened to turn bust. In contrast, China and India seem relatively unperturbed by so-called economic contagion. As it is a premise of this book that international agricultural trade can spur development and generally improve the terms of trade for developing countries, it is important to determine how they can avoid instability and maximise gains under the aegis of GATT/WTO.

Those suspicious that unimpeded capital movements have resulted in capital fight and even world economic contagion should think twice before forsaking the ideal of free trade in goods, services & capital. Abandoning trade in capital along with goods & services could be like throwing the baby out with the bath water. Although free trade brings risks it can also accelerate sustainable growth.

Since the 1997 downturn began in Asia, critics of capitalism renewed calls for reforms to prevent capital flight from relatively healthy economies during regional panics. Point taken. Perhaps some sound economies did suffer from a 'demonstration effect' by countries rife with nepotism and waste. Of course 'blaming the victim' is unfashionable and usually unwarranted. However, government reforms in tendering public works contracts, and more transparent accounting in investment were long overdue in many countries. In fact, economic historian Michael Bordo[1] disputes the concept of 'contagion', claiming that 'full information' reassures investors against panic, preventing capital flight from healthy economies. Bolstering Bordo's argument is Argentina's assertion that its sound economic policies give it immunity against contagion from Brazil – though this claim was negated in Argentina's crisis of 2000-1. But transparent accounting and what the World Bank and IMF call 'good governance' can act as security blankets when economic trouble looms. Let us now range a bit freely in our discussion of world trade, which can shed light on India's development.

The trebling of India's milk production in Operation Flood is evidence that, although the country's status as a dairy exporter is small its potential is tremendous. But future gains depend on the ability of importers to pay for Indian exports. Because these conditions will be increasingly affected by the GATT/WTO it is worth tracing its effects in other scenarios.

Back in the ex-USSR

Some wags maintain that conditions in Russia matter no more to the world economy than those in The Netherlands, since the countries have approximately the same size output. But that is nonsense for several reasons beyond the subtle but real psychological effects that one market can have on another: Vast Russia has a population 10-times that of tiny Holland; Russia retains thousands of nuclear arms; and 1917 is just one year that springs to mind when Russian economic problems had worldwide impact.

Russia's post-1989 crises have been occurring in a time of relative peace, when the United Nations, the World Bank, the International Monetary Fund and other multilateral institutions are committed to assisting the restructuring of the former mainstay of the Soviet empire from communism to modern transnational capitalism. The success of this transformation is far from assured.

Already explanations are mooted for its presumed failure. Although formerly state-run parts of the former USSR economy such as the chemical and gas sectors were 'privatised', these plans are said to be stillborn because they were sold as monolithic, or monopolistic, blocs and - crucially - not broken up into competing entities. True, they were sold, but often to the same officials, the same old communist *nomenklatura* with a capitalist makeover, who had managed them poorly under communism. But more than new management was need according to this analysis. Privatisation wasn't enough, they needed to be disaggregated into competing organisations. If, after free marketeer Boris Yeltsin succeeded Mikhail Gorbachev, Soviet state enterprises had been broken up properly, in the manner of the dismantling of telecommunications monolith American Telephone and Telegraph (AT&T - affectionately called 'Ma Bell' after its well-known logo of a bell) in the United States, the economy would have been positively stimulated. Redundant staff and outdated equipment could have been cut, in rationalisations needed for productivity increases. (Theoretically, sacked staff would find new jobs in other productive enterprises.) The existence of competing rivals would have encouraged good management, reflected in continual price and quality improvements to products offered Russian consumers.

In the break-up of telecom behemoth AT&T, which was viewed with trepidation by all but neocapitalist purists, such as devotees of Friedrick von Hayek and Milton Friedman, efficient management of Ma Bell was needed to ensure its survival against the many decoupled 'Baby Bells'. But in early-1990s privatisations in the ex-USSR, the former state monoliths remained largely intact, and too many managers tried to survive simply through barter, suspending payrolls, and seeking ways to exploit their virtual monopolies in the new, nominally free market. Lack of true competition doomed the post-Soviet economy to market failure.

Decentralisation, deregulation and privatisation were bywords of the policies of Margaret Thatcher in Britain and Ronald Reagan in the USA during the 1980s - and to a significant extent, PM P.V. Narasimha Rao in India after 1991. Fortunately, productivity gains quickly became obvious in the UK and US reforms - so much so that they encouraged further deregulation of telecommunications. Telephone rates to consumers fell and quickly led to adoption of mobile telephones, faxes and Email worldwide. Successful telecoms reforms spurred deregulation of the airlines in the USA and other countries. Airline deregulation was also largely successful in that, despite a wane in direct flights and the development of 'hub & spoke' logistical plans by airlines such as Delta (spawning the joke that one couldn't fly from Boston to New York City without flying first through Delta's hub airport much further south in Atlanta, Georgia), and the isolation of Minneapolis in a 1998 labour dispute with Northwest Airlines (which despite deregulation had gradually obtained control of a majority of landing slots in the Twin Cities), it doubled US domestic and overseas air travel. US fares fell in real terms while air travel in Europe, where airlines were still predominantly highly-regulated national carriers, remained relatively expensive. Drops in the cost of domestic airfares and telecommunications undoubtedly contributed to a rise in US business productivity. Seen in the 1970s and 1980s as a sick giant, the USA now has the image of an efficient economic superpower.

Compared to flawed privatisations in the ex-USSR, successful US deregulation suggests that success depends more on productivity gains made in *competition* than on privatisation itself. At any rate, economic growth in the Reagan-Thatcher years encouraged global adoption of free market policies. This included short term investment capital in and out of poor countries, although Joseph Stiglitz (2002: p.65) points out - and US history shows - that the USA and 'advanced industrial countries' feared tariff cuts and 'capital market liberalisation until late in their development'.

It is important not to confuse the neoliberal, *laissez-faire* reading of Adam Smith by Reagan and Thatcher with what they regarded as the watered-down conservatism of certain predecessors in their respective Republican and Conservative (*aka* Tory) parties. The strict monetarism and horror of inflation shared by Reagan and Thatcher were a far cry from the nominally free market economies overseen by earlier leaders of their respective parties, Richard Nixon and Edward Heath, who ran their countries with an eye to sustaining certain levels of output and employment, sometimes ascribed to Keynesian monetary policies. (Like holy writ, a passage in Keynes can often be found to support any viewpoint.) Nevertheless, the difference between monetarism and Keynesianism can safely be stated so: monetarists feel social welfare cannot be sustained without strict control of the money supply and inflation; Keynesians generally believe that control of inflation is secondary to maintaining sufficient levels of investment - *via* private and especially government spending - to sustain output and employment. Ironically, although the champion of Star Wars was ideologically identified with monetarism, Lester Thurrow[2] observed that: 'President Reagan proved that Keynesian economics still works, but President Mitterrand also proved that no country in Europe is big enough to go it alone.'

Certainly Reagan and Thatcher tolerated much higher levels of unemployment (ca. 5-10 per cent) than their predecessors (ca. 2-5 per cent). Full employment was one war promise Franklin Roosevelt and Winston Churchill used to inspire their troops. In candid moments the advisors of Reagan and Thatcher argued that higher levels of employment were not just needed to correct economic imbalances, but existed also because the social welfare net that rose after World War II had not only improved unemployed people's ability to survive joblessness - but also made them choosier about work. As for international currency controls, one illustration of how times have changed is that at times during the Vietnam War, the US economy was so closely managed (or centrally-planned) that major US corporations were prohibited from exporting investment capital to their subsidiaries in Europe and elsewhere.

Many of Reagan and Thatcher's ideas on decentralisation, deregulation and privatisation scorned by their critics soon spread across Europe (spurring a reversal of French President François Mitterrand's socialist policies in the early 1980s), and thereafter inspired restructuring in South America, the Eastbloc and the Third World. Despite touting decentralisation as superior to central planning, Reagan and his ex-Wall Street cabinet members, e.g. George Schultz and Donald Regan, pushed integration of world financial systems claiming that transnational joint ventures or private finance to commercial companies could be a development boon to poor countries parched for investment.

Meanwhile, though Thatcher espoused decentralisation she cut the funding authority of local councils to ensure that monetarist policies replaced what she deemed years of their Keynesian overspending and debt. Thatcher's promotion of London as a centre for financial and other services ironically helped spur European integration. But her hard-headed resistance to what she popularly characterised as meddling of *dirigist* super-integrationists like Commissioner Jacques Delors, helped establish the principle of subsidiarity (*aka* devolution) in which EU member governments in, say, The Hague or Helsinki, have authority in all matters that cannot better be handled by EU authorities in Brussels. The concept characterises the federal relationships between Länder and the Federal Government of Germany. Subsidiarity also reflects federal principles in the Tenth Amendment of the US Constitution: 'The powers not delegated to the United States by the Constitution...are reserved to the States respectively, or to the people.' The triumph of subsidiarity was one victory by British 'Euro-sceptics' against Brussels *dirigisme* that may well be savoured by other EU members with less clout in Brussels than heavyweights France and Germany.

European integration & enlargement

Just as dairists in Gujarat might complain of meddling from Delhi, rural farmers and managers worldwide wage continual war with national governments (and now perhaps with the GATT/WTO) over agricultural policy. Germane to our purposes is the fact that European dairy surpluses were 'monetised' in India's Operation Flood. So a glance at European integration can explain how that lactic largess materialised in the first place.

After the post-World War I failure of the League of Nations degenerated into the Great Depression and World War II, much faith was placed on supranational institutions such as the United Nations to prevent World War III. Optimists heartened that two world wars had not totally destroyed the earth were nay-sayed by pessimists: *Third time's a charm!*

But what about Europe? How would it restructure, and what relationships would the chastened powers enjoy with their remaining and former colonies? Returning Europe to pre-war levels of output had first priority.

1951

With leadership by Jean Monnet and Robert Schuman the European Coal & Steel Community (ECSC)[3] was established in 1951 to foster economic cooperation rather than military confrontation between France and Germany. With its 6 founding members of Belgium, France, Germany, Italy, Luxembourg and The Netherlands, the ECSC achieved prosperity as well as peace, paving the way for further integration in the EEC.

1957

Under the 1957 Treaties of Rome, the 6 ECSC members established the European Economic Community (EEC), The EEC's Common Agricultural

Policy (CAP) regained Western Europe's food self-sufficiency, and produced the surplus Butter Mountain and Milk Lake that eventually flowed toward India. The European Community of Atomic Energy (ECAE, sometimes known as Euratom) was also established. Germany was somewhat out of the bargain on account of its sins during World War II.

But it contributed to Britain and France's development of military and peaceful (if polluting) uses of the atom. France used ECAE under President Charles de Gaulle to enhance national *gloire* through foreign policy carrots in the Third World - accompanied by the nuclear sticks of its *force de frappe*. Britain maintained its more cooperative 'special relationship' with the USA. In fact Labour cabinet member Tony Benn later claimed Britain never enjoyed any autonomy in its nuclear relationship with the USA: London could not launch missiles on Moscow (or even Paris) without Washington's permission.

But whether or not Britain became a US 'nuclear poodle', both Britain and France enjoyed greater prestige from nuclear development. Hanrieder & Auton[4] wrote that de Gaulle believed nuclear membership would help France to 'regain the independent and dynamic role' it deserved 'regardless of whether the cost' was justified on purely strategic grounds.' This argument apparently was not lost on developing countries including China, India and Pakistan.

1973

About 3 years after the advent of Operation Flood in India, on January 1, 1973, Denmark, Ireland and the UK joined the European Community, bringing membership to 9. Britain had clung on to trade relationships in its Commonwealth, and resisted EEC integration by promoting the European Free Trade Area (EFTA), before joining the EEC. In the 1990s Britain remained arguably the EEC's most belligerent-but-important bedfellow, despite PM John Major's assertion that it belonged 'at the heart of Europe'.

1981

Greece joined in 1981, making the EC-10 and prompting interest by other less industrialised countries with softer currencies that EEC membership was a possibility.

1986

After making democratic reforms Portugal and Spain were admitted to what was now the EC-12. At this time the passage of the Single European Act and the *Jean Monnetesque* zeal of Commissioner Jacques Delors in promoting the lucrative potential of the Single Market gave EC membership coveted status. Turkey applied (1987), Cyprus (1990), Malta (1990), Switzerland (1992), Poland (1994) and Hungary (1994).

1995

However, it was Austria, Finland and Sweden who joined the Community with its new name the European Union (EU) making the EU-15. The familiar blue flag with 12-encircled stars remained the official symbol. Voters in oil-rich Norway rejected EU membership in a referendum; although that denies Norway policy influence in Brussels, it retains access to the EU Single Market through the European Economic Area (EEA). Further 'deepening and widening' of what was became commonly known as the European Union (EU) was planned. By this time EU dairy commodity aid to India had virtually ceased although technical assistance to a smaller scale dairy development project was underway in China.[5]

Agenda 2000

About a dozen former Eastbloc countries applied for membership. Under EU Commission President Jacques Santer the Czech Republic, Estonia, Hungary, Poland and (the Mediterranean island of) Cyprus are in advanced discussions on admission. Bulgaria, Latvia, Lithuania, Romania and Slovakia may spend longer on the waiting list. While this portends a historic political enlargement of the European House and underscores the end of the Cold War, it could break the budget.

After progress in transition from communism, Poland grew so lax about needed restructuring, that Brussels forced a warning shot, cutting ECU60m earmarked to retrain unemployed miners and shipbuilders. The EU also banned some Polish dairy products from EU trade after sanitary rules were ignored. These approximate the sanitary & phyto-sanitary measures (SPMs in WTO jargon) that India has been meeting in annual dairy exports of 2000-9000 metric tonnes to other countries. (Neither India nor Poland can afford to rest, because with continuing food scares in Japan, the USA, the UK and elsewhere, food safety will be an ongoing battleground in trade warfare.) Poland's dairy trade embarrassment is symptomatic of difficulties faced by former Eastbloc countries face in EU admission. Their large agricultural sectors could overwhelm the budget at present levels of CAP farm subsidies. To obviate that scenario and simultaneously meet GATT/WTO demands, agricultural reform has high priority in Agenda 2000. Direct income support to farmers from social funds, and payment to farmers to perform environmentally beneficial services is expected to replace the former production focus of the CAP. National governments are likely to get responsibility for many agricultural subsidies now stemming from Brussels.

EU (dis)integration?
Creative policy wonks foresaw that deepening European integration in the 1990s could release Europe from projects on other continents that elicited charges of neo-colonialism. But EU integration is stressed whenever economic cycles tempt national governments into beggar-they-neighbour policies. In some respects Europe is as ethnically diverse as India, and it is understatement to say European integration has been opposed at various times by all political stripes. Britain's Labour Party opposed joining the EEC for years, although recently most of Britain's Euro-sceptics have congregated in the Conservative party, e.g. members of PM John Major's cabinet including Norman Lamont, Michael Portillo and John Redwood, or Major's successor as Tory party leader William Hague. But in time many business and political leaders came to favour it, believing that if Europe was to match USA or Japanese performance, further economies-of-scale would have to be achieved in Europe. At the time of writing, Tory leader David Cameron emphasises cooperation with Europe.

In the mid-1980s European Commissioner Jacques Delors launched his campaign for the European Single Market with strong support from *dirigistes* in France and Germany. Despite hand-wringing, Margaret Thatcher and John Major signed treaties establishing the Single Market. In the post-colonial world this could be seen as a triumph of geography over politics. UK trade with continental Europe was much greater than with former colonies Australia or Canada, and all these countries reformed immigration laws to attract needed investment, workers and - not least - set the legal basis for multiracial, pluralist societies.

The new geopolitical realities set the scene for other further political and economic union in the Maastricht Treaty, although Britain typically balked at the costs of social welfare provisions in Maastricht's 'Social Chapter'. European Monetary Union (EMU) was another shibboleth by which to distinguish Britain from the Franco-German drive toward integration. After problems in the early-1990s, Britain was understandably wary that the country might enter EMU at rates with the D-mark or other currencies that could damage its economic welfare. Predictably, Euro-sceptics fanned populist fears that losing the pound (£) was tantamount to burning the Union Jack flag - or losing sovereignty itself. Although the 1992 Programme has not by itself raised EU output 4 per cent, or cut unemployment as predicted in the early-1980s' report to Brussels by economist Paulo Checchini, the Single Market is generally seen as successful. In late 1998, head of the British National Farmers Union Ben Gill said, 'It's in British farmers' interests to make EMU work.' (This reflects weakening of farmers' traditional preference for the Tories over Labour.) Although Tony Blair's Labour Government maintained its coyness on joining EMU which was set to start on January 1, 1999, agriculture minister Nick Brown[6] announced UK traders and farmers would have the option of receiving CAP market support in Euros (i.e. European Currency Units or ECUs set in Brussels) by autumn 2000. EU integration advanced and Euro-sceptics retreated.

Perhaps because Italy (once deemed poverty-stricken) was a member from the beginning, its per capita GDP eventually surpassed that of Britain which joined late. Poorer members such as Ireland, Greece, Portugal and Spain have also profited economically from integration. All EU members benefited from increased business and employment opportunities for their people, and increased prestige and economic muscle in competition with Japan and North America. Through frequent consultation among members and (occasional) unity of voice expressed through Brussels, ECSC/EEC/EC/EU governments gained prestige. Although it has largely gone unmentioned, EU integration translated into greater economic and military security (partly due to NATO membership) in the dangerous years as Russian hegemony ebbed, and communist and social-democratic Germanies reunified.

But European political and economic union was far from complete. Commissioner Jacques Delors had to fight for representation at G-7 and other top economic summits. The EU suffered humiliation after premature recognition by Germany of the sovereignty of Croatia and Slovenia allowed the civil war with Serbia to get out of hand in former Yugoslavia. Had EU governments spoken with one voice, and if Germany's constitution had permitted the deployment of its armed forces[7] within a framework of EU foreign policy, it is doubtful that Yugloslav President Slobodan Milosevic, and the former president of Bosnia's Serb Republic Radovan Karadzic, would have initiated over four years of civil war that (despite the presence of NATO troops and mediation by the USA and the UN) remains unresolved. To victims of the ensuing violence and genocide of the Muslim population of Bosnia-Herzogovina early in the 1990s, and later of Albanians in the Serbian province of Kosovo, the political, economic and military integration of the European Union appears unimpressive.

The EU also faces sensitive relations with many countries, especially Turkey which sought admission to the EEC as early as 1964. Although about 1 million Turks live in Germany, and Berlin hosts one of the largest urban Turkish enclaves in the world, many Germans are dubious of Turkish membership in the EU, maintaining that cultural - not religious - differences make integration problematic.

Greece opposes admission of its traditional rival Turkey as long as they contest occupation of Cyprus. Turkey's real GNP growth was about 8 per cent in 1995 and maintained a rate of about 5 per cent thereafter.[8] Its secular constitution devised under Kemal Ataturk remains a modernising influence and, doubtless, has helped meld trade relations with the EU.

Turkey has supplied millions of guestworkers to Europe and been a staunch NATO ally in the Korean and Gulf Wars. The denial of EU membership to Turkey could potentially polarise sentiment of Muslims both inside and outside Turkey against the supposed Christian majority of the EU. Yet given Turkey's human rights abuses of its Kurdish and Armenian minorities, it is unsurprising Turkey was denied fast track to EU membership. But EU-Turkish relations improved when the coalition Government of SPD Chancellor Gerhard Schroeder and Green Party foreign minister Joschka Fischer succeeded long-time CDU Chancellor Helmut Kohl in 1998, and Berlin eased citizenship requirements for the children of guestworkers.

The possibility that trade will bring Europe and Turkey, and by extension, Greece, closer together encapsulates the chicken-or-egg nature of integration. What comes first: trade or political union? Wherever people engage in trade they begin to feel their political stripes are not incompatible.

Economic integration around the world

In the 1980s and 1990s the Association of South East Asian Nations (ASEAN) was formed by Brunei, Indonesia, Malaysia, the Philippines, Singapore, Thailand and Vietnam to become a borderless economic zone and to form a lobbying group capable of swimming with the two biggest economic tigers in the region - China and India.[9] The United States (where schoolgirls and boys expect the twenty-first century will see more business in Asia than Europe) was alarmed and a little jealous at being excluded from ASEAN. So the USA began the Asian-Pacific Economic Cooperation (APEC) agreement, its own association of Pacific Rim nations (including Canada, Indonesia, Japan, Korea, Malaysia, New Zealand and the Philippines) to ensure the country that Boeing and Microsoft call home gets a fair hearing abroad. Nor are just jumbo jets or computer software in the APEC pipeline. Increased sales to Pacific Rim countries like Japan and Korea have boosted US dairy products to about 8 per cent of total world dairy trade in 1997, up from 4.4 per cent in 1990 according to the US Dairy Export Council.[10] Whether or not India will have enough surplus milk to export some to these markets, the USA hopes it can capture more world market share, and its Department of Agriculture (USDA) has given the nod to biotechnology research to boost productivity. Pharmaceutical and biotech companies such as Monsanto are eager to participate.

In the 1990s integration was spurred in Latin America by MERCOSUR, which despite a slow start, seems to be contributing to a decade of peaceful development in services, industry and agriculture - notably dairying. Trade ties between Argentina, Brazil and Uruguay were strengthened. Later discussions in this book will refer to the GATT view that regional trade agreements ultimately sacrifice a measure of global potential. Who can doubt, however, the present value of a regional trade relationship between sometimes warring neighbours, compared to the future value of some theoretically perfect agreement?

The most momentous blow for free trade in the Western hemisphere in the 1990s was the North American Free Trade Agreement (NAFTA). It was derided by US information systems magnate-cum-presidential candidate Ross Perot who warned NAFTA would lead to 'a giant sucking sound' as manufacturing jobs fled the USA for cheaper conditions south of the Rio Grande. Nevertheless, Canada, Mexico and the USA did form NAFTA - a common market that partly owed its existence to rivalry with that other, increasingly-competitive Common Market across the Atlantic Ocean. NAFTA advocates also saw it as a much-needed measure to invigorate the Mexican economy which, after a 1970s oil boom went bust, was characterised by legal and illegal emigration for jobs in the North. NAFTA did attract a great deal of short term investment to Mexico which partly due to a strong peso resulted in a brief export boom for US suppliers, mostly near the border. As Perot predicted, a number of turn-key electronics and other manufacturing plants were constructed just south of the border but, all things considered, NAFTA has not harmed the US or Canadian economies.

One hopes some net long-term investment in productive infrastructure was made in Mexico, because NAFTA dreams turned into nightmare with the devaluation of the peso and overnight capital flight around December, 1994. The US Government somewhat stabilised the Mexican economy with a $50 billion bailout, but it was unable to stave off painful recession and disillusion, south of the border. This nasty episode illustrated that while Mexico was perhaps an 'emerging economy' in the same league with India and the Little Tigers of Asia, it was no candidate for G-7 status. Mexico's set-back casts significant doubt on unfettered capital flows.

William Greider[11] presents Mexico as a cautionary tale of how US policy can inadvertently cause trouble elsewhere. Greider says 'Mexico's false boom' was fuelled by the US Federal Reserve's 'supplying easy credit' to bail out America's 'troubled commercial banks.' Cheap credit from New York made otherwise unattractive Mexican bonds for marginal projects a bargain. As long as the Mexican bonds maintained a high rate of return, this lucrative arbitrage thrived. When cracks appeared in the Mexican boom in 1994, it quickly went bust. Because the case of Mexico sheds light on more recent troubles in East Asia and Russia, it will be discussed further below. It also helps elucidate why China and India remain relatively unscathed.

Capital offences?

In the Reagan-Thatcher years, governments on all continents and multilateral institutions such as the IMF and World Bank accepted the gospel of free trade in goods, services and even short-term capital. They echoed the depiction by Wall Street bankers and influential publications such as the *Economist* that the best hope of spreading investment to needy countries was in what may be called a liberalised extension of neo-classical economics. The Club of Rome's calls in the 1970-80s for a 0.7 per cent of GDP contribution from rich countries to investment in the Third World were muted. Drawing focus from the dangerous, wasteful nuclear arms race back to economic development was probably useful, but even the Club of Rome's most illustrious member, Willy Brandt, never fully believed such a First-to-Third World version of the Marshall Plan would work. Doubters in muttered that the Club of Rome was more a sideswipe at US foreign policy by lesser European allies (particularly France) than a serious attempt to rectify Third World inequities. There had been decades of disappointing results from many projects assisted by institutions such as the World Bank (Operation Flood not among them!). Perhaps strictly profit-oriented capital investment, as long-advocated by development iconoclast Peter T. Bauer, was the one true path after all. Publications like the *Wall Street Journal* and the *Economist* pointed to the virtue-enhancing effect upon governments of having to contain state-owned enterprises and inflationary wage increases to public employees, and to avoid crippling tax burdens on MNCs if countries were to attract investment. One of the brighter themes of early-1990s economic trends was a swing to internationally-recognised accounting standards. Internationally 'transparent' accounting could, as in Michael Bordo's analysis given above, bring closer the ideal of 'perfect marketplace information' - thus avoiding waste and the shock of capital flight when unwise investments proved faulty.

But in late 1998, the trend of free market policies to make a better world seemed at least temporarily stymied. It is true that the shift to free markets has gone acceptably well in the Czech Republic, Hungary and Poland where the economies have benefited from contract work from the West, e.g. in textiles.[12] Even though Germany's *Wiedervereinigung* and reconstruction of former East Germany has proceeded less miraculously than hoped, it continues. Yet the relatively greater success of Eastbloc countries compared to Russia in adapting to capitalism seems hinged on this: their pre-World War II history of working within the international capitalist community and the fact that some of the attitudes and expertise necessary for survival in such an environment endured.

This cultural legacy seems lacking in Russia. As a top US foreign policy advisor[13] said in *The Cold War* documentary TV series, adopting free market policies without the necessary financial attitudes, institutions and other infrastructure is fraught with peril. Perhaps its inexperience with capitalism and the hope-inducing examples of the Czech Republic and Hungary (along with blandishments from Germany and France who dangled the vision of a prosperous 'European House' in front of a country which had only temporarily abandoned this chic illusion after the Bolshevik revolution of 1917) made Russia try to run before it could walk. But dozens of clever Western economic advisors including Jeffrey Sachs had advised Russia that a slow Gorbachev-style transition from communism to capitalism would be more painful than a short, sharp shock. Perhaps that explains why Russia appeared a fanatic new true believer in the *laissez-faire* religion, at least until the 1998 meltdown of its stockmarkets, fall of the currency and capital flight when former rouble-billionaires were rumoured to join pensioners selling plastic carrier bags in the Moscow subway.

At any rate, economist Kazimierz Poznanski[14] has suggested that the USSR's focus on 'output-maximisation' and neglect of quality-control contributed to its greater need than some of its Eastbloc comrades to resort to barter rather than cash sales for its often shoddy goods. (In contrast to poor USSR-quality goods were internationally renowned Zeiss lenses from East Germany, and machine tools, motorcycles and weapons from former Czechoslovakia.) Poznanski wrote:

> After years of gradual catching up, it [USSR] has come to the equilibrium technological gap. Gomulka (1985) reveals that up to 1975 Soviet rates of labour productivity growth, while declining, were still high enough to bring Soviet industry closer to the productivity level of the United States. However, since that time the rates in both countries have equalised, but the absolute level of Soviet labour productivity remains about 25 years behind…

This is a telling point for all countries. It doesn't pay to fall too far behind in a race. Not only were Soviet car, chemicals and computer industries inferior to those of the USA and Asian tigers, but they would never catch up as long as central-economic-planning (CPE) was clung to. Of all the bright economists in the USSR many must have realised that even if the economy was not reformed overnight, reform was inevitable in the long run. Even if a majority of citizens accepted a mediocre standard of living as long as it guaranteed economic stability, the invisible hands of a minority of entrepreneurs would surely keep hammering for free market reforms. (The image of Hungarian-American billionaire speculator George Soros attacking a weak currency comes to mind.) The Soviet Union's parallels with other countries sharing its penchant for socialist planning - India and Sweden -

are striking, are they not? Economic liberalisation for all three arrived around 1991. Even rich Sweden has difficulties adjusting its mixed public/private economy to the realities of global capitalism. It can be argued that although India was starting out from a lower economic base than Sweden and also Russia, it has a better chance of steady growth than Russia.

Perhaps the unkindest cuts to Russia's body politic came from its mafia which seemed better at extorting payoffs from entrepreneurs than Moscow was at collecting taxes. Nor was the country Russia defeated good for ready cash. After years of handouts from Germany, the coffers in Bonn and Berlin are too empty to offer more succour to Russia. The IMF's credit line has been strained by problems in East Asia. The chief Russian financial auditor claimed proof that previous IMF loans worth billions of dollars had been squandered or stolen and warned that no further loans should be made until his country puts its house in order.[15] A former World Bank boss questioned whether specific funds fronted by the West had actually been stolen, but predicted that future loans would (instead of simply being allocated to the government's central fund, where accounting is difficult) be targeted at specific projects as is routine procedure for the European Bank of Reconstruction and Development (EBRD) and the World Bank. Whether or not this is an affront to Russia's prestige, it may be a necessary step toward recovery. It is also worth noting that these procedures reflect the transparent funding relationships that existed among bilateral, multilateral and NGO players in India's Operation Flood.

Melancholy Russian folk tales feature amiable peasants doomed to servitude by a weakness for vodka and other diversions. But it was fervently hoped that a well-educated population produced by seven decades of socialism could adopt free market disciplines and thrive. Of course there is hope for Russia. After all, the countries that popularised the terms *gangster*, *mafia* and *embezzlement* later established law & order, and now enjoy excellent standards of living. That hope is shaky in Russia - not due to the haplessness of the people, but because true economic reform entailing competition as well as privatisation was not achieved. But as the average life expectancy of men and other quality of life indicators plummets toward the Russian soil, we ought to be alert to comparatively healthier performers in these 'interesting times'.

China & India exhibit growth & stability

China has continued to grow, like several Asian countries before it, with internal reforms and development borne along by export-led growth. Its foreign account balance is in the black chiefly due to the USA, which now has a greater trade deficit with China than it long complained of with Japan.

The jury is still out on whether Shanghai will not just supersede Hong Kong as preeminent financial centre following the June 1997 handover from Britain, or whether democratic reforms made shortly before the departure of Britain's last governor Chris Patten will be completely quashed. The big question after the world economic meltdown of 2006 was whether Shanghai can join the banking and finance club heretofore reserved for Tokyo, New York, London and (occasionally) Frankfurt. After two decades China has not outlived outlived censure for its 1989 Tiananmen Square massacre of pro-democracy dissidents, after which Deng Xiaoping named Jiang Zemin his successor.[16] But there were signs of progress on autumn 1997 visit by Communist Party Gen. Secretary and President Zemin to the USA, when he performed cooly in candid question-and-answer sessions with journalists and university students. On President Bill Clinton's early-1998 visit to China his speech maintaining that history showed human rights and political freedom were important for development was broadcast widely in Chinese media. Coming a decade after China's first professed interest in joining GATT, there were signs (e.g. a willingness to cut farm export subsidies, if not internal farm supports[17]) that China saw membership in GATT/WTO as more advantageous than ignoring it and thereby endangering that organisation's effectiveness by acting outside it.

India finally begun to make a serious attack on Government corruption in the mid-1990s, according to *Economic Times* consulting editor Swaminathan Aiyar. After the 'tarnishing' of Congress, the Bharatiya Janata Party (BJP) barely managed to patch together a coalition Government, but that didn't stop economic growth from touching 7 per cent in 1995-96. (Even if India's GDP growth was lower at 5 per cent in 1995-96, that is still well ahead of ca. 2 per cent population growth and could likely be sustained indefinitely without fuelling inflation.) Aiyar deplored the 'plethora of subsidies…most of which never get to the poor'. But he adds that 'with a more energetic rule of law' (clearly indicating property rights and transparent rules for investment) 'the future looks ever brighter'.

There is no guarantee China and India will continue inexorably toward prosperity. Beijing has always had a tenuous hold on the provinces, and sporadic reports of warfare between companies (privatised from former socialist communes and collectives) are disturbing. Record flooding and portents of a stockmarket crash are bad enough without reminders of the warlordism and civil war before the 1949 Communist Revolution.

India's too-often inefficient Government fritters funds in boondoggles, when economic development is crying out for further improvements to health care. While India nearly halved its child-mortality rate for children aged under-five from 173 to 85 per thousand in the period 1980-1996, it remains double that of China - and perhaps highest among emerging economies.[18] Throughout this book the case is made for bringing educational levels of boys - and most of all girls - up to those of China. A lack of good roads and the sporadic provision of electricity sap productivity in town and country. Well-meaning programmes providing free electricity to rural Punjab, and subsidising it to farmers in Harayana have turned into power blackouts when state electrical grids make such large losses (US$2.8b[19] nationally in 1996) that they cannot afford to maintain burnt-out transformers. The World Bank recommends either raising rates or privatising utilities and cutting over-manning, but unsurprisingly, farmers and utility workers find such capitalist logic unpalatable. Yet recurring droughts remind us that although food stocks staved off starvation in the 1987 drought, both arable and dairy agriculture need improvements to maintain food security. In line with analysis elsewhere in this text, economist Ashok Gulati[20] is reported by *India Today* to suggest rectifying a long-skewed domestic policy in which: 'industry has enjoyed a 45 per cent tariff protection while agriculture has been taxed at 22 per cent.'

By late 1997 PM Inder Gujral's minority United Front Government, a coalition of 15 parties, had achieved several foreign policy successes with India's neighbours. The 'Gujral doctrine'[21] was credited with solving a river water dispute with Bangladesh and signing a hydroelectric power deal with Nepal. But as mentioned previously in this text, India's dispute with Pakistan over Kashmir and other issues took a more bellicose twist as Gujral's successor PM Atal Bihari Vajpayee initiated a series of nuclear tests in early 1998 - soon reciprocated by Pakistan. While Delhi can afford this spitting contest more easily than Islamabad, neither country really wishes to continue costly nuclear development. (N.B. There are hints that the tests were a signal to third parties such as China or Afghanistan that neither India nor Pakistan would suffer bullying.) India's 1996 per capita GDP of $360 cries out for improvement. While Pakistan's GDP per head of $520 is almost 50 per cent higher than India's, its economy suffers worse inflation. *The Economist*[22] 1997 forecast was GDP of $350 billion for India and $71 billion for Pakistan. So with an economy just one-fifth the size of India, an arms race is proportionately more expensive for an already-tremulous economy. Fortunately, reason may prevail: *Make milk, not war.* By many measures China and India appear less precarious than some of the world's flashier emerging economies. A prime reason may be their conservative approach to policies on capital, currency and investment controls which receive our attention below.

When US economics writer William Greider published his 1997 book *One World, Ready or Not: The Manic Logic of Global Capitalism* warning of overcapacity in world automotive, computer and other industries the

Economist backhandedly honoured his volume of caveats by deriding it as a 'populist tome' in its lead editorial. In light of current world economic woes, he might have responded: *Caveat Victor!* Greider had written:[23]

> The great virtue of capitalism - the quality that had always confounded socialist critics and defeated rival economic systems - is its ability to yield more from less.... But this expanding potential to produce more goods also poses the enduring contradiction for capitalist enterprise: how to dispose of the surplus production. You can make more things, but can you sell them.... The problem of surplus capacity drives not only the competition between firms for market shares but also the imperative to discover new markets.

Of course making more widgets (or kilograms of butter & ghee) with fewer workers releases more people available for other industries, making it possible for an economy to grow. But this virtuous circle ends when there is insufficient capital to establish new jobs. No jobs, no consumers. In the 1950s, the view that overcapacity can lead to job loss and *deflation* was a common view of what caused the Great Depression of 1929-39. But deflationary fears went out of fashion in the inflation and stagflation of the 1970-80s. Additionally, establishment of the World Bank and IMF after the 1944 Bretton Woods conference was supposed to fulfil the crucial role of 'lender of last resort. Charles Kindleberger wrote in his classic work *The World in Depression, 1929-1939* that:[24]

> It is a theme of this book that part of the reason for the depth of the world depression was the inability of the British to continue their role of underwriter of the system and the reluctance of the United States to take it on until 1936.

Greider (despite his critics) released the spectre of deflation from the attic:[25]

> During the last generation the world's 500 largest multinational corporations have grown sevenfold in sales. Yet the worldwide employment of these firms has remained virtually flat since the early 1970s, hovering around 26 million people.

That is a small number compared to a world population over 6 billion people. What Greider calls 'the dirty little secret about technological revolution' is that it 'depresses a firm's rate of return per unit'. Lenin also saw the drive to new markets, partly to assuage the decline of return on investments, as the driving force behind imperialism. Eric R. Wolf writes:[26]

> Lenin's argument therefore connects monopoly capitalism, the need to export capital, the political seizure of colonies, and the outbreak of war among contending capitalist powers in one chain of cumulative causation.

According to this it would be safe to say that since the fall of the Berlin Wall signalled the triumph of capitalism, we live in fear that if Lenin was correct about how capitalist powers compete militarily for new markets, we might as well prepare for World War III. Fortunately not, for Wolf adds: 'Since Lenin wrote, some of the links in this chain have been shown to operate as contingent features of particular circumstances, rather than as sequential and inevitable stages.'

GATT/WTO for prosperity, not war

Phew! Perhaps the fall of communism does not relegate the capitalist world to inevitable wars fought with bullets, bombs and missiles. Almost as cheering is evidence that the USA, IMF and World Bank now combine to fill the role of 'lender of last resort', the player Charles Kindleberger saw as crucial to preventing recession from turning into a major Depression on the order of 1929-39.

It is the position of this book that, while humans are innately competitive (ready to revert to barbarism to protect themselves, their kin and communities) that this competitive drive can be expressed as well in economic competition (not to mention sports or music) as in military conflict. Further, individuals and nations can advance their needs for food, clothing, shelter and subjective needs (e.g. security and good reputation) through economic cooperation, i.e. trade. That is why all countries, rich and poor, weary of a century of world wars, would do well to endow international trade with the glamour we once, to our grief, ascribed war. In a similar vein science writer Matt Ridley argues that although evolution has equipped us with (what Richard Dawkins coined) 'selfish genes' we paradoxically have 'social instincts' to 'exchange goods and information, and to divide labour.' As Ridley[27] says: '…trade between countries is the best recipe for friendship between them…'

The hoary observation that 'all boats rise on a rising tide' suggests that, as long as conditions improve, politicians need not express people's economic frustration in military means. The best way to improve people's welfare is through mutually beneficial trade. Of course, trade can degenerate into trade war - not a pretty thing either. One ugly example is the trade embargo on Saddam Hussein's Iraq, where the consequences include malnutrition among children and infants. The stand-off between the UN and Iraq over inspections to uncover 'weapons of mass destruction' is military in nature, and the GATT/WTO process can have little effect until a UN-Iraq agreement is complete.

However, GATT/WTO jurisdiction is extremely useful in defusing many disputes that in the past could have blown up into harmful trade wars. The 'banana war' begun in November, 1998 between the USA and the EU over fruit tariffs launched little more than amusing newspaper headlines. Although the consequences are serious for banana farmers in storm-damaged Central America and elsewhere, the likelihood is the dispute will be resolved in a straightforward manner according to the 1994 Uruguay accords. Nor will the USA always get its own way - even though it is the world's biggest economy and many Honduran plantation owners are US-based MNCs.

The burgeoning, dynamic nature of international trade promises no dearth of disputes. The efforts of more *laissez-faire* dairymen in Britain, Denmark, Italy and Sweden[28] to abolish EU milk quotas - or of US dairists to accomplish the same in Canada - will arouse great ire in marginal farmers clinging to milk quota. World trade struggles are now too convoluted to reflect the great power imperialism of Lenin's day. Granted, the USA has a larger economy than Canada. Similarly, Germany far outweighs Denmark and Sweden who are attacking its position on EU milk quotas, in which the German dairy sector consumes the biggest share of EU dairy subsidies. In all likelihood, Canadian and European quota issues will provide additional examples of disputes settled according to transparent, internationally-agreed GATT/WTO rules.

Here lies a subtle, overlooked benefit of making agriculture part of the Uruguay settlement: total world welfare will improve because GATT/WTO unleashes the principle of comparative advantage and nullifies the rent-seeking activities of special interest groups. Farmers and their linked partners in the food supply chain can now focus on improving productivity and competitiveness within the GATT/WTO framework instead of wasting resources on the unpredictable results of special interest lobbying.

Suspicion abounds in the Third World that GATT/WTO exists only as a means for rich countries to penetrate their markets. But some of the earliest cases brought to the WTO for adjudication demonstrated it did not automatically rule in favour of the strong. The WTO upheld the complaint of countries including India in an important fishing dispute. Environmentalists in rich countries had successfully lobbied for regulations on nets, requiring them to be woven so as not to endanger certain species. The aim sounded laudable: to prevent dolphins from unnecessary drowning. But the WTO ruled these regulations could act as an illegal non-tariff-barrier (NTB) against poor country fishermen. The WTO ruling allows time for them to amortise present nets and buy expensive new ones in due time, if indeed they prove environmentally desirable.

This example suggests that if and when the need arises, India will be successful in appeals to GATT/WTO to enforce rules against predatory pricing or 'dumping' of surplus foreign milk in India's domestic market, and to increase access for dairy and other exports to rich countries like the USA, where India enjoys a significant production cost advantage. The theme of this book is that, ideally, the GATT/WTO process is not necessarily a tool of Wall Street, Tokyo, Frankfurt and other world bourses to extract ever more profits from India though clever financial scams including short term capital loans or currency manipulation. On the contrary, GATT/WTO can be a judicious force protecting the livelihoods of India and other developing countries. A good policeman is your friend; GATT/WTO is the policeman of international trade. And if that is so there exists the prospect not only of long term domestic growth in India's dairy industry - but also the possibility of export growth that could benefit rural farm families as well as big city processors. But more on that later.

In any event, the *Economist's* sniffing over Greider's pessimism did not prevent a dramatic East Asian downturn involving the fall of the Thai bhat; the implosion of the Suharto regime in Indonesia in 1997-98, and the bankruptcy of Japan Leasing Corporation (September 1998) while venerable companies such as Mitsubishi and Nissan flirted with the same; the fall of the Japanese yen against the US$ (and threat that if Tokyo allowed it to slide any further, Beijing would retaliate with a devaluation of Chinese currency to maintain its lucrative export trade); economic crisis in South Korea and withdrawal of Korean investments such as Hyundai and Samsung from England and Wales.

Nor did it prevent a virtual crash of the world's computer industry, as microchip prices fell (from $55 in 1995 to under $3 in 1998) to the extent that German firm Siemens[29] abandoned a £1.2 billion (ca. US$2b) state-of-the-art semi-conductor plant at Newcastle, England a year after the Queen opened it to great fanfare. This was followed six weeks later by closure of a Fujitsu[30] electronics factory in PM Tony Blair's own constituency near Durham. Savage price-cutting in electronics components by South Korean companies prompted fears of a global deflationary spiral. Meanwhile, US-owned electronics plants were relocated from Britain to eastern Europe where wages were much lower. GATT/WTO specialists Bernard Hoekman & Michel Kostecki[31] note 'the very large nominal wage differences' that induce such factory relocations - and calls for protection by special interest lobbyists in rich countries: 'In 1995 the hourly average cost of unskilled labour in Thailand, Russia, or China was less than $1, as compared to $25 in Germany and $15-17 in France, Japan, and North America.'

The lure of lower wages has naturally spread production across the world and led to, for instance, approximately double the total world capacity for auto production compared to average yearly demand. The same disturbing pattern of overcapacity extends to other industries including high-tech agriculture which periodically faces slumps or massive restructuring in the manufacture of combine harvesters, etc. Overcapacity, a fall in demand and world deflation on a scale not seen since the Depression of 1929-39 were predicted by Greider, and by October 1998 the setting for such 'wrenching calamities' was well underway. Although he saw no replacement for the 'wondrous machine' of global capitalism, or resolutions to capitalism's abiding contradictions, he did offer suggestions to mitigate its most violent oscillations. These included debt relief for the poorest nations, and international labour agreements to prevent recurrence in emerging economies of the 'ancient abuses renewed in the 'dark Satanic mills' seen in Britain's industrial revolution.[32]

Greider's most provocative idea was to 'restore national controls over global capital' establishment of a small gatekeeper's tax on capital movements; as little as a fraction of 1 per cent could be enough to slow computerised movements of institutional investment portfolios (e.g. trade union pension plans, retained earnings invested by MNCs or huge private speculators like George Soros' Quantum Fund). Slowing the frightening daily shifts of such huge funds could increase security, and the funds accrued could perhaps be invested in the poorest countries which had not so far attracted capital. Of course, the accrual of such funds was bound to breed bureaucratic competition to gain their control. Instead of a small damping effect on turbulent capital flows, the rate of tax could become as serious a burden on investors as the unreasonably high interest rates imposed on the US economy in the Great Depression. Who was right about the merits of *laissez-faire* capital movement, William Greider or the *Economist*? Some major capitalist titles considered Greider's view that allowing the completely free movement of capital which can disappear overnight is as safe as letting infants play in a herd of buffalo. Supposedly benign beasts can stampede on short notice. In a September, 1998 article *Wall Street Journal*[33] reporters David Wessel and Bob Davis noted that:

> Until now, the prevailing view among the world's economic policy makers was that money should move freely around the globe, allowing capital to find the most profitable and productive investments, no matter where they happen to be.... But it's now clear that foreign money had its costs. Much of that money was in short-term investments, and could leave as quickly as it arrived.... Empty

office buildings in Kuala Lumpur and Bangkok testify that at least some of the foreign money was wasted.

The article claimed Paul Krugman and Rudiger Dornbusch (both at MIT) and even the supposed doyen of *laissez-faire* economics Jagdish Bhagwati (Columbia) questioned the recent orthodoxy - oft attributed to Austrian economists Friedrick von Hayek and Joseph Schumpeter - that transnational capital movements should be completely unleashed. As he is not only widely-respected, but often lionised as a free trader by the *Economist*, it was stunning to read that while he remains 'one of the USA's most ferocious advocates of free trade in goods and services' Bhagwati says: 'Any nation contemplating the embrace of free capital mobility must reckon with the costs and also consider the probability of running into a crisis.' The *WSJ* also quoted the venerable John Maynard-Keynes, putably siding against rampant movement of capital in international economic life: 'It is widely held that control of capital movements, both inward and outward, should be a permanent feature of the system.'

Moreover, a mid-1998 Goldman Sachs financial newsletter acknowledging that India, China and to a lesser extent Chile had escaped global economic influenza: 'So far, countries whose currencies have not been freely convertible have done best.'

This is straight talk from a capitalist icon that, in the manner of capitalists supposedly willing to sell the rope with which to hang them, admits the prime sufferers of capital controls are 'US multinationals - particularly financial institutions'. The European Single Market mantra of the 1980-90s was *the free movement of people, goods and capital.* Many question whether the mantra should include all three, that is whether *capital* movements can be made less damagingly volatile. The *WSJ* quoted Montek Singh Ahluwalia, who helped lead post-1991 free market reforms in India as Finance Secretary (and like Bhagwati continues to advocate free trade in goods and services) thus: 'In Indonesia, the moment people knew the rupiah would slip, anyone with real money took their money out. In India that couldn't happen: The rich in India couldn't move out $20 billion.'

Ahluwalia said that in the context of India capital controls are 'a nuisance but in this transition phase, it is necessary.' His balanced comments are persuasive. But not all are convinced. David Folkerts-Landau, who heads emerging market research at Deutsche Bank after serving as a top IMF official, called controls 'catastrophic ' because they would drive away investment. Folkerts-Landau echoed many Wall Streeters in explaining the almost primal fear that he believed made controls counter-productive: 'The fear of being trapped is all-consuming for foreign investors.' Bolstering the anti-controls view was Gabriel Singson, governor of the Philippines' central bank who said his country's experience in the early-1990s showed: 'Controls are unmanageable…'

But that did not prevent PM Mahathir Mohamad from sacking deputy PM Anwar Ibrahim and banning trade of Malaysia's currency outside its borders in early September 1998. If the US Federal Reserve chair Alan Greenspan was correct saying that the New York stockmarket suffered from 'irrational exuberance', the same could be said of bourses in China and India. In the last decade, stockmarkets in China and India have been described as over-buoyant by those fearing their stock bubbles will burst as spectacularly as Japan's did in the late 1980s. However, both China and India are weathering post-1997 economic storms better than many other emerging nations. Referring to China's insulation from cold showers, Paul Krugman urged in an open letter in *Fortune* magazine that currency controls, whether in Malaysia or elsewhere, be temporary - because their distorting effects magnify over time - and that controls be accompanied by reform, in line with Michael Bordo's call for reform, above.

Chile has little better reputation than China as a bastion of democracy, but World Bank chief economist Joseph Stiglitz argued in the *Financial Times* of London, and at the Brookings Institution in Washington, DC that Chile's tax on short-term foreign borrowing and China's discouragement of short-term currency trades or bank loans have sustained important long term investment in infrastructure while decreasing economic volatility. Stiglitz' view on short-term capital coincides appears to coincide with that of William Greider (see above and below). Russia is said to be considering reforms more on the Chinese than Indian model. China's GDP growth in the year to August 1998 was 6.8 per cent - over 50 per cent higher than India's at 4.3 per cent.[34] China's currency has remained strong on exports to the USA, while India devalued the rupee 35 per cent in 1993-1998 and about 19 per cent to mid-1998.[35] Another reason Russia may be impressed by Chinese economic performance is that, after years of liberalisation since 1991, India had attracted a pittance of investment from its expatriates, while mainland China's booming economy (+6.8 per cent GDP growth 1997-98) attracted impressive investment from overseas Chinese. Of course, China exports more than India to the USA. Perhaps it is only a matter of time until Indian expatriates ('USA-return' Indians are, reportedly, already fuelling an economic renaissance around Bangalore) increase the flow of remittances and investment in the sub-continent.

Greider on capital flows since Bretton Woods

But what heralded the current era of capital flows? In 1971 US President Richard Nixon devalued the dollar and abandoned the gold standard (US$35/ounce in 1971) and 'closed the gold window' after 1973. Thereafter the American apostle of free markets Milton Friedman cogently argued the merits of 'floating exchange rates'[36] determined by global markets. Before Nixon unilaterally cancelled the Bretton Woods system of fixed exchange rates notes William Greider: '…the foreign-exchange market existed mainly to facilitate commercial trade and its size was trivial - a turnover of $10 billion to $20 billion a day - compared to $1200 billion a day two decades later.'

World capital (currency, bonds, derivatives, etc.) movements have increased more than most people imagine. A McKinsey report enumerated what William Greider calls an 'epic shift' in the ability of governments to control their domestic inflation, money supply and other aspects of their economies. In 1983 the world's five predominant central banks (the USA, Germany, Japan, Britain and Switzerland) held $139 billion in foreign exchange reserves for average daily turnover of $39b in the world's major foreign exchange markets. By 1992 these central banks' reserves had doubled to $278b, which sounds impressive until one realises that this was against a *16-fold* increase to $623b 'in daily trading activity'. By the mid-1990s daily currency trading had passed $1.2 trillion says Greider[37], with the City of London accounting for $460 billion, nearly double that of Wall Street.

This is phenomenal. In 1983 major government central banks held a 3-to1 advantage in reserves against daily activity. After international capital and currency controls eased, reserves roughly equalled daily trading by 1986. By 1992 the market situation had been *reversed* by institutional traders, as well as private currency traders scorned as 'golden boys' by Jacques Delors and epitomised by George Soros. Financial traders had reversed their situation: they now held a 2-to-1 advantage over five of the biggest central banks in the world. Noting the loss in job security to communities around the world threatened by capital flight, Greider wrote the most insidious effect of unfettered global capital flows 'is not the speed or volume, however. It is the price.'

Against historic rates, Greider finds that real interest rates (i.e. nominal rate of interest discounted by inflation) have doubled at 4-to-5 per cent in the USA; a report for the finance ministers of the world's 10 largest economies found real interest rates of 4 per cent were 'a full percentage point' over rates of a few decades before. Of course the positive side of higher real rates is the increased availability of capital for worthy investments. But the dark side is that finance consumes a larger portion of the economy. Even more insidiously, central banks may be forced to raise baseline interest rates *not* because domestic agriculture and manufacturing are fuelling inflation, but because dubious cross-border speculation has made capital scarce and dear. This was probably the case in Mexico.

Many financiers agree that Mexico's early 1990s NAFTA boom had less to do with actual production and employment than a frenzy of arbitrage - e.g. buying New York money at 5-6 per cent and investing in short-term Mexican Government notes or stocks appreciating at 12-14 per cent.[38] (Alternatively, foreign investors might be tempted by privatised former-state assets at fire sale prices.) The bubble that grew from this arbitrage popped in late 1995 after US interest rates rose too high to finance 'rolling over' short term loans south of the Rio Grande. The Mexican debacle illustrates the ratcheting to a higher scale of the boom and bust effects of macroeconomic cycles on industries (e.g. jute) that were deplored by Karl Marx, Thorstein Veblen and Mohandas Gandhi[39] for their negative effects on employment and ancillary industries - particularly when demand for products such as jute had not been fully met. It was a wrenching experience for Mexico's farmers; before agricultural price supports were cut in NAFTA-induced economic liberalisations, the country was a net food exporter; in the early NAFTA boom Mexico imported about 9 million tonnes of grain (about one-third of its consumption) and an unprecedented amount of dairy products from USA. In the year after the crash of the peso, 1995, Mexican exports rose 27 per cent, but total national output plunged 7 per cent. India is capable of better than what has been disparaged as its 'Hindu rate of growth', but Mexico's crisis is evidence that India should remain wary of short-term investment.

If the activities of George Soros were capable of forcing the devaluation of the pound and Britain's abandonment of the Exchange Rate Mechanism (ERM) on Black Wednesday in 1992, it becomes yet clearer why China and India question notions about the unalloyed benefits of free-roaming capital.

Barry Eicheringen, an economist from Berkeley, has pointed out that until the early-1980s only the USA, Britain and Switzerland allowed free capital flows, until Germany loosened controls around 1984 (presumably in the spirit of the Single Market) and Japan followed later. The world depression of 1929-39 occasioned a global desire for tight regulation which only ebbed with sustained World War II prosperity, the spread of bank depositor insurance, lower interest rates - and the ideological shift personified by Reagan and Thatcher in the 1980s.

In another article Paul Krugman said that Eicherungen's 'classic book' *Golden Fetters* showed the Great Depression was unnecessarily spread by the 'dogged determination' of countries to 'remain on the gold standard at all costs'. Laymen who accuse economists, like meteorologists, of perpetual disagreement are being too unkind. Like weathermen, the degree of agreement among Eicherungen, Krugman and Charles Kindleberger on causes of the Great Depression is impressive. Briefly, they agree that there was no single cause for the 1929-39 economic crisis; that though there remains disagreement on whether the 1929 crash stemmed from Europe or Wall Street there is no doubt that the 1937 crash was precipitated from America; and that *the Depression lasted much longer than was necessary* - given the current level of expertise in international finances. The last point gives grounds for optimism in the current slump.

From their consensus we can draw hope from Krugman's analysis on how to avoid another one. He says raising central bank interest rates - as the US Federal Reserve did so damagingly after 1929 - to lower inflation, maintain previous levels with other benchmark currencies - or in puritan zeal to punish past economic mistakes - can also lead to long-term disaster. Krugman adds:[40]

> In the end, a global slump is quite an easy thing to prevent. The only way it can happen is if the people who have the power to prevent it fail to take the risk of such a slump seriously, and continue to cling to ideologies inherited from a more benign era.

Previous examples of economic damage control included Fed head Alan Greenspan's sustenance of US monetary liquidity after the Wall Street crash of 1987. Another was the US-led $50 billion bailout of Mexico after the December 1994 fall of the peso, and ensuing crash of the Mexican economy which according to William Greider[41] depressed Latin American stock markets by 38 per cent and some Asian markets by 10-21 per cent in what the *Financial Times* called a 'Tequila Effect'.

The world's top capitalist newspapers indicate the ideological consensus may be shifting toward Greider's pessimism. Voltaire's Dr. Pangloss is wrong about this being the best of all possible worlds. It is yet to be seen whether British Labour PM Tony Blair's advocacy of IMF economic reforms in a 'third way' betwixt the free market and old style socialism offers practical reforms. Russia's recent experience demonstrates that the less insulated a country's economy is from the global economy, the more attention must be paid to raising its competitiveness; this includes not just high productivity in a few industries but (more and more) flexibility to meet changing conditions. Yet Greider dourly points out that the higher average rates of world productivity become, the harder it is for developing countries to rise to these levels - and that when falls do come, they come ever more swiftly.

If that sounds too pessimistic, query workers in Northeast England. Although many of their parents were turned out of jobs with British Steel, coal or shipbuilding when former PM Margaret Thatcher removed subsidies in the 1980s, the magic of neo-classical economic restructuring was supposed to usher them into 'lean manufacturing' jobs exporting

Nissan cars to continental Europe, or even high-tech 'post-industrial' or 'clean manufacturing' computer industry jobs with Fujitsu, Hyundai, Samsung and Siemens. Most of these plants were attracted by local tax concessions – but closed within years. The Nissan factory in Sunderland, known globally for best practice in the fashion of Toyota, put one-quarter of its workforce on furlough in the winter of 2008/9. The call centres that supposedly hailed Sunderland's entry into the information age are leaving for India, as pictured in the film *Slumdog Millionaire.*

As the East Asian economic slowdown begun in 1997 coaxed the world to flirt with recession and deflation in late 1998, the US exhorted finance ministers of emerging economies to adhere to the current free market paradigm - including freely convertible currencies. But although the US is today generally portrayed as the world's preeminent free trader, Charles Kindleberger details how sporadic that record has been; just 6 decades ago the US sought to dampen the effects of the world crisis on its domestic economy by passing the Smoot-Hawley tariffs into law in June 1930.

Previously, many nations engaged in beggar-thy-neighbour rounds of tariff imposition and competitive currency devaluations. Britain's Conservatives retreated into a policy of Empire Preference which, when European wheat prices fell 1925-26, precipitated a 'Battle for Wheat' among France, Germany and Italy.[42] Although the USA resisted the heavy mantle of economic role model and sought to recoup bonds on World War I war debt owed by its allies including Britain - even while making sympathetic signals toward the easing of war reparations demanded by France from Germany - many nations watched the progress of the bill in hopes the USA would set a proper tone. Alas, the 1930 signing of Smoot-Hawley by President Herbert Hoover (against the urging of 1028 US economists to veto the bill, and despite 30 foreign official government protests) torpedoed prospects of a world tariff truce and reductions that had been negotiated since the World Economic Conference of 1927. Whatever the precise reasons for the Great Depression, there is scant disagreement that Smoot-Hawley was more than a nudge toward the abyss. Kindleberger[43] wrote that it 'let loose a wave of retaliation'. Jeffrey Sachs pinpoints it as a contributing cause of foreign defaults and other woes.

Some foreign retaliation may have preceded the actual signing of the bill. Kindleberger notes that India raised its tariff on 'piece goods in February 1929', and France and Italy raised auto tariffs a month later. But as in any storm, exact cause and effect are hard to determine. Europeans tended to blame the Depression on the Wall Street crash and unwillingness of Washington to forgive debts. But Republican President Hoover principally blamed the Depression on European sources (and thus tended to support higher tariffs in agriculture and other trade). His 'new deal' Democrat successor Franklin D. Roosevelt tended to blame the Wall Street crash and Smoot-Hawley for problems (although FDR too was occasionally willing to blame Europe and accede to demands by US farmers for higher tariffs).

Economics may be, as John Kenneth Galbraith is credited with saying, a dismal science. But its study is more utilitarian than just for putting university students to sleep at night. Well-run economies can avoid war and even promote democracy and cultural development. After World War II Sir Dennis Robertson quipped that when the USA sneezed, Europe caught pneumonia. Kindleberger says that wherever the root causes of the Great Depression, 'ignorance'[44] prolonged it - and faulty US economic policy was much to blame for the resumption of woes in 1937. The bright side of this thought is that intelligent economic policy can prevent a recurrence of depression, fascism and war.

By the late 1930s conditions had been rotten for so long in the developed countries (e.g. hyper-inflation and Nazism in Germany, fascism and foreign adventures by Italy, civil war and purges in the USSR, earthquake and recession in Japan and unemployment in Britain) that the 1937 American recession was felt mostly in less developed countries. In the British Commonwealth, Australia and New Zealand had recovered and against a 1929 base of 100, 'reached the 80s and 95' respectively by 1935, according to Kindleberger but: 'The recovery in British India prices was much less extensive - from 58 in March 1933 to 65 in 1935 and 1936.'[45]

Coffee and banana exporters did better than did wheat in spotty Latin and Central American performance, but revolutions and coups were endemic; Brazil began moves toward autarky. But The Netherlands East Indies (tied to the gold bloc *via* the guilder) did even worse than India: against the 1929 base of 100, performance of only 49.6 in March 1933 prices fell to a paltry 44 in 1936. The following year held little economic salvation, least of all for economies tied to the gold bloc. (This is evidence for Paul Krugman's recent injunction to worry more about employment and human welfare indices than inflation or adherence to fixed exchange rates.) Even in the classic cases of 'banana republics' where farms and facilities were wholly foreign-owned, the Depression had an inimical effect upon the indigenous population, affecting employment, training, schooling, social welfare and other parameters that could have prepared human capital for decolonisation. Needless to say, in parts of the poorer countries where the people still controlled their own means of production, their exports generally suffered with incomes and development.

Why did the US recession of 1937 hurt less-developed countries more than Europe and Japan? The less offensive answer first: because declines in USA demand for freight and shipping rates lowered costs in Europe. Now the underlying reason: because Europe and Japan had artificially invigorated their economies in preparation for war - proof that deficit spending on wicked projects can boost prosperity at least temporarily. Recent books based on the diaries of Nazis Joseph Goebbels[46] and Albert Speer[47] leave little doubt many contemporaries believed the reconstruction of Germany's war machine was investment as productive for the economy as construction of the first *Autobahn.*

In a metaphysical sense, it is impossible for us to do the moral calculus on all the effects of World War II on all the world's countries. In any case we shall never know. But the thought persists that without the conflagration of World War II the worst evils of colonialism and racism would have persisted longer in the developing world. How long would Indian independence have been forestalled without the war? Perhaps the lesson is that hunger and unemployment are such overwhelming present evils that governments are tempted to risk future annihilation by constructing battleships as well as roads in order to placate their citizens. Civilisation is safer when people are supplied so adequately with food, clothing and shelter that they have more to lose than gain by going to war. That is why it is every country's interest to make GATT/WTO work for them. Hope remains that, if rules are honoured, the WTO can work for all.

Post-World War II planners tried to construct institutions to prevent a recurrence of the Great Depression or at least mitigate the recessions that attend world economic cycles. They were largely successful in Europe and North America. But economies are only slightly more controllable than the weather. A storm always threatens. By 1997 the strength of the British pound roused calls from British business leaders for devaluation *vis-à-vis* the German mark, and in 1998 factory layoffs were blamed on the high pound. As we discussed above, one of the greatest obstacles to European unity was the advent of European Monetary Union (EMU) scheduled for 1999. As economic shock waves epi-centred in Moscow reverberated with those coming from Jakarta, Kuala Lumpur and Singapore, and knocked on stock markets and banks in New York, one recalls that not long ago our worst fear was collapse of the new, over-heated stock market in Shanghai. The economic boycott of Iraq over 'weapons of mass destruction' made front page headlines - ignored by many readers who turned to the NASDAQ or DOW to see how inflated their stock portfolio had become since yesterday. India was seen as foolish for risking financial sanctions with its spate of nuclear tests. Now financial papers portray China and India as cool heads in world financial turmoil.

Are we sliding again into the abyss? It is just eight decades since President-elect Herbert Hoover promised to assist American farmers by raising tariffs on food imports. Charles Kindleberger[48] notes how this purported assistance to domestic farmers resulted in the 1930 Smoot-

Hawley Tariff Act which exacerbated the international trade situation and led to defaults on agreements made in the 1918 Treaty of Versailles. Will the current recession tarnish India's status as an emerging economy, and harm its new industries in software and other services? Could it reverse gains so painfully won in the Green and White Revolutions?

Fortunately, economic problems once thought intractable are now better understood. *We are all Keynesians now* is common currency. Kindleberger showed that maintaining greater liquidity in the US banking system would have relieved the Great Depression domestically and that, without Prisoner's Dilemma-like mistakes such as the Smoot-Hawley Tariffs, the Depression need not have lasted worldwide 1929-39 until war broke out. Paul Krugman correctly argued that maintaining banking liquidity and open trade could prevent the global recession of 1997 from turning into a depression. To combat financial crises wrought by unfettered capital flows, William Greider suggests a small tax on short-term capital investment to mitigate volatility - although Joseph Stiglitz (2002: 266) noted during the dot.com and post-9/11 recessions that such a Tobin-like tax was problematic unless it is 'imposed universally'.

In 2009 the British Government warned banks to retain more capital reserves against risks, base bonuses on long-term not short-term profits, and planned a windfall tax on bankers' bonuses in 2010. As spectacular growth in Dubai edges toward default, economists urge transparent accounting. Some lessons are straightforward. *Moral hazard?* Separate commercial from investment banking, as was the case before America's 1933 Glass-Steagall Act was repealed in 1999. *Capital flight?* Scrutinise short-term investment and make government and business reforms. *Depression?* Maintain liquidity and avoid trade wars.

With luck, we will emerge from the real estate-base debacle signalled by the failure of Lehman Brothers in the USA in 2007, and the nationalisation of Northern Rock in the UK in 2008.

The future is murky, dark. So let us further examine the past. If history does not make the case for *laissez-faire* economics, it often guides against the opposite extremes of autarky and even import substitution.

Chapter 3

Mercantilism to WTO

Why rich & poor drop protection for tariffication

An earful of complaints awaits anyone encountering jobless workers outside the locked gates of a factory or commercial farm. The pain of unemployment makes it difficult to see gains from free trade. It is no wonder the mercantilist idea that development is a zero-sum game, in which one nation gains only at another's pain, lingers on. Wherever free market reforms face downturns, protectionists are ready to return to mercantilism.

But, claim market economists, mercantilism and protection give just temporary relief, leaving a society further behind in competitiveness and development. Rich and poor countries alike prosper most when all the barriers (i.e. tariffs) affecting trade are made transparent, i.e. 'tariffied' in a process of tariffication', in the rules-based multilateral framework of GATT/WTO. Today the cut-throat tactics of mercantilism, epitomised by Francis Drake's plunder of gold from Spanish ships, appear rather juvenile attempts at nation-building. But have times really changed?

Countries may be less ready to scuttle each other's navies but they still launch broadsides at rival economies. US President Ronald Reagan's costly 'Star Wars' initiative in the 1980s, it is now argued, ultimately bankrupted the Soviet economy. More subtly, countries deploy industrial policies such as overt and covert aid to auto industries by the Governments of France, Italy and Japan – and arguably to aviation by the USA to Boeing, and the EU to Airbus. The EU and, to a lesser extent the USA, funded farm price supports and export subsidies at great cost to their consumers and - most germane to our discussion - to farmers in developing countries.

Compared to the piratical mercantilism of Drake's day - and the tariff hikes and competitive currency devaluations that prolonged the Great Depression from 1929 until World War II - the General Agreement on Tariffs and Trade (GATT) began in 1947 to make the world a kinder, gentler place. Only since the 1994 Uruguay Round Agricultural Agreement

(URAA) have rich countries begun to dismantle subsidy regimes that skewed world farm trade. GATT repudiates mercantilist notions that national welfare is improved by maximising exports and minimising imports in order to accumulate bullion or maintain a strong currency. The establishment of the World Trade Organisation (WTO) after the GATT/WTO-1994 accord to administer agreements on tariffs and trade in GATT and - without getting too technical - other agreements on trade in services (GATS) and intellectual property rights (TRIPs) made many developing countries full members of the GATT club for the first time.[1] (After 4 decades, the acronym GATT is well known; so while WTO has formally assumed some tasks charged to GATT, our text uses the terms almost interchangeably - or as GATT/WTO-1994.)

Cynics argue poor countries made risky concessions on MNC-owned biotechnology patents, in return for farm reform in rich countries. But GATT/WTO-1994 does rectify major imbalances in world trade relations, and additional issues can be redressed in negotiations culminating after the year 2000.

A decade before the Uruguay settlement Lester Thurrow (MIT) identified the Achilles heels of the world's three main regional trading rivals. Thurrow[2] said America faced a 'productivity problem'; Europe faced an 'employment problem' with structural unemployment in France and other countries of about 10 per cent; and Japan had a 'trade imbalance problem' with an economy that depressed domestic consumption and depended on exports. Certainly the USA suffered a drain on its economy in its chronic trade deficit with Japan; Japan lacked natural resources or military muscle; and Europe suffered low productivity and high structural unemployment of around 10 per cent, although its social safety net kept more Europeans from homelessness than in the USA. Thurrow warned that unless America exerted leadership, the world threatened to disintegrate into three trading blocs of Europe, Japan and itself - lowering output and chances for development. But what a change a decade makes! US leadership did bring Europe and Japan to the GATT bargaining table on agricultural reform and some expected the 1994 agreement can be a boon to some poor farm exporters.

Since the Cold War the USA is called world's top military superpower (Paul Kennedy's 1987 caveats on over-extension notwithstanding.) This is less remarkable than the resurgence of US export performance, after the Reagan-Bush administrations (1980-92) marked by rapid business restructuring according to the edicts of business gurus such as Peter Drucker, and influenced by Japanese models of 'lean manufacturing'. US 'down-sizing' and 'right-sizing' cut layers of unproductive corporate fat, i.e. sacking middle managers and personnel in rationalisations that would have been impossible given the corporate traditions and laws of Japan and Europe. Unfortunately, the patients - US workers - were conscious during the operation. Accomplished with a minimum of anaesthetic, the painful economic surgery was followed by a surprisingly swift recovery, based on Keynesian deficit spending in the Reagan military build-up (for which taxpayers are still paying - whether or not the US arms build-up was what won the Cold War). Most workers found new jobs even if in real terms they earned less than before. More women had to work in the formal economy. But the impact for the rest of the world was that US industry and services were more productive than before and therefore more competitive on world markets.

Europe was enjoying a surge of prosperity partly due to efficiency gains and market expansions made possible by the 1992 Single Market campaign. However, Europe's clamber toward 'full employment' was interrupted by German reunification (officially begun October 3, 1990), which added around 1 million former state workers to the dole.

Japan's economy had seemed impregnable - despite frequent wrangling with the US over trade - but the late-1980s revealed faults. The Japanese 'bubble economy' was reportedly based on inflated urban real estate valuations. Corruption involving the Japanese mafia (*Yakuza*) was rumoured. Overvaluations in equity encouraged banks to make loans for Japanese acquisition of Hawaiian and New York property, Hollywood movie companies, artworks (ca. $40m for Van Gogh's 'Irises') and other spectacular investments. But in the late-1980s, the bubble began deflating inexorably until it showed the need for real structural reform in banking, investment and labour practises. It was a measure of how rich Japan had become that it took a decade for its real estate debacle to affect leading firms' 'lifetime' employment practices, or for official unemployment figures to approach 3 per cent. After two decades of fear that Japan was overtaking it as a world power, it appeared the painful US economic shakeout of the 1980s and early-1990s had launched the USA into a higher echelon of economic power than it had enjoyed since the Vietnam War forced US abandonment of the Bretton Woods system in 1971.

Into 1997 the world economy grew, fuelled by hope for transition in Russia, and driven by solid growth in automobiles, aviation, construction and electronic components. Exports of raw materials such as timber from Brazil and Thailand (more controversial today than past British, Canadian and US forestry and mining) fuelled growth. Strong food and grain prices fattened export accounts of many countries. But as mentioned above, Thailand's devaluation of the bhat was the first thread of the skein of East Asia's 'economic miracle' to unravel. Indonesia, Malaysia and others soon followed in devaluations to stimulate sales abroad - a classic response to slowdowns by economies based on export-led-growth. As long as the thriving US economy can absorb this flood of electronic goods, appliances, cars and computers, recovery looks more likely. But tax cuts and cash vouchers granted citizens in late 1998 by the Japanese Government looked inadequate to reverse the East Asian crisis. And as the USA entered recession again in 2006, more countries were tempted into competitive devaluations of the 1929-39 ilk.

The Banker's Dilemma

In these supposedly enlightened times, government central bankers are still tempted by what Matt Ridley calls, 'the most famous game in all of game theory,' adding, ' The game is known as the prisoner's dilemma, and it applies whenever there is a conflict between self-interest and the common good."[3] Like a prisoner who has promised co-conspirators to remain silent but fearing one will inform on him if he is not *first* to make a deal with the jailers, central bankers know global stability is threatened by tariff hikes or currency devaluations - but are tempted to act unilaterally to relieve their citizens' unemployment and other distress.

Until Britain's abolishment of the Corn Laws in the nineteenth century, self-sufficiency seemed the norm for national development policy. From the end of World War II until the fall of the Berlin Wall many governments frightened by high or volatile prices of imports (e.g. oil, machinery) attempted 'import substitution'. The end of the Cold War affords the world a chance to increase overall efficiency and output *via* specialisation of labour, according to comparative advantage. But this economic quest is (as we saw in the last chapter) endangered by difficult conditions in East Asia, Russia and to a lesser degree Germany.

History records why most policy makers came to believe that maintaining open international trade according to market forces rather than trying to 'manage trade' for short term advantage is worth temporary pain. Furthermore that non-discriminatory trade, according to transparent rules negotiated in multilateral negotiations and administered by the GATT/WTO, is the best way to sustain development.

Throughout this discussion will be offered corollary evidence for one of our main themes: Indo-European cooperation in dairy development in Operation Flood 1970~1996 was an admirable use of existing resources. It was the best exception to the rule that food aid does more harm than good.

Historical Background

In eighteenth and nineteenth centuries the keen intellects of Adam Smith, David Ricardo, Thomas Malthus and Karl Marx wrestled with problems of war, peace, hunger and prosperity like those John Maynard Keynes struggled with in the Great Depression, and with which Jagdish Bhagwati, Amartya Sen and others remain engaged at the end of the twentieth century. While the problems are of similar type their scale is magnified. World population is much greater than in the age of Adam Smith. Moreover, the composition of labour markets in all countries has seen dramatic shrinking of the farm sector, breaking the tie to subsistence agriculture which characterised human life for millennia. In itself this is no bad thing, except that in times of economic stress they lack the option of returning to family farms to sit out recessions until urban jobs reappear. Gradually more people gained livelihoods from manufacturing or services. (Of course farming increasingly depends on services - from AI and ET to IT - but the discussion is best left simple for now.) However, as national economies became more interdependent, workers became more vulnerable to forces from abroad. In recessions they wondered if their lives were truly any better than their grandparents.

So let us briefly reckon with ideas relevant to ongoing debates on economics, population and world trade. Particular attention is paid to the post-World War II period of the Cold War, when Western efforts - often influenced by Walt W. Rostow's 'take-off' theory - frequently failed to achieve their goals, and food aid programmes could even be counterproductive. Resistance to ideological interference from the West and the Eastbloc resulted in Jawaharlal Nehru's declaration of a non-aligned 'Third World' in 1955, and establishment of UNCTAD and formation of the 'Group of 77' developing nations in 1964. The critiques of development programmes from, e.g. Peter Bauer on the Right, and Susan George and Arturo Escobar on the Left, are worth examination.

The agricultural 'protectionism' which Jagdish Bhagwati says was originally built into GATT-1947 by the USA began to be removed in the controversial GATT-1994 accords. In the Uruguay Round, agriculture and dairy trade were brought under GATT aegis for the first time. Kym Anderson and Rodney Tyers'[4] work suggests that developing country exporters which lost world market share from 1961 to 1986 could profit by removal of rich country agricultural subsidies and tariffs against their products. A synopsis of the GATT-1994 agreement and creation of the WTO will inform our discussion with some best case/worst case scenarios for rich and poor nations. The benefits of free trade are far from universally recognised. Trade often takes lower precedence to other values of ethnic groups or countries. History is replete with examples of groups valuing ideological purity and self-reliance over unrestricted commerce, such as the Puritans who settled New England. Until Britain repealed the Corn Laws in 1846, Government policy favoured agricultural self-sufficiency over free trade. Although the Bretton Woods conference in 1944 inaugurated the post-World War II era of expanded international trade, 'import substitution' remains common sense to many people. Many countries including Albania, China, India, Korea and Burma (*aka* Myanmar) have for lengthy periods adopted policies of virtual autarky. Bhagwati[5] writes:

> The virtues of division of labour and exchange, noted even in Plato's Republic, had been lost to oblivion. Mercantilism and its legitimation of autarkic protective policies seemed to be only common sense, reminding one that common sense is what makes a person assert that the earth is flat, for that is how it appears to the naked eye.

Free trade is often opposed on the basis that it harms domestic farmers or even the nation (or region) as a whole. Even in rich countries farm lobbyists insist their nation's welfare depends at least partly on its thriving agricultural sector. (Such an assertion might be closer to the truth if lobbyists for protection argued that the future of the governing leadership depended on their continued political support.) Writing in a survey of agriculture in the *Economist*, a publication that was instrumental in the repeal of the English Corn Laws in 1846, Edward Carr[6] wrote:

> Every age has found a pretext to protect its farmers. In the nineteenth century that pretext was unfair competition from cheap American and Australian wheat. In the 1930s it was farm poverty. After the Second World War it was food security. In the 1960s it became preservation of the rural character. The farm lobby is quite capable of finding something new for the 1990s.

Mercantilism

In Europe, after the decay of feudalism (weakened by the formation of city states and the other manifestations of the Enlightenment), the preponderant 'mercantilist' philosophy of new nation states such as France and England included the tenet that self-sufficiency in food (as well as iron, textiles, etc.) was a pillar of national power.[7] In the starvation-prone time of Thomas Malthus (1766-1834), when food production limited population and hence the numbers of well-fed soldiers that could be fielded, this argument was intuitively apparent. An army marches on its belly.

In the 'zero-sum' economics of the age of mercantilism one country's loss was another's gain. When Francis Drake seized a Spanish ship, Spain's pain was England's gain. It seemed one country could be rich only if another were poor. This was partly due to widespread confusion equating *specie* - usually gold or silver coins - with wealth of the state and (secondarily, if thought of at all) the yeoman farmer. The goal of trade policy, including tariff rates and issue of export licenses was maximisation of gold controlled by the realm. (Today the relative strength of a nation's currency is similarly confused with national welfare - a point addressed in Chapter 2.) In mercantilist philosophy notes Paul Kennedy, 'lessening the outflow of specie'[8] by substituting domestic 'textiles, iron, grain', and even taking measures to deny rival powers profitable trade relationships, seemed nearly as important as maximising wealth (**Table 3. 7**).

Wealth of Nations

The name associated with the first great erosion of what Kennedy called 'the mercantilist, protectionist state' is Adam Smith.[9] Because Smith saw that every economic activity did not require a loser he deemed mercantilism foolishness. In *The Wealth of Nations* (1776) Smith argued (albeit in a more limited way than contemporary neo-liberals do) that the 'invisible hand' of individual self-interest was the best guarantor of aggregate local, regional or national wealth. Smith argued that wage and price controls imposed domestically (i.e. intranationally) by national governments hindered productivity and hence national wealth. Acceptance of Smith's free trade philosophy was a precursor to the dismantling of centrally planned economies (CPE) of the COMECON countries in central Europe and around the world after 1989.[10]

But it is a long way from an *intranational* policy of liberal trade within territory controlled by the British Crown in the eighteenth century to a policy of tariff-free trade *internationally*. To the consternation of mercantilists, Smith advocated both. While the Crown enjoyed gains from trade with its colonies and less powerful nations, it was loath to see rivals such as Spain or France profit from trade with Britain. Additionally, the landed aristocracy, whose income depended on rents from tenant farmers, lobbied the Crown to retain protective tariffs on food imports from other countries that would compete with domestic production, lowering their prices and rents.

A century ago J.D. Nicholson noted that although consumers had suffered from a dearth of imports from 1765, Britain did not become a net food importer until 1788. This demonstrates that markets moved much slower two centuries ago - as well as the probability that the purchasing power of English workers limited the aggregate demand they exerted in the marketplace. Notwithstanding that, Nicholson asserts that even Adam Smith, who noted the harm to consumers (i.e. failing to import food) had missed an important *raison d' être* of the protective tariffs known as the Corn Laws: *to bolster the power of the Crown.*[11] Mercantilist policy protected the Crown through the ability, in emergencies, to commandeer British merchant ships as temporary warships. This was also an era long before the imposition of income taxes *and regular collection* - a task that continues to challenge revenue agents in Russia, Italy, India, China - and every other country in the world. Another abiding attraction to the Crown of a mercantilist, closely-managed trade policy was the fiscal power to raise monies through the granting of import and export licences, and levying tariffs on exports and imports.

The English Crown finally concluded that more revenue could be raised by liberalised policies (i.e. by levying tax on a greater quantity of freely traded goods instead of selling licences to conduct trade) than mercantilism. The death knell of came when enough policy makers agreed with industrialists - influenced by the writings of David Ricardo, and later John Stuart Mill - that free trade would increase national power and wealth. Bhagwati[12] claims free trade profits a nation: 'whether its trading partners were free-traders or protectionists. Unilateral free trade emerged as the prescription from this corpus of thought.

Today this concept remains intrinsic to GATT/WTO. In the nineteenth Century acceptance of free trade was a landmark defeat for Britain's 'agrarian protectionists' according to E.J. Hobsbawm.[13] Of course free trade has troubled high-cost producers in all countries from the age of mercantilism to the present, liberalised GATT/WTO world trading system. But even if some producers (e.g. farm or factory owners and their workers) suffer under free trade, Smith, Ricardo, Bhagwati and a host of others have shown theoretically that the gains to consumers and the government outweigh their loss - and that resources can be reorganised to ameliorate those losses in new enterprises.

In the real world, however, things are not always as they seem. In a 1988 address to Amul, the National Dairy Development Board (NDDB) and allied farmers' cooperatives that trebled India's milk production in the 26 years of Operation Flood, Dr. Verghese Kurien[14] pointed out that some of the countries that beat the drum loudest for *Free Trade!* protect their own dairy markets, while doing their best to penetrate markets such as India and erode Amul's market share. Considering the fact that India's dairy farmers already operate with a 30-40 per cent cost advantage compared to Europe or America, and that Amul offers an impressive and growing range of high-value-added products (HVA 'luxury' products often are the wedge used for market penetration) from baby food to ice cream, foreign multinationals would seem to pose little threat to Amul's market dominance in India. Perhaps two or three years of widespread drought could dramatically increase foreign market share in a few products. But in a country of nearly 900 million milk lovers, it would be a major loss to the aggregate Indian economy (not just to dairy farmers) to lose its current state of effective self-sufficiency in milk. The chances of that happening are nil, unless and until highly-capitalised dairymen in the USA and other rich countries succeed in their hopes to cut their own production costs.

But a move toward *laissez-faire* in US farm policy has formidable potential to lower dairy production costs. The 1996 US Federal Agricultural Improvement & Reform (FAIR) Act[15] and recent victories by proponents of biotech products (e.g. genetically modified soybeans and dairy hormones such as rBGH/rBST) in the relevant sanitary-and-phytosanitary and veterinary committees of the EU and WTO are significant. To prepare for this and other exigencies - such as the EU invoking unreasonable hygiene standards as a non-tariff barrier to Indian exports - Kurien's annual report urged his colleagues to 'engender' ever better quality. He underscored the benefits to the Indian economy by cooperatives which reinvest in the productive potential of members, unlike some profit-taking commercial rivals which after the 1991 economic liberalisations tried to act as *free riders* on NDDB investments by luring deliveries from farmers previously nurtured by coops. Perhaps the most telling point Kurien made in reiterating the importance to farmers of coops is this: about 85 per cent of milk produced by dairy powerhouses the USA and New Zealand is produced, processed and marketed by coops. A word to the wise is sufficient.

Industry versus Agriculture

As hinted above, it was the growth of industry within rising nation-states that prompted a paradigm shift away from zero-sum mercantilism. Britain, whose power was enhanced by its leading role in the Industrial Revolution (making it well-placed to profit from exports to the continent in the era of revolution and Napoleon[16]), experienced structural shifts that were later mimicked by nations worldwide.

As Britain's textile, coal, steel, armament, shipping and rail industries raised national output, and manufacturing and industry grew more important to the tax base, the relative weight of agricultural interests declined. (Perhaps it is politics, not economics, that truly is a 'zero-sum' competition.) Although Thomas Malthus' predictions of apocalyptic famine were later disproved (or at least delayed!) his assertion that humanity is limited by the food available to keep it alive is self-evident, as well as tautological. But Malthus did not anticipate increased agricultural productivity due to technological change, which is why his dismal logic of the arithmetical growth of the food supply lagging behind the geometric growth of the human population was faulty.

In our own time increased productivity wrought by the Green Revolution has helped food supply keep pace with demand, as world population doubled in the period 1950-1988.[17] Yet, Malthus' dire warnings linger on. Paul Kennedy, whose book *Preparing for the Twenty-First Century*[18] refers often to Malthus, is pessimistic. Citing the research of Lester Brown and the World Watch Institute, Kennedy writes that droughts of the 1980s, along with an estimated 500 million 'seriously undernourished' people, a wedge of world population believed by Brown and apparently by Kennedy to be rising, could be neo-Malthusian harbingers of a new era when population outstrips food production.[19] Pessimists claimed that in the early 1990s, world grain production was rising at only 15 million metric tonnes annually, when 28 million MT were needed to match world population growth. Better harvests in the mid-1990s reversed this trend and began restoring depleted stocks of grain, etc. But hunger returned with a vengeance in the first decade of the new millennium.

Late 1998 reports were that US and world prices for maize (called *corn* in the US, though corn has long been a synonym for grain in Britain, as in the 'Corn Laws') were depressed because China had begun a policy of self-sufficiency in this product in order to avoid import dependence. Whether or not China succeeds in meeting its long-term demand is contingent on factors including record flooding (which reportedly made 2m people homeless in 1998), soil suitability for maize, the amount of wheat and other grains that continue to be imported, etc. What this report tends to indicate, happily, is that Chinese authorities are optimistic about pushing out their country's food production possibilities frontier. Malthus may have to wait a bit longer for alimentary apocalypse.

In the Industrial Revolution witnessed by Malthus in the late-nineteenth and early-twentieth centuries industry competed with agriculture for scarce workers. Wages must minimally be sufficient to feed and clothe workers, but shrewd industrialists knew that if cheaper sustenance were available, the cost of 'a living wage' could stabilise or even fall, reducing overhead. According to E.J. Hobsbawm[20] manufacturers believed food prices: 'were kept artificially high by the monopoly of the landed interest, made even worse by... the Corn Laws.

So in their own interests, industrialists and the Anti-Corn-Law League fostered a mass campaign[21] to abolish the Corn Laws in Britain, and permit the import of cheaper grain from North America and elsewhere. This was resisted - to no avail - by the landed aristocracy, who argued that relying on food imports would subject their island nation to embargo and siege. But the ability of the British navy to defend its sea lanes was too well known, and the political influence of industry had so far exceeded that of agriculture that the arguments of the agricultural gentry were to no avail. Food shortages were never entirely forgotten. As late as the year 1842, unemployed workers reportedly died of starvation on the streets of Manchester.[22] Typical of most of history's so-called famines, starvation in Manchester stemmed more from structural defects in food distribution - limited 'entitlements'[23] to food in the vocabulary of Amartya Sen - than food shortages. At any rate, the horror fuelled public support for reductions of tariffs on food imports. By 1846, most of the listed Corn Laws were rescinded.

Eric R. Wolf[24] notes that meat consumption had been at a 'relatively high level' in Europe before the Industrial Revolution, when it fell. But railroads and steamboats reversed industrial workers' slide in meat consumption from new 'livestock frontiers' - foremost the American 'Wild West' by 1860 and (funded by British capital) the Argentine pampas after about 1875. The advent of refrigeration accelerated the trade in meat and also contributed to expansion in the supply of fresh liquid milk to customers in cities such as London, as described by Peter J. Atkins.[25]

As capital-heavy Britain turned from textiles to iron, steel and railways, repeal of the Corn Laws freed labour from the farm sector.[26] Crucial to this structural shift was a 9 per cent drop in food prices between 1850 and 1869. Further drops in real food prices after 1882, due to cheaper freight and efficient foreign producers[27], convinced many remaining doubters of the advantages of free trade. Domestic farmers responded to foreign competition by rationalisations (e.g. drainage of marshes) that increased productivity in the 1850s and 1860s. Because the influx of foreign grain forced down domestic farmgate prices, some British farmers switched production from cereals to higher-value-added (HVA) milk and cheese, which improved the diets of industrial workers.

Free trade policies were part of a 'virtuous circle': the increased profits on sale of British manufactures (cheaper to produce, since workers' living wage was stabilised or even lowered in 'real terms') on world markets provided a richer tax base. Taxes funded the navy, which in turn protected the commercial sea routes in which flowed the life blood of the Empire. The British accepted a principle earlier recognised by the Dutch: in the long run, military power is based on commercial power, not vice-versa.[28]

Comparative Advantage

The British embraced free trade with perhaps more fervour than the Dutch, after many policy makers accepted the theory of 'comparative advantage', a refinement of Adam Smith's trade theories advanced by David Ricardo in the early nineteenth century. By comparative advantage, Ricardo's proofs showed that even if England were *absolutely* more efficient than Spain in *all* types of production (i.e. both corn and linen) it would still benefit from free trade.[29] For example, if Spaniards were *comparatively* better at producing corn than linen, then England should trade its cheaper linen for Spain's cheaper corn. In a leap from zero-sum mercantilism, policy makers now agreed that both countries would be wealthier than they were before they forsook autarky, adopted specialisation of labour and engaged in international trade. Although comparative advantage is counter-intuitive, mathematical proofs of it are simple and convincing. It applies to India as much as to England. According to Paul Samuelson: [30]

> the theory of comparative advantage is a closely reasoned doctrine which, when properly stated, is unassailable. With it we can identify gross fallacies in the political propaganda for protective tariffs aimed at limiting imports. With it we can identify the germs of truth that sometimes pop up in the heated claims for tariff protection.

Protection of Infant and Strategic Industries

Of course the real world is more complex than Ricardo's proof, and intelligent people continue to argue whether or not to protect sectors of an economy by taxing imports, or to adopt less restrictive policies for international trade. Such disparate industries as steel, consumer electronics, military production, agriculture, and baby formula frequently entertain surprisingly similar arguments both for protection and for free trade.

It is difficult for any government to impose unpopular policies indefinitely, if the governed remain unaware of gains from those policies. Governments are routinely lobbied by domestic special interest groups for subsidies, protection from foreign competition, or both. But even proponents of comparative advantage and free trade occasionally excuse tariffs on imports, to protect infant industries. Economists including John Stuart Mill and Jagdish Bhagwati have argued that indeed there are instances when temporary protection of infant industries from foreign competition is justified[31] if returns to society outweigh the costs of protection *in the long run.*

This rationale was offered for India's infant steel industry which benefited from direct government subsidies and tariffs on imports for decades after independence. Despite–their preference for heavy industry, planners occasionally made wiser concessions to dairy development, instituting some protection when domestic production started of skimmed milk powder, baby food, etc. which had been supplied by low-cost foreign producers such as Glaxo and Nestlé.[32] These efforts (later subsumed under Operation Flood, 1970-96) did involve heavy investments along with commodity aid from the EEC, WFP, etc. - but they originated partly out of a desire to save foreign exchange. Indeed, after 1976, India virtually stopped commercial imports of milk powder, saving millions of rupees on its balance of payments.

The Republic of Ireland offers a European instance of staunch defence of its farm sector. For reasons including factorial advantages in land, temperate climate and labour costs, the dairy industry played a more strategic role in Eire's economy than in more industrialised EEC (*aka* the EC or EU) countries. In the early 1980s, over a decade after Ireland entered the Common Market in 1973, the European Commission was planning mandatory milk quotas to cap the burgeoning Butter Mountain, Milk Lake and beef stores. Eire correctly saw this as a significant threat to its welfare, and negotiated fiercely. Like China and India, Ireland knew that long-term economic diversification would proceed more securely upon a prosperous base of agricultural development. Margaret Thatcher herself expressed admiration for the Irish Government's vigorous defence of its 'strategic' national interest in dairying.[33]

In the end, Brussels made Irish dairy farmers less subject to cutbacks than their continental counterparts. Half a decade after the 1984 introduction of EC milk quotas, statistics reflected Eire's successful defence of its farm sector: agriculture still accounted for 12 per cent of Ireland's GDP - a portion exceeded only by Greece (13.2 per cent) within the EC-12. Moreover, 68 per cent of Ireland was in permanent pasture, 14.4 per cent of its labour force in agriculture (in the EC only Portugal with 17.5 per cent, and Greece with 25.5 per cent, had more) and food comprised about 32.5 per cent of exports. In fact, some room for expansion was allowed Irish dairymen after 1983-84, whilst those in other countries, notably France and Germany, had to contract. Nevertheless early-1980s milk quotas and cuts in guaranteed beef support did not totally vaporise dairy mountains. As late as 1991 (seven years after cuts in beef support and imposition of milk quotas) a near record 700,000 tonnes of beef was in storage, and EC dairy surpluses exceeded 500,000 tonnes.[34] (The drain on EC taxpayers by storage costs of continued surpluses surely prompted renewed offers to India for continued monetisation as dairy aid, past original cut-off dates.)

More significant CAP reforms awaited the knife wielded by EC (*aka* EEC or EU) agricultural commissioner Ray MacSharry in 1992. From its beginning, the Common Agricultural Policy (CAP) was a compromise between the industrial Germany and more rural-oriented France. Germany needed France as a market - and also badly needed a partner to enhance its prestige after the reproach it earned in World War II. Gallic peasant culture remained so strong that Henry W. Ehrmann[35] remarked: 'In a sense, France never repealed its Corn Laws.'

John T.S. Keeler wrote that post-World War II French agricultural policies were fashioned according to 'neo-corporatist' policy, which in turn influenced the design of the CAP.[36] Thus, until 1992, the CAP little discriminated between rich and poor farmers, but–subsidised them on a simple *pro rata* system according to acreage or livestock numbers. This explains why the CAP produced such prodigious food mountains, and why EEC commissioners resorted to export subsidies, surplus disposal and dairy aid programmes involving India and other countries to clear its expensive storehouses.

Calculated thus, a rate guaranteeing survival of small-holders entailed generous incomes for larger farms. French neo-corporatist philosophy envisioned medium-sized family farms, a compromise between unviable small-holdings of the peasant past and much larger agri-businesses in the USA - viewed with apprehension by Gallic farmers.[37] But various factors inhibited rationalisation, keeping nearly a million holdings under the 50 acres considered viable. Needless to say, such smallholdings drained an alarming portion of EC farm expenditure. At its peak the farming accounted for an untenable 70 per cent of Community spending, with milk programmes accounting for 30 per cent of that.[38]

In a landmark CAP reform in 1992, EC farm commissioner Ray MacSharry broke with tradition and 'differentiated' between rich and poor farmers in eligibility for income supports. (The synonym 'modulation' replaced 'differentiation' in the EU Agenda 2000 campaign.) The other chief point of MacSharry's CAP reform was that for the first time CAP income subsidies were 'decoupled' from farm production.[39] Europe's agriculture was a mature industry, ripe for the removal of subsidies, as long as intolerable structural or social dislocations could be avoided - as they were in Eire.

Deciding if protection of industries (whether portrayed as 'infant' or 'strategic') is justified is difficult enough for economists, but even more so for politicians vulnerable to lobbying by special interests. As mentioned above, the Government of India, a continent away from Europe, imposed protection against commercial imports of dairy products such as baby food and milk powder (by more than one definition an infant industry) after domestic suppliers such as the NDDB began competing with Glaxo, Nestlé and other low-cost foreign suppliers.[40] Economists making the case for protection of Indian dairying might argue that there were more potential gains from India's dairy industry than its steel industry, partly because milk powder, baby food and sweets had a steady domestic market making it less cyclical than steel. (I.e. milk has a higher inelasticity-of-demand than steel.)

Protectionists might properly argue, as did the NDDB, that dairy production was likely to bolster India's foreign exchange reserves by substituting domestic products (e.g. baby formula) for foreign imports; and that dairy processing was less capital-intensive than steel. In fact these were some of the rational reasons motivating dairy development in India. Although the White Revolution was sometimes criticised for an over-emphasis on capital investment in processing and transport infrastructure, Operation Flood's 'stainless steel temples' were dwarfed by the heavily-subsidised factory complexes of heavy industry such as steel - the latter far less likely than dairying to absorb India's surfeit of surplus labour.

Aborted LDC 'Take-offs' compared to the Marshall Plan

After World War II dozens of former colonies of various European powers gained national independence and took responsibility for their own macroeconomic planning. Many Third World countries tried a variety of strategies to reach the stage of development that in an influential 1956 article the author Walt W. Rostow coined 'The Take-Off into Self-Sustained Growth.'[41] Briefly, Rostow termed his five stages of growth: 'traditional society, preconditions, takeoff, drive to technological maturity, age of mass consumption.' Rostow's takeoff theory found wide acceptance among rich, industrialised country (IC - also known as rich or developed countries: DC) interests concerned with poor, less developed country (LDC) progress in the Cold War. Rostow's takeoff theory has also been blamed (unfairly or not) by critics such as Peter T. Bauer for waste and failures of IC aid to solve LDC development problems. Before Rostow became internationally prominent, many LDCs including India had chosen to adopt USSR-style centrally planned economies (CPEs). Emphasis on heavy industry, it was hoped, would help their countries leap-frog from what Rostow termed 'traditional society [over the] preconditions' for takeoff into self-sustaining development.

Michael P. Todaro wrote that according to Rostow's theory, the main obstacle to - or constraint on - development was the relatively low level of new capital formation or savings in most poor countries. (N.B. The Reagan-Thatcher paradigm advocating unbridled global capital movements increased the availability of capital to many LDCs, but as seen, the average real cost of capital may have increased and the short-term nature of some cross-border investments has led to economic instability and recession in Mexico and Asia.) In Todaro's[42] reading of Rostow, if a country wanted to grow: 'then it could seek to fill this 'savings gap' ...either through foreign aid or private foreign investment. Unfortunately, this strategy often met with disappointment. Modern commentators suggest part of Rostow's theory was incomplete or flawed from the onset. Although he was not referring to Rostow, remarks in *India Today* by Jairam Ramesh[43] are pertinent:

> Our methodology for estimating savings is deeply flawed. For example, official figures for household savings do not include assets like jewellery and gold. Even so, India's overall savings rate of about 25 per cent of GDP is remarkable for a poor country. At around 19 per cent of GDP, our household savings rate is comparable to that prevailing in Asia. Our private corporate savings rate is rising and currently around 4 per cent of GDP.

Although their savings rates were 'identical' South Korea developed twice as fast as India during the 1960s and 1970s notes Ramesh, concluding, 'The villain is public and government sector savings.' He claims public saving is under 2 per cent of GDP and 'that awful term, *dissavings*' by government administration is nearly (minus) -3 per cent of GDP. Here Ramesh is criticising the BJP-led coalition's advocacy of raising the domestic savings rate to 30 per cent, while rubbishing their populist plan to commit 60 per cent of public investment to agriculture and rural development. Get back to basics and stop trying to fool us, he urges the Government. As hinted previously, Ramesh supports liberalisation of the Indian economy, a fiscally-neutral approach to agriculture and (long-pampered) industry, and transparent accounting of public funds - all eminently sound policies.

Our present discussion need not tarry much longer in this dense macroeconomic thicket. But the fact that the average savings rates of households in Europe and North America has declined to a level *below* India's 19 per cent, while public and government savings rates are significantly *higher* than India's, suggests that fiscal policies and formal financial structures in rich countries encourage maximum household consumption, while the lack of a formal government 'safety net' in countries like India prompts a high rate (i.e. 19 per cent) of household savings - much of it in the form of gold or jewellery which is easily liquidated in emergencies and holds value in inflation. At the same time it suggests public and government institutions in the North include future investment in their budgets, while India's public and government institutions depend on external sources for investment.

This simple comparison of rich and poor country savings rates holds few surprises for many readers, but it may illustrate relationships between savings, investment and national output. Planners of Rostow's era correctly noted a positive correlation between rising investment and rising output. This was evident in the USSR after 1917, Germany in the 1930s, and Europe during the Marshall Plan, 1948-52.[44] The inference was that a massive Marshall Plan-like transfer of capital to poor countries could launch them into self-sustained growth. Unfortunately, correlation did not coexist with causality when countries have different mixes of social capital and institutional embeddedness.

Although Third World observers sometimes see no appreciable difference between the worldviews of Left and Right political factions in rich countries, longstanding differences exist. In the United States (which despite its late-twentieth century free trade rhetoric, developed behind a frequently-erected tariff barrier in the nineteenth century) it is true that Democrat President Harry Truman launched the Marshall Plan successfully in Europe, but by no means all Democrat Party members -or their Republican rivals on the Right - believed similar results could be easily achieved in poor countries such as India. And it is fair to say that while the pro-business Republican Party in the USA Right and far-Right energetically pursued overseas markets, most thought Third World development was more likely *via* internal economic liberalisations and sale of cash crops and other exports than *via* 'foreign aid'. Leftish Democrats supported foreign aid much more than Republicans. In their heart of hearts more Republicans than Democrats believed free market reforms in poor countries must precede their rise to modernity, and that the 1974-75 demands by 150 poor countries for a new international economic order (NIEO) were fraught with nonsense. Personified by 'the Yankee trader', the American Right's views were similar to those of British economist[45] Peter T. Bauer: the best way for a country to enter global trade was to develop cash crops for export, as Malaya had in rubber, and West Africa in cocoa, etc. A major difference between the American Left and Right was that intellectuals on the Left might consider analyses of *dependencia* economists such as Raul Prebisch (that poor countries suffered from skewed 'centre-periphery' relationships with rich ones), but the Right blamed government corruption, illiteracy, disease and - above all - socialist policies for lagging growth. But 2 decades after the NIEO was proposed, the GATT/WTO-1994 improved terms-of-trade between rich and poor and partially *reconciled* the views of Left and Right in that, while trade relations *indeed had been tilted against poor countries* (particularly in agriculture), trade reform - not just aid or wealth transfers - was the safest route to development.

What overly-optimistic proponents of foreign aid on the Left (often suspicious of business and sympathetic to the tenets of democratic socialism) in rich countries missed in the early-post-World War II years was historical fact: that prior to instances of massive investment leading to growth in Germany, Europe in general, and parts of the USSR, these areas had *previously* experienced post-takeoff stages of what Rostow termed 'technological maturity' characterised by 'modern attitudes and motivations, as well as modern technologies'. Significant portions of these industrialised countries had even entered the 'age of mass consumption' (i.e. Rostow's fifth stage, marked by consumer durables such as motorcycles and family automobiles.[46]

Yet more auspicious for post-World War II recovery in Germany, most of Europe and much of the USSR was that there already existed productive networks of physical capital in the form of harbours, railroads and other transport and communications infrastructure. Even if burnt-out, they could be rebuilt on the same patterns. And crucially, European labour had already entered one of the post-takeoff stages of growth (marked by widespread literacy, modern education and attitudes toward work such as punctuality) which Rostow called 'the drive to technological maturity'. Thus, these societies converted investment into output more efficiently than poorer 'traditional' societies, marked by low literacy and a dearth of scientists, engineers and entrepreneurs.

Bauer points out that while Marx accused metropolitan countries of plundering their colonies, he also regarded them as a progressive force of modernisation.[47] In the early post-colonial era following World War II the consensus of policy makers in developing countries was probably that colonialism stymied their historical drive toward modernity and that in the case of the Raj, the British effectively looted India by transferring high-value-added textile operations to factories in England. There is evidence to support both views and undoubtedly different areas experienced varying effects. Whatever the verdict of economic historians on the ratio of outright exploitation-to-net investment by colonialist powers, some Third World economists now acknowledge certain benefits accrued during the era of European colonialism. These include development of transport, communications and services (e.g. the highly-regarded Indian Civil Service), as well as investment in other industries. At any rate, while significant aspects of modern economies operated in major Indian cities (e.g. Bombay, Calcutta, Delhi, and Madras - nodes pertinent to this book), India *in toto* had by no means been modernised as thoroughly as European areas that regenerated quickly *via* Marshall Plan aid. And many countries were poorer than India.

Bauer's dissent on Harrod-Domar and Rostow's 'take-off'

Many underdeveloped Third World countries, aspiring to economic take-off and impressed by the reconstruction of Europe with the Marshall Plan, were influenced by variants of the Harrod-Domar growth model.[48] Briefly put, the H-D model assumes a positive significant correlation between increases of net investment and GDP growth (according to an economy's underlying capital/output ratio). Peter T. Bauer attacked the limitations of the Harrod-Domar model, along with Rostow's stages-of-development theory, under the heading 'Two Unsuccessful Approaches' in his 1971 book[49] *Dissent on Development.* Bauer pointed out that Harrod and Domar were concerned with 'advanced industrial societies', and their models being 'largely Keynesian in their main aims and assumptions', were inappropriate for underdeveloped countries. Bauer wrote that an over-emphasis on capital accumulation contributed to the failure of development policies and he castigated schemes that raised capital through unnecessary 'compulsory saving', unduly restricting consumer spending and domestic markets. Bauer scorned 'large-scale foreign aid' (i.e. grants or soft loans) that was often wasted by LDCs: '[without the] recognition that expenditure does not become productive simply because it is termed investment.'

In a 1969 essay, Bauer attacked the 'spurious consensus' 'of contemporary development economists' whose main tenets he depicted as 'invalid' and 'not even generally accepted.' These tenets included the supposition that through 'historical accident' and 'colonial exploitation', it is 'a vicious circle' of 'extreme poverty' that blocks 'the capital formation required for raising income.' Bauer said planners were wrong to assume that post-colonial development hinged on: 'comprehensive central planning...compulsory saving...large-scale foreign aid.'

On the contrary, Bauer thought genuinely productive projects could attract investment by domestic or foreign commercial banks, bypassing the 'aid trap' completely. Although quantities of monies and materiél in aid programmes seemed large, they seldom amounted to more than 1 per cent of the GNP of the economies they were supposed to improve. Thus, said Bauer, what in reality were relatively small amounts often had less potential to improve poor countries than to destabilise them. According to Bauer it better to rely on commercial capital formation and investment. Bauer invoked Karl Marx in his synopsis of the gap between neoclassical economists and the aforementioned 'spurious consensus':

> classical writers, including Adam Smith and Marx, closely related capital accumulation as an engine of development to...particular groups, organisations and classes, such as traders, governments and the bourgeoisie, and to social attitudes, relationships and institutions, and to changes in these. Some of the most influential growth models abstract these forces, and apparently treat long-term progress as dependent on capital expenditure alone; and this abstraction differentiates this modern approach from that of the classical writers.

The above passage is important to our later discussion of contemporary dairy aid. It suggests food aid was safer in the hands of a pluralist organisation composed of knowledgeable dairy practitioners such as the NDDB - rather than being disbursed by a central Government ministry. It informs our analysis of attempts to ensure that such capital (in the form of commodity dairy aid and loans to India) was deployed appropriately by farmer cooperatives to raise the country's dairy output, avoiding direct or indirect taxes and administration costs that would decrease aid efficiency. So poles-apart was Bauer from Rostow's take-off theory that Rostow[50] once remarked: 'If Professor Bauer did not exist, it would have been useful to invent him... '

Certainly Bauer dissented on the received wisdom that all societies were limited to the five steps choreographed by Rostow. Bauer suggested that when his formulations were not tautological they were 'so vague and open-ended as to be unserviceable.' He derided Rostow and like-minded theorists for ignoring the anthropological uniqueness of societies (one point on which Bauer and Arturo Escobar concur), the unpredictability of historical forces such as technical innovation and other factors more important to LDC development than external aid. The difficulty of separating the causes of growth from mere co-variants helps explain the seemingly endless, often politicised debate on development in the Third World. As hinted above, one side of this debate was personified on the Right by Bauer claiming LDCs are often unable to absorb massive external investment flows. Bauer acted as a Right-wing gadfly to Rostow, a mainstream[51] establishment figure in the USA (the world's largest aid-donor) Democratic administration of President Lyndon B. Johnson. Rostow, on the US Left, generally represented the pro-foreign aid viewpoint. This was the 1960s' era of the Vietnam War, a foreign adventure Johnson inherited from the assassinated President John F. Kennedy, and earlier the French. In the 1950s, bloody colonial retreats from Vietnam and Algeria had almost brought France to civil war. In the 1960s and early 1970s, at the apogee of post-World War II US power (when Americans still believed implicitly in their own country's positive role as an anti-colonial force - since their own revolution in 1776 - and its ability to improve conditions in the rest of the world), Vietnam lead to its nadir. The unpopular war polarised politics and rent the US cultural fabric (Pres. Dwight Eisenhower, Kennedy's predecessor, admitted in his memoirs that most Vietnamese would have voted for Communist leader Ho Chi Minh, if they had the opportunity in the 1950s.).

The financial cost of the war depleted the resources to fight Johnson's domestic 'war on poverty' and promote better race relations, fuelled inflation, necessitated deficit spending in Washington - and forced Johnson's successor Richard M. Nixon to abandon the gold standard and other aspects of the Bretton Woods system after 1971. Abandonment of Bretton Woods, was a body blow to the international trading system that was not fully healed until the establishment of the World Trade Organisation after 1994. Fortunately, the WTO is an improvement on Bretton Woods: although the latter fostered a quarter century of fairly stable world economic growth (1944-1971) its gold standard was not designed to withstand the vortex of transnational capital flows and floating exchange rates that the present flexible GATT/WTO system is capable (despite 1990s' examples of capital flight) of handling.

For the purposes of further discussion we shall refer to the Bauer and Rostow camps. Of course additional camps engaged in the debate - notably before the end of the Cold War, after which the Uruguay GATT trade talks superseded strategic nuclear arms limitation talks on the world stage. To the Left of Rostow were 'world systems' theorists such as Immanuel Wallerstein, ideologically close to Susan George and Arturo Escobar[52] who criticised food aid and development schemes generally, and Shanti George who critiqued Indian dairy development specifically. Todaro cites other views to the Left of Rostow, e.g. 'the neo-Marxist school - Baran, Sweezy, and Magdoff'.[53] Not to be forgotten were official Communist Party theorists in the USSR and China who fuelled propaganda that Western capitalism and neo-colonialism were principal obstacles to LDC development, while ignoring flaws in their own centrally-planned economies. To varying degrees, critics on the far Left viewed the Rostow/World Bank nexus (nominally further Left on the political spectrum than the Bauer camp on the Right) as being too preoccupied with Cold War strategy to be effective promoters of Third World development if not, as evidenced by British and US support for the apartheid regime in South Africa, actually inimical to it. Nevertheless, Washington Cold Warriors knew that demonstrating US-fostered development in poor countries undoubtedly would promote their interests in the ideological war with Communism. Rostow[54] conceded that:

> demonstrating that underdeveloped nations - now the main focus of Communist hopes - can move successfully through the preconditions into a well-established take-off... resisting the... temptations of Communism... is I believe, the most important single item on the Western agenda

Whatever the efficacy for LDCs of Rostow's stages-of-growth theory, it so profoundly influenced Cold War policy that it is understandable why Bauer termed it a 'spurious consensus.' Their debate on investment echoes the proverbial question: *What came first - the chicken or the egg?* Both Bauer and Rostow camps identified a concomitant surge in investment as economies experience the preconditions for take-off. But: *What came first - the investment or the growth?* Bauer (described as iconoclastic by many; less benignly by Club of Rome or NEIO adherents) believed historical accident and technical innovation, such as made possible the rubber industry and consequent development in colonial Malaysia[55], are stronger determinants of long-term growth than development strategies (i.e. foreign aid) touted by the Rostow camp. Late in his career Rostow[56] defended himself against critics such as Bauer and Simon Kuznets:

> My colleagues insisted on regarding the rise in the investment rate in the take-off as a primal cause in the matter, say as a Harrod-Domar growth model. If I had it to do over again, I would state emphatically, right at the beginning, what I wrote...in 1960: '...The emergence of a rate of net investment sufficient to outstrip the rate of increase of the population and to yield a positive net rate of growth is at least as much the result of prior [sectoral] growth as a cause of growth.'

Here Rostow agrees with Bauer that previous indigenous growth is 'at least as important' as what might be provided by external investment, but he leaves the door open to foreign aid - Bauer's regular object of scorn. After decades of experience, perhaps the positions of Rostow and Bauer began to converge. They are near agreement that investment alone is no guarantor of growth, but rather a covariant, along with a society's ability to treat historical accident and technical innovations as opportunities for growth. It does seem obvious (comparing, say, the different historical paths to modernity taken by South Korea and Britain) that peoples are not consigned to preordained paths. What is incontrovertible is that many of the detailed (generally 'top-down', centrally-planned) blueprints for development in Third World countries, often relying on large-scale investment, failed. But not all - or at least not entirely. As we shall see, India's White Revolution programme Operation Flood probably benefited from a mix of ambitious top-down, government-sanctioned planning and investment in urban centres, while measures of democratic, bottom-up procedure augmented the formation of rural milk cooperatives and encourages their adaptation of the Anand model to local conditions.

It may, however, be useful to add that, where investment or aid has failed to fuel growth (perhaps in a crude application of the Harrod-Domar model), blame may be due to inappropriate or ill-timed investment. Logical fallacies befell some politicians, e.g.: *Britain is rich and has a large steel industry; therefore to be rich our country must build a steel industry.* Investing in steel often had less benefit to nationhood than investing in domestic farming. In the post-colonial era, many LDCs attempted 'take-off'[57] by squandering scarce resources on heavy industry. J.P. Cole[58] wrote:

> a political goal in many developing countries... has been the establishment of an iron and steel industry. A heavy industrial base has also been considered essential in most socialist ones.

This was true of post-World War II India and China, influential models for smaller LDCs.[59] Perhaps due to India's large domestic market its state steel industry has enjoyed some success. Yet, neither has it - beset by over-manning and other inefficiencies draining government coffers - been a rocket to growth (at least until the early-twenty-first century). China, whose overall post-World War II growth has roughly doubled India's[60] growth also mistook steel production for progress. Consequently, China wasted labour, and the landscape suffered long-lasting degradation–from the embarrassing 'back-yard' steel furnaces of the Mao era. Unfortunately, many smaller countries with factorial advantages of iron ore and coking coal but smaller domestic markets followed similarly unrealistic industrial policies, but were less able to afford them. *They neglected agriculture and consumer goods and textiles based on farming.* They wasted on metallurgy what Hobsbawm[61] termed: 'the very heavy investments required by even quite modest ironworks (compared to quite large cotton-mills).'

Countries such as Nigeria suffered the curse of petroleum, relying on oil exports instead of improving domestic productivity. Others, finding deposits of bauxite (like iron ore and coking coal, ubiquitous on the planet), over-invested in the aluminium industry. Output usually exceeded domestic demand and had the bad fortune to come on line when the cyclical world market was unremunerative. In many cases, centrally-planned industrial policies impoverished farmers and consumers, leaving LDC Governments deeply in debt. Unable to sell commodities abroad, they could not afford food and other imports. After ignoring their farm sectors, many countries completed the vicious circle, becoming dependent on food aid.

Over-valued Currencies

As in many countries, agriculture in India suffered worse than benign neglect. *India Today* columnist Jairam Ramesh[62] notes: '…industry has been pampered. Ashok Gulati, the noted economist, has shown that industry has enjoyed a 45 per cent tariff protection while agriculture has been taxed at 22 per cent.' Historically, most rich countries grew by expropriating wealth from their farm sectors. But greater measures of appropriate agricultural investment would have contributed more to national output than did heavy industry. India is just one example of LDCs which taxed farmers too heavily without returning commensurate Government services.

'Indirect taxes' could be even more harmful than direct taxes. LDC governments often hurt domestic agriculture by maintaining national currencies at artificially high rates of exchange against the currencies of the major industrial countries (e.g. the US dollar and the German mark). This acted as a subsidy to industry - *exacted from agriculture* - because it effectively lowered the prices of machine tools and other capital-intensive imports desired by Third World industrialists from richer countries - while making farm exports dearer. Of course farming also uses imported equipment but far less than is characteristic in heavy industry. Over-valued currencies could sabotage the growth of cash crops for export. Rural economies were stunted when produce became artificially expensive and uncompetitive on world markets. That is one reason Bhagwati described over-valued currencies as prime 'disincentives' to LDC agriculture.[63]

Meanwhile, subsidised heavy industry and high-tech factories in urban centres made cities employment magnets. More migrants from the disadvantaged countryside than would ever find jobs in the formal economy flocked to the cities. This was a mixed blessing. A few urban workers mastered high-tech jobs, but cities hardly grew into urban utopias as job seekers rushed in. Migration reduced rural unemployment, but robbed the countryside of productive workers.

According to Michael P. Todaro, early research tried to explain excessive rural-urban migration in Third World countries in terms of 'social, cultural and psychological factors'[64] but he determined that the chief motivation for migration was the chance of high-paying jobs in urban centres. Operating from the economist's perspective that given perfect information most consumers make rational decisions, he postulated that farmworkers moved to cities because of 'urban-rural differences in expected rather than actual earnings.' Todaro's theory of rural-urban migration explained: 'the apparently paradoxical relationship (at least to economists) of accelerated rural-urban migration in the context of rising urban unemployment.'

In other words, even if rural migrants did not immediately find better jobs (typically paying 3-to-4-times the average rural wage), Todaro showed their behaviour was not naive, but rational if their urban income eventually exceeded the opportunity costs of income they forsook in rural employment. Flocking to the cities appears even more rational in the context of over-valued national currency rates, condemned by Bhagwati for depleting rural agricultural sectors in LDCs.

Import Substitution versus Exports

When steel, aluminium and other commodity exports from too many LDC producers swamped the world market, or during ebbs in world business cycles, world prices fell, jeopardising national development plans. An LDC's economic crisis was compounded if it was short on cash to pay for imports. Import substitution policies were often imposed to meet domestic demand, stimulate employment and save foreign exchange. (These were arguments for manufacturing milk powder in India, but in this case import substitution was sensible because India had a comparative advantage in dairying. Import substitution in industries without a comparative advantage, e.g. design and manufacture of jumbo jets, might be disastrous.) Unfortunately, import substitution often proved counter-productive to all its espoused goals[65] and in the long-term left LDCs less competitive than before on the world market.

Another trenchant development argument long embroiling agronomists, economists, geographers and politicians is the cash crop vs. food crop debate. It somewhat resembles the debate on industrial policy in developing countries, i.e. whether it should-be top-down and monolithic or bottom-up and pluralistic. Should a nation concentrate on export crops or self-sufficiency? Such a controversy over oilseeds (from cotton, rapeseed and other plants) vexed policy makers in India over the last decade, and the question bears brief discussion here. When Operation Flood, the White Revolution programme in India (utilising high input fodder, nutrients and concentrates to raise milk yield) got underway, oilseeds had long been an adjunct to cattle fodder. Thus, to observers like Martin Doornbos, it was a 'paradox'[66] that, just when development of the Indian dairy industry required additional intensive inputs including oilseeds, liberalised economic policies of the Indian Government allowed export of oilseeds as a cash crop. Fortunately, what Paul Samuelson[67] called the 'substitution-effect' comes into play. India is a relatively large country and oilseeds are just one of many products palatable to cattle. Moreover, it has a huge, relatively diversified domestic market which can buffer world market fluctuations more easily than smaller, single-crop LDCs. When India sells inputs abroad, other products generally can substitute for them. At any rate, Indian oilseeds production has risen in the 1990s, fostered by cooperatives on the Anand model.

Small economies depending on just one or two exports were more vulnerable to world market fluctuations than multiple exporters like India. For instance, many non-petroleum exporting LDCs suffered serious trade deficits after the OPEC oil embargoes of 1973-74 and 1979-80. Typically dependent on widely-available commodity exports such as coffee, poor countries were helpless to raise prices on their commodities enough to pay higher oil prices imposed by cartels. Later we will discuss further the economic austerity (prompting a temporary resumption of dairy aid imports) forced upon India by oil price rises in the Gulf War of 1991.

Oil shocks prompted calls by 150 Third World and developing countries in 1974-75 for a new international economic order (NIEO) whose demands were: (1) debt renegotiation; (2) redefinition of the terms-of-trade and better access to rich country markets; (3) IMF reform; (4) increases in development aid to UN recommended levels. Generally speaking, the fall of communism in the USSR weakened the redistributive elements of the NIEO platform. Debt relief has been addressed sporadically, getting renewed attention after Hurricane Mitch devastated Latin America in autumn 1998. Responding to clamours for debt cancellation, UK development (DfID) head Clare Short repeated that it would be extended only to countries making structural reform. The IMF has made some reforms, but many poor countries chafe under structural adjustment. GATT/WTO-1994 did increase their access to rich markets. Debt cancellations agreed by the Group of 8 major powers in Gleneagles, Scotland in 2005 offered some relief, but the signatories' plan to 'end poverty rang hollow.

Liberalisation of Farm Trade

At the beginning of this chapter we discussed the similarity between the Prisoner's Dilemma and the difficulty central bankers face in recessions. Avoiding the temptation to raise tariffs or devalue currency can achieve an ideal state which Hoekman & Kostecki[68] call a 'Pareto-optimal situation'. They explain: 'A Pareto-optimal situation is one where no party can be better off without another party being made worse off.'

Of course acting selfishly and restricting trade unilaterally (like a prisoner informing on cohorts to secure individual freedom) can benefit special interest groups (e.g. protected-farmers or industries) in the short run and perhaps even improve a country's aggregate welfare temporarily. Almost inevitably, the resulting harm to its trading partners returns to haunt countries that try to prosper at others' expense.

Retaliation can come *via* competitive devaluations of currency, as it characteristically did in the Great Depression. Global output shrinks along with trade. Many national leaders have come to realise that they must side-step domestic lobbying of the type that can thwart free trade. The means to do so are rules made in multilateral negotiations begun in the GATT in 1947, and carried on since 1994 in the permanent negotiating forum of the WTO. Hoekman & Kostecki[69] sum up the utility of the GATT/WTO neatly: 'In instances such as these, where individually rational behaviour by governments is not efficient, the creation of an institution or regime can help solve the dilemma by fostering cooperation.'

The survivors of the Great Depression and World War II knew prosperity and peace depended on improved international monetary and trade relations. The Bretton Woods gold standard helped reestablish monetary stability. But hope for an International Trade Organisation (ITO) was dashed by the US Congress' refusal to ratify it in 1948. Isolationist tendencies were still rife in America. After the stillbirth of the ITO, its older but less promising sibling, the GATT tariff reductions negotiations claimed a shaky but growing lease on life. GATT did not achieve the formal institutional importance envisioned for the defunct ITO, but periodic proclamations by die-hard protectionists that 'GATT is dead' proved premature, and GATT achieved its apotheosis in the WTO in 1994. This book is written not to relate how that bureaucratic development took place, but to show why the agricultural ramifications of the Uruguay settlement are important to rich and poor alike, especially during world recession.

Global food trade is at unprecedented heights. Food is rapidly becoming as freely traded a primary commodity as coal, or manufactured commodities like steel. Until recently, however, agriculture was too sensitive a political and social issue for most countries to consider dismantling the array of overt and covert subsidies and tariffs that made it one of the world's most regulated activities. This was true - to a surprising degree - of even the powerful industrialised areas of Europe, Japan and North America. Jagdish Bhagwati[70] writes that agriculture was: 'Exempted from most of GATT's discipline...right from the start.'

In fact, when the General Agreement on Tariffs and Trade (GATT) was first drawn up in 1947, it was the USA (which in the nineteenth century specialised in farm exports in order to buy manufactures from Europe) that led efforts applauded by France and other farming countries to write loopholes into Articles XI and XVI, removing agriculture from the GATT agenda.

In 1955, the Eisenhower administration pleased farm lobbyists when it was granted a further waiver from agricultural liberalisation. In the early decades of GATT, Bhagwati suggests their 'small role in overall world trade and their low political profile and clout' deemed LDCs unable to block IC waivers on farm trade. Bhagwati[71] also identifies political fall-out from overemphasis on industry: 'the major developing nations were protecting their manufactures instead and therefore were not interested in lobbying for agricultural trade liberalisation.'

Slowly at first, global trade underwent a tectonic shift. Led by Japan, the Little Dragons (*aka* Tigers) among developing countries began to export manufactures. First small–toys, textiles and inexpensive appliances and, as the decades rolled by, more reliable, better performing - and still cheaper - motorcycles, cars and electronic branded products. World trade saw annual real growth of 7 per cent in the period 1948-1970[72], but despite growing trade deficits suffered by the USA, the idea persisted in many quarters that agriculture was unique and should be treated separately from manufactures. Little move toward free trade in agriculture was made during the Kennedy (1964-1967) or the Tokyo Round (1973-1979) of GATT, although some tariffs were reduced in 1967. In the incipient spirit of *détente* Poland became the first communist country to join GATT in 1967. This reflected more than a thaw in Cold War relations (before 'Prague Spring' ended in the 1968 USSR invasion of Czechoslovakia). It also reflected the GATT/WTO principle that trade can be profitable *via* fair, *rule-oriented* agreements - irrespective of the *structures* of the individual economies involved.

Naturally, like farm lobbyists around the world, most in the USA touted the uniqueness of farming, the need for tariffs against cheaper imports and the wisdom of promoting US exports with subsidies. But Washington got a dose of macroeconomic reality in the inflationary oil shocks of the 1970s. The Nixon administration began to favour the liberalisation of farm trade. The succeeding Ford and Carter administrations also tried to combat domestic 'stagflation' in the 1970s by playing the farm card internationally. In the 1980s the Reagan administration began a subsidy war against EEC Common Market agricultural policy (CAP), demanding that all measures skewing farm trade be withdrawn 'within 10 years'. The USA would no longer humour its European allies on farming.

Simultaneously, US policy shifted from mere 'containment' of Communism to outright winning of the Cold War by all the economic and military means at its disposal. Early in the 1980s, President Ronald Reagan upped the ante against what he called the 'evil empire' of the USSR by announcing the costly 'Star Wars' weapons programme which horrified peace activists, but now is widely credited with convincing Moscow that it could not afford a new arms race. The EEC (*aka* EC, EU) saw its CAP not just as farm policy, but as a non-negotiable part of its social policy. Washington saw the CAP as a means by which its European allies were selfishly enriching themselves at the expense of the economic strength of the USA, whose political and military leadership was vital to winning the Cold War. Hoekman & Kostecki[73] note that:

> Throughout the 1960s and the 1970s, agricultural discussions between the two major players - the EU and the USA - were based on two totally different world-views. The EU basically sought to manage world trade in a way that facilitated the functioning of the CAP, while the USA - supported by countries such as Australia, Canada, and New Zealand - wanted to achieve significant liberalisation.

Between them, the EEC and the USA controlled about 40 per cent of world food exports. But CAP export subsidies were eroding US market share. Among the negative effects of Community export subsidies was a general lowering of world market prices, including milk powder. Europe suggested a compromise akin to the Eastbloc's reliance on managed trade.

Table 3.1.

GATT-1947 to WTO-1994[i]

1947: Geneva Round (23 countries). GATT records tariff negotiations of 23 countries. Rules reflect US farm policies. Unlike trade in manufactures, neither Quantitative Restrictions (QRs) nor export subsidies are forbidden in agricultural trade.

1949: Annecy Round (11 countries).

1950: China withdraws from GATT.

1951: Torquay Round (32 countries). Germany joins GATT.

1955: US granted GATT waiver on agriculture. US "client" Japan joins GATT, but Bandung Conference proclaims non-aligned Third World movement in the Cold War.

1955-1956: Geneva Round (33 countries).

1957: EEC begins with Treaty of Rome.

1960-1961: Dillon Round (39 countries).

1964: UNCTAD presses for trade reforms to benefit developing countries.

1964-1967: Kennedy Round (74 countries).

1967: Poland first Eastbloc country to join GATT.

1973-1979: Tokyo Round (99 countries).

1974-75: New International Economic Order (NIEO) demanded by poor countries

1986-1994: Uruguay Round (103 in 1986; 128 early-1995). Many GATT functions permanently consolidated in WTO. Agriculture, textiles & clothing brought into GATT for the first time. General agreements on trade in services (GATS), trade-related intellectual property (TRIPS) and trade-related investment measures (TRIMS) are notable (if limited & controversial) liberalisations agreed by many developing countries.

[i] Hoekman & Kostecki (1995): pp 14-17, 24, 200.

The Eastbloc used barter, i.e. international agreements on cereals, dairy, rice, etc. In GATT parlance the Community wanted the Uruguay Round Agricultural Agreement (URAA) to be 'outcome-based' while the USA and its partners desired a 'rules-based' outcome.

By now the zeal for truly unrestricted trade had mounted in the West, as the laissez-faire aspects of Smith's and Ricardo's ideas asserted themselves over those upstarts Marx and Keynes. The USA rejected the Community's proposal for such trade-balancing requirements. Dramatic changes came in the GATT Uruguay Round (1986-1994) spurred by the earlier rise of the Cairns Group.[74] In the 1980s New Zealand and Argentina joined a coalition of a dozen mostly poorer countries led by Australia in the Cairns lobby boosting free world farm trade. All Cairns members, irrespective of their level of 'development' (*via* industrialisation or expansion of the services portion of their economies), shared one trait: a comparative advantage in agricultural production that could be exploited if world trade were liberalised, particularly if the USA, and especially the EEC, reduced farm subsidies. Paul Kennedy[75] wrote that the 'greatest beneficiaries' of a farm subsidy phase-out would be Australia, New Zealand and Argentina - in contrast to some US farm communities that might 'wither away'.

Others suggested liberalisation would depress US dairying while cereals sectors prospered - although export growth in value-added dairy products like pizza cheese to Asia might sustain it. Nevertheless, despite threats to individual localities and sectors, US trade representatives Carla Hills and (later) Clayton Yeutter believed agricultural liberalisation would benefit the US economy in the aggregate. The USA joined in Cairns Group demands that the European Community, Japan and other countries should dismantle their trade-distorting agricultural regimes.[76] Kennedy's gloom over the prospects of individual communities is already borne out by massive restructuring in the US dairy industry (i.e. farm closures or amalgamation with neighbouring farms, mergers and enlargement of dairy cooperatives, and mergers among processors). The campaign to maximise US farm export earnings is further discussed below. Ironically, this superpower initiative is *via* GATT/WTO, a potential boon to developing countries such as India - where in late 1998 the National Dairy Development Board (NDDB) announced export of Amul products to the USA.

Cold War Agri-politics

Changes in US trade policy were forced by the costly over-extension of its military hegemony in a pattern Paul Kennedy compares to the demise of the Portuguese, Spanish, Dutch and British empires.[77] Robert Gilpin fully agrees that functioning as military linchpin of the Western Alliance became an economic burden to the USA and precipitated its abandonment of the gold standard and overall Bretton Woods system. Whatever the merit of 'Asian values', Gilpin and many or most observers agree that US patronage and openness to exports from Japan, and later the newly-industrialising-countries (NICs, e.g. South Korea, Taiwan) was a fundamental basis of the Asian economic miracle. Whether or not it follows that Japan and the NICs profited economically from US Cold War policy is arguable. (Certainly Vietnam did not.) But access to the US market gradually raised Asian competitiveness, threatening US industrial dominance. Gilpin[78] accepts this and identifies Cold War geopolitical initiatives by the USA for its open-door policy to Asian imports:

> there were no large, neighbouring non-communist economies to which the Japanese economy could be attached. In order to overcome this problem...the United States took several initiatives. One was to expedite the decolonisation of Southeast Asia; after all, one cause of

> the Pacific War had been that European colonisers had closed Southeast Asian economies to the Japanese. The USA also sponsored Japanese membership in the 'Western Club.' [e.g. IMF, World Bank] ... In addition, the USA gave Japan relatively free access to the American market and American technology without an economic quid pro quo, although it did require strategic concessions (i.e. air and naval bases) from the Japanese.

Frances Moore Lappé and Joseph Collins, the authors of *Food First* (1980), appear in agreement with essential parts of Gilpin's analysis. Lappé & Collins relate two-US export responses to rectify the persistent balance-of-payments deficit wrought by: (1) imports of consumer goods from allies on the Pacific Rim, e.g. Japan, Korea and Taiwan, whose access to the USA fuelled their export-led-growth; and (2) the one-half trillion dollars spent by the USA - much of it overseas - on the Vietnam War, not to mention its network of bases abroad, and the nuclear umbrella over its allies.

One response was to raise exports of high-technology products. The USA has been successful in this. Despite challenges from the European Airbus[79] consortium, the USA has maintained its lead in civil and military aviation, and is also first in world arms exports - followed by Britain. While Chinese, European and Russian rockets are successful at boosting satellites, and the space station Mir has demonstrated Russian resilience in space, the NASA space shuttle symbolises US dominance in space technology. The approaching end of the shuttle programme is a public relations problem, but mitigated by the lack of a serious challenge by other countries.

The other response noted by Lappé & Collins was a package of 'Food Power' policies to increase US agricultural exports.[80] They list several initiatives taken by the Nixon administration and the USDA in the early-1970s, to unleash its 'Food Power':

The USA renounced the Bretton Woods system of fixed international currency rates, in which the dollar was pegged at US$35/ounce of gold in 1971[81] This was followed by devaluations of the dollar (11 per cent in December 1971, and a further 6 per cent in early 1973) making US exports more attractive.

The USA would 'tempt potential buyers' with low prices and cheap financing by the Commodity Credit Corporation (CCC). The concessionary terms of these sales made them hard to distinguish from soft loans in food aid programmes and they shared another potential effect: promotion of US commodities exports. The USA brandished the banner of free trade in urging other countries to accept its exports, pointing to plans to abolish US domestic farm price supports as evidence of its good faith.

Then USDA ordered cutbacks in crops acreage, almost ensuring that world market prices would rise (irrespective of bad weather in other grain exporting countries, which as fate would have it, catapulted world prices beyond USDA predictions). Secretary Earl Butz used carrots and sticks in his encouragement of US farmers. He told the *Washington Post* that the need to keep price supports low gave farmers the choice to 'adapt or die', but he also used flattery, calling the American farmer 'the man of the century', and he urged farmers to plant 'fence post to fence post'.[82] This carrot assuaged their objections to subsidy cuts with reassurances of profits to be made from selling food to a 'hungry world'.

By these steps the USA buoyed its balance-of-payments account, prepared foreign acceptance of US exports, and weakened the position of highly-subsidised EEC exporters. (Note: Since World War II, China, India, the USSR and the USA have dominated world cereals production. But North America and Western Europe have been big exporters, while China, India and Russia have often been heavy importers. High CAP price supports and the mechanised implements, fertiliser and other inputs they encourage have increased European production to an extent that confounds expectations: although Canada's vast prairies dwarf the arable acreage of France, France grew more wheat than Canada 1970-1993. Canadian total cereals production did not surpass CAP-protected France until about 1990.[83] Overproduction of cereals in Europe entailed cheaper feed for beef and dairy farmers, encouraging surpluses in those sectors too. In this vicious circle the CAP often consumed 70 per cent of the EEC budget.

European Food Mountains were already on the horizon when the USA hit its first great post-World War II financial crisis in the Vietnam War, setting the scene for the huge 19 million metric tonnes (MT) sale of US grain to the USSR in 1972-73.[84] *In Merchants of Grain* (1979) Dan Morgan tells the saga of US grain sales made in Leonid Brezhnev's era of communist 'gerontocracy' to satisfy consumer demand for grain-fed swine and poultry. (Then as in the 1990s, the Russian dairy herd was being sacrificed to provide meat.) The historic sales had multiple effects on international political and economic relations. Food prices rose precipitously in the USA - a country used to cheap food. Milk soared past $1 per gallon. Whereas in 1961-72 the USA enjoyed a dairy trade surplus of nearly $100 million per annum, the import picture in 1973-74 switched to a deficit of ca. $60 million ($89m imports minus $28.6m exports).[85] Consumers scorned the sale as 'the great grain robbery' and blamed grain cartels who prospered from it, along with OPEC oil boycotts, for fuelling double-digit inflation.

The point here is this: an overall growing trade deficit, domestic inflation and disgruntlement following the US-Soviet grain deals and OPEC oil shocks induced the US Government to exercise muscle on world grain markets. This trade initiative served as a model for the expansion of US dairy exports in the 1980s (following the second OPEC oil boycott), as Butter Mountains and Milk Lakes formed in the USA and Europe. From a 1979-81 base dairy exports rose 38 per cent by 1992. Like grain, US dairy exports were assisted by financing from the Commodity Credit Corporation (CCC) arm of the USDA, in what is now called the Dairy Export Incentive Programme (DEIP).

US guaranteed 'soft' loans were instrumental in countering EEC dairy 'dumping' on world markets in the 1980s. Washington obviously determined that waging this costly 'subsidy war' against Brussels was worthwhile not just for political support it garnered among American farmers, but for world market share the USA had lost due to the subsidised exports of Europe's Common Agricultural Policy (CAP). And although the USA had been an industrial power since at least the early-nineteenth century, it is often overlooked that the preponderance of US exports were *not* manufactures but actually commodities such as cereals, beef, minerals and timber until the mid-twentieth century. The rise of the USA as an exporter of raw materials should give second thoughts to those maintaining the only route to national power is via manufacturing, industry and services. With its balance-of-payments accounts in red ink due to Cold War spending on weaponry and overseas military bases – not to mention a trade deficit with a list of countries headed by Japan - it is understandable why the USA waged a subsidies war with Europe and Japan in order to put its foreign exchange accounts back in black. Although the GATT-1994 agreement was to phase out CCC and DEIP export subsidies for US grain and dairy, it was ironically the muscle of such soft loans that helped bring Europe to the GATT table in the first place. The opening of Japan to American rice, and other gains being made by the USA on the Pacific Rim (e.g. in Australia and New Zealand's traditional dairy export enclaves such as Malaysia) testify to the inexorable success of the US 'Food Power' drive.

It was ironic that Japan, Asia's top industrial power (whose export-led growth had thrived on access to American markets, and whose security benefited from the US nuclear umbrella) also had some of the world's highest rates of protection for rice, beef and other US exports. Frances M. Ufkes details how Japan's 'state sponsored beef sub-sector' and protection against other US farm products were 'highly-politicised' issues in US-Japan trade negotiations.[86] The US attitude to the EEC was similar. Within the USA, even opponents of the country's military policies resented the fiscal ability of the EEC (which spent a smaller proportion of its output on defence than the USA - or even Japan) to protect its own farmers while subsidising sales abroad. A combination of factors was pushing the USA into the arms of the CAIRNS group. Together, they would pester Europe and Japan into liberalising farm trade (for even those sacrosanct commodities, sugar and milk) in the GATT-1994 agreement. Particularly important to our discussion is the analysis of Anderson & Tyers (1991) which explicates trade barriers to LDC exports. But first let us compare the classic 'wheat trap' of Nigeria to the case of India.

Nigeria's 'wheat trap' compared to India's situation

Food policy is a touchy subject. Although Smith, Ricardo, Malthus elucidated some truths, policy makers in this century have, as always, peered through a glass darkly. Noble or greedy, neither government officials nor commercial traders can ever foresee–all the results of their actions. Their hands are guided by more subjective motives - enrichment and security for themselves and their families. It is difficult to apply a conventional moral calculus to historic trading events, when past players understood even less about food security than we do today.

But, as those who do not learn from history will probably suffer insults to their food security, let us compare the cases of India and Nigeria. India is more populous and almost bereft of costly oil. In this century both countries have been in the mainstream of international food systems, but India has had to make every effort to raise its self-sufficiency, while Nigeria could afford to exchange oil earnings for imported foodstuffs. How wise was Nigeria's decision to buy food abroad than from domestic farmers?

The USA bypassed Germany as the world's largest exporter in the 1980s. Although Germany briefly regained the top spot, the USA plied ahead, with farm exports a crucial component of its export drive. US farm sales abroad in 1989 were worth $40 billion.[87] Most of this was wheat, with the USA accounting for nearly half of world imports. US penetration of foreign markets in this century is illustrated dramatically in Nigeria where little wheat was grown and the population relied on indigenous grains such as barley grown on the Jos Plateau. In 1910, only 20 per cent of Nigerian wheat imports came from North America, with the remainder originating in Britain and Germany. Yet by 1936, US traders accounted for 98 per cent of Nigerian wheat imports. The USA continued to dominate Nigerian imports, although after World War II France and the EEC made inroads with subsidised sales comprising 5-10 per cent in imports of mostly soft wheat. Andræ and Beckmann[88] point out that due to its oil exports:

> It is true that in Nigeria wheat imports have nearly always been on fully commercial terms. When in the 50s and 60s, great subsidies were

given to many Third World countries, notably through the PL 480 campaign, Nigeria was not among the major beneficiaries. The trade has expanded enough by other means.

In the early-1970s period of drought, civil war, and famine in Biafra, Nigeria did accept some food relief, e.g. 56,000 tonnes, predominantly wheat, in 1971. Wheat donated during the famine probably accustomed an even greater share of the population to the taste of wheat and lured them away from indigenous grains. Andræ & Beckmann claim US wheat imports led to 'under-development' in Nigeria by severing the backward linkages between urban mills and bakers to traditional farmers. But conspiracy theorists would be wrong to assume the 1970s famine was the only wedge to maintenance of market penetration and increases in wheat consumption in Nigeria. After all, the USA had sold wheat to Nigeria for several decades. True, US food aid functioned as a promotional 'loss leader' for future commercial sales in many poorer countries. But Nigeria could *pay* for most imports on a commercial basis. Furthermore, oil price rises following the second OPEC oil embargo of 1980-81 made the USA more aggressive in promoting commercial sales, with oil exporters like Nigeria high on the list. Assiduous plotting of possible market prospects by the USDA office in Lagos developed commercial sales of maize, rice, tallow and (mostly) wheat. Andræ & Beckmann[89] write that the Nigerian market was further opened by: 'the classical means of official support for US wheat penetration.'

The USA had supplanted French interests by establishing the first flour milling plant in Lagos in the early 1960s, and in 1980 a 'Great Plains Wheat Team' of millers and bakers associations held courses promoting wheat-based foods. Andræ & Beckmann[90] quote the following USDA memo to illustrate how crucial was the establishment in Lagos of a US-Nigerian Joint Consultative Committee (AJCC) to eliminate:

> the major constraint to the rapid expansion of US agricultural commodity exports to Nigeria…the lack of physical infrastructure, i.e. port facilities, feedmills, integrated poultry/piggery/livestock operations, flour mills, etc. The AJCC will facilitate private US investment in the Nigerian agrobusiness sector (USDA 1981).

Needless to say, dairy marketeers around the world were familiar with the methods employed in US wheat promotions and sought to emulate them.

Food self-sufficiency matters more to India than oil-rich Nigeria. The table below (Agrostat/FAO/1994: Trade/Index) compares the food imports of Nigeria and India and reveals facets of their relative degrees of food self-sufficiency. Nigeria's 1979-81 (=100) *import value* of dairy product imports soon halved to a level still held in 1992, whereas the *import volume* of Nigeria's dairy imports gradually fell to 19.1 in 1989, rising to just 38.6 in 1992; meanwhile the *import unit value* of dairy imports rose to 128.4 on the scale of 1979-81=100, by 1992. Nigeria's dairy import trend was generally up in the early 1990s.

India's dairy import value hit a low of 3.6 on the 100 index in 1990 as European Community (EC *aka* EEC or today EU) dairy aid to Operation Flood virtually stopped. Just two years later India's dairy import value index rose to 52.7 (close to Nigeria's) begging the questions: (1) Did EEC-Indian politics affect low dairy import value in India in 1990?[91] and (2) Was the rise in value of imports to Nigeria in 1992 due to a surge in US dairy exports? Both connections seem likely, in (1) because of pressure to halt EEC-India dairy aid flows; and in (2) because after the US *dairy product exports* index dropped to 127.8 (due to severe drought in 1989) it rebounded to an impressive 138.0 in 1992. As for US dairy *production*, the index figures generally precipitate the pattern of exports, showing a dip in the drought year of 1989 (112.8 in 1989 compared to 113.4 in 1988) before a steady rebound to 118.74 in 1992.[92] These figures trace the US '99' drive to pressure Europe into liberalisation of farm trade under GATT.

In the case of cereals, Nigeria's 1979-81 (=100) *import value* of cereals fell to 17.1 in 1989 and 34.1 in 1992, whereas the *import volume* of Nigeria's cereals hit 24.9 in 1989 (lowest point was 20.8 in 1990) and rose to just 49.0 in 1992; meanwhile the *import unit value* of cereals changed little (1989: 68.9) between 1985 and 1992 when it was 70.2. **Table 3.2** shows that as the Green Revolution progressed 1961-92, India became a net cereals exporter while Nigeria relied more on cereals imports.)

Observers wary of the similarity of the 'top-down' establishment of transport and dairy processing facilities in India's Operation Flood to infrastructure-building in Nigeria (i.e. the wheat processing plants built by the USA in Lagos, etc.) were understandably fearful that India's White Revolution could likewise be coopted by the EEC for its own benefit. In this counterfactual scenario, European equipment manufacturers lobby for construction in India of plants to process endless shipments of dairy surpluses for sale to India's urban consumers - supplanting the roles of India's millions of rural cattle. Nor did food traps disappear in the twentieth century – in 2007 the charity CARE rejected $45 million in US funding, claiming monetisation of US wheat and vegetable oils harmed Kenya.[93]

Table 3.2 shows that compared to Nigeria whose oil exports paid for food imports, India was moving toward self-sufficiency in cereals and dairy products. Meanwhile, the section below recounts Anderson & Tyers' analysis of the damage done to the world's poor country farmers by rich country protectionism.

Table 3.2.

India & Nigeria dairy & cereals imports: 1961, 1986, 1992 (1979-81=100)			
	1961 import value dairy	1989 import value dairy	1992 import value dairy
India	12.6	52.4 (1990=3.6)	52.7
Nigeria	6.0	23.4	51.7
	1961 import volume dairy	1989 import volume dairy	1992 import volume dairy
India	58.6 (1970=46.9)	45.2 (1990=2.9)	55.5 Gulf War crisis
Nigeria	22.0	19.1	38.6
	1961 import unit value (u/v) dairy	1989 import unit value (u/v) dairy	1992 import unit value (u/v) dairy
India	20.1 (1970=20.8)	94.1 (1990=104.1)	96.4
Nigeria	34.0	90.9 (1990=121.5)	128.4
	1961 import value cereals	1989 import value cereals	1992 import value cereals
India	no data	no data	no data
Nigeria	1.8	17.1	34.1
	1961 import volume cereals	1989 import volume cereals	1992 import volume cereals
India	no data	no data	no data
Nigeria	4.0	24.9	49.0
	1961 import unit value (u/v) cereals	1989 import unit value (u/v) cereals	1992 import unit value (u/v) cereals
India	27.5	85.1	66.5
Nigeria	44.9	68.9	70.2

Source: Agrostat/FAO/1994[1]

Agrostat/1994/FAO: Trade/Index/ India, Nigeria.

Anderson & Tyers on LDC Export Losses

In the cornucopia of arguments by Kym Anderson and Rodney Tyers for liberalising world farm trade is one appealing to geographers, geneticists and health workers as well as practitioners of the dismal science of economics. They argue for a more diverse network of food exporters, because dispersed production is less liable to supply and price fluctuations due to the vagaries of climate and disease. Thus world food security and the gene pool of plants and livestock would be safeguarded by more geographically-dispersed LDC farmer suppliers.

The thrust of Anderson & Tyers'94 thesis is economic, addressing the inequity of the terms-of-trade suffered by poor countries and the consequent need for reform under GATT/WTO. They relate how rich industrial market economies (here denoted ICs for industrialised countries) eroded the world market share of developing countries (LDCs) after World War II, by examining trade in the most important agricultural commodities traded on world markets - a weighted selection of grains, meats, milk products, and sugar measured in US$. In the early 1960s rich countries, i.e.

the First World, held about 50 per cent of world of world market share, with the other half divided between centrally-planned eastern Europe (i.e. the Second World) and developing countries (i.e. the Third World). By the mid-1980s, the First World held an astounding 70 per cent[95] of world market share, while Eastern Europe and developing countries combined had to settle for just 30 per cent.

Ominously, terms-of-trade worsened for the centrally-planned Eastbloc as well as the developing world. From the period 1961-64 to the period 1983-86 the food situation in the Eastbloc went from surplus to deficit, dropping to -1 per cent to -2 per cent to -5 per cent. This was a disappointing result for a region gifted with fertile soil and large expanses of arable land. Most alarmingly for developing countries in principally the Third World, what had been a food surplus of 2 per cent to 3 per cent in 1961-64 plunged to -2 per cent to -3 per cent in 1983-86.[96]

Because the food security as well as the export competitiveness of poorer countries was falling, the CAP has been seen as an instrument of neo-colonialism by LDCs who not only were blocked from exporting to the European Community (EC *aka* EEC and EU) by its high tariffs on their products, but often could not afford to compete on world export markets against subsidised food exports from the EEC. Not only did the CAP ruin the export picture of some developing economies, it also made them dependent on rich world food surpluses. Dependency theorists needed no further evidence to depict the 1957 Treaty of Rome and the CAP (then seen as an admirable attempt at European food self-sufficiency) as symbols of unfair trade practises by the EEC.

Anderson & Tyers charged that past (i.e. pre-GATT-1994) export and production subsidies in the EEC *cost poor country farmers nearly 50p in lost earnings for every £1 spent on EEC protection.* That may have been a boon to European agribusiness, but by harming the buying-power of farmers and citizens in poor countries, it also cost European industries and workers lost export opportunities. Once noted, industrial lobbyists in the First World echoed the grumbles of farmers in the Third World. Anderson & Tyers' charge was grave. But it is a fact that the EEC subsidised its farm exports more than any other exporters including the USA. The USA stepped up its subsidy war against Europe with the Food Security Act of 1985 using export subsidies as a crucial component of a drive to double US world dairy exports share from 4.4 per cent in 1990 to 7.9 per cent in 1992. *But even then, US farm subsidies rose to just half EEC levels.* At the same time that the EEC claimed (rightfully) to be alleviating poverty in India with its donations of dairy aid, France and other highly-subsidised wheat producers were dumping cereals on world markets. Although the EEC made some trade concessions to ACP countries under the Lomé Conventions, protection remained high against food imports from many other poor countries.

EEC apologists claimed their food mountains were a buffer against world shortages, but the EEC was criticised by potential cereals and dairy exporters among LDCs and the Cairns Group as a hypocritical player robbing the poor countries of export opportunities and - worse - even sabotaging their domestic agriculture. Anderson & Tyers[97] and many other food systems analysts rightly argued that sporadic EEC dumping led to price fluctuations that whip-lashed poor farm exporters, contributing to a long-term downward trend on real prices:

> [All of this was] of serious concern to the majority of the world's poor, namely farmers in low-income countries who account for almost three-quarters of the world's farm workers and over a third of the world's workforce.

This consensus fuelled such widespread demands for reform that agriculture was brought under GATT aegis for the first time in 1994. **Table 3.3** below shows how dramatically the distribution of world food trade shifted against LDCs and the Eastbloc over 1961-64 and 1983-86. Granted, the GATT process that virtually endorsed quantitative restrictions on imports (quotas) and high tariffs on farm commodities, clothing and textiles until 1995, was viewed with suspicion by developing countries. But as the new WTO dismantled some barriers to LDC exports in 1995, there were grounds for hope that this supranational institution would be more friend than foe to Third World development.

Agrostat/FAO/1994 statistics on agricultural products trade[98] back the viewpoint of Anderson & Tyers. Leaving aside the matter of Centrally-planned Eastern European Countries (CEEC, also losing market share), several conclusions can be drawn from Agrostat[99] data in **Table 3.3** and **Table 3.4** below. Initially poor country (LDC) value of all agricultural product exports did not lag very far behind rich country (IC) exports, 1961-64. Thence, trends worsened. From minuscule levels in 1961-64, LDC agricultural imports grew an enormous 8-times by 1983-84, supporting Anderson & Tyers' claim that poor country food imports grew dramatically.

As for exports, Agrostat data show that while LDC exports grew almost 5-times from 1961-64 to 1983-86, they were, starting at a lower base than ICs, far outpaced by rich IC exports owing partly to export subsidies. The fact that IC farm imports soared 5-times from 1961-64 to 1983-86 may be explained by rises in specialisation of labour and horizontal links in agriculture *among rich countries* - most notably European countries. In other words, rich countries engaged in higher levels of transnational food

Table 3.3.

Anderson & Tyers'[i] research shows: Industrial Market Economies (ICs) eroded world market share of Centrally-planned Eastern European Countries & Developing Economies (Eastbloc & LDC).		
	ICs	LDCs & Eastbloc
1961-64 food exports	<50% (i.e. less than 50%)	>50% (i.e. more than 50%)
1983-86 food exports	70%	30%
1961-64 food imports	>50%	<50%
1983-86 food imports	40%	60%

Source: Anderson & Tyers (1991)

[i] Anderson & Tyers (1991) Global *Effects of Liberalizing Trade in Farm Products*. This is a revised account of research prepared by the authors for the World Bank's *World Development Report* for 1986.

processing likely increased their agricultural imports *from each other* more than from poor countries. But this interesting new sub-plot was a diversion from the real drama: First World farm price supports and export subsidies were effectively robbing Third World farm families.

Chart 3.1. LDCs outpaced by ICs in world ag products trade

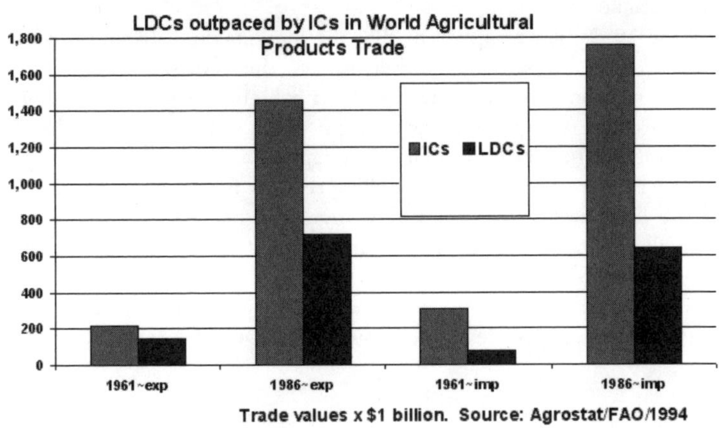

Table 3.4.

Agrostat/FAO supports Anderson & Tyers'[1] claim that Industrial Market Economies (ICs) eroded world agricultural products market share of Developing Economies (LDCs) (x US$100,000)		
	ICs Developed	LDCs Developing
1961-64 food exports	$212,842	$144,066
1983-86 food exports	$1,456,100	$715,294
1961-64 food imports	$309,440	$75,580
1983-86 food imports	$1,755,921	$639,251

rson & Tyers (1991) *Global Effects of Liberalizing Trade in Farm Products.*

Tables show the value of food imports into poor countries increasing much faster than their exports. Developing countries (LDCs) also had more difficulty recovering from the early-1980s recession induced by oil price rises than did rich-developed countries (ICs). Not only had the real price of the oil they imported risen, but the real unit value of their exports (which were chiefly farm commodities) had fallen.

Because commodity food exports are one of the chief means by which poor countries can purchase high-value-added (HVA) rich country exports like jumbo airliners, machine tools, computer software and biotechnological products, this diverging trend has disturbing implications for poor and rich countries alike.

By the 1980s, it was apparent that the inequitable distribution of world income would be skewed further unless the terms-of-trade for poor countries were improved. Moreover, in enlightened self-interest, some rich country exporters expected that if farm trade were reformed, the Third World could afford more of their HVA exports.

This was one of the most compelling reasons for developed countries to seek the liberalisation of world farm trade in the GATT Uruguay round that finally got underway in 1986. Greed is not always good. But when it can be put to good use, why quibble?

Table 3.5 below shows how subsidised industrialised country (IC) exporters outpaced less developed countries (LDCs) 1961-89.

Table 3.5.

Agrostat shows ICs outpacing LDCs in food trade. (1979-81=100)			
	1961 Import Unit Value (u/v)	1986 Import Unit Value (u/v)	1992 Import Unit Value (u/v)
ICs developed countries all	30.1	101.1	134.9
LDCs developing (not Eastbloc)	30.8	75.8 (u/v imports peaked 1981: 108.8)	91.9
	1961-64 Export (u/v) mean Unit Value	1983-86 Export (u/v) mean Unit Value	1989-92 Export (u/v) mean Unit Value
ICs developed countries all	34.0	90.0	123.3
LDCs developing countries	28.6	84.9	94.8
	1961 Import Value	1986 Import Value	1992 Import Value
ICs developed countries all	13.0	101.5	159.6
LDCs developing countries	10.2	82.5	126.5
	1961-64 mean Export Value	1983-86 mean Export Value	1989-92 mean Export Value
ICs developed countries all	12.8	90.8	140.1
LDCs developing countries	16.7	102.1	131.4
	1961 Import Volume	1986 Import Volume	1992 Import Volume
ICs developed all	43.2	100.4	118.3
LDCs developing	33.4	109.5	138.6
	1961 Export Volume	1986 Export Volume	1992 Export Volume
ICs developed all	34.6	98.3	117.7
LDCs developing	55.9	123.8	126.5

Source: Agrostat/FAO/1994/Trade, Index, Economic Groups, Food

1980s: USA Adopts CAIRNS Stance

Over the protests of domestic lobbyists the US Government agreed with the Cairns position that agriculture should be high on the agenda in the Uruguay Round of GATT. In language hearkening to Smith and Ricardo, the Cairns Group wished to 'liberalise' agriculture. Cairns countries demanded that just like tariffs on industrial goods, all the erstwhile hidden non-tariff trade barriers (NTBs) to their food exports should be converted into explicit tariffs (i.e. taxes levied on commodities at customs borders). This meant that all forms of assistance to all of the world's farmers and food exporters - including explicit subsidies, hidden income subsidies, tax relief, export subsidies and tariffs on imports - ought to be clarified in a process eponymously dubbed 'tariffication'.

That tariffication terrified marginal producers in highly-subsidised countries is no exaggeration. But the industrial and services sectors in rich countries had become so preponderant that they overwhelmed the rear-guard lobbying of farm protectionists, adding impetus to farm reform.

Cairns countries argued that non-tariff barriers (NTBs) could be as effective constraints on trade as high import duties. By this time, many of the guises developed in the 1970s and 1980s as NTBs for non-farm goods were well known. They were typified by voluntary export restraint (VER) agreements between Japan and the USA over semi-conductors, or between Japan and France and Italy over cars. These supposedly voluntary agreements were (and are) usually agreed *via* strong-arm diplomacy. Ironically, they often benefited exporters (who could charge more for the limited quantity of their exports) while consumers suffered. Before the Uruguay agreement agricultural trade found its equivalent of automobile VERs in managed, results-oriented bilateral trade deals[100] such as the US-USSR grain deals of the 1970s.

Another non-tariff barrier was typified by bureaucratic bottlenecks, which persisted in the European Community even after the signing of the Single European Act after 1986. A typical example comes again from France. After Spain was admitted to the Community in 1986, inspection of Spanish tomatoes and other fresh produce on France's Pyrenees border was at times conducted in such a desultory manner that it guaranteed spoilage of shipments before they reached Gallic markets.

Nevertheless, the principal non-tariff barriers to agricultural imports, such as imports of Argentine grain to Europe, were invisible government subsidies to domestic farmers, resulting in price differentials that were insurmountable to outside goods. Harder to identify than price support programmes, agricultural protection often took the form of hidden income subsidies or tax relief which, like explicit tariffs or customs duties, effectively raised the price of imported food. Formerly, plaintiff countries had asked, simply and rather naively, that others lower their import tariffs. In the Uruguay Round, the Cairns group and others demanded more substantive measures: that all hidden subsidies and non-tariff barriers be laid plainly on the table (i.e. 'tariffied') to make trading costs more calculable. According to Hoekman & Kostecki[101] the US and Cairns demands were addressed but remain far from met: 'Agriculture remains "special", but has at least been put on a progressive liberalisation track. The goal is not free trade but to reduce trade distortions.'

Tje 1994 accords were successful in reintegrating agriculture (12 per cent of world trade in 1993), and textiles and clothing (7 per cent in 1993) into the GATT process. Tariffication is a historical accomplishment that bodes well for future agricultural liberalisations. Pending ratification by all signatories (128 in early 1995, 153 in mid-2008) to the 1994 Uruguay GATT agreement, most international food trade came under the governance of the new World Trade Organisation (WTO; Although many functions prior to 1995 managed by the GATT were subsumed by the WTO, common parlance equates GATT and WTO as synonyms which is why they are used here almost interchangeably - or as GATT/WTO.[102])

After January 1995, the WTO became a permanent institution and is the principal forum for conflict resolution in the continuing GATT process. The Dispute Settlement Body (DSB) distinguishes legitimate sanitary and phyto-sanitary measures (SPMs) on trade from covert trade barriers.[103] This is a focus of activity as biotechnologically-enhanced products such as milk from cows injected with rBST[104], and soybeans, tomatoes and other biotech exports–enter world markets from the USA. It is also a forum for monitoring instalment of spurious SPM barriers in rich countries against products such as cheese from India. In brief, the WTO is 'a far more powerful mechanism for resolving disputes' such as dumping and non-tariff barriers than was the GATT with, acknowledges the *Economist*, signatories making an 'implicit surrender of sovereignty'. The publication claims it is a small surrender that could 'permanently raise global welfare by $100 billion a year.'[105] But the WTO is fiercely contested by people who fear it grants too much power to transnational corporations.

There is also occasional backsliding. For instance, after 2001 the USA raised tariffs against EU steel; the WTO ruled against the USA in that instance. In the recession year of 2009 the EU reimposed dairy export subsidies; the WTO response to that is pending at the time of writing. But most people in rich and poor countries have a vested interest in the ongoing success of GATT/WTO. Hoekman & Kostecki[106] echo F. Roessler (1985): 'The WTO is somewhat analogous to a mast to which governments can tie themselves so as to escape the siren-like calls of various pressure groups.'

Dairy comes under GATT

After decades of waivers dairy trade was brought into the multilateral GATT process, although like sugar, dairy remains somewhat protected from GATT/WTO supervision compared to cereals. Nevertheless, the Uruguay agreement was a landmark for international dairy product trade which has possible ramifications for dairy commodity aid as trade rules continue to reduce subsidies and protection of dairying in countries, primarily in Europe and North America that have been the main sources of surplus commodities utilised as dairy aid.

According to David R. Harvey[107] the South has a comparative advantage in production of fruit, some vegetables and dairying (due to composition of the labour force, if not climate). Harvey identifies the chief Northern comparative advantage as cereals (due to climate and soil composition). It is difficult to predict the global effects of a complete liberalisation of world dairy trade, but several countries in the South including India and Mexico could become bigger players on world export markets. If the North is to respond, its dairists must take full advantage of temperate climates, cost-effective inputs, and efficient technology in order to produce dairy commodities at or below world price levels.

GATT/WTO 1994's winners & losers

The results of the agricultural liberalisations agreed in the 1994 GATT accords are still becoming clear. The international situation is complex, and in some respects more dynamic than in previous decades. Prosperity in China and other emerging economies is reaching income 'thresholds' where national demands for grain imports to feed farm animals follows is spurred by increased consumer demand for livestock products. This phenomenon has affected world food stocks and price levels since at least the early 1990s. It is also important to bear in mind that the draconian demands of the USA and Cairns countries for liberalisations were ultimately watered down by deft negotiations on the exact time-periods used as bases for cuts, and the exact wording of agreements. Chief beneficiaries of these sophisticated tactics were France and other EU countries. Of course poor countries that are potential food exporters are critical of ongoing protectionist tactics by what they call 'Fortress Europe'. For instance, while the EU may be adhering to the letter of agreements on aggregate dairy subsidy cuts and has indeed cut subsidies on some exports, dairy marketeers in India complain that the EU violates the spirit of GATT/WTO by aggressive promotion of other product lines with all permissible export subsidies until they are outlawed completely. They also accuse the USA of using every tactic to block imports from poor countries, even as it touts free trade.[108] Of course EU and US Governments would face rebellion from their farmers if they did not exploit all remaining export promotions. Such is the case with US DEIP dairy export promotion. But in concurrence with complaints of foot-dragging in 1998, Hoekman & Kostecki[109] warned in 1995 that 'decades to come' will reveal 'the intentions of its [WTO] Members' to dismantle remaining barriers and that in new WTO rounds: 'There is still very much that needs to be done on services and on agriculture and textiles and clothing…' Not least of these issues are the setting of minimum labour rights for workers employed by multinationals (MNCs), and the education of children involved in farming and textiles. Meanwhile, observers generally expect the success of the 1994 agreement to be proportional to genuine liberalisation by rich OECD countries.[110] So far the USA is leading the EU and Japan by example with its 1996 Federal Agricultural Improvement & Reform (FAIR) Act, hearkening to early-1980s reforms in New Zealand that virtually abolished subsidies. FAIR (which evolved from *laissez-faire* proposals in the 1995 Freedom to Farm Bill) abolishes set-aside, deficiency payments, and decouples US price supports from production in seven yearly fixed but falling' production flexibility contract payments'.[111]

In examining the 'fair' or 'foul' implications of FAIR, David R. Harvey[112] praises the **'internal coherence'** of the 1996 Act insofar as it decouples income supports from prices. But he notes the concern of Stuart & Runge[113] (1997) that FAIR does not stop 'larger farmers getting the bulk' of remaining payments. (N.B. Agenda 2000 proposals for 'differentiation' or 'modulation' address this anomaly in the EU.) As to the **'external legitimacy'** of FAIR, Harvey finds it 'consistent' with the Uruguay 'spirit' insofar as Aggregate Measures of Support (AMS; see Synopsis of GATT-1994 below) for wheat and rice are falling in the USA. However, Harvey claims 'neither milk nor sugar AMS' get reform and supports stay in line with former Producer Subsidy Equivalents (PSEs). This might dismay low-cost producers considering export. But US delays in dairy and sugar liberalisation may be only a bargaining chip to prompt reform of these sectors in Japan and the EU. Additionally, the plunge[114] in US dairy farms from 131,535 (1992) to just 99,413 (1997) is evidence that that, not only are American dairists suffering a painful cost-price squeeze, but they are bracing for further liberalisation. Reports of rising cheese[115] imports to the USA - and launch of the-Amul brand[116] product line including butter and ghee by the NDDB in the USA in 1998 - suggests the USA is acting in the Uruguay spirit in dairy trade as well as in cereals.

Harvey says judgement must wait on the 'long-term sustainability' of FAIR, because 'suspension' of US agricultural safety net legislation from 1938 and 1949 does not equal 'elimination'. If market volatility increases violently or if US competitiveness suffers abroad, political lobbyists will press for reinstitution of subsidies. Can the US stay the course? Cynics chortled as drought and low US milk prices brought pleas for a reversal of FAIR - but complaints muted as milk and other prices rebounded.

Harvey[117] hails the FAIR commitment to a Commission to analyse the role of government in agriculture, and suggests that just as the OECD devised a useful definition of PSEs for the Uruguay Round, it might provide a 'multilaterally acceptable specification of the appropriate role of government' for WTO talks beginning in 1999. Indeed this *could* inform debates on agriculture as environmental and social concerns replace the former production focus of the EU's Common Agricultural Policy. Two factors drive the EU Agenda 2000 reforms: (1) GATT/WTO liberalisation; and (2) EU enlargement (as ex-Eastloc countries join the EU). These could drive: more support cuts, relegation of farm aid from Brussels to national governments, an end to milk quotas, and the end of remaining food export subsidies - as well as a struggle with the USA over biotechnology.

Because subsidy cuts generally result in lower national food stocks, upward pressure was expected on world commodities prices. In the long run this may not be as serious as it sounds because as Anderson & Tyers point out, *real* international prices now are 25-50 per cent lower than in the year 1900.[118] Hoekman and Kostecki[119] note it was the opening of the American heartland that lowered world grain prices in the nineteenth century, prompting Holland to specialise in livestock and dairying, while Austria-Hungary, France and Germany protected their farmers and subsidised exports in a pattern not unlike the CAP after 1957. Most economists expect net benefits to the world's consumers to outweigh costs to producers. GATT/WTO-mandated cuts in farm subsidies could also be translated into additional investment in other industries and services that raise world prosperity. Of particular interest is the observation by economists that the richer societies grow, the more 'high-value-added' food products their citizens may purchase. The inference, that rich country farmers should 'shorten the food chain' by investing cooperatively in processing, packaging, branding and marketing of specialty foods to survive subsidy cuts is obvious. Turning dull commodities into rare 'brands' can capture more value for farmers. David R. Harvey[120] and associates have researched how to lend Northern Uplands English Beef cachet like that of branded French 'champagne' and Yorkshire's 'Wensleydale Cheese'. The USA, UK and Europe experienced a renaissance in organic and/or local production of fruit, vegetables and dairy products.[121] However, by 2009, production by huge 'organic-industrial' operations threatened the sustainability of many small family farmers who feared their last bastion against agribusiness was weakening.

Food riots in 80 cities worldwide confirm warnings that 'food-deficit-low-income' countries such as Peru could suffer from agricultural liberalisation. For such countries, food aid advocates including Hans W. Singer[122] and James Ingram (WFP) suggested an expanded role for food aid - albeit with sensitive 'early-warning' field reports to minimise market price distortions and disincentives to domestic farmers. Countries such as Peru could receive food aid to improve their balance-of-payments accounts as African countries have to alleviate structural adjustment programmes. It goes without saying that poor governance can render such programmes counter-productive. Discussions below reveal lessons from India.

Although this author was originally sanguine on the prospects of GATT-1994 liberalisation, the case for pessimism grew. One of Paul Kennedy's[123] main themes in *Preparing for the Twenty-First Century* is the critical importance of biotechnology 'for farming in general and for North-South relations'. Kennedy accepts that biotechnology is necessary if an ever more-populous world is to escape 'the Malthusian trap' but sees little evidence societies will easily make a 'large-scale switch to biotech farming and food processing'. Unlike the Green Revolution of the 1960s says Kennedy, biotech-advances are mostly funded by MNCs which carefully guard their patents from firms unless fees are paid and generally make it: 'more difficult for the developing world to acquire those research techniques.'

Countries including India and China are suspicious of protection for Trade-Related Intellectual Property Rights (TRIPS) on biotechnological products such as rBST to increase milk yield, and high-yield-variety (HYV) or genetically-modified (GM) seeds which obligate farmers to long-term contracts. LDCs suspect TRIPs are a wedge by which MNCs such as Geigy and Monsanto penetrate poor country agriculture, in a process that Ben Fine *et al.*[124]term: 'appropriationism…the encroachment by capitalist products and processes within agriculture itself.'

In assessing GATT/WTO-1994 even the *Economist* magazine - a bulwark of free trade since abolition of the Corn Laws in 1846 - admitted after the establishment of the WTO that Third World fears on copyright and patent provisions (TRIPs) might prove to have some basis in fact. Hoekman & Kostecki[125] write: 'There are no definitive empirical estimates of the impact of the TRIPs agreement on developing countries…. Market structure and conduct is very important.'

Patents and so-called intellectual property rights will be a battleground for the foreseeable future. As for the overall effects of agricultural liberalisation, some major studies are more definitive. **Table 3.6** below gives 'Three Scenarios for Liberalisation Effects on LDCs'. A study by the Economic Research Service (ERS) of the USDA found that GATT liberalisation by OECD countries *alone* would have a negative effect on LDCs, although LDCs would share in world welfare gains of about 2.6 per cent if they also completely liberalised their trade. Another ominous, but

Table 3.6.

Three Scenarios for Liberalisation Effects on LDCs					
	Anderson and Tyers		UNCTAD	(SWOPSIM) (by ERS of the USDA)	
	OECD only	Global	OECD only	OECD only	Global
Net change in welfare ($US billions)	11.5	56.3	-0.6	-4.5	2.6

Source:: Raymond F. Hopkins in William P. Avery, 1993[126]

perhaps less thorough, report from UNCTAD predicts losses for developing countries in OECD-only, and even in complete global liberalisation of world agricultural trade. The UNCTAD study may be unnecessarily gloomy. Looking at the GATT-1994 agreement *in toto*, perhaps more credence is due the scenario by Anderson & Tyers, about whom Raymond F. Hopkins[127] explains:

> They disagree that effects of OECD liberalisation would have a net negative effect [on LDCs). The difference may be explained, possibly, by noting that the other models were based on immediate effects, whereas the Anderson and Tyers model runs over several years to 1995. Further, there were differences in base years, commodity coverage, and elasticity estimates among the models.

Although the point is disputed, some developing country farmers potentially gained more from GATT/WTO-1994 than rich country farmers. Long-term beneficiaries include: (1) Third World and former-Eastbloc farmers with a comparative advantage in agriculture. Raymond F. Hopkins points out that LDC members of Cairns, e.g. Chile and Fiji, would be expected to gain. Anderson & Tyers (1991) expect liberalising agricultural trade to go far in rectifying imbalances in the terms-of-trade suffered by most poor countries if rich countries cease dumping surpluses on world markets. (2) Farmers in rich countries which enjoy comparative advantages, e.g. the USA in wheat[128] and Argentina in beef and wheat. (3) OECD dairy farmers specialising in high-tech, efficient dairying, e.g. some in the USA, Britain and Ireland.

This is not to say the future is clear. Depending on peso-dollar exchange rates, Mexico has imported large quantities of US milk, but its national dairy output has grown tremendously in recent decades (as Mexican migrants take a large share of new jobs in the US dairy industry). If WTO rules are enforced, Mexican dairy exports could grow in North America.

Synopsis of GATT-1994

After 1947 two rules characterised the GATT process: (1) tariffs must be non-discriminatory (though exceptions can be made for regional integration agreements such–as the EU and MERCOSUR); and (2) GATT members should 'bind' tariffs, i.e. not raise tariffs above previous levels following a multilateral trade negotiation (MTN).[129] Violating these rules by overt or covert means is grounds for complaint and compensation. Applying non-discrimination and binding to agriculture was a historic advance of free trade. But because of the complex, frequently invisible nature of supports in many countries, the Uruguay negotiations went further. Irrespective of uncertain future benefits, changes mandated by the Uruguay accords are well known. A synopsis[130] of the Uruguay GATT/WTO settlement from the National Farmers Union (NFU, Britain) gives the salient points of the agreement which came into effect in 1995 for the following six years. The accords address areas of: (1) internal support; (2) export subsidies; and (3) 'tariffication'[131] making explicit the hitherto hidden forms of protection against foreign farm imports:

(1) Internal support: All industrialised countries (ICs) including the EU and USA must reduce their internal support (i.e. domestic subsidies) of farmers by 20 per cent over six years, on a base period of 1986-1988. Highlights:

- These subsidies are assessed by a calculation called Aggregate Measure of Support (AMS) which quantifies the value of all non-trade-distorting support given directly or indirectly to farmers.[132]

- Special concessions have been made to developing, or less developed countries (LDCs) in the Third World. Preferential agreements were negotiated with Central and Eastern European countries (CEECs) as well as North Africa.

- The least developed countries (LLDCs) are not obligated by the Uruguay agreement to make any farm support cuts.

(2) Export subsidies: The NFU report acknowledges what Third World and Cairns critics charged: 'Effectively only the European Union and the USA subsidise their exports.' Therefore, the EU and USA are the only blocs affected by new rules mandating reduction of export subsidies - although the USA, whose internal (i.e. domestic) prices were closer to world prices, would find it easier to comply. (The rice industry of Japan, the third trade bloc in question - with prices abut seven-times world levels, was more

vulnerable to cuts on domestic subsidies and tariffication rules than cuts of subsidies of food exports, which were minuscule compared to its automotive and electronic exports.) Generally speaking, the agreement requires that, in regard to export subsidies:

- ICs must reduce subsidies on farm exports by 36 per cent over six years, on a 1986-90 base. ICs must cut 21 per cent of their volume of subsidised exports over six years on the same base. These cuts must be to each line of dairy products, e.g. 36 per cent of butter, 36 per cent of milk powder and 36 per cent of cheese, not simply a 36 per cent cut in aggregate dairy products. (Volume export cuts probably hurt the EU worse than 'tariffication'.)

- Non-subsidised exports are not subject to volume reduction.

- Food aid is not subject to any cuts.[133]

While direct export subsidies are outlawed under the WTO, trade boosterism in the form of trade fairs and high-profile trade missions coordinated according to information gathered by government agencies remains legal, and continues to be vigorously pursued by Britain, France and the USA. The US food lobby ensures that two-thirds ($186m) of the $250 million export promotion budget is allocated to food.[134]

(3) Tariffication: All barriers to foreign agricultural imports (e.g. variable levies in the EU or import quotas in the USA and Canada) must be 'tariffied' into tariffs of equivalent effect. (See also above.) Here are more highlights from the NFU synopsis:

- In the aggregate, tariffs on imports must be reduced by 36 per cent over six years, with no tariff on individual items being cut by less than 15 per cent. Tariffs will be cut in six equal steps.

- Because the base period (1986-1988) for many agricultural commodities was marked by low world price (FOB) levels, it was expected that tariffication would leave the EU with a high remaining level of external protection (supporting critics of 'Fortress Europe'). However, minimum access rules would ensure that if import volumes of meat, SMP, butter and cheese do not rise by 3 per cent to 5 per cent of internal EU consumption by the year 2000, tariffs on these imported commodities must be cut by up to 32 per cent. (See below *re* USA.)

- The EU would cut tariffs on beef and pig liver 100 per cent, cut those on skimmed milk powder (SMP) 20 per cent, and cut tariffs on products with sugar or SMP components 20 per cent.[135]

The Uruguay agreement allows stronger measures (quotas, tariffs, etc.) against fruit, vegetable and other farm exports from non-GATT members such as the People's Republic of China[136]- a stick to encourage China's eventual acceptance of multilateral trade disciplines with membership at the end of 2001. Although China has the world's largest domestic market - and in the 1990s reverted to being a net food importer before a mid-1990s policy shift attempting to reverse this status - making it less vulnerable to international pressures, its desire for foreign exchange motivated it to join the WTO.

In the view of this book it is easier to envision a prosperous, populous China as a continuing grain importer, but not a top dairy exporter - although Sino-EU cooperation on dairy development is ongoing. Early twenty-first century land acquisitions in Africa suggest that China plans imports as one component of long-term food security.

Before the GATT agreement, domestic milk (and sugar) producers in the USA (sparsely populated, compared to China) were protected by quotas on foreign imports. These quotas were stipulated in Section 22 of US trade law, permitted in pre-Uruguay GATT agreements. Canada and Europe went beyond the US example (of setting quotas on imports under Article XI of the pre-Uruguay GATT[137]) by their installation of domestic production quotas and pricing. My own research found milk quotas were attractive to US dairists but rejected by the Reagan administration.[138]

Similarly, Japan subsidised inefficient, if picturesque, small-scale rice farming and protected it from imports under similar GATT loopholes, claiming rice was part of its cultural tradition. However, the exorbitant level of domestic rice prices relative to world prices made the scale of Japanese protection indefensible, when many rich and poor countries complained of chronic trade deficits. Prying Japan's market open to rice imports was a symbolic achievement of the Uruguay Round.

Upshot of GATT/WTO-1994

Now that protection is being tariffied (i.e. made transparent) Canada's domestic milk quota regime is having difficulty accepting the extra 5 to 6 per cent volume of imports mandated by the Uruguay agreement. Canada is also under pressure to accept more milk from the USA under the terms of the North American Free Trade Agreement.[139] If this trade issue were not settled within NAFTA, it would be adjudicated by the WTO.

Across the Atlantic Ocean, EU milk quotas became less financially untenable after the year 2000, as former Eastbloc countries with farm sectors providing ca. 27 per cent of all employment[140] were admitted to the Single Market. EU Agricultural Commissioner Franz Fischler expected milk prices to fall 25 per cent between 2000 and 20004, driven by the twin forces of EU enlargement and GATT/WTO. Within the EU-15 a coalition of Britain, Denmark, Italy and Sweden sought abolition of quotas[141] while some of the new members of the EU-25 expect to be able to compete as low-price producers. My research finds that most countries of the EU-25 remain hostile to licensing of rBST in Europe, for reasons of animal welfare, as well as the likelihood that this GMO would disrupt labour markets and milk supply.[142]

Relying upon its efficiency in milk production and marketing ability, the USA was confident it could adjust to rules mandating import of an additional 2.5 per cent equivalent of its domestic volume.[143] From a 1979-81 base, it raised dairy exports 38 per cent by 1992. The US Dairy Export Council predicted a 14 per cent annual rise over the five years to 2003, bringing total US dairy exports to 7.7 billion pounds (ca. 3.5 billion kilograms or 35,000 metric tonnes/slightly fewer litres[144]) US exports to China, Japan and Mexico might double - even quadruple to Brazil - if world economic malaise can be reversed.

The US share of world dairy exports nearly doubled from 4.4 per cent in 1990 to 7.9 per cent in 1992. Such developments convinced the EU it could not win a subsidy war against the USA, ushered in CAP reform under Commissioner Ray MacSharry in 1992 in the lead-up to GATT/WTO-1994, and spawned Agenda 2000. Soon after GATT ratification by the US Congress, the Clinton administration reacted to congressional calls to cut dairy surplus storage costs by expanding exports. This US export initiative helped mollify those who opposed Clinton's championing of NAFTA and GATT. If not all US actions were in the spirit of Uruguay, they generally adhered to the letter of the agreement - including a phase-out of export subsidies. It is fair to say that most US export gains were made by stimulating - almost creating - demand for dairy products in countries such as Japan and South Korea which traditionally marginalised dairy consumption. Exporting cheeseburger and pizza culture helps sustain US farmers and lower the country's trade deficit.

On January 20, 1995, USDA announcements of Dairy Export Incentive Program (DEIP) allocations of 335.3 million pounds for the first half of 1995 included more than 22,000 US tons of first-time allocations for the Asian region, including 15,000 tons of non-fat dry milk, 7000 tons of milk fat and 300 tons of cheese. New Zealand and Australia, traditional suppliers to Oceania, protested the new US export wave. DEIP shipments included 17.8 million pounds of non-fat dry milk to Malaysia, Thailand and the Philippines, and were reflected in stronger domestic prices for US dairy farmers.[145] Motivated by its chronic trade deficit and emergence as the world's biggest creditor nation since the costly arms build-up under President Reagan, the USA manifested eagerness for commercial competition with other countries. This was doubly so in the case of New Zealand; not only did the archipelago nation enjoy a large dairy trade surplus with the USA, but it tweaked Uncle Sam's beard by banning US nuclear-equipped warships from its harbours in the 1980s. The US export drive continued after President Obama inherited the historic budget deficits generated in the administration of his predecessor George W. Bush.

The extent the USA can carry its dairy export offensive on the Pacific Rim depends on its adherence to the rules of GATT/WTO; trade countermeasures that its competitors in Oceania and Europe might take to maintain their traditional markets. As discussed above, India is a new exporter to world markets, shipping mainly to the Middle East, and has potential for more. But it was significant that India began shipping dairy products to New Zealand about2009.

Free Trade repudiates Mercantilism

We have discussed motivation for trade from pre-history to the present and how various participants perceived it. Nationalist and mercantilist theory of trade as a weapon in a zero-sum rivalry has given way to understanding that the wealth of nations is maximised by free trade according to division of labour and comparative advantage. Autarky, irrational protection of infant or so-called strategic industries, overvaluation of currency and neglect of farming and rural development have been repudiated. Since the Cold War, what P.T. Bauer called 'the spurious consensus' of development economists influences international policy less than neo-classical trade theory.

The signing of the Uruguay Round Agricultural Agreement (URAA) in GATT/WTO demonstrated a world consensus that free trade benefits all nations, and that IC obstacles (industrialised country farm price supports, export subsidies and unfair tariffs) to LDC agriculture should be phased out in the new millennium. Notwithstanding such commendable reforms in farm trade, the uncomfortable truth is that a large portion of the world remains in poverty. What 1998 Nobel Prize for Economics winner Amartya Sen terms 'entitlements' to food security are not enjoyed fully by hundreds of millions of people.[146] It is true that in accordance with free market strategies, China began liberalising its agriculture in the late-1970s, and India did likewise in the early-1990s. But these processes are not complete, and the fact that grain reserves dwindled for a few years before 1996, as world grain production lagged behind population, obscures the future of agreements on grain and dairy trade. Reports of rice shortages in Indonesia, following the 1997 economic crisis and resignation of perennial President Suharto, are sobering reminders that world food and financial systems are a complex and fragile web whose survival may depend on shelter by the WTO, IMF and World Bank.

Disturbingly, William Greider[147] sees evidence that China, with its large domestic market, is in a position to flout WTO conventions such as the Most-Favoured-Nations (MFN) rule on non-discrimination in trade if it wishes to do so. That is problematic because as Hoekman & Kostecki say, 'MFN is one of the pillars of the GATT.'[148] If Greider is correct, China could wreck the WTO when its economy rivals that of the West.

Into the forseeable future, suspicion that the terms of trade still favour ICs (e.g. in patents owned by industrialised country agribusiness interests on biotechnological goods in the Green and White Revolutions) over LDCs will prompt requests by less developed countries for exemptions to the trade-related intellectual property (TRIPs) provisions of GATT/WTO; there will also be calls from LDCs for constraints against agribusiness in domestic farming. But tariffication of barriers is already increasing dairy trade. International dairy trade is headed for on-going battles over hormones in beef and dairy agriculture.[149] WTO rulings on Sanitary and Phyto-Sanitary Measures (SPMs) involving safe use of antibiotics; gene manipulation of hormones such as BST; pathologies involving E. coli, salmonella, TB and BSE (*aka* Mad Cow Disease) could have unexpected impacts on trade. How long it takes international dairy trade to reach a new equilibrium level accommodating increased demand for cereals, the uncertain effects of global warming, disease, biotechnology, animal welfare issues and other factors is greatly contingent upon the authority that the WTO is able to exert over competing dairy trading countries.

Periodic world economic downturns and fears of deflation give pause for thought. The recession following Pres. George H.W, Bush about 1993, which Pres. Bill Clinton called the worst crisis since World War II, was just a portent of the debacle confronting Barack Obama when he was inaugurated in January 2009. Our discussion has assumed the GATT/WTO system will survive and even thrive. But in Asia economic meltdown of 1997, Malaysian PM Dr. Mahathir Mohamed invoked currency controls, saying: 'The free market system has failed and failed disastrously.'

This chapter was launched with references to the swashbuckling exploits of Francis Drake in the Age of Mercantilism. Could global economic woes portend a return to protectionism and 'beggar-thy-neighbour' policies? Paul Krugman has compared the mercantilist fallacy (wherein national governments valued bullion over their citizens' welfare) to the current fallacy of governments sacrificing jobs, education and nutrition (*aka* human capital) on the altar of low-inflation. Like Charles Kindleberger, who discerned a pattern of slavish adherence to the gold standard in the Great Depression of 1929-39, Paul Krugman warns that policies prioritising a strong currency or low inflation over economic indicators such as the Gini co-efficient are short-sighted. The post-1997 slump spawned consensus that of the free trade in goods, services and *capital*, the latter should be assayed in future trade talks to limit its volatility. This conviction has deepened since toxic sub-prime mortgages, distributed by Wall Street, infected banks worldwide.

The USA and the IMF appear guilty of too much, too soon, in touting unimpeded capital flows to countries like Malaysia and Mexico. Despite potential benefits of liberalised capital to investors and poor countries the *Financial Times*[150] admits current problems exhibit the dangers to countries with weak financial systems: '[although this should not mean] a broader loss of faith in free markets.

'So far, multilateral institutions are more effective than they were in the Depression preceding World War II. In a joint statement advocating 'greater coherence in global economic policymaking' as envisioned in the Uruguay Round, the WTO[151], IMF and World Bank IMF claimed: 'Trade liberalisation has yielded enormous benefits to the world over the past 50 years; we must be on constant guard to counter any tendency to slip back into protectionism which would be a tragic mistake…'

Our discussion has focused on agriculture with some reference to textiles, since these are often the next sectors explored by developing countries. Altogether, agriculture, textiles and clothing account for more than 20 per cent of all world trade and strongly impact the terms-of-trade for developing countries. Insofar as the Uruguay agreement reduced trade barriers in goods and services, it can improve the welfare of poor countries. But capital and investment rules merit study. In late-2009 UK PM Gordon Brown (whose doctoral thesis reportedly analysed the Great Depression) called for a version of the Tobin Tax on global investments.

There is reason to fear 'appropriationism' of Third World food sovereignty by multinationals under the patent and intellectual property provisions of GATT/WTO-1994. Sales of African farmland to Chinese investors beg analysis. Certainly the World Bank's promotion of dairy development in Africa begs scrutiny. Many such questions can be addressed in the WTO Doha 'development round' if and when it resumes.

Table 3.7.

MOTIVATIONS: factors in expansion of international dairy trade & aid		
MOTIVATOR	EFFECT	LEGACY
Age of Mercantilism (16th-18th Century)	National gov'ts encouraged rationalisations (e.g. enclosures) raising agric. productivity. Peasants became indust. Proletariat.	Speeded nationhood. Now repudiated for *zero-sum economics & beggar-thy-neighbor* trade policies.
Adam Smith's *Wealth of Nations* (1776).	Showed *invisible hand* of individual ambition *in free markets* motivated national economic output more than mercantilism.	Attacked as passé by Marxists in Industrial Rev. Rehabilitated by CPE failures of 1970s-90s.
David Ricardo's *Principles* & theory of *comparative advantage* (ca. 1817).	Showed that even if England was more efficient than Spain in *all* production, trading specialities raised output for *both*.	Blunted arguments that national power depended on import tariffs. Inspired free international trade.
Industry forces repeal of English Corn Laws (1846).	British political power shifted from landed gentry to industrialists.	Showed free trade raises nat'l power better than autarky.
Bretton Woods (1944-71~)	Reformed post-WW-II finance & trade relations.	Gold std. left (1971). IMF, WB aid dev't.
ECSC (1951), EEC-6 (1957), EC-12 & Sngl. Eur. Act (1986) EU-15 (1995).	Cut war threat & helped recovery. EEC GDP overshadows Eastbloc in 1970s.	Success spawns *1992 Single Market*, NAFTA pact, etc.
GATT process (1947-94) follows defunct ITO.	Framed int'l trade principles, e.g. MFN. Barred quotas 'cept milk, sugar.	LDCs demand dev't & trade reform in UNCTAD (1964).
USSR joins GATT (ca. 1987). China considers membership.	Debunked bipolar socialist vs. GATT trade blocs.	Most ICs & LDCs accept GATT.
Rio Summit (1992) Uruguay GATT agreement ushers in WTO era (1994-)	1992 EC reforms enable WTO to govern ag - to US & Cairns approval.	LDCs, China fear copyr't & patent rules (e.g. biotech).

Compiled by: B.A. Scholten (2009)

Table 3.8.

CONSTRAINTS: potential limitations on international dairy aid & trade		
N.B.: Phytosanitary & eco-issues could be misused as nontariff barrriers to trade.		
ISSUE	STATUS	OUTLOOK
Foot & mouth disease (FMD)	Chronic; contained by slaughter & compensation.	Same for foreseeable future.
Brucellosis	Same as above.	Same as above.
Tuberculosis (TB)	Worsening?	Research. Curtail antibiotics misuse?
Chron's disease	Milk-borne link to human Johne's disease?	Same as above.
Rabies	Improving - but endemic worldwide (UK free *via* quarantine). Contained by culling, vaccination.	Vaccinated bait may control in wildlife. Electronic tagging begins UK in 1998.
Bovine spongiform encephalopathy (BSE)	Beef link to human CJD. "Mad Cow" disease drops, as human CJD reports rise.	Unknown. Slaughter & compensation, safer rendering needed.
Over-/Misuse of antibiotics leading to immunity of pathogens	Increasing virulence of diseases *possibly including the above* plus salmonella, E.coli, & gluten allergies.	Limit over-/misuse in animal agriculture. Use *different* drugs in animals & humans.
Refrigerants (e.g. CFCs)	Montreal Protocol (1987) CFC ban probably ameliorates greenhouse effect.	Must develop substitutes for CFCs & refrigeration itself.
Bovine somatotropin (rBST)	Legal in US (1994) & many non-EU countries.	Bellwether of radical biotech, e.g. cloning.

Compiled by: B.A. Scholten (2009)

Chapter 4

Food & Dairy Aid
Post-war effects on poverty & development

After tracing the rise in farm trade from the Age of Mercantilism to World War II, we discussed the struggles of poor countries to develop in the Cold War, before the historic Uruguay Round Agricultural Agreement (URAA) brought farm goods under the aegis of the GATT/WTO system in 1994. The war and subsequent decolonisation acutely disrupted food systems in many countries - just as the agricultural capacity of North America increased.

Whatever the mission statements showcasing post-war food and dairy aid, the material facts were that an apparatus of mass food production in North America coexisted with food deficits in Europe and elsewhere. Like nature, the world food system abhors a vacuum.

The stage was set for huge transfers of food aid, first to Europe as part of the Marshall Plan, later as surplus disposal until 1954 when America's PL 480 Food for Peace programme began, and has evolved to the present day. Once Europe regained its feet, political pressure increased to utilise cereal and - increasingly - dairy aid in the developing world.

But as leaders including food aid innovator Hans W. Singer, and National Dairy Development Board (NDDB) Chairman Verghese Kurien well knew, food aid is a two-edged sword. Utilising European dairy aid to stimulate India's dairies while avoiding disincentive effects on domestic farmers was so difficult that it was tempting to abandon the attempt and spurn it as a Trojan Horse to aid dependence.

Proceeding from a stagnant pre-Operation Flood base of barely 20 million tonnes per annum, the monetisation of dairy aid led to domestic production of about. 70 million tonnes in the 1990s and 100m in 2009 – an achievement inviting examination by food deficit countries. Kurien recalls it was a hard-fought victory that critics - including some in the World Bank - predicted would fail as badly as many less ambitious efforts. It is crucial to understand how and why OF augmented India's food sovereignty.

Fortunately, after decades of effort, and economic reforms following the first Gult War of 1991, Kurien[1] could say in 1997:

> In fact, a recent World Bank study - and the World Bank during the last decade has been no friend of cooperatives or of NDDB and Operation Flood - suggests that India's milk production is as much as 40 million tonnes per year higher than it would have been without Operation Flood.

Let us now get an overview of food and dairy aid programmes which became part and parcel of bilateral (country-to-country) initiatives such as the US PL 480 programme, and multilateral efforts by the Food and Agricultural Organisation (FAO) and World Food Programme (WFP) of the United Nations (UN), to stimulate development in poor countries.

Just as food aid is a subset of overall international food trade, dairy aid is a subset of overall food aid. Both food and dairy aid are relatively recent phenomena in the annals of recorded history, and dairy aid in particular was not viable until the advent of modern processing technology. Centuries ago, international dairy trade was virtually limited to bulky cheeses. The introduction of dry milk powder sprayers revolutionised dairy trade and made use of milk in aid programmes possible in remote areas.

Although grain trade reached massive levels after the repeal of the British Corn Laws in 1846, it was a century before the advent of large flows of aid. John Shaw and Edward Clay define food aid as, 'aid supplied as food commodities on grant or concessional terms.'[2] Studies of food aid are divided on its origins. Some historians identify its earliest instances as small shipments of grain from the USA to friendly governments in South America, a century ago. In *Merchants of Grain* Dan Morgan[3] relates that after the closing of the Dardanelles in World War I, Europe relied more on the USA and Canada which, 'emerged as the dominant factors in the world grain markets.' US wheat exports soared from 4-to-9 million tonnes 1913-21. Future president Herbert Hoover had organised US food assistance to the Allies in World War I, and after the Bolshevik revolution and Russian civil war involving foreign forces, Hoover organised US food assistance to Russia.[4] But observers agree it was not until the 1940-50s that formal food aid drastically altered global consumption.

Morgan writes that after World War II: 'dozens of countries that had once fed themselves began to depend on a distant source - the United States - for a substantial part of their food supply.' The USA did more than simply dominate commercial grain trade in this new era. It is no exaggeration to say it was progenitor of the means and philosophy of post-war cereals aid. Shaw & Clay[5] write that India, the largest recipient, but later a net food exporter after the Green Revolution, was the focus of early discussion and that: 'Until the early 1960s, food aid was (correctly) seen as almost synonymous with US food aid.'

Selections from the literature

Most of this book's sources on international dairy aid and trade are experts in academia or institutions such as the FAO, WFP, IFPRI, IMF and World Bank. Hans Singer, Edward Clay, John Shaw, John Cathie *inter alia* are eminent advocates of food aid. As noted previously, Peter T. Bauer was a Right-wing iconoclast *vis-à-vis* post-World War II aid and development paradigms. Free trade advocate Jagdish Bhagwati, as well as Jeffrey Sachs continue to reflect Bauer's view that even when external aid can assist development, it countries should adopt market-oriented policies.

Although university libraries stock large sections on development and much on food aid, the literature on dairy aid per se is relatively limited. Nevertheless, a significant body of work was inspired by the White Revolution in India, and its leading programme Operation Flood (OF) - both pro and con, if tending toward the latter. Sources tending toward acceptance (if not blanket approval) of dairy aid in India include Harold Alderman, Peter J. Atkins, John Empson, and John W. Mellor. Less enthusiastic observers of European dairy aid in India include John Cathie and Edward Clay. Perhaps the leading commentator on Operation Flood has been Martin Doornbos. At the Institute for Social Studies (ISS) Indo-Dutch Programme on Development Alternatives (IDPAD) Doornbos published numerous books and articles with co-authors including Liana Giertsch; Manoshi Mitra; Piet Terhal; K.N. Nair; and Frank van Dorsten which are among the best researched and argued works on the subject. When this text differs from the critical views of Doornbos, it is often on the basis of data unavailable at the time of his writing.

Acting as iconoclasts from the Left are Susan George on food aid in general, and Shanti George and Claude Alvares on Operation Flood in particular. Joining them in his radical indictment of world food systems, if not dairy *per se*, is Arturo Escobar, remarkable for the ferocity and scope of his attack on the post-war aid and trade regime. Because in my view (reflecting Bauer, Bhagwati and Sachs) the effectiveness of aid programmes is less important to development than simply 'getting the prices right' in poor countries, this book explores the prospect that liberalisation of agricultural trade can enhance food security. Thus frequent reference is made to GATT/WTO experts such as Kym Anderson & Rodney Tyers, and Bernard Hoekman & Michel Kostecki. Hernando de Soto's views reflect the belief - seen in the 'third way' philosophies of Tony Blair, Bill

Clinton and now Barack Obama - that the aims of socialism can sometimes be won by harnessing the productive impulses of capitalism.

Also cited, as in preceding chapters, is journalist William Greider who, while accepting most market principles, joins historian Paul Kennedy and currency trader George Soros[6] in concern that restless capital threatens stability. Books by M.V. Kamath on Operation Flood, and Dan Morgan and Anthony Sampson concerned with the grain trade, as well as publications such as the *Economist* (est. 1843), *Hoard's Dairyman* (est. 1885), and historical sources document the role of food aid in the Cold War.

Reference is made to Geeta Somjee & A.S. Somjee, Dilip R. Shah and others who investigated the microeconomic domestic effects of dairy cooperativisation on rural dwellers including women, children and tribals in India. Because of the opportunity to access empirical evidence on macroeconomic dairy performance in the FAO Agrostat·PC database, this book highlights the aggregate performance of India compared to other countries, to reach conclusions on the interrelationship between international dairy aid and trade. Because researchers such as Andræ & Beckmann, Stephen Hellinger *et al.*, Stéphane Jost and John Tarrant have outlined ways in which food aid systems could be improved, they are additional points of reference. Since some of their suggested reforms began in the mid-1990s, e.g. decentralisation of programmes and early-warning networks to speed emergency response, food aid is more likely to offer timely disaster relief. However, as mentioned above, in 2007 the *International Herald Tribune* reported criticism by the charity CARE of US food monetisation in Kenya. This observation underlines the importance of understanding how monetisation of EEC dairy aid succeeded in India.

Organisation of food aid

Food aid has generally taken three forms:

(1) Emergency aid: provided on an ad hoc basis for relief of food shortages due to war, drought, flood, disease or other disasters. NGOs such as CARE, Catholic Relief Services and Oxfam have long been active in emergency food aid.[7] Traditionally, emergency aid composed about one-third of the world total.

(2) Programme food aid: began in post-World War II surplus disposal policies of the US. Later formalised under PL 480, programme aid was granted on a bilateral basis to foreign governments as a gift or on concessional rates. Ideally, it was sold at prices that did not unduly discourage domestic farmers. Its purpose was to displace commercial imports that would otherwise be a macroeconomic burden on the economy in the form of external balance-of-payments problems, or internal inflation.

Resources saved could be reinvested in the economy, eventually 'trickling down' into rural development. Such ideal results were not always forthcoming from these 'top-down' schemes, and too often programme aid acted as a disincentive to domestic farmers - as Anne M. Thompson[8] discovered among Egyptian wheat farmers. Shaw & Clay say programme aid is 'always supplied on a bilateral government-to-government basis.'[9] However, as James Ingram, Hans Singer and others continue to urge the use of food aid for 'attenuating the costs of structural adjustment programmes' (SAPs) of poor governments, presumably managed by the World Food Programme (WFP) on a multilateral basis - the precise definition of programme aid seems amorphous. Shaw & Clay acknowledge the line between programme and project food aid has become blurred.

(3) Project food aid: is a sort of magic bullet aimed to transfer additional nutrition and income to target groups such as the rural poor, women and pre-school children, school lunches, and workers in Food-For-Work (FFW) projects, etc.[10] that were often missed by programme food aid. Principal provider of project aid is the WFP, although other multilateral[11] and NGO efforts are significant. As John Cathie points out, food aid is not limited to commodities; a prime example of non-commodity aid that increased food security in a target country was assistance by the NGO Oxfam which joined the FAO in funding 50 per cent of a feed mixing plant five miles from Anand[12] which became headquarters for India's White Revolution. In the case of India, *project* food aid totally supplanted *programme* aid in 1978, when the last such agreement was signed. India, which had been an early focus of programme aid, next served as a testing ground for project aid. Such project food aid later accounted for about 10 per cent of official development assistance. Ram Saran and Panos Konandreas note that project aid can relieve macroeconomic 'foreign exchange burdens' and allow 'additional domestic resources' for domestic development[13] just as outmoded programme aid did. As it gained experience the WFP refined project aid to assist local microeconomic development in schools, health centres and in dairy development. After World War II, food aid flows began almost entirely as cereals shipments from the USA to Europe.

Once European recovery was assured, India became a main recipient. Cereals will probably always constitute most of the aid basket. Dairy aid took longer to develop. It took time for milk surpluses and technology (e.g. sophisticated powder-spraying developed in Scandinavia and refined by cooperatives for buffalo milk in India) to reach levels where dairy aid accounted for more than a trickle in post-war streams. The lead role of Europe in dairy aid is recounted below. But the earlier story of post-war trade and aid brings dairy aid into focus.

Susan George and Anderson & Tyers on Poverty

Of fundamental interest is the interrelationship between trade and aid. Some theorists claim the use of food aid as loss leaders, or enticements to later commercial sales, attacked the agricultural base of poor countries, precipitating a gradual post-World War II decline in the terms of trade for the developing world. Even food aid advocate Hans Singer readily acknowledges counterproductive instances of food aid. Susan George made the apocalyptic claim in her 1984 book *Ill Fares the Land* that, 'the relative and absolute numbers of hungry and destitute people have vastly increased'[14] since the advent of aid programmes. Yet, by the early-1990s her claim that the number of malnourished people was rising *relative* to total world population[15] (i.e. the percentage was rising) seemed doubtful. That millions of people in the world suffer malnutrition is unquestioned, but by the Rome Food Summit of 1996 it seemed a greater proportion of world population was escaping food poverty. Complicating the matter is the fact that basic nutritional needs in calories and dietary composition vary among people, occupation and climate.

According to a 2006 FAO report by Edward Gillin, food inadequacy affected 20 per cent of the total world population in 1990-92 compared to 35 per cent two decades before, although developing countriy populations swelled by 1.5 billion people in this period.[16] In 2009 FAO Director-General Jacques Diouf agreed the world's portion of hungry people fell 1970-96, but had risen since, with projections of a historic high in 2009 with 1.020 million people going hungry every day, and that, 'The silent hunger crisis - affecting one sixth of all of humanity - poses a serious risk for world peace and security.'

Exact numbers and percentages are debatable. But it is incontrovertible that food riots in about 80 cities worldwide 2006-08 support Susan George. She has long warned that subsidised rich country food surpluses disguised as aid must not corrupt Third World agriculture through kickbacks to bureaucrats, or skew progress by forcing inappropriate technology on recipients. All reputable experts join George in condemning the pitfalls of 'tied aid', i.e. food commodities granted on the condition that recipients reciprocate by buying other goods such as seeds, equipment or consultancies from the 'donor' country. Tied aid is typically 15-20 per cent less efficient than outright grants or loans.

Phillip C. Abbot and F. Desmond McCarthy[17] condemn aggressive marketing, especially export subsidies and dumping, for Europe's encroachment of developing countries' share of markets. They conclude their study on tied aid: 'Hence one should not assume that aid with conditions attached will benefit a recipient, and even if there is benefit, the real value of the aid to a recipient may well be less than its nominal value.'

Anderson & Tyers[18] seem to perceive food aid as less distorting to trade than European subsidies on commercial exports to world markets, where Western Europe gradually displaced Third World and CAIRNS competitors. They write that since World War II, the grey area has widened between commercial sales and grants of food commodities with no-strings-attached. While Anderson & Tyers share most of Susan George's concerns on development their remedy is *reform* not rejection of GATT principles. Detractors of food aid correctly charge that aid in commodities had its origins in surplus disposal, and that there are instances when food aid is merely an inducement to commercial sales.[19] Raymond Hopkins found that the US and many countries continue to utilise surplus disposal in food aid programmes.[20] In fact, surplus disposal of EEC (*aka* EC, EU) dairy aid was the original compulsion behind Operation Flood in India. But that was not the whole story. Martin Doornbos *et al.* [21] see it thus: 'From the donor side, while the compulsion of surplus disposal and the interests of export promotion through aid were certainly the basis of EC dairy aid, other motivation became increasingly important.' If we imagine ourselves in the roles of past policy makers without the benefit of hindsight, the history of food aid in general, and dairy aid in particular, is neither so venal nor as simple as its detractors portrayed.

There are many reasons why food aid became part of the post-World War II scene. Foremost among them is: *because it could.* North American agricultural production boomed during hostilities. Lend Lease, comprising mostly war *materiél*, was cancelled in August 1945, but it was soon apparent Europe required continued assistance. Fear of communism was intrinsic to US policy but Secretary of State George Marshall[22] downplayed ideology, stating: 'Our policy is not directed against any country or doctrine, but against hunger, poverty, desperation and chaos.' Loans and aid for European recovery became known as the Marshall Plan, running from ca. 1947 to the mid-1950s.[23] Much of Western Europe suffered renewed food shortages, as the bad harvest of 1947 preceded a bitterly cold winter.[24] It was not until a decade after the Treaty of Rome established the EEC in 1957 (and owing much to the intensifications of farming spurred by EEC agricultural commissar Sicco Mansholt) that it regained food self-sufficiency. After World War II, countries that had lost farm machinery - and labour - in the conflict needed time and assistance, before they could resume normal production.

But while the need for food aid was real, it would be a mistake to underestimate the influence of the US farm lobby in the late 1940s and early 1950s. The desire for foreign markets by US farmers helped shape Washington's foreign policy. The farm lobby pressured presidential administrations to keep agriculture off the agenda of the original GATT-

1947 negotiations (thus maintaining their protections), and to extend food aid first in European recovery and then in programmes around the world (stabilising US farmgate prices by surplus disposal). While the country as a whole enjoyed a sense of victory, hearing frequent hubristic assertions of an 'American Century', excess production amounted to a 'farm problem' that muddied US political waters for decades. Gradually, post-war euphoria ebbed into a sober realisation that Allied victory had not healed all the hurts of the world. Most ominous were communist movements[25] promising bread and peace and threatening Governments such as Greece which the USA and Great Britain recognised as legitimate. Against this propaganda the USA (prompted by Britain and France clinging to empire) found itself on the ideological defensive against the socialist world. Churchill's 'iron curtain' speech, delivered in Missouri on March 5, 1946, had a long-running effect on public opinion and presaged new President Harry Truman's[26] 'Truman Doctrine' speech on March 12, 1947 resolving 'to assist free peoples'[27] beyond the western hemisphere – a departure from the geographically narrower Monroe Doctrine. This identification of faraway Greece and Turkey with the freedom of American citizens set the rationale for the peacetime use of US military power and *materiél* around the world. Besides military aid, the USA was to help restore, 'Livestock, poultry and draft animals…' as well as railways, ports and other infrastructure destroyed by the Germans, and threatened by Greek communist partisans. The stage was set for programme food aid, i.e. long-running shipments as opposed to short-term disaster relief. Farmers in Europe and America took note.

At a high-level meeting in early 1950, US leaders prepared a top secret document of principles that guided Cold War strategy for decades.[28] It also established the ideological rationale for the use of food aid. The country's complacency on security had been jarred by the communist victory in China in 1949, and the Kremlin's unexpectedly early development of an atomic bomb. Labelled 'NSC 68'[29], the document was inspired by George Kennan who urged 'containment' of the USSR but later rued the unremitting US response. NSC 68 defined policy on political, economic and military means deployed by the USA in the Cold War. The planners reckoned the USA could triple military expenditure without grievous inflation, but knew the USA and its Western allies lacked manpower, materiel and primarily public support to 'contain' Russian and Chinese revolutionaries by arms alone. NSC 68 described a subtler approach: (1) while maintaining pressure on communist expansion through a diplomatic, trade and military strategy of 'containment', (2) 'an affirmative programme' of 'political and economic measures' would wrest the ideological initiative from the Soviet Union and China: 'by the steady development of the moral and material strength of the free world....[NSC 68 concluded that]...the cold war is a real war in which the survival of the free world is at stake.'

The outbreak of the Korean War in the spring of 1950 prompted Truman to sign the document that directed pro-active military-economic strategies thereafter followed by the US Government in concert (usually) with its allies. When NSC 68 was made public, decades later, it was clear that the US breadbasket was part of the arsenal of Western democracy. Of course making food aid a foreign policy weapon neatly disposed of the farm surplus problem. Truman could fight communism and assuage farmers in one fell swoop. Twenty years later, the EEC put a similarly noble front on shifting European dairy surpluses overseas. Thus came the Butter Mountain and Milk Lakes to India.[30]

The detractors of food aid claim accurately that post-war food aid was a surplus disposal policy administered in an ad hoc manner. Reform was a priority in the Public Law 480 Food for Peace[31] programme established in 1954, but the geographical obstacles to delivering food aid in a timely manner meant that it often arrived just in time to wreck farm incomes in recipient countries. Alongside its altruistic impulses, food aid was designed to complement US domestic farm policy. In the 1970s, Secretary of State Henry Kissinger touted PL 480 as a weapon to deploy against the OPEC oil cartel, as well as the USSR in the Cold War. US food aid often violated the conditions later described by John W. Mellor[32] as prescribing 'reliable' amounts, administered to minimise disincentives to indigenous farmers and to distribute welfare effects 'evenly' through recipient societies.[33]

Problematisation of Poverty

President Harry Truman's deployment of food in the Cold War was not bereft of humanitarian concerns. In a major speech, Truman said that despite a great victory against Nazism many people of the world's people suffered hunger and material 'misery'. Truman's speech went on to portray poverty almost as an engineering problem, such as smashing the atom or building a dam that could be solved by American ingenuity, resolve and resources.

Although it is wrong to question Truman's altruism, he might be accused of naiveté. It is now clear that eradicating world poverty is a fundamentally more complex problem than building atomic bombs. Anthropologist Arturo Escobar[34] mocks what he calls Truman's 'problematisation of poverty' as if the USA suddenly awoke and - noticing the rest of the world in abject poverty - scribbled a prescription for its eradication, congratulating itself on its contribution to the 'development discourse'. Drawing mostly from the history of development efforts in Colombia, Escobar argues strongly that, not only was the Western (i.e. First World) response to poverty in the so-called Third World hubristic, but it harmed the 'development' of poor countries. Truman's prescription for poverty is painted as naive. Hindsight suggests Escobar's verdict on the faults of Western policy is on many counts correct. Its weakness is that it scarcely holds the Second World, i.e. the Eastbloc, including the USSR and China, accountable for its sins in the Third World.

Escobar was not alone. According to the *Economist*[35] the USA and its Cold War allies spent $1,400,000,000,000 ($1.4 trillion in 1988 dollars) in foreign aid, 1960-94. Right-wing critic P.T. Bauer claimed this formidable sum was most effective at disrupting poor countries or 'killing them with kindness'. Escobar derides top-down programmes devised by First World 'Lords of Poverty' and their client Third World 'elites' that frustrated people's efforts to devise their own solutions to want.

Table 4.1.

A Brief History of the PL 480 Era

- Spring 1950: President Truman signs NSC 68 after outbreak of the Korean War.
- Establishment of the original PL 480 Food for Peace programme, 1954-66.
- As the complexity of food aid effects (both pro and con) was better understood, the US revised the original PL 480 with a refined "surplus utilisation policy" calculated to raise reliability of shipments and cut disincentives to recipient country agriculture.
- According to Edward Clay, the period from 1971 through the 1980s could be termed a "residual policy" further fine-tuning PL 480 not just to improve welfare effects in recipient countries, but also to minimise costs to the US which was suffering serious budget deficits, partly due to the Vietnam War.
- In 1990 the US completely rewrote PL 480 legislation.[i] Principal changes established direct management responsibilities, new bilateral grant programmes (some using local currencies) and debt forgiveness. A greater delineation was made between agencies responsible for the new PL 480: USDA was to be responsible for Title I and AID was to administer both title II (donations) and the new Title II, i.e. the government-to-government grants programme. Formerly, Titles I/III and II were managed by interagency committees headed by USDA and AID - clearly a troublesome arrangement.

The decades following World War II unleashed a succession of development paradigms. The USA led Britain, France and initially the USSR in the establishment of several international institutions which continue to function today. One of these was the International Monetary Fund[36], a lending institution established at the Bretton Woods conference in July 1944. The IMF was designed to avoid or mitigate future depressions, by acting as the 'lender-of-last-resort'[37] - a role borne by Britain before its financial depletion in World War I. Part of the reason for America's activist foreign policy after World War II was recognition that the 1930s' Depression and 1940s' world war resulted partly from US refusal to assume financial and military burdens borne by Britain before 1914. A multilateral institution akin to the IMF, but reflecting relatively more US influence, is the World Bank which fosters development and, as we have discussed, made successful loans to India's Operation Flood.

Another institution envisaged at Bretton Woods was the International Trade Organisation (ITO). One of its goals (a harbinger of the similarly doomed New International Economic Order or NIEO, 1974-75) was to stabilise world prices of a basket of commodity exports from Africa, Asia and Latin America to ensure 'fair' prices to these producers. In any event, the ITO was scuttled a few years later by the US Congress which rejected its purported infringement on US 'sovereignty' – a recurrence of its rejection of the League of Nations after 1918'. Similar cries of *Sovereignty!* are heard worldwide today from opponents of the WTO.

But scuttling the ITO did not mean an utter dearth for supranational institutions. We have already examined how the GATT process evolved to oversee agreements on tariffs, trade and finally agriculture in 1994. The United Nations was to serve as chief forum for Third World interests, and a number of subordinate bodies were created to implement UN policy. These included the International Fund for Agricultural Development (IFAD). The chief UN agency concerned with rural poverty, IFAD has approved over 300 development programmes in nearly 100 countries. Although great disagreement remains over many aspects of hunger and economic development, a surprising degree of consensus exists on the relative success or failure of policies initiated since aid flows began in earnest after World War II: 'centrally-planned', 'top-down' or 'trickle-down' ideas eventually fell out of favour. Unfortunately, according to an IFAD report in 1992: 'For the past 40 years, development thinking has been dominated by a paradigm in which the growth of the overall economy is believed to lead automatically to wealth "trickling down" to the poor.'[38] Policy revamps from one decade to the next were dramatic, and IFAD (1992) depicted the parade of development paradigms thus:

1950-early 1960s: 'emphasised growth alone as defined by the rate of growth of GNP - not GNP per capita, which caught on later.'

1950s: Lewis and others 'defined the problem as how to achieve growth with an unlimited supply of labour'.

Early 1960s: Rostow argued that traditional societies needed to acquire surplus savings to finance an economic 'take-off' into modernity.

1980s' Structural Adjustment Programmes (SAPs): SAPs were mandated by the IMF and World Bank. The 1980s were a 'decade lost to development' in Africa, simultaneously hit by drought, debt and SAPs - endangering human capital. According to Shaw & Clay unanticipated needs in the former-USSR meant, 'Food aid is therefore more needed now than it was three decades ago when the WFP first began operations.'[39] Hans Singer, sometimes called the father of food aid, agreed with IFAD (1992: p 10) that, 'food aid is being viewed by recipients as an important source of development finance.'[40] Such 'counterpart funds' were monetised in Operation Flood.

Lana Hall claims proceeds from PL 480 wheat sold in Brazil were used effectively in supporting indigenous wheat price supports, which increased farmer and consumer welfare. The chief downside was displacement of commercial imports[41] from farmers in other countries. In contrast, Anne M. Thomson shows the sporadic nature (and disincentive effects to domestic farmers) of PL 480 wheat shipments to Egypt which were doubled by the Carter administration before Egypt's 1979 peace agreement with Israel.[42] Hans Singer and IFAD would probably approve PL 480 effects in Brazil more than in Egypt; Egypt is a middle-income country compared to Bangladesh and India, although Egypt was the top recipient of cereals aid over 1970-97 (**Tables 10a,b,c**).

More generally, IFAD criticised outmoded prescriptions that expected all so-called traditional societies to follow similar paths, regardless of their starting points. Such Western notions gall critics like Arturo Escobar who see the cultural heritage of developing countries as paramount. Whether they were better or worse than the forced-industrialisation policies of China and the USSR awaits the judgement of history.

Variants on dominant paradigms

In the 1950s and 1960s era of 'import substitution' rapid industrialisation with infant industries protected by high tariffs was popular in Latin America, Pakistan, etc.[43] Unfortunately, not only did many of these inefficient industries produce negative value-added[44], but they also sacrificed rural development and exacerbated rural-to-urban migration, which reached 3-4 per cent annually in the 1970s in Brazil, Chile and Colombia, *and nearly 4 per cent in Mexico, Peru and Venezuela.* Although 'mega-cities' such as Calcutta (*aka* Kolkata) grew in India, the country's Green and White Revolutions ameliorated urbanisation. Countries using import substitution almost to the point of autarky include China until the 1970s and Albania until the 1990s.

In the 1960s and 1970s the 'export-led growth' model was successfully followed by 'Asian tigers' such as Taiwan, Korea (ROK), Singapore, Hong Kong and to some extent, Indonesia and Malaysia. William Greider[45] and Robert Gilpin[46] note most Asian Tigers benefited from US Cold War strategy, which opened American markets to their goods, and supplied them with aid of all kinds. IFAD agrees that massive aid helped, although this international institution avoids explicit references to Cold War politics, in its assessment of land reform, and aid paradigms. Most of these 'tigers' adopted capitalist economies.[47]

'State-led growth' characterised policy in several countries, 1950s-1980s. IFAD notes: 'India's second five-year plan was famous for its emphasis on heavy industries under public sector management. Pakistan's second, third and fourth five year plans were [marked by]...a low allocation for agriculture and...the private sector.' In 1978-81, as the Reagan-Thatcher doctrine of privatisation began to sweep the world, many countries in 'the South' had preponderant public sectors: Zambia (61 per cent), Bangladesh (41 per cent), Ivory Coast (40 per cent), Ethiopia (37 per cent), India (33 per cent), Pakistan (45 per cent) and Venezuela (36 per cent).[48] The burden of state-led policies upon the rural population is illustrated by the case of Ghana where direct and indirect taxes accounted for nearly two-thirds of value added in the 1970s.[49] Over time, the negative effect of state-led growth policies became apparent, but fears of rising urban unemployment kept many of them in place. It was not until the early 1990s that Indian Prime Minister Rao began to reverse policy, and privatise state industries - a benchmark in Third World economic trends.

Jeffrey Sachs[50] writes that in the 1960s, the fad at the World Bank and among many donors was development planning. In the 1970s, this gave way to 'basic needs', a doctrine which led the Bank to back non-market economies such as Tanzania.

IFAD[51] calls basic needs one of the 'challenges to the dominant paradigm', adding social engineering to earlier approaches that touted GNP growth without regard to distribution among different social classes. As popularised by the International Labour Organisation (ILO), basic needs plans taxed the rich above certain income levels, and redistributed it in food, clothing, etc. to the poor. It was partly successful in India, where 3 per cent of rural employment came to be funded by the Employment

Guarantee Scheme of Maharashtra in 1984-85. But basic needs were not the final answer because according to IFAD: 'For all its merits, this strategy emphasises the consumption needs of the poor, rather than their productivity.' Criticism of the neglect of the productive potential of the rural sector was echoed by sources as disparate as Jeffrey Sachs and Arturo Escobar. Anderson & Tyers[52] also criticised such policies when governments set artificially low price controls on domestic food sales or allowed the farm sector to stagnate because food aid was available.

Structural Adjustment Programmes (SAPs) came to prominence in the 1980s. Higher prioritisation of balanced government budgets marked monetarist policies to fight inflation. But the emphasis on privatisation of previous institutions of rich fordist welfare states and socialist developing countries hailed the dawn of neoliberalism. By 1982 many Third World countries could no longer avoid debt problems. Mexico was one of the first to flirt with defaulting on overseas loans. The largess that followed the first and second OPEC oil embargoes spawned billions of petrodollars in loans from OPEC countries to developing nations, and even though many of these loans were on 'soft' terms, they increased the already burdensome debt of many. More to the point, the conservative economic philosophies of the Reagan and Thatcher administrations - essentially hostile to socialist planning - rippled through the World Bank, the IMF and eventually the UN itself. This culminated in the replacement of Secretary-General Boutros Boutros Ghali of Egypt by Kofi Annan of Ghana whose management record was more acceptable to the USA.

The apparent failure of decades of top-down, state-managed economic plans induced governments of poor countries to 'bite the bullet' when the World Bank and IMF unveiled the painful SAPs to be agreed to before they would 'roll over' these countries' debt. In most instances SAPs demanded adoption of free market policies, such as privatisation of state-owned industries, downsizing of the civil service and cuts in subsidised services to citizens. Needless to say, these austerity measures were politically unpopular. But few poor governments in the 1980s could say no. Many had to adopt SAPs entailing, loss of subsidised food and health programmes for women and children and cutbacks in education. Some LDCs in Latin America and Asia continued to make halting progress, but Africa suffered net disinvestment, its development in stasis.

'Good Governance' was the mantra of the 1990s. It is still in fashion and permeates US and UK discussions on how to deliver Afghanistan, Iraq and Somalia from status as failed states. Good governance extended the strict financial accounting of SAPs to political accountability. Jeffrey Sachs writes that frustration with earlier paradigms - 'development planning', 'basic needs', 1980s-era 'structural adjustment', etc. - prompted IMF and World

Bank insistence on government reform in debtor countries. This is not an abandonment of SAPs, but an intensification of SAPs that might have been politically untenable in the Cold War.

Jeffrey Sachs[53] says the 1990s' paradigm shift to 'good governance' is well intentioned, but remains 'deeply flawed.' It is too burdensome on poor economies. For example, the World Bank set 111 conditions upon Kenya, before granting one loan. Under SAPs, debtor governments are urged to reduce external debt and domestic budget deficits. This is done through cuts in subsidised services, imposition of new taxes and user fees and greater transparency in customs administration (thus becoming more receptive to imports) - along with the privatisation of state enterprises and civil service reforms already underway. They claim the IMF's obsession with price stability blinds it to all else. Poor economies that could be growing at 5 per cent annually are held to only 1-2 per cent because of the Bank's unreasonable fear of inflation.

Of 53 countries in Africa, only Botswana, Mauritius and Uganda have enjoyed healthy growth since the end of the Cold War. In the years 1980-88, Sub-Saharan Africa as a whole suffered with GDP growth of just 1.5 per cent - compared to the healthier GDP growth of 5.7 per cent in India despite a serious drought in 1987.[54] Although Sachs believes SAPs have a purging effect on some governments, he urged debt relief for the poorest countries to mitigate hunger and loss of the 'human capital' of women, children, etc. By some macroeconomic estimates, Africa suffered net disinvestment of $40 billion annually, because more money went to the North in debt relief than was invested on the world's poorest continent. According to former UK Department for International Development (DfID) head Clare Short, interim debt relief plans for several poor countries, in and out of Africa, were agreed in 1996-97. More was promised at the G8 Summit in Scotland in 2005, but the signatories have been slow to deliver.

Before we go on, it is worth considering that SAPs could reinvigorate the neglected potential of food aid. Hans Singer is figurehead of a group (including Shaw, Clay and James Ingram of the WFP) who advocate the use of food aid to ease the plight of poor countries undergoing structural adjustment. Invoking the concept of 'additionality'[55] developed in his 1978 WFP study, Singer is in full agreement with John W. Mellor that 'donors must supply large amounts', entailing a net supply larger than before aid began - while recipients must give priority to their own farmers and minimise disincentives to them.[56] In the case of sub-Saharan Africa (SSA), Singer identified nine ways that food aid could ease SAPs. Recognising the danger of food aid as a disincentive, Singer still claims, 'the real limit is not aid capacity, but absorptive capacity. Further, Singer[57] maintains a need: 'for additional food aid, subject to assurance that food aid helps to provide incentives for increased local production and physical and human investment in recipient countries.'

The food, obtained from Western donors or triangular transactions from other Third World countries in surplus, can be sold by recipient governments to supplement their budgets, or simply fight hunger among their citizens. Triangular transactions do ease suspicion that food aid is just a cover-up for Western surplus disposal. However, Clay & Benson write that, 1983-88, triangular cereals aid purchases or trilateral exchanges tripled from under 500,000 tonnes to nearly 1.2 million tonnes - from 4.5 per cent to 8.9 per cent of total cereals food aid.[58] Local triangular food aid operations can sometimes be more cost-efficient and timely than aid from the USA or EU. Until a decade ago, Zimbabwe exuded potential as a breadbasket for triangular operations; sadly that has faded in the nebulous political situation.. Some countries could utilise assistance, but questions remain: *Will aid be a disincentive to farmers? Will it create dependence?*[59]

Susan George[60] identifies three paradigms of hunger and development: (1) 'trickle down' with benefits emanating from entrepreneurs and modernising elites which may correlate to the views of the IMF and World Bank; (2) 'dependency theory' of a centre (or 'core' as Immanuel Wallerstein refers to rich North America and Europe) and periphery of the Third World, that has been consistently exploited since colonial times. As George describes it, dependency theory seems fairly consistent with Arturo Escobar's view of the 'development discourse'. (3) Beyond the second model lies 'class analysis' that appears more Marxist than Escobar's rather anthropological (or postmodern) worldview.

George says that because the NIEO is incomplete, First-Third World relations (in which IC elites support LDC elites, *aka compradores*) will be characterised by conflict, not harmony. George calls for economic independence and 'empowerment' rather than interdependence or integration of LDCs into the global economy. She is not alone in calling for fairer pricing of food commodities through formation of a new international economic order for food. Indeed, much has been written about the fair trade movement among companies in the USA and Europe and coffee coops in Latin America and Africa.[61] But recurring calls for a global food cartel to safeguard poor country producers appear doomed. William Greider notes that OPEC 'struggles constantly' to enforce production and price controls for oil - a commodity scarcer than food.[62]

What is the upshot of the paradigm parade? After examining the cornucopia of aid and development paradigms and of national development plans spawned by them from World War II until the end of the Cold War, it appears that top down philosophies were passé by the 1990s. With more emphasis on rural development including alleviation of poverty, education and women's empowerment, the new paradigm might be called 'trickle up'. Fortunately for India, its White Revolution programme Operation Flood (OF) combined such positive 'trickle-up' features to microeconomically enrich rural dairy farmers, along with enough 'top-down' planning to macroeconomically improve the efficiency of national infrastructure. OF was an unusual fine-tuning of previous food aid schemes, and the magnitude of its eventual success - against the auguries of doomsayers - suggests that some of the sins of omission or commission of aid practitioners in earlier, failed programmes might be forgiven, in light of the unique circumstances they encountered.

After the fall of the Berlin Wall in 1989, and successive dismantling of the USSR and Eastbloc countries, prospects were any government attempting central planning. Denis MacShane[63], a British labour MP and metalworkers union official summed up the post-Cold War outlook: 'For years socialists used to argue among ourselves about what kind of socialism we wanted. The choice of the left is no longer what kind of socialism it wants, but what kind of capitalism it can support.'

Many developing nations were criticised for turning their backs on political, commercial and trade relations with their former colonisers in favour of self-reliance or central planning (if not state-led growth). Perhaps a temporary rejection of capitalism was a necessary part of nation-building, fulfilling a collective desire to punish foreign companies that had profited from colonialism. But after the Cold War, this anti-capitalist, anti- trade attitude became passé. In post-apartheid South Africa, President Nelson Mandela led a charm offensive to attract the return of foreign direct investment (FDI) by MNCs including Ford Motor Company. Greider writes that today developing countries from Malaysia to Paraguay clamour for investment from MNCs like Ford and Motorola, and bemoans the MNCs' ability to blackmail countries into labour and tax concessions.

Arturo Escobar's book *Encountering Development*[64] does for post-WW II development what Shanti George's volume[65] did for Operation Flood. Although they treat different levels (global versus national) of development, both books are thorough critiques of 'First World' development strategy in the 'Third World'. While George was concerned with mismanagement of economic, political, and genetic factors of India's dairy development, Escobar addresses mismanagement of 'development' itself by the First World in the Third World, drawing evidence from the post-war period to contemporary Colombia. What distinguishes Escobar's approach is his attempt to assess the North's policies in the South in terms of anthropology and postmodernism. This approach is not alien to George, but Escobar goes further, railing against the very term 'sustainable development'.

Table 4.2.

EEC dairy aid commitments & deliveries to India 1978-83		
Period & Commodity	EC Commitment	Agrostat/94 data
1978-80 SMP	150,000 MT	134,934 MT (mean)
1978-83 SMP	same as above	129,634 MT
1978-80 B O	45,000 t	39,756 MT
1978-83 B O	same as above	37,294 MT

Source: Agrostat/FAO/1994

Like George, Escobar spares no effort in criticising misjudgements by the Lords of Development. Typical flies in the ointment of Northern schemes include: overlooking the danger that White or Green Revolution programmes founder if the cost of inputs is too high; if peasants have no access to credit; or if irrigation systems are in disrepair. But shouldn't such issues, in Colombia or elsewhere, be treated less as philosophical conundra and more as everyday, empirical problems solvable by rational decision makers? The image of 'ignorant' peasants resisting new technology has given way to realisations that they can make better risk-benefit assessments of new initiatives than the development practitioners who tout them. Where, say, a switch to hybrid seeds carries not only the prospect of greater yield but also entails even a slightly greater risk that pests could ruin the crop, a 'conservative' peasant is understandably cautious. That said, if hybrid seeds are as resilient as native varieties, most farmers switch. Escobar praises the refusal of Colombian peasants to comply with ill-conceived schemes. This is reminiscent of the reluctance of India's small farmers to switch to Friesian cross-breds which were maladapted to local climate, fodder and disease.

Escobar observes that lack of credit can bottleneck development. But new approaches to increasing credit among the poor are proving successful, notably the Grameen Bank. Neglect of Third World culture, and links to traditional agriculture, were addressed by institutions such as the UN's International Fund for Agricultural Development (IFAD).[66] Decades of evidence suggest rural development is necessary not just to bring lower quintiles of Third World societies into so-called modernity, but also because aggregate national economic growth might actually be led by rural agriculture, small manufacturing and services. Rural development may be best option for countries – including some in Africa - that cannot depend on export-led growth to grow their economies.

The failure of many development efforts is contrasted by the success of India's White Revolution. European aid could have disrupted its dairy sector if it were not been monetised as additional. But Edward Clay[67] was sanguine on, at least, the *reliability* of shipments:

> The EC commitment since 1980 of 1.65 million tonnes is shared between the bilateral aid programmes of member states (730,000 tonnes) and the programme of 'Community Action' organized by the Commission (920,000 t). The Commission also administers virtually all dairy aid. Informal administrative practice has fixed commodity commitments since 1978 at 150,000 t of SMP & 45,000 t of butter oil. These levels have no developmental rationale, but represent an approximate balance of processed dairy products in terms of fresh milk equivalent earmarked for export as aid. Such practice is, however, more satisfactory than commitments fluctuating with the short-run surplus position (**see Table 4.2 above**).

Conclusion of the War of Three Worlds

Critics on Left and Right found plenty to criticise in food aid regimes. Alongside 'Northern' theorists including Susan George, John Mellor, and Hans Singer, we considered 'Southern' theorists Arturo Escobar and Hernando de Soto.

Escobar decries interventions by First World 'Lords of Poverty' in the Third World. But de Soto vaunts grassroots cooperation of Latin people to meet their needs, despite damage by developed countries and their 'mercantilist' Left- *or* Right-wing governments. De Soto argues that people - Vikings or mestizo Indians - share similar goals: 'adequate food, clothing, shelter, transport to work, security for their families, and a stake in decision-making. Food aid can sometimes help such people.

Where food aid has been unsuccessful, it is often because delivery was poorly timed. This is why early warning systems on drought and famine conditions are important. It is also why efficient transport and logistics are necessary to speed relief – as the Government of India demonstrated in domestic drought relief in the late 1980s – a dramatic success compared to the tragedy of famine in Rajasthan in 1968.

Many problems can be ameliorated by use of Geographic Information/Positioning Systems (GIS/GPS). Such systems have been used by NGOs such as Riders for Health (www.riders.org) for medical outreach in rural Africa.[68]

At other times, food aid fails when commodity control is lost to unauthorised groups, as happened in Afghanistan and Somalia. In the case of Nigeria's *Wheat Trap* told by Andræ & Beckmann, aid was a loss leader to commercial sales which disrupted forward and backward linkages between domestic farmers and markets. This not only weakened the livelihoods of grain farmers in Nigeria's hinterlands, but it also weakened the food security of urban consumers in a country in which the most significant export is petroleum.

Tables 3a, 3b and 3c below relate major cereal aid recipients by caput and volume, against the history of food aid and development since the mid-twentieth century. India was not a top 10 per capita cereal recipient 1970-97, partly because it made progress in famine relief in these years.

Table 4.3a.

Main cereal food aid recipients per capita: 1988-1997			
Country	**Kilogram per head**	**GNP per capita PPP$ 1996/7**	**percentage food deficit 1990-92**
1. Jamaica	63.0	$3480	5.6%
2. Jordan	50.7	$3430	0.5%
3. Guyana	48.5	$2490	5.6%
4. Liberia	45.9	$1110	23%
5.Mozambique	28.0	$ 520	29.2%
6. Ethiopia	27.3	$510	28%
7. Mauritania	25.4	$1870	4.4%
8. Suriname	24.3	$3150	4.9%
9. Malawi	23.0	$700	16.4%
10. Bolivia	22.6	$3000	11.9%

Source: FAO[69].

Table 4.3b.

Major cereal food aid recipients by total volume: 1970-97			
Country	**Million Tonnes**	**GNP per capita PPP$ 1997**	**percentage food deficit 1990-92**
1. Egypt	33.5	$2940	0.9%
2. Bangladesh	32.7	$1050	8.8%
3. India	15.9	$1650	4.9%
4. Ethiopia	13.6	$510	28%
5. Pakistan	12.6	$1590	3.5%
6. Indonesia	10.5	$3450	2.2%
7. Korea Rep.	9.1	13,500	0.1%
8. Sudan	8.6	$860	10.9%
9. Mozambique	8.1	$520	29.2%
10. Sri Lanka	7.9	$2460	6.4%

Source: FAO[70].

Table 4.3c.

Landmarks in food aid & development
* **1954**: US reorganises its bilateral food aid donations with PL 480. Till early 1960s: food aid synonymous with US food aid.
* **1956-76**: US 59m tonnes programme food aid to India (1993 value = $4.8 b).
* **1961**: World Food Programme (WFP) created as multilateral food aid agency.
* **1967**: Food Aid Convention (FAC) consolidates donor commitments.
* **ca. 1968**: Indian famine in Rajasthan.
* **1969-81**: Afghanistan receives dairy aid from WFP. Plans for "monetised" dairy aid dropped due to poor project control, after 1979 USSR invasion.
* **ca. 1970-71**: Nigerian Civil War and famine in Biafra.
* **1971** (independence) to late-1970s: food aid critical in Bangladesh.
* **November 1974**: : UN World Food Conference called for improved food policy. Minimum annual target of 10 million tons cereals set. WFP restructured, creating Committee on Food Aid (CFA) to govern WFP. Goal is to coordinate multilateral, bilateral and NGO aid programmes. CFA becomes "world focus for discussion on all aspects of food aid." (James Ingram in Shaw & Clay, 1993, World Food Aid: pp ix-x)
* **August, 1982**: Mexico cannot service debt, triggering Third World debt crisis.
* **1987**: India withstands worst drought this century in all regions.
* **1988**: Increased rice production brings Bangladesh close to self-sufficiency.
* **1988**: dairy products comprise ca. 340 thousand tonnes total food aid.
* **1989**: dairy products comprise ca. 156 thousand tonnes aid.
* **1990**: dairy products comprise ca. 137 thousand tonnes aid.
* **1991**: dairy products comprise ca. 234 thousand tonnes aid.
* **Early-1990s**: ex-Eastbloc receives more food assistance than Africa. But Gulf War-spawned oil price rises increase need for food aid in India, etc.
* **1994**: Uruguay GATT accords signed, ushering in WTO era.
* **1997**: Ex-USSR dairy production falls (HD, 10 Aug'97) as red meat demand rises. Russia bypasses Japan in queue for New Zealand butter, etc.
* **1998**: India (expected 71m MT) passing US as #1 world milk producer. US promises Russia US$639 in food & other aid to quell opposition to Iraq policy.
* **1999**: US-EU "Banana War" pressures ACP countries & tests GATT/WTO rules. Battle in Seattle protests of the WTO show contestation of globalisation.
* **2008**: World Bank announces plan to replicate India's dairy revolution in Africa.

Sources: FAO/Agrostat; BAS.

In the next chapter we compare India's dairy production and consumption records to other developing countries. We will see how Operation Flood improved dairy self-sufficiency, despite cries that it was a subterfuge to trick the subcontinent out of its lactic birthright.

3. Cattle at dusk near Anand.

4. Dr. Verghese Kurien interviewed by the author.

5. Mother Dairy Gandhinagar at Ahmedabad.

6. Technicians, Vidya cheese plant. 7. Amul, the brand of GCMMF coop.

8. Amul range including butter, infant milk substitute and cheese.

9. From left: Siddharth (Kurien's grandson), Dr. Kurien presents *I Too had a Dream* to President A.P.J. Abdul Kalam in 2008. Between is Kurien assistant P.A. Joseph; Mrs. Molly Kurien right.
This picture courtesy of Kurien collection; others are Scholten photos.

Chapter 5

Data on India & Comparators

Beyond expectations 1960s ~ 1990s

We have seen the flows of international agricultural trade and the symbiotic evolutions of post-World War II trade and aid regimes in the Cold War. Although large-scale international grain trade was established centuries ago, food aid is a recent phenomenon, almost peculiar to the twentieth century, and has been promulgated out of commercial, geopolitical and ideological imperatives alongside humanitarian concerns.

The vulnerability of milk products to spoilage makes them a special sub-set of food, far more delicate than most commodities in world food trade and aid which is dominated by hardier cereals. Containing 82-88 per cent water, milk is almost instantly perishable, and cows should be milked twice a day. The expansion of dairy trade was contingent on advances in transport technologies and refrigeration. Fine sprayers for buffalo milk powder were developed in India in the 1950s. Others such as ultra high temperature-processed milk (UHT) emerged more recently.

Now let us examine changes in production, consumption, trade, population and other aspects of dairy development on the global, continental, and regional scales, making reference to changes in India, primarily from 1961 to the late-1990s.

Meanwhile, a brief discussion of India's quality-of-life indicators in the late-1990s illuminates the time-frame of this study. India is a natural touchstone for any global discussi

on of dairy development because this large, populous country has traditionally engaged in dairying as an ancillary activity to crops production, and it has also been a crucible of post-colonial development paradigms - a focus for trade and development theorists.

India was the largest 'non-aligned' nation of the Third World and fortunately - a point this book highlights - adept at turning potentially disastrous foreign trade or aid initiatives to its benefit.

Selections for our Country Comparison Group

The principals in our comparison group are Bangladesh[1], Egypt, Pakistan and Zimbabwe - like India, all listed by Agrostat/FAO as 'low-income' countries. Bangladesh and Pakistan were selected also because they border India and share some of its heritage. Egypt was selected because it has been the largest recipient of dairy aid besides India.[2] Zimbabwe was chosen because, like India, it has been the object of cooperative dairy development programmes studied by Shanti George, one of the principal commentators on contemporary dairying. Occasionally we refer to Turkey, long an aid recipient in Food-for-Work programmes, is among countries mentioned. Located on the right periphery of our maps - the target of marketing efforts by the USA - are South Korea and China, which are becoming important players in dairy trade. Many of the misconceptions, failures and successes experienced by India shed light on other countries. In any event, India's cultural affinity for bovines, milk and dairying presents a natural theatre for dairy development. We begin by examining its lack-lustre economic development in the post-colonial era.

Status as the world's largest democracy has been a source of pride to India since independence in 1947. Of less merit is 'the Hindu rate of growth', a phrase used by domestic and external observers in attempts to explain the country's slow rate of development compared to other Less Developed Countries (LDCs). Democracy has at times been blamed for India's failure to reach its potential. India boasts more infrastructure per capita than countries with quite autocratic regimes such as China and Indonesia, but has lagged behind them in output.[3]

On the other hand, democratic checks and balances, along with the limited powers delegated to the states, in India's federal system, may have saved India from costly misadventures of autocratic systems, such as misconceived initiatives in steel and agricultural sectors, and the political upheavals of Mao's Cultural Revolution in China, or the political purges that followed the demise of socialist Indonesian leader Sukarno in the mid-1960s. Many observers would insist that, while India's economic development has not been as rapid as some Asian tigers, this big country retains a cultural heritage of richness and diversity. William Greider[4] and also Robert Gilpin[5] point out that economically successful Asian tigers functioned as clients of the West in the Cold War, unlike India, which took pride in non-alignment.

Nevertheless, by the mid-1990s it was clear that compared to many other LDCs, India could do better. There had been sufficient time to pursue its individual path to prosperity, but remained quite poor. After the secession of Pakistan, India enjoyed relative tranquillity in its domestic and foreign affairs, aside from acute crises such as the incursion by China in the early

1970s (which happened to stimulate the milk industry), and chronic unrest by Kashmiri nationalists. One legacy from the British Empire era that the country continued to benefit from was the Indian Civil Service (ICS), an institution noted for accurate record-keeping - a distinct advantage in pursuits such as cattle breeding. India also developed some world class universities - but primary and secondary education languished. According to the World Bank, over 50 per cent of India's adults were illiterate in the 1990s - compared to just 20 per cent in China, or 10 per cent in Thailand. Jean Drèze and Amartya Sen[6] show that in the period 1986-87, 51 per cent of females, and 26 per cent of males aged 12-14 and living in rural areas had never enrolled in school. In rural Uttar Pradesh, fully 68 per cent of females and 27 per cent of males aged 12-14 had never enrolled in school. According to an *Economist Survey* by Clive Crook[7]:

> Between 1960 and 1990 India's GDP grew by an average of a little under 4 per cent a year - the 'Hindu rate of growth', as it came to be known. In round numbers, Pakistan's GDP over the same period grew by 5 per cent a year, Indonesia's by 6 per cent, Thailand's by 7 per cent, Taiwan's by 8 per cent and South Korea's by 9 per cent.

Blaming a 'Nehruvian socialism' that he says had to be abandoned after oil price rises in the Gulf War prompted a balance-of-payments crisis in 1991-93, Crook[8] continues:

> India's planners had laid great emphasis on rapid industrialisation, the ostensible reason for interfering with a more market-driven course of development. Yet in India between 1960 and 1990 industrial output grew on average by only 6 per cent a year. In Pakistan it grew by 8 per cent a year, in Indonesia by 9 per cent, in Thailand by 9 per cent, in South Korea by 10 per cent and in Taiwan by 12 per cent. In 1960 South Korea's income per head was roughly four times bigger than India's - $800 at 1990 prices, compared with $200. By 1990 South Korean income was 20 times bigger - $8000 against $400.

How could more wealth be created among India's poor? In what amounts to a repudiation of the development paradigms of previous decades, market-oriented observers and economists in the mainstream of the current IMF and World Bank paradigm - such as Crook, Jeffrey Sachs[9], and Kazimierz Z. Poznanski[10] - blame laggard development of the Indian economy, like the demise of Eastbloc economies, on isolation from competition, *dirigist* central planning, and failure to adopt market disciplines – especially before the reforms (albeit half-hearted, says Crook) begun under PM Narasimha Rao in 1991-93. More germane to our discussion, Crook claims India's farm productivity 'has risen markedly more slowly' than most other Asian economies, that the Green Revolution has not been taken to its limits and that there is a general need for agricultural reform - which it may be inferred, would stimulate the White Revolution. Crook says individual farmers *not fertiliser manufacturers* should be subsidised. At the Institute of Rural Management Anand (IRMA) Katar Singh[11] notes: 'quite a lot of so-called farm subsidies go to the private industries and public undertakings manufacturing farm inputs to cover up their inefficiency and mismanagement.'

Crook's laundry list of reforms looks reasonable to anyone who has visited India. Public Sector Electricity grids should be improved. PSEs suffer chronic blackouts; faltering voltage necessitates frequent, costly rewiring of pumps, leading to widespread reliance on environmentally-dirty petroleum powered generators. State irrigation departments, rife with corruption, call out for reform, writes Crook. Singh[12] agrees that: 'it is unethical to penalise irrigators [i.e. farmers] ...due to widespread inefficiency and mismanagement in Irrigation Departments.'

Reforms prompted by the economic crisis in the 1990s stimulated internal investment in the agricultural sector. The Jain Group, which makes farm equipment, reported a 400 per cent increase in turnover in the three years after reform began, and a rise in the number of its workers to 3000 people.[13] External investment surged. Janairus Banaji[14] details how India's new openness to foreign direct investment (FDI) attracted large commitments by MNCs which are diversifying from tobacco into food. FDI might benefit both Green and White Revolutions, but the effects on rural employment were uncertain. There are also fears that countries such as India are test-beds for risky experiments in genetically-modified (GM) crops. Years later the *Economist*[15] reported an epidemic of 1200 farmer suicides linked to crop failures of biotech (Bt) cotton in Maharashtra in the 18 months preceding 2007; citing this phenomenon, dairy cooperative leaders testily noted no such suicides among their members.

Singh[16] warned also that exports should be managed by farmers' coops, not MNCs, to ensure that the desire for trade gains does not supersede the need to improve nutrition of the rural poor who have benefited less from Government food subsidies than urban consumers.

OF mistake avoidance

Calls to redirect fertiliser subsidies from inefficient manufacturers to cost-conscious farmers have a bearing on the White Revolution. Fertiliser and other inputs (especially water) are critical factors in crop production, and crop wastes are the chief form of fodder for 'landless, small and marginal farmers, numbering about 70 million'[17] who produce much of India's milk. (More crops = more crop wastes = more fodder for cows.) There are also parallels between fertiliser plants and plants such as those run by the NDDB producing cattle cake.

Attempts at reform were made, but although government subsidies for fertilisers were cut from a remarkably large 0.9 per cent of GDP in 1991 to 0.6 per cent of GDP about 1997[18], there was still too much waste. Why? Moral hazard. Subsidies flowed to indigenous fertiliser manufacturers, not farmers. Subsidies discouraged cost-cutting by fertiliser makers. They keep input costs high for farmers, when imported fertiliser, or fertiliser made by foreign-owned firms, could be cheaper. This boondoggle benefits special interests, not farmers and food production. If Crook's market-oriented reforms were put in place, tariffs on fertiliser imports would fall (repudiating 'import-substitution' policies long entertained by the GOI - and fostered by the lobbying efforts of manufacturers seeking subsidies) and farmers would receive tax credits, or perhaps vouchers, leaving them free to buy more cost-effective inputs - whether they were of domestic or foreign origin.[19] Thence, competition would likely drive down input costs to individual farmers, leading to greater productivity in Indian agriculture. Lower tariffs on machinery used in fertiliser plants could allow recapitalisation of more efficient domestic fertiliser plants if this were necessary. The chief advantage of pursuing Crook's recommendation is that it would reduce macroeconomic waste and raise productivity.

Lessons learned from this analysis of waste in the fertiliser industry, and the benefits of liberalisation can be extended to the supply of inputs for the White Revolution. Crook and other free-marketeers would likely recommend that all dairy inputs (including breeding, feeding and training) be opened to foreign competition.[20] Critics of Operation Flood charge that OF is sometimes guilty of waste, monopolistic practises or price distortions, comparable to the case of fertiliser that Crook is critical of in the Green Revolution. In a system as large as OF it would be surprising if there were *no* instances of inefficient practices or even impropriety. But serious charges of kickbacks and other malfeasance have been convincingly denied by OF officials.[21] And it should not be forgotten that the cooperative nature of OF, as well as the democratic checks-and-balances in it, not only capture the rents of any public subsidies available to OF *for farmers*, but also help guard against corruption.

In the early 1990s, Edward Clay and Olav Stokke[22] wrote that studies of 'the very expensive development programme' show 'no dramatic nutritional impact, either negative in the producing communities, or positive in the consuming urban areas.' They agree with critics that income benefits from

OF were distributed 'inequitably, following a pattern of other major Indian development programmes', adding that:

> The increase in milk production achieved by the so-called white revolution seems to have been brought about by a combination of factors. Retail price controls...Producers have been subsidised. None of the evaluations of Operation Flood taken from a donor perspective has been able to conclude unequivocally that the benefits have justified the considerable transfer of resources financed by European taxpayers through the Common Agricultural Policy and the European Community Aid Programme.

Defenders of Operation Flood would naturally accept Clay & Stokke's grudging admission that Indian milk yield rose and retort that, of course OF was costly - after all, many crucial aspects of OF are traceable to dynamics (e.g. surplus disposal, market penetration and export promotion) made inevitable from milk mountains that grew from rich country subsidies in the EEC. This can hardly be stated too strongly. Furthermore, as shown by a host of reputable economists including Jagdish Bhagwati (1988), Kym Anderson & Rodney Tyers (1991), and Bernard Hoekman & Michel Kostecki (1995), rich country farm subsidies gradually weakened the terms-of-trade of poor countries - effecting a considerable transfer of resources from poor countries to rich ones.

That OF did not meet all the hopes of observers from disciplines outside agriculture is not surprising. NDDB head Verghese Kurien[23] observed that although cooperative dairying is a good way to fight rural poverty, it is not the only way and that, to be effective, OF had to be managed primarily as an agricultural initiative, not a social programme. What must be borne in mind is how much happier the present state of Indian dairy development is today compared to what it was before 1970: milk rationing in the cities, no milk production increases in any region of India, and dependence on EEC and US dairy commodities. This scenario of dependency, redolent of neo-colonialism, easily could be present reality - had Indian dairy leaders not defended their dairy autonomy. Facing a subsidised EEC capable of devastating Indian dairy price structures with a mountain of 'free' dairy aid, it is to India's credit that it looked this gift horse in the mouth, refused to be cowed, and negotiated terms with Europe that reflect credit on both donor and recipient today.

Crook should be pleased that India's dairy development benefited from incidents of waste avoidance. These wise but controversial choices ran contrary to official import-substitution policies, and eventually contributed to rises in GDP, reductions in balance-of-payments accounts and bolstered its dairy autonomy. A prime example was the insistence by officials in Anand (a decade before the NDDB was established there in 1965) on importation of the most advanced technology appropriate to the coops' needs. A benchmark decision in the 1950s was the purchase of milk powder spraying equipment from Denmark (more on this later) which, like the case of fertiliser reform above, violated policies of import substitution, but raised productivity to a new plateau. The exposure of Indian dairy equipment manufacturers to foreign competition probably spurred development, long before early-1990s economic reforms.

Businessman Rahul Bajaj testifies to the retarding effect of over-protection from imports. The leader of a large family concern specialising in small motorbikes said previous central planning by GOI stifled innovation, allowing Bajaj to make profits on shoddy scooters. After a quarter-century alliance with Japanese manufacturer Kawasaki has improved Bajaj offerings in India and, with son Rajiv Bajaj at the helm, is exporting Bajaj products to the Philippines and other ASEAN countries. Jagdish Bhagwati compares the '**pro**scriptive Government' of India which often stifled innovation and entrepreneurship - to the '**pre**scriptive' approach of Japan whose MITI fostered 'Symbiosis between Government and private entrepreneurs' leading to innovation and export-led growth.[24] (Bhagwati's analysis is cogent. But Robert Gilpin's analysis might also note that while non-aligned India stagnated in mercantilism, Japan could hardly fail to prosper with the USA as a willing target for its exports.

Bear in mind, about 65 per cent of India's labour force remains on the land, compared to 5 per cent of Japan's.[25] Relatively few Indians have been engaged in the production of consumer durables such as scooters, but that is changing. Today India ranks as one of the world's largest emerging economies with a burgeoning middle class that (upwards of 350 million) nearly equates the population of Europe. But rural-to-urban migration could accelerate, worsening conditions in already crowded cities, unless living conditions and opportunities for employment improve in ruralities. Although India still enjoys a surplus pool of rural labour, pressure increases to raise farm productivity to match rising consumer demand. Hence, the case for opening of the economy. Free-marketeers such as Clive Crook and Jeffrey Sachs argue that opening economies to the importation of farm implements, e.g. generators, pumps, tillers, small tractors, and welding equipment can stimulate what a previous paradigm termed integrated rural development. India's White Revolution shows that in start-up situations, hardware imports can improve macroeconomic performance, even if they temporarily worsen national balance-of-payments accounts.

While joint ventures pose the long-feared danger of foreign control and repatriation of profits abroad, they also offer the chance of technology transfer - and a goad to domestic producers to improve their competitiveness. Recent experience of improvements in domestic production indicate that opening markets has a net benefit to the national economy, especially when foreign firms such as Suzuki set up high-tech (compared to the old-tech Ambassador autos and Royal Enfield motorcycles that India has outgrown) joint ventures. Nevertheless, while economic liberalisations spur competitiveness and raise productivity, improvement (whether by Government or private means) of public provision of water and electricity would provide a more fundamental boon to human health - and base to economic growth.

According to Crook, India's capacity-licensing regime, which was constructed to ensure that growing firms did not control an 'unduly large share' of India's scarce resources, was disastrous, because it (explicitly) ignored the price signals necessary to raise market efficiency, and national productivity.[26] Crook's dour analysis of India's performance and his prescriptions for reform (reflecting IMF and World Bank-mandated SAPs in other developing countries, including, abandonment of price controls, tariff reductions, and subsidy cuts to special interests such as fertiliser makers) is persuasive on many counts.

However, some points should be made in defence of India's past efforts in agricultural development, and dairy development in particular. First, while it is true that India's agricultural output has not risen as fast as most Asian countries, it should be noted that several countries around the world (some with better factor endowments than India) have comparatively worse records in both the Green and White Revolutions. Second, India is a vast country with relatively few navigable rivers in its interior, with a huge, growing, heterogeneous population, so the fact that there has been *any* rise in Indian output is sufficient to improve world aggregate figures. Third, although Indian agricultural growth has lagged behind China in the post-Mao era (and that points to the need for further reform of its farm sector), it stands to the credit of GOI, and to the cooperation of the WFP, FAO and other multilateral, national and NGO actors in world food trade and aid regimes that post-independence India has not suffered to quite the extent of China, where an estimated 20-30 million people died during famines in the Mao era. After unconscionable deaths in the famine in Rajasthan and other parts of India around 1968, GOI set about improving stockpiles and logistics for distribution of cereals and other food stocks in emergencies - winning kudos for its relief efforts in the drought of 1987-88. Gulati *et al.*[27] explain how Indian dairy cooperatives developed Decision Support Systems (DSS) to deal with procurement gluts and lows and that: 'despite the worst drought [1987-88] in recent history, cattle deaths were almost totally averted as were outbreaks of epidemics.'

It is disappointing that by OECD and IFPRI development markers such as infant mortality, female and overall literacy, India's performance has been poorer than China's. Yet, in the case of dairy development, India has done rather better than many competing countries, owing in part to shrewd decisions on infrastructure investment, utilisation of what could have been problematic dairy aid, and attention to farmgate prices paid to rural farmers, as well as affordable prices for urban consumers. The White Revolution employed some realistic pricing and marketing policies more in line with Clive Crook's ideal state than other sectors characterised by what he called: 'India's insanely repressive system of domestic planning and regulation.'[28]

View of this book

Next to Clive Crook's dark landscape of a sub-continent-sized Third World country, complacent in its status as a democracy of great cultural richness with a thrifty, hard-working population bound in economic misery because of governmental *dirigisme* – this book sees dairying as a font of optimism. According to Alderman[29], Mergos & Slade:

> Total milk production in India increased at a rate of 5.5 per cent a year between 1970 and 1985, yet only 6.0 per cent of total milk production was handled through cooperatives at the end of this period. Thus it is clear that progress must be occurring throughout the sector.

Delineating the positive effects of Operation Flood in a virtuous circle with improvements in the non-cooperative sector is a classic chicken-or-egg question. But considering the fact that India, beset by milk droughts, suffered a decade of dairy stagnation before 1970, it is unimaginable that OF was any sort of boondoggle. Barrages of attacks on India's attempts at making its dairying 'vertically integrated from producer to consumer'[30] (Doornbos, Gertsch & Terhal's 1991 phrase) have identified shortcomings - but cannot disprove evidence of notable improvements in India's overall dairy production and per capita consumption.

One of the chief purposes of this book is to investigate the varying degrees of success or failure in terms of increasing milk supply, guarding national 'dairy autonomy', spurring rural development, or bringing minorities into the cash economy, that can be attributed to Operation Flood. From the time of writing in 2009, it seems ridiculous, but so rife was the scorn heaped on India's White Revolution, that for decades it was questioned whether milk consumption increases were domestically based – or entirely a sham based on EEC dairy aid. So let us now examine empirical evidence - which generally supports positive assessments on all counts -

from charts and maps representing international dairy production, trade, and consumption, from the 1960s to the 1990s, drawn from the Agrostat·PC computer database distributed by the UN's Food and Agricultural Organisation (FAO) in 1990 and 1994 version, as well as later sources such as FAOSTAT.

Examination of Charts & Maps

World Charts

This section offers graphical representations of India's dairy progress in the principal years of our study, 1961~1996. Data from the mid- and late-1990s from the Food and Agricultural Organisation of the United Nations (FAO) explicates world dairy developments and provides evidence for the achievements of Operation Flood. Colour versions of these illustrations will be uploaded on: www.durham.ac.uk/b.a.scholten

Chart 5.1. World Milk Production & Population 1961-1990 below shows world population rising faster than milk production well into the 1970s, when OF began. Immediately apparent is the dramatic rise in milk production represented by a steepening of the curves for Asia and the World as a whole. Asian production starts at a low level but climbs to intersect the curve of North & Central America, and approaches that of the USSR.[31] The rate of increase of World output falls behind population growth, 1990-1993. Production plateaus or falls in Europe, the ex-USSR and, to a lesser extent, Africa restrained output, although (**Table 5.1**) it is still increasing.

Newer data show India propelling World milk output as Northern markets mature. A drop in world milk production occurred around 1963, roughly coinciding with the first major sale of US grain to the USSR during the Kennedy administration. This block-sale to the USSR, whose purpose was to expand beef and dairy production there, subtracted from fodder stocks available to dairy producers in other countries. A similar phenomenon was seen after Pres. George W. Bush made biofuel part of national policy. This led to a doubling of prices for maize and other cereals, in a spiral of price inflation that challenged dairy farm families as well as consumers.

Another plateau in world production is discernible in the years 1966-71. This period is that of the 1968 Indian famine, and also a time of milk rationing in Indian cities, but the graph of Asian milk production shows little drop - probably because overall Asian production was still at a low base. Although the drop in aggregate world milk production around 1968 appears attributable more to a slump in North & Central American output

Chart 5.1. World Milk Production & Population 1961-1990

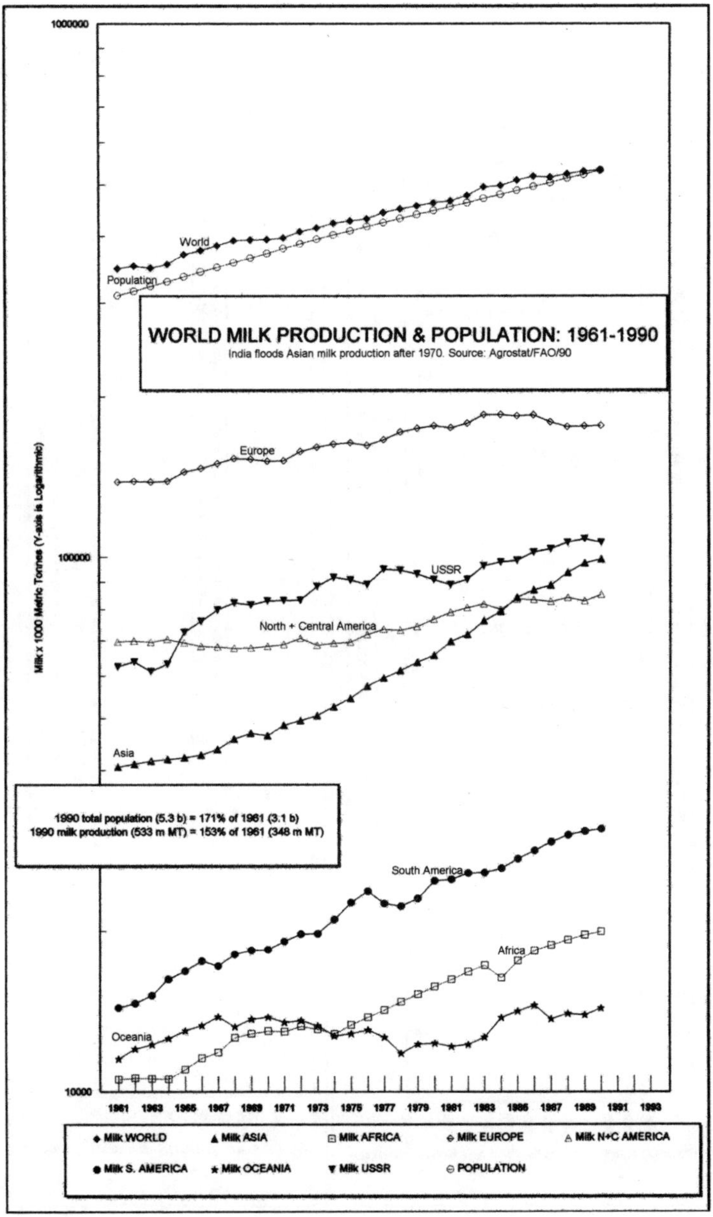

Chart 5.2. Imports Selected Third World Milk ex. Butter 1961-89

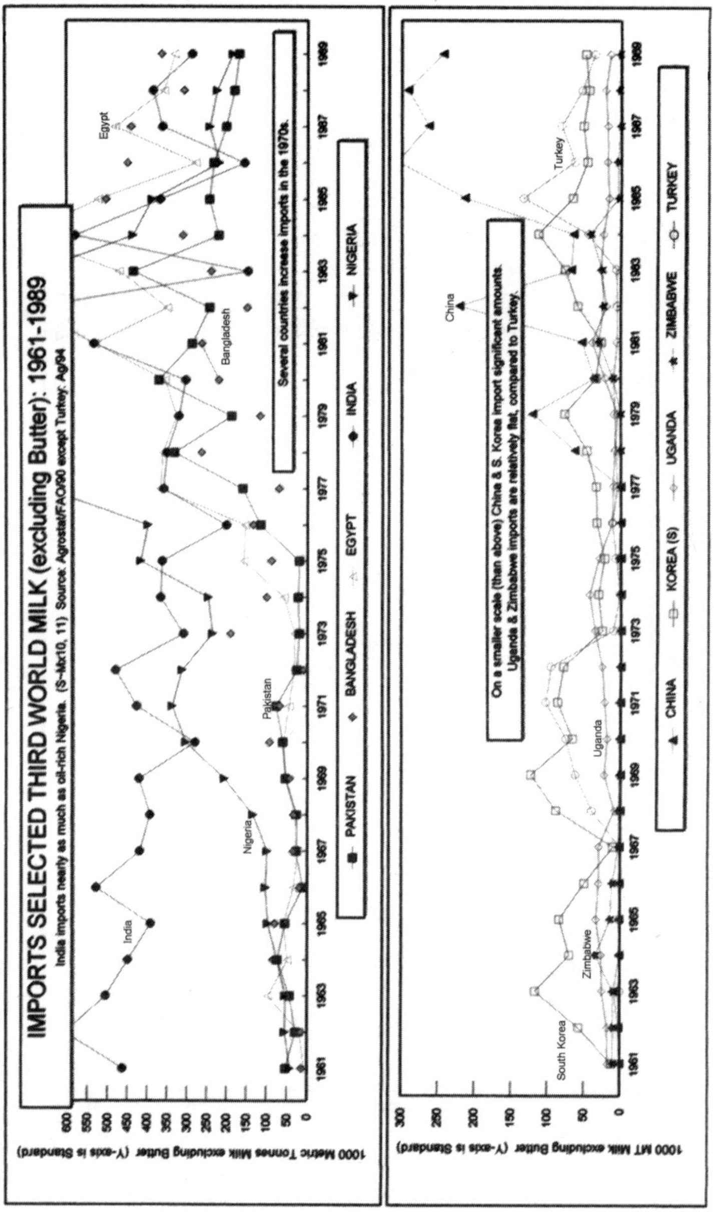

Chart 5.3. Imports World Milk (ex. Butter) 1961-89

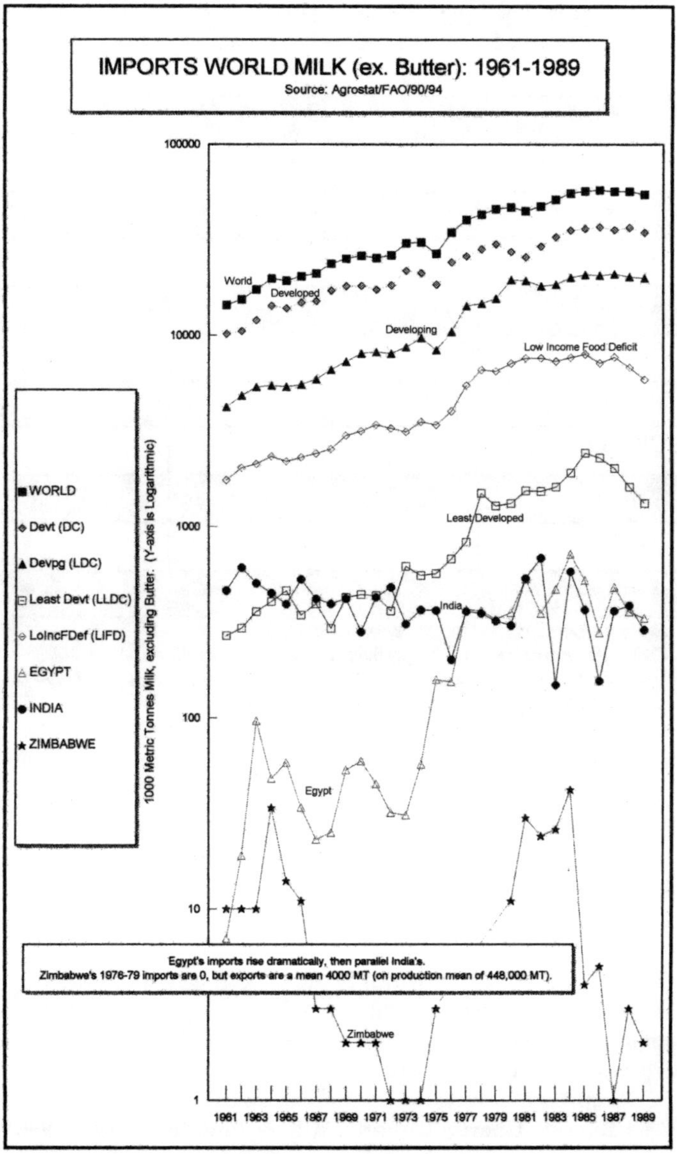

Table 5.1.

FAO MILK PRODUCTION (million tons) est. forecast[i]			
	1996	**1997**	**1998**
WORLD	539	547	555
EU/EC/EEC	125	125	125
USA	70	71	71
India	68	71	74/actually 70.8
Russia	36	34	33
Pakistan	20	21	22
Brazil	19	21	22
Ukraine	16	15	14
Poland	11	12	12
NZ	10	11	12
Australia	9	9	10

Source: FAO *Dairy Outlook Report* (June 1998)
(N.B.: Argentina's total milk production was ca. 6.80 million MT in 1993; Uruguay's was ca. 1.17 million MT in 1993. *Source: Agrostat/FAO/1994*)

[i] FAO (June 1998) *Dairy Outlook Report*. N.B. Agrostat/FAO/94 estimated 1993 520.955 million MT.

than in India, these charts show that as Indian production becomes an ever greater portion of world production, it has a progressively greater effect on overall world performance. Thus, India's drought of 1987-88 correlates with a dramatic dip in world milk production.

However, it must be noted that this dip in world output was also a result of policies in rich countries, which reduced both dairy production and the numbers of farmers engaged in it. The effects of policies including long-term milk quotas imposed in 1984 in Europe (*aka* EEC, EU), as well as the US herd-buyout of 1986 (in which thousands of cows were sent to China), and the cheap food policies of the Reagan and first Bush administrations, are traced above in **Chart 5.1. World Milk & Population 1961-1990**[32], and in the upper of two horizontally-grouped charts labelled **Chart 5.2. Imports Selected Third World Milk (excluding butter)**[33] **1961-1989.**

Third World countries including Pakistan, Bangladesh, Egypt and especially Nigeria increased milk excluding butter imports, mostly skimmed milk powder (SMP), during the 1970s. This was probably due to a variety of factors including oil price rises after the 1973-74 OPEC boycott, which enabled petroleum producers such as Nigeria to import more SMP, and saw OPEC countries make massive 'petro-dollar' loans to other developing countries whose deteriorating foreign reserves also increased their need for dairy aid, at a time when Europe's Butter Mountain was on the rise. The surge and eventual fall in India's dairy commodity imports is traced in **Chart 5.3. Imports World Milk (ex. Butter) 1961-89.** According to INTERFAIS[34], Asia Including India) was the top food aid recipient in the 1970s, but Africa, including Egypt and other North African countries, took that position in the 1980s, to be followed by Sub-Saharan Africa in the 1990s - except temporarily for the ex-USSR countries.

So, for a variety of reasons, OF officials were concertedly trying to stop importation of foreign dairy commodities by the late 1980s, but a temporary resumption of imports was advisable because of the 1987-88 drought.[35] As Egyptian imports also rose steeply around 1988, it is likely that a burgeoning surplus in the USA (the 1986 herd buy-out[36] effectively managed the US surplus for only 2-3 years) and still-untamed production in the EEC led to concessionary sales of milk powder, etc.[37] On the bottom chart with its lower scale, the import curves of China (nearly 300 thousand tonnes in 1988, from zero in 1977) lend credence to this analysis: as India began to refuse further dairy commodity imports, the USA and EEC sought new markets/recipients in surplus years.

Interestingly, 1987 coincides with a slackening of imports by Bangladesh, and a stabilisation of milk (ex. butter) imports by Nigeria following a sky-rocketing of Nigerian milk imports 1976-84. One possible explanation for this is that an American trade and foreign policy initiative prioritised opening China (following President Richard Nixon's 1970s visit) to US dairy exports over supply of concessionary sales or aid to countries such as Bangladesh, Pakistan or Turkey. Meanwhile, for geopolitical and other reasons, after President Jimmy Carter brokered a peace treaty between Israel and Egypt in 1979, Egypt continued to be a prime recipient of US dairy aid.

In the early-1990s John Empson[38] predicted India would be the world's number two–dairy producer (behind the ex-USSR countries) within a few years - a prediction that was easily met (**Table 5.1**). By the mid-1990s, India (68 million MT in 1996, by some estimates) had passed the fragmented ex-USSR (thence called Newly Independent States (NIS); later Commonwealth of Independent States (CIS)) and was already vying with the USA for number one status. The mature US milk market was essentially flat at 70-71 million metric tonnes (MT), although consumption rises of about 1 per cent were propelled by the late-1990s economic boom. As the New York stock market broke records in early-1999, many US families could afford meals in pizzerias and other restaurants where cheese was a prime ingredient - often followed by ice cream and cappuccino containing more dairy products. The FAO[39] reported the situation among CIS countries in 1998-99 was the obverse. Milk production on former collective farms in the two major milk producing countries, the Russian Federation and the Ukraine, had been unprofitable since about 1990.

A huge flow of dairy aid to Eastern Europe and ex-USSR countries began with the fall of the Berlin Wall in 1989 (moderating briefly in 1991) catapulting these ex-communist countries past Sub-Saharan Africa in the ranks of recipients. INTERFAIS[40] recorded the Russian Federation as the world's top food aid recipient with 46 per cent of deliveries in the region and 18 per cent of the global total in 1993 and, as is customary in relief situations, dairy aid composed an unusually high percentage of aid. After its 1993 peak of 'the exceptionally high level of 17.2 kg. per capita in 1993', INTERFAIS[41] notes that deliveries to ex-USSR countries decreased to 8.7 kg. per capita in 1994, and 6.1 kg. per capita in 1995. (Poor countries were 'hard hit' notes INTERFAIS[42]: Low-Income-Food-Deficit-Countries (LIFDCs) received just 2.1 kg. per capita in 1995.) Food aid from the West likely displaced some production in the Russian Federation and Ukraine, where unprofitable cattle were slaughtered to meet demand for beef. The prospect of production increases in Belarus and Uzbekistan, however, hints at a reversal of the overall decline in the ex-USSR/CIS dairy picture around the year 2000. Altogether, due to declines in the ex-USSR and relative stasis in the US market - but largely due to heroic advances in Indian dairying - World production curves amplify the satisfied belches of Indian dairying more loudly today than they did in 1970.

Continents: Milk Production Charts 1961-70-80-90

Chart 5.4. Continents Milk Production: 1961-70-80-90 shows in pie charts below that production stabilised in the mature milk markets of Europe, North & Central America, and ex-USSR/Russia compared to Asia (including India) as a whole, and Africa. Africa has much more scope for milk consumption and production than seen presently due to the lost decades of the 1980-90s, when drought, lack of investment and debt depressed development - not to mention economic collapse in Zimbabwe where, in 2009, political power-sharing perhaps presages improvements. South America, whose economic performance rose after desultory output in the 1970-80s, may, partly because of cultural predispositions toward milk, continue to grow in a pattern similar to that of the USA.

Brazilian milk production rose 40 per cent from ca. 14.5 million MT in 1990 (15.06m MT was estimated earlier by Agrostat/FAO/1994) to 20.5 million tonnes in 1997, booming on the economy which increased consumer demand. However, a fall in consumer demand, a rise in subsidised imports from the EU and duty-free access for milk powder and cheese from MERCOSUR countries, mainly Argentina and Uruguay in late 1997, led to problems and 'producers' milk prices dropped abruptly' according to the FAO.[43] (Note: Argentina's total milk production was ca. 6.80 million MT in 1993, and Uruguay's was ca. 1.17 million MT in 1993 (*Source: Agrostat/FAO/1994*) As in countries including Thailand, and India before Operation Flood, concerns have been raised about adulteration in Brazil's informal sector, although one observer states that simply because milk is sold in the informal sector does not necessarily mean it has not been pasteurised; nevertheless many consumers boil purchased milk to ensure hygiene. In 1999 it was reported that Thailand was attempting to regulate the market by selling inexpensive licenses to shops.

However, quibbles over sanitation were less worrying than the fall of the Brazilian real and general economic crash of early-1999. The real was almost the penultimate currency to weaken in a worldwide economic malaise which originated in Thailand in 1997, spread to Malaysia and Indonesia in 1998 - thereafter having a domino effect in Russia. Fortunately, by April, 1999 (as NATO bombed Serb targets in Yugoslavia) a recurrence of the 1929-39 world Depression was forestalled, partly owing to increased IMF aid, democratisation in Indonesia and finally, after a decade of slow restructuring in Japan, the prospect of 1 per cent GDP growth in that country which, like the USA, acts as an 'importer of last resort' and lender to countries in recession such as Thailand.[44]

Although much of its economy was managed according to the Washington consensus, Argentina's dairy sector was severely impacted by the Brazilian devaluation (75 per cent of dairy exports went to Brazil. Powder export prices to Brazil fell from US $1900 to $1500 a tonne.) Farmgate prices fell from ca. $0.20 litre in 1998 to just $0.13-$0.16 litre, i.e. below production costs, at a time when hot weather in the Santa Fe region cut maize and other fodder growth. In 1999, Argentina's dairy exports suddenly became 10-15 per cent more costly than those of Australia and New Zealand - fellow CAIRNS countries which, despite their rivalry on dairy markets, shared the demand that the EU and USA relinquish all their dairy export subsidies, tariffs and other protections in the WTO.

Meanwhile, in Peru, an LIFD country with few pretensions to dairy exports, farmers honoured a principle of Operation Flood's Anand Pattern, i.e. that milk production is as much a factor of fodder as breeding: Peru[45] imported heifers chiefly from countries with pasture-based systems, e.g.

Argentina, Uruguay, Chile and New Zealand, rather than its former supplier, the USA, where most heifers are bred for intensive farming.

The importance of Argentina[46] and Uruguay as exporters onto world dairy markets could increase further if the Doha round of WTO talks, which were halted at Cancun in 2003, eventually succeeds in removing vestigial import tariffs, production subsidies and (especially) export subsidies on cheese and other dairy products which European and other countries continued to exploit, even after the 1994 URAA. As recently as spring 2009, the EU reinstated dairy export subsidies – embarrassing backsliding by an economic supranational organisation with far more resources than the developing countries which suffer from dumping.

According to the Dairy Farmers of Canada, whose quota system has been challenged by the USA and New Zealand, Canada is a minor exporter to the world market, while the EU is the main exporter and much EU trade has relied on export subsidies - a target of GATT/WTO.

As the population of China develops a taste for dairy ice cream, yoghurt or (less likely, given Chinese cultural familiarity with soya products, and the lactose-intolerance of many children and adults) liquid milk, Asian figures for consumption could dwarf those of other continents. Although it can be assumed that, especially since World War II, the USA has had much influence on the diets and consumption habits of people on the island groups of Oceania[47] such as Samoa and Vanuatu, Agrostat's inclusion of strong dairy producers and exporters Australia and New Zealand in the continental group Oceania makes it difficult to discern the discrete effects of US marketing for the years 1961-90. However, dairy marketeers in the USA and elsewhere have designs on untapped parts of Asian. Their tactics are not limited to advertising, concessionary sales or food aid. Science may also come to the fore, with the development of low-lactose milk products agreeable to Asian palates.

Although India is seen as a milk-loving land and Japan is stereotyped as lactic-averse, the FAO estimated in 1998 that Indian per capita milk consumption was 'still a relatively modest 65 kg. of milk equivalent per year, less than that of, for example, Japan.' In 1997, according to a Japanese contributor to the FAO's Email Dairy-Outlook-Link[48], there were over 616 items of canned coffee on the market from 121 manufacturers, most containing milk or milk products (SMP, WMP or whey powder) - 70 per cent of them available from street vending machines. Where there is milk there will be markets.

Be that as it may, the big question for North American dairists is whether high-technology and firm world market prices can maintain their status as big exporters to (mostly) Asia and North Africa.

While the USA exploits any niche markets abroad to remedy its negative trade balance, its dairy exports constitute only about 1 per cent of total production - a lower percentage than those of Australia and New Zealand. Australia and New Zealand, like Argentina[49], Uruguay and other potentially major dairy exporters are counting on WTO negotiations to cut remaining US and EU dairy export subsidies. Argentina, particularly, sees US and EU subsidies as thorns in the side of its natural comparative advantage in farm trade.

The EU, Canada, Japan, Norway and Switzerland restrict milk output. The question for the EU is whether if, as agreed in 2007, milk quotas will actually end in 2015. Like Mark Twain's death, the demise of quotas has often been exaggerated.

The question is also pertinent to Canada whose milk quota has been challenged by the USA under the NAFTA trade agreement. The USA and New Zealand won agreement from a WTO panel in March, 1999 that Canada's classified pricing system violates rules on export subsidies, but the findings do not impact domestic milk supply management *aka* quotas. Canada appealed.[50]

Pie charts on **Chart 5.4. Continents Milk 1961, 1970, 1980 and 1990** show that after stasis of 11.7 per cent to 11.8 per cent shares of world production in the years 1961 and 1970, Asian world production share rose rapidly to 14.2 per cent in 1980, and 18.6 per cent in 1990.

(Note: Accompanying the pie slices are figures of gross world milk production, rising from 348m MT in 1961 to 533m MT in 1990.) Recall that the charts labelled World Milk & Population 1961-1990 traced Asian milk production - whose curve assumed a permanently positive slope after the advent of Operation Flood in 1970.

Rich/Poor (DC/LDC) Milk Production Charts

The group-of-four pie charts labelled **Chart 5.5. DC/LDC Milk 1961, 1970, 1980, 1990** tell us nothing about per capita intake, i.e. consumption, but they do reflect significant growth of dairying among Less Developed Countries.

Production figures next to pie slices show that LDC production rose little from 1961 (65m MT) to 1970 (77m MT), but climbed much faster thereafter. Coinciding with the main thrust of Operation Flood, LDC milk production reached impressive levels in 1990 (148m MT).

Between 1961 and 1990, LDC production more than doubled as LDC world milk production share rose from 18.6 per cent to 27.8 per cent. Due to Indian growth Asia now produces about one-third of world production - a stunning rise from less than one-fifth in 1961.

Continents, Countries & Econ. Groups: Milk (ex. B.) Intake Charts

If food production doubles in a period when population triples, there is a loss in availability. More indicative of food security are data on per capita intake (*aka* consumption), though it must not be forgotten that aggregate food supplies do not guarantee 'entitlements', in Amartya Sen's word, for all groups. That said, per capita intake is one indicator of food security.

Chart 5.6. World Milk (ex. Butter) Intake 1961-89 notes average Asian intake of milk (excluding Butter, in Agrostat/FAO terminology) starting at a very low level compared to all other 'continents' groups in the Agrostat grouping, but climbing steadily. The Asia intake curve nears Africa's about 1990.

Chart 5.7. Selected LDC, LLDC, LIFD Milk (ex. Butter) Intake: 1961-89 reveals more about per capita intake because it disaggregates relatively rich Asian countries such as Korea from less economically developed ones such as Bangladesh. Although the idea can not be proven from this chart, an expectation of a positive relationship between income level and milk (ex. butter) intake is apparent. As incomes rise, the assumed cultural indifference of some Asian countries to liquid milk may be bypassed by greater availability and marketing of products like pizza.

Besides showing intake trends of selected sub-groups of poor countries, **Chart 5.7. Selected LDC, LLDC, LIFD Milk (ex. But.) Intake 1961-89** shows intake trends of Bangladesh, Egypt, Pakistan, Zimbabwe and South Korea - in relation to India and the World as a whole. After a flat period in the 1960s, milk (ex. butter) intake rose noticeably. This has implications for future commodity flows, particularly cereals, which are used in concentrated inputs in dairy fodder. As the caption notes, milk (ex. butter) intake rose dramatically in Pakistan and South Korea (ROK).

Trade embargo, as the Rhodesian regime held out against sanctions and civil war (1969-81) and regional drought (ca. 1982-late-1980s) remain evident in Zimbabwe. Zimbabwe's milk (ex. butter) intake curves are roughly paralleled by (though lower than) Low-Income-Food-Deficit (LIFD) countries. About 1962-65, Zimbabwe had close to the average of about 27kg. annual per capita intake of LIFD countries, but then fell, likely owing to political and climatic difficulties. Agrostat shows Turkish intake was double average world levels, higher than developed countries (DCs) but fell thereafter except for 1979-81. Still, Turkish intake including yoghurt is higher than in Pakistan or India.

Health conscious Western consumers have boosted yoghurt sales - but although milk intake is rising fast in India, French attempts to market yoghurt there have fallen flat (personal communications from New Delhi). Dahi, a traditional, low-cost product made by souring boiled milk with lactic bacterial culture, remains the staple.

Continents, Countries & Econ. Groups: Butter & Ghee Intake Charts

Butter and ghee are favoured forms of milk fat turned into products storable without refrigeration. Butter, made by churning cream of ca. 32 per cent fat, is the dairy spread most used in Western countries and the ex-USSR. Ghee, clarified butterfat similar to butter oil, with almost 100 per cent moisture and solids-not-fat removed, is favoured in India, although Dairy India Yearbook editor/publisher P.R. Gupta [51] noted: 'Butter & Ghee are luxury foods consumed by a very small percentage of population in the Indian subcontinent. The Number One dairy product is liquid milk, largely as a whitener for their morning cup of tea or coffee.'

Gupta's point taken, this book uses 'Milk ex. Butter' and 'Butter & Ghee' in its charts, graphs and maps because: (1) Agrostat/FAO disaggregates dairy trade and aid primarily into these two categories. (2) Most EEC dairy commodity aid recombined as liquid milk & other products in India was whole or skimmed milk powder (WMP/SMP) & butter oil (BO). (3) Simply because ghee *has* long been a luxury to most Indians, any consumption rise (that is unconnected to dairy aid) is a proxy for production increases.

Chart 5.8. Selected DC, LDC, LIFD Butter & Ghee Intake: 1961-92 shows a dramatic drop (often 40 per cent) in butter & ghee intake in rich, more economically developed countries. These data correlate well with **Map 5.1** and also **Map 5.2. Butter & Ghee kilograms per capita Intake**. Butterfat in cheeseburgers, pizzas, 'yuppie cheese' and ice cream has displaced much 'table butter' in the USA and other rich countries since 1961. As Ben Fine *et al.*[52] demonstrate, the existence in a food system of a commodity, whether fat or sugar, guarantees it will be consumed in one form or another - no matter what diets are trendy.

Meanwhile, as Westerners fooled themselves that they were adopting low-fat diets, intake of butter & ghee generally rose in poorer countries, 1961-1992, although not as fast as milk (ex. butter).

As ghee is expensive for many Indans, the 20 per cent rise in intake of butter & ghee, from 1.0 kg. per capita in 1961, to 1.2 kg. per capita in 1991 and 1992, is significant in **Chart 5.8.** The rise is more impressive after intake plunged to just 0.7 kg. per capita in 1973 and 1974. India surpassed average world intake of butter & ghee in 1990 and approached Egyptian levels. Except for 1973 and 1981, India's butter & ghee intake seems to parallel the loftier curve of Pakistan (which once enjoyed a superior national milch herd and fodder growth). The rise in India's butter & ghee intake since 1973-74 contrasts the slowly rising intake of Low-Income-Food-Deficit (LIFD) countries, and the declining butter & ghee intake of Least-Developed Countries (LLDC) and Bangladesh. The fastest rising intake shown on **Chart 5.9** is that of South Korea, which rose from zero in 1970 to near-Indian levels in 1991, and surpassed world levels in 1991.

Chart 5.4. Continents Milk 1961, 1970, 1980, 1990 (4-pies/stats)

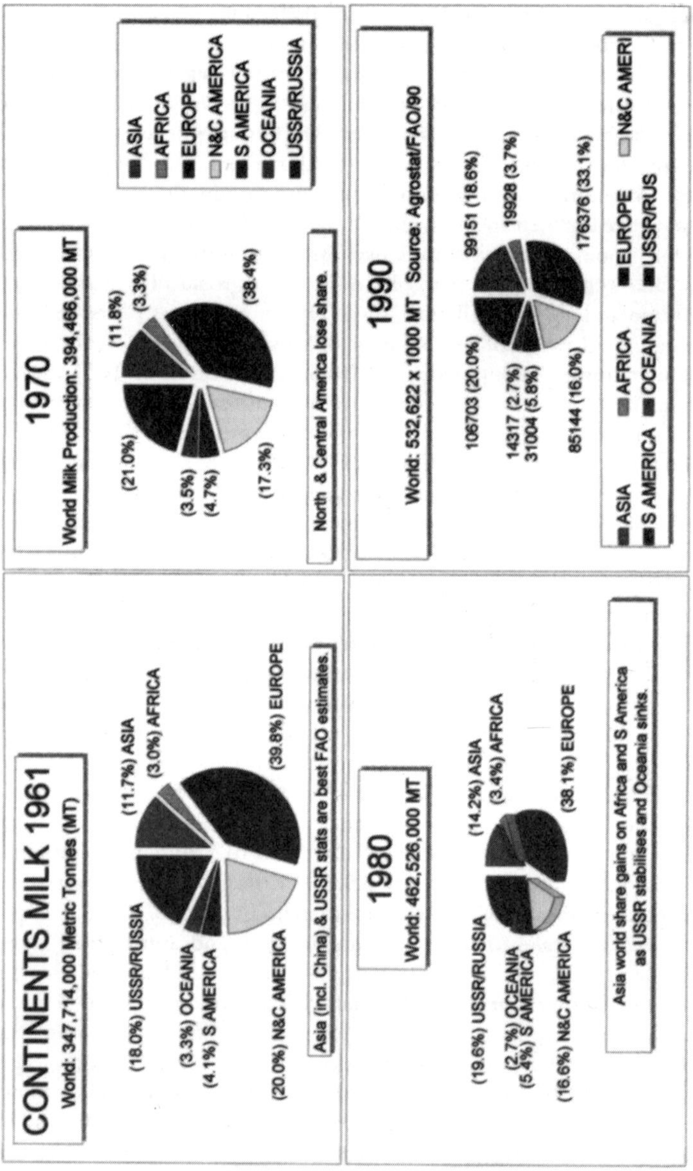

Chart 5.5. DC/LDC Milk 1961, 1970, 1980, 1990 (pies/stats)

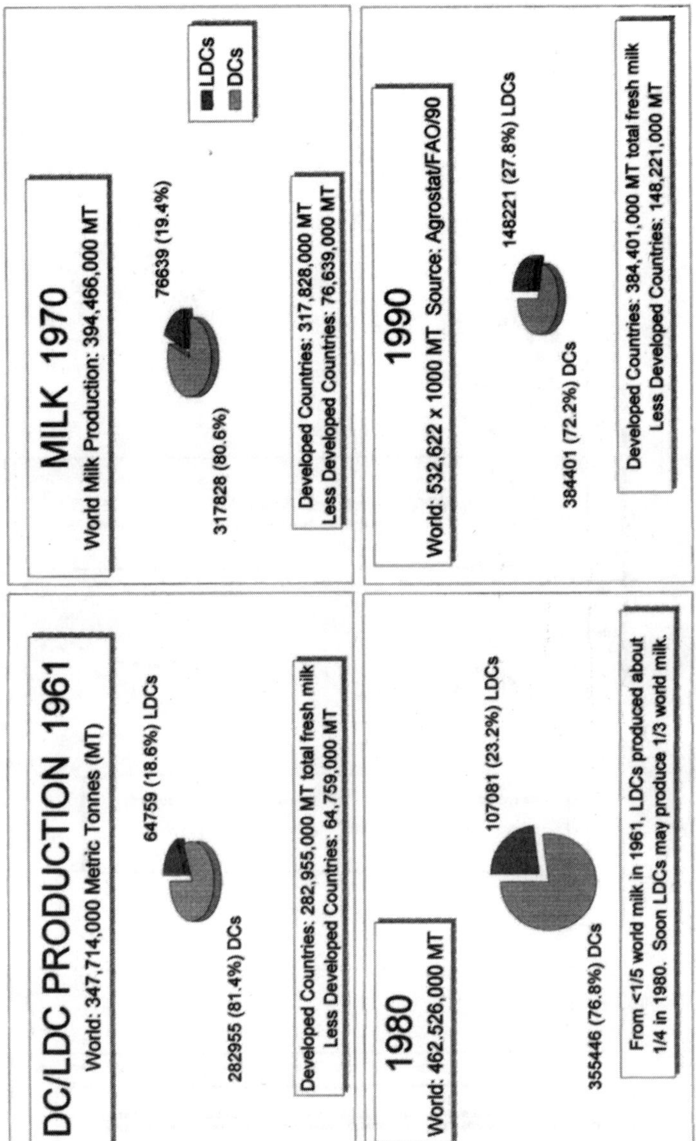

Chart 5.6. World Milk (ex. But.) Intake 1961-89 (cont/stats)

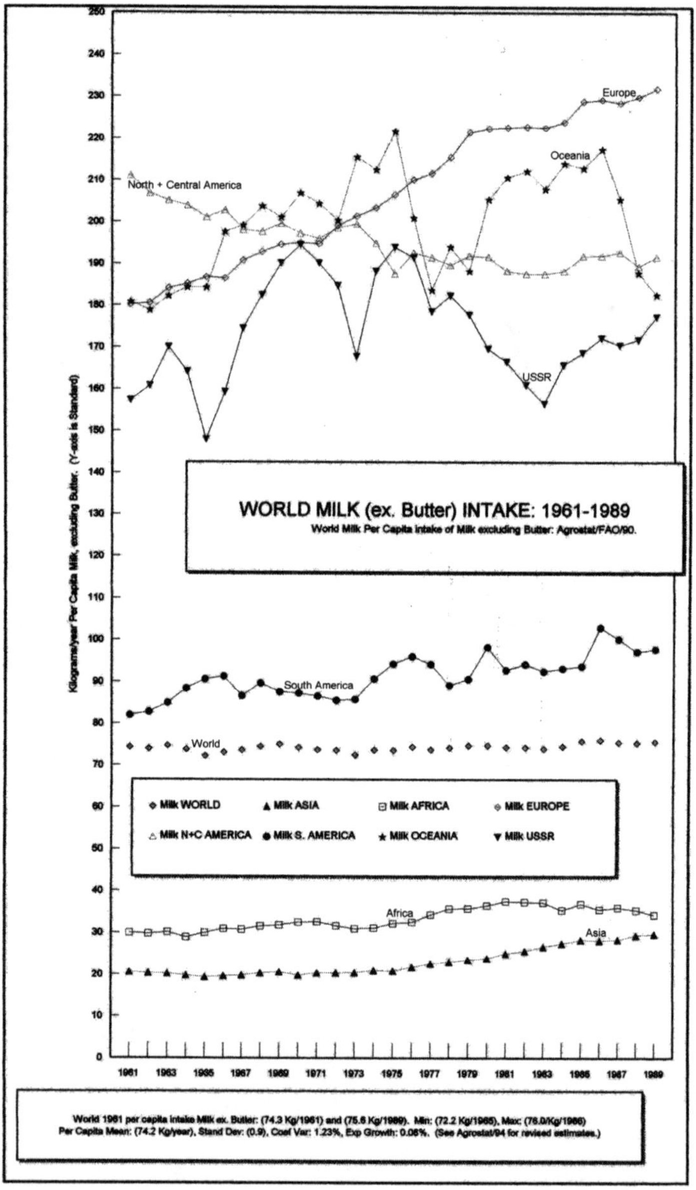

Chart 5.7. Select LDC, LLDC, LIFD Milk (ex. But.) Intake 1961-89

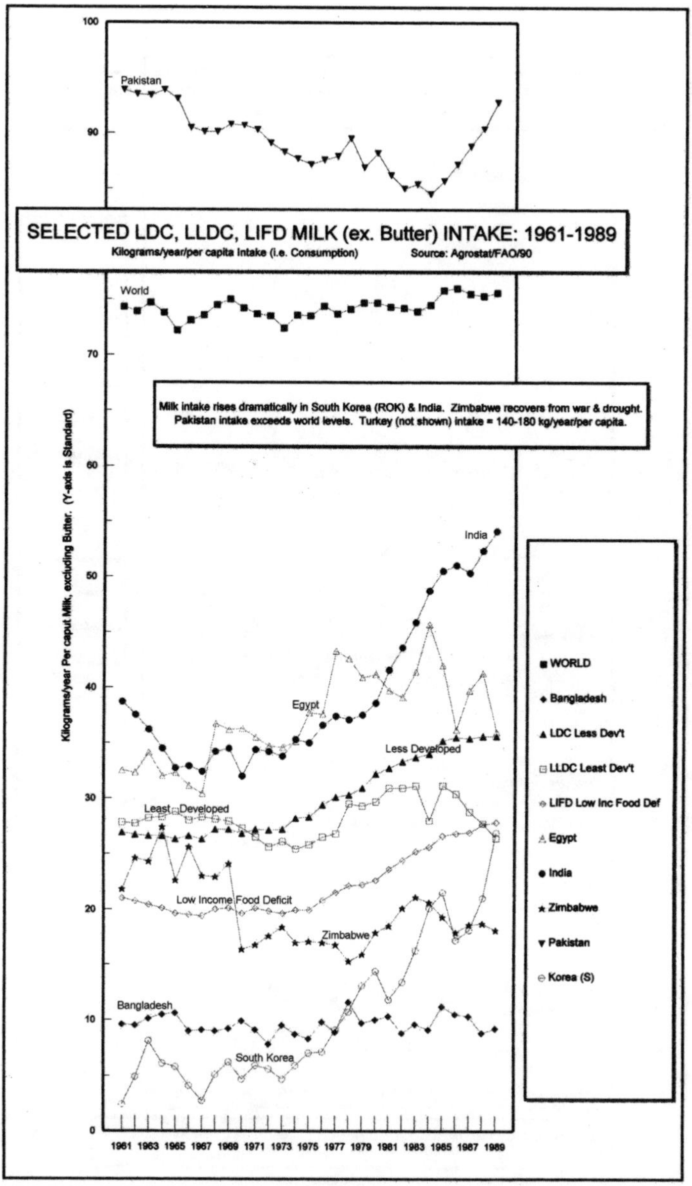

Chart 5.8. Select DC, LDC, LIFD, Butter & Ghee Intake 1961-89

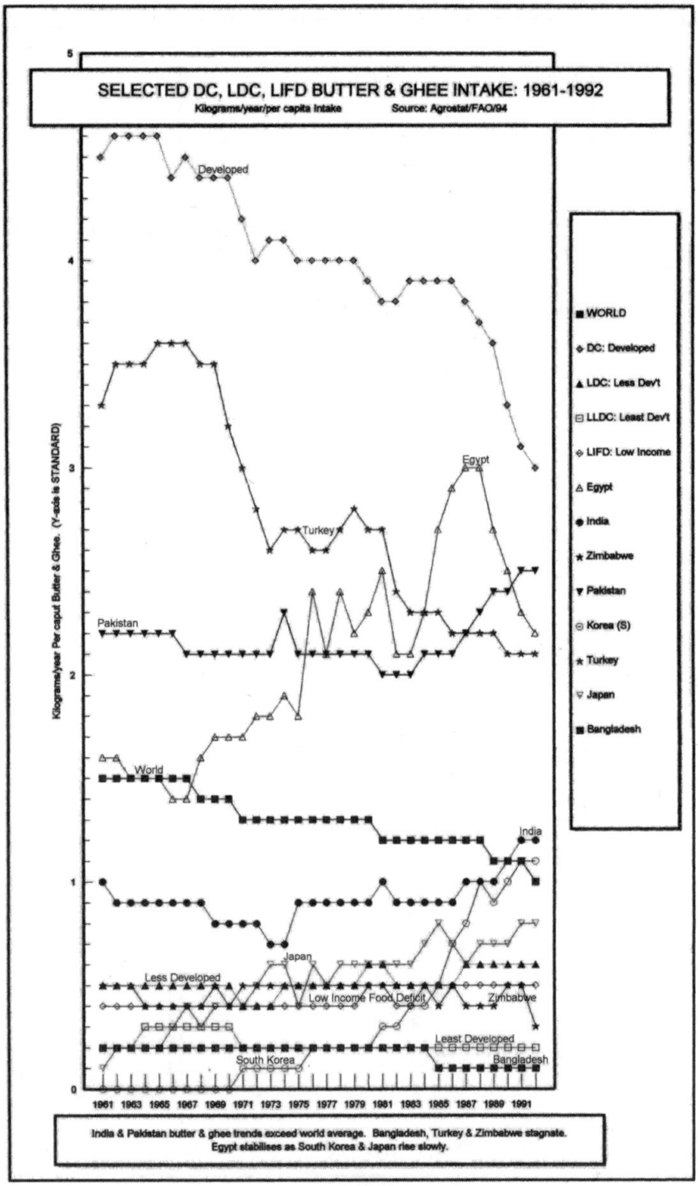

Maps

Butter & Ghee per capita Consumption exp. gr. 1961-92 map

The maps below highlight India's dairy success since the rationing of the 1960s, while data on many world countries can along with companion maps on milk ex. butter, stimulate study. Growth of intake is shown below in **Map 5.1. Butter & Ghee per capita Consumption exponential growth 1961-92.** Despite a consumption slump in 1973-74, India managed 0.7 per cent growth. While a rise under 1 per cent might seem modest, it represents a considerable achievement in that production outpaced rapid population growth. India's consumption in this period stands in contrast to Bangladesh (-2.4 per cent exponential drop) which experienced difficulties after separation from Pakistan.

India's progress also compares well to Zimbabwe whose exponential drop in per capita consumption (-0.2 per cent) of butter & ghee was almost as dire as that of Bangladesh. Zimbabwe's consumption improved after the settlement of the civil war in the early 1980s, and the establishment of dairy development programmes, which Shanti George[53] praised for greater sensitivity to local conditions than Operation Flood, which sought to replicate the Anand model throughout India. Unfortunately, political turmoil and unsuccessful land reform have troubled Zimbabwe's dairy sector since the turn of the century.

Pakistan's exponential growth 1961-92 was just 0.2 per cent, but is worth noting because it began at a higher base and remained above Indian levels of intake of butter & ghee - actually exceeding US levels. The same could be said of Turkey, which began in 1961 with high levels (3.3 kg. per capita) of butter & ghee intake, but later saw negative consumption of -1.9 per cent, eventually plateauing at 2.2 kg. per capita in 1990-92, below Egypt (2.2 kg. per capita). Egypt, which began with butter & ghee per capita consumption, of 1.6 kg. in 1961 - barely above the world average (though 50 per cent above India's intake - experienced 2.2 per cent exponential growth. This was likely due to petrodollar loans in the mid-1970s, and US concessionary sales under PL 480 after the peace settlement with Israel in the late-1970s. It is worth noting that, unlike consumption of butter & ghee in Egypt, almost all of India's consumption is produced domestically.

Map 5.2. Butter & Ghee kilograms per capita Intake for 1961 and **Map 5.3** for **1992** below, focusing on India's performance relative to comparable developing countries, are below. Interesting patterns can be discerned, e.g. the rise of dairy consumption in the Pacific Rim, initially owing to a combination of exports from Australia, New Zealand and the USA. It would be fascinating to delineate what other forms (e.g. cheese, ice cream, yoghurt, etc.) dairy fat consumption took in Western countries as butter consumption fell, but here our focus is on India. Because ghee has always been one of the most valued items in India's diet, **Map 5.2** and **5.3** are strong evidence that Indian dairy development (not imports) was responsible for long-term improvements in its food security in the White Revolution. Of course these aggregate figures for per capita intake tell little about distribution, i.e. consumption rates for landless and marginal groups in the hinterlands, or the poorest urban dwellers. But higher per capita rates of intake (1.2 kg. per person in 1992 compared to just 1.0 kg. in 1961) increase the likelihood that entitlements improved for all socio-economic groups.

Again, India's performance is contrasted by negative figures for comparators. Consumption of butter & ghee in Turkey fell one-third.

In Zimbabwe - suffering first trade embargo when as Rhodesia it left the British Commonwealth in 1965, and then civil war - consumption fell about 40 per cent to the low level of 0.3 kg. per capita butter & ghee intake.

Even more disturbing is the fall in butter & ghee consumption in Bangladesh, from 0.19 kg. in 1961 to half that, or 0.1 kg. in 1992. Fortunately for Bangladesh, food security for its rapidly growing population improved as rice production in its Green Revolution neared self-sufficiency, although Shaw & Clay noted 'low levels of food intake in the poorest 60 per cent of the population.'[54]

Map 5.2. Milk ex. Butter kgs. pc Intake 1961 and **Map 5.3** for **1989** above also reflect continuing high levels of of butter & ghee intake in Pakistan, whose good fodder base and high domestic production were augmented by food aid from the USA after the invasion of Afghanistan by the USSR in 1979.[55]

Egypt's per capita intake of butter & ghee jumped from 1.6 kg. in 1961 to 2.2 kg. in 1992. Egypt availed itself of a higher level of imports of milk excluding butter during this period, and the Agrostat/FAO database shows that Egypt received dairy aid including SMP, BO and other dairy products from the USA and the EEC (*aka* EC/EU) through 1992.

A historic shift is shown by China. Just as a journey of a thousand miles begins with one step, China's acceptance of dairy products including butter & ghee began with an intake rise from about zero in 1961 to 0.1 kilogram per person in 1992. Recently, China has developed dairying faster than any other country, joining the top 10 world producers with 35 million tonnes in 2007. After the close of the 2008 Olympics, dairy exports slumped when melamine adulteration was found, but the industry is expected to rebound.

Map 5.1. Butter & Ghee pc Cons. exp. gr. 1961-92

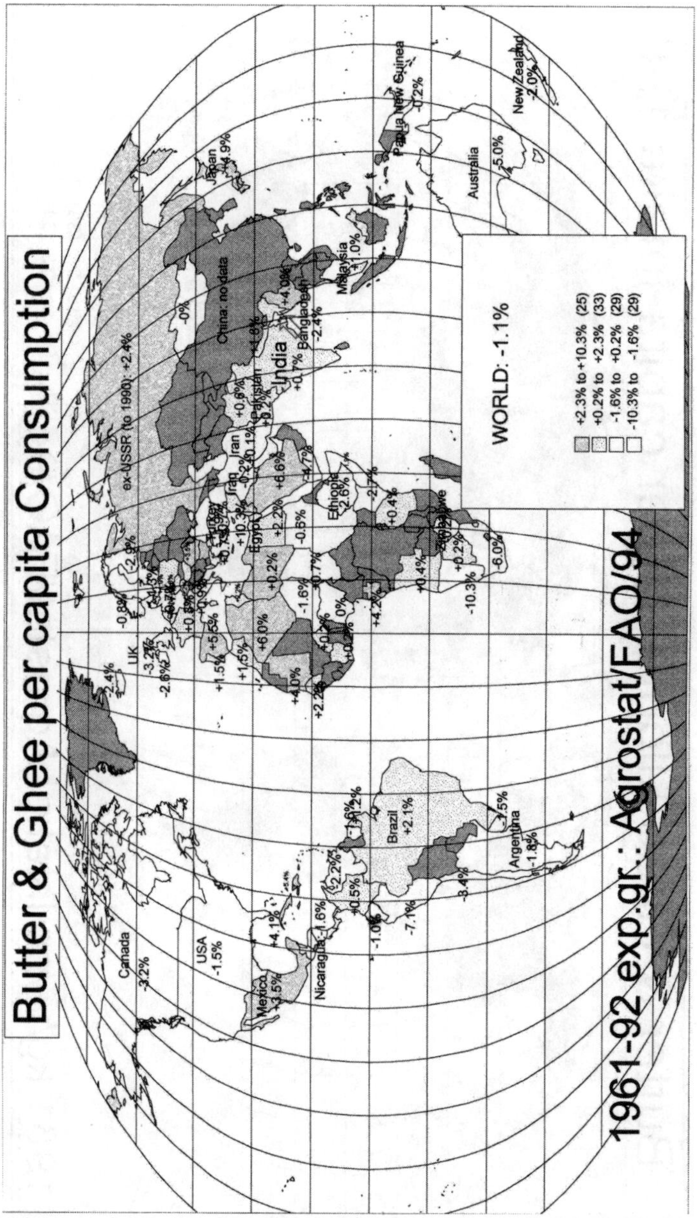

Map 5.2. Butter & Ghee kgs. pc Intake 1961

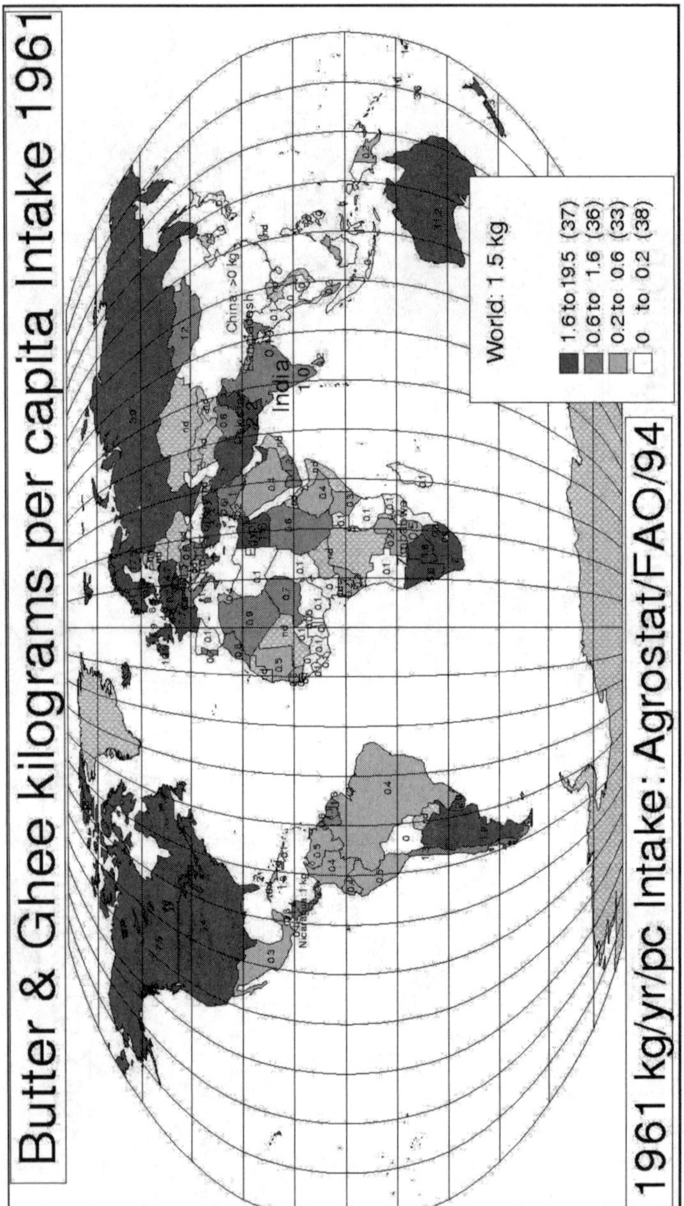

Map 5.3. Butter & Ghee kgs. pc Intake 1992 (India focus)

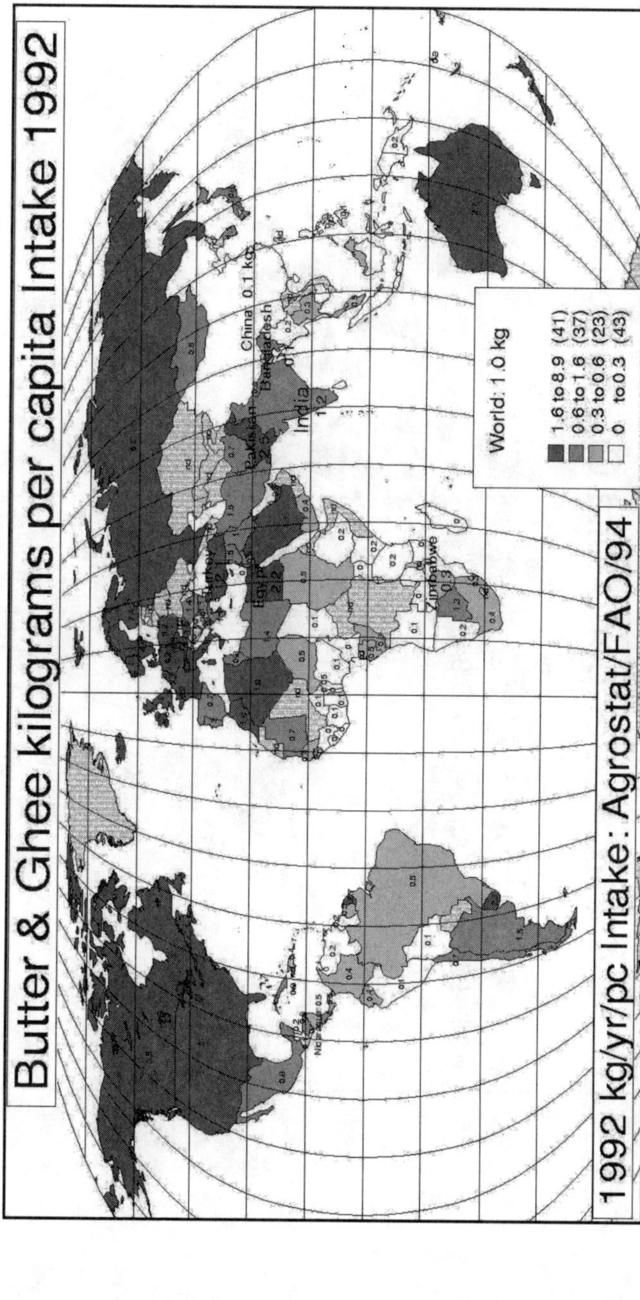

Map 5.4. Milk ex. Butter pc Cons. exp.gr. 1961-92

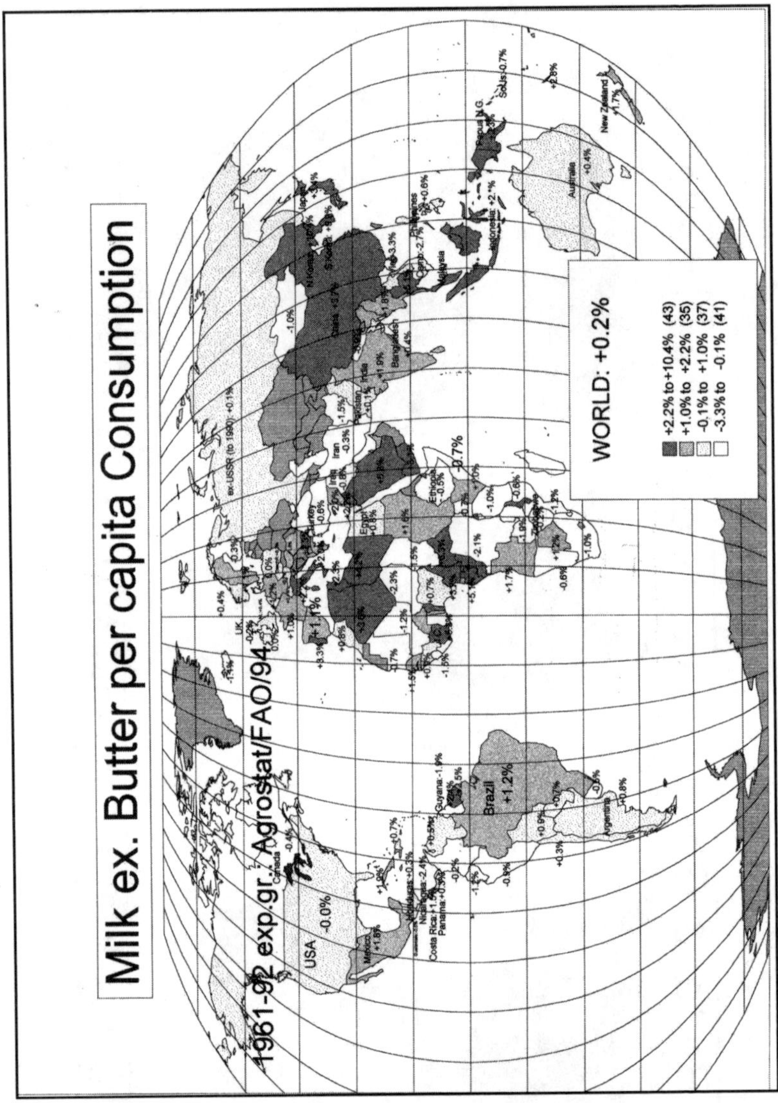

Map 5.5. Milk ex. Butter kgs. pc Intake 1961

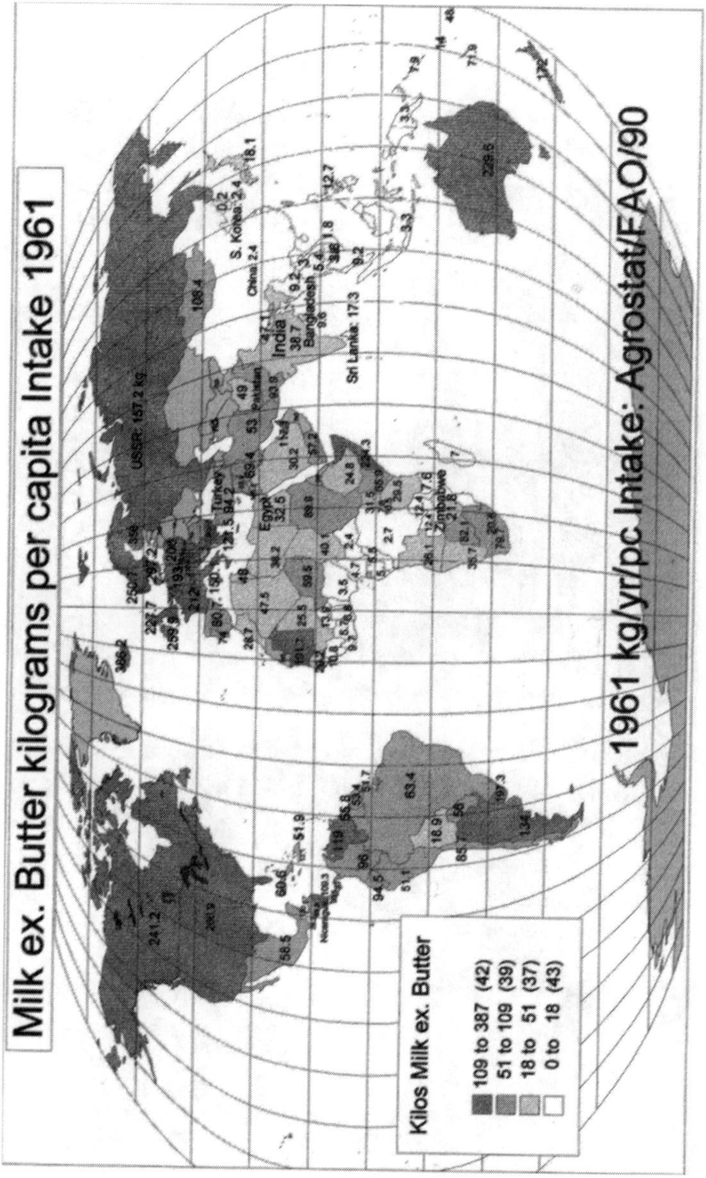

Map 5.6. Milk ex. Butter kgs. pc Intake 1989

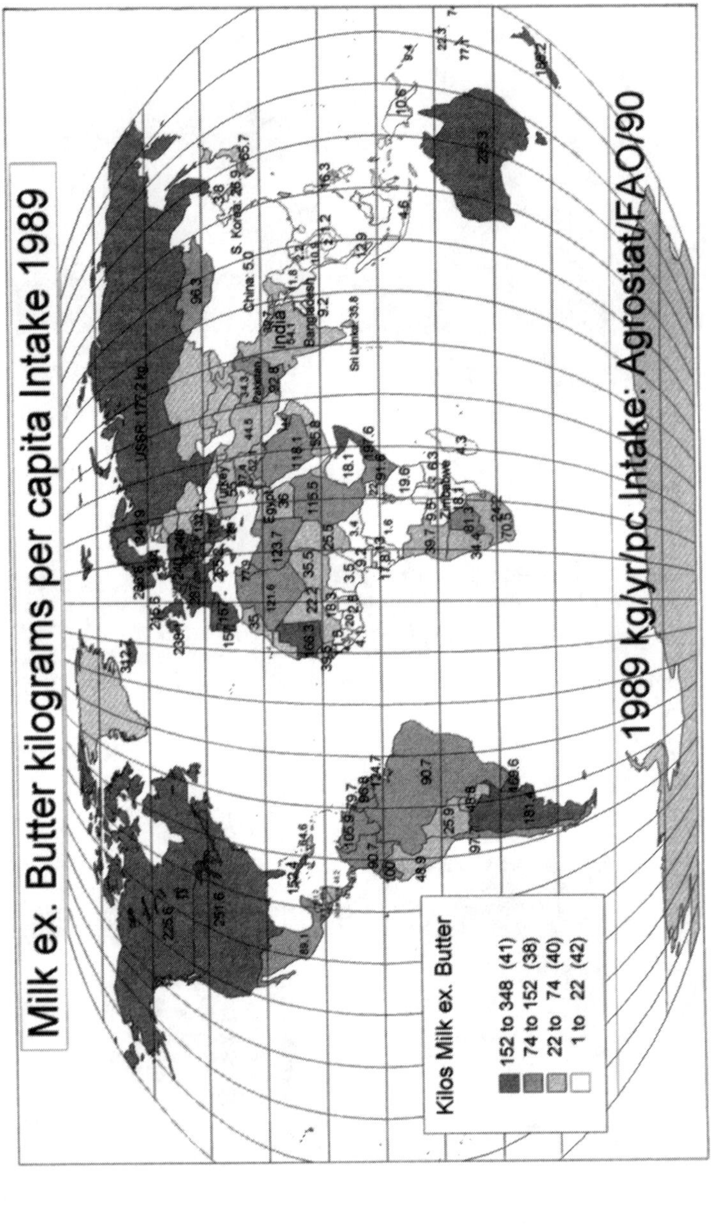

Milk ex. Butter per capita Consumption exp. gr. 1961-92 maps

Exponential growth of intake is shown above on **Map 5.4. Milk ex. Butter per capita Consumption exp.gr. 1961-92**. The world rate for consumption of milk ex. butter is positive (0.2 per cent) unlike that for butter & ghee, which was negative (-1.1 per cent). One reason for this is that health conscious consumers in the USA and other Western countries cut butter from their diets while continuing to favour milk in liquid low-fat (1-to-2 per cent) form. (Note: Finnish scientists report data suggesting heart disease is more due to bacteriological infection by *Chlamydia pneumoniae* in arteries rather than plaque build-up from butter.[56])

In our comparison group, India (1.9 per cent) again shows a high rate of per capita consumption growth next to Bangladesh (0.4 per cent), Egypt (0.8 per cent), Pakistan (0.1 per cent) and Zimbabwe (-0.2 per cent).[57]

Turkey (-0.6 per cent) is in the map's lowest quartile of shading, reflecting falling consumption.

Sri Lanka (1.9 per cent) shows identical growth to India in its rate of intake rise in **Map 5.4**. It should not be forgotten that India achieved a 20 per cent consumption rise as the population burgeoned by nearly 50 per cent: from 539 million in 1970 to 797 million in 1988.

Although China (3.7 per cent) and South Korea (9.9 per cent) started from a low consumption base, their high rate of exponential growth is a harbinger for increased trade flows. Because of the large populations in these emerging economies, hefty domestic or foreign supply increases will be needed to meet even a small change of taste in diets

Milk ex. Butter kilograms per capita Intake maps for 1961 & 1989

Map 5.5 and **Map 5.6**, based on the 1990 version of Agrostat, testify to progress in Indian food security from 1961 to 1989. India's consumption of milk excluding butter shines relative to our comparison group. While Pakistan records a slight drop in its high level of per capita consumption from 1961 (93.9 kg.) to 1989 (92.8 kg.), India increased its consumption nearly 40 per cent from 1961 (38.7 kg.) to 1989 (54.1 kg.).

Egypt rose slightly from 1961 (32.5 kg.) to 1989 (36 kg.), but Zimbabwe lost nutritional ground from 1961 (21.8 kg.) to 1989 (18.1 kg.).

India's neighbour Bangladesh fell from 1961 (9.6 kg.) to 1989 (9.2 kg.). Agrostat hints that demographics contributed to lower availability in Bangladesh where 1961-93 exp. growth of production (1.8 per cent) lagged behind population growth (2.7 per cent).

The 1994 version of Agrostat/FAO is in accord with the 1990 version, and unveils dramatic data. Indian per capita milk ex. butter consumption increased dramatically to nearly 60 kg. in 1992. The FAO estimated Indian consumption of about 65 kg. per capita *total milk equivalent* (TME) in 1998.

Yet more statistics point to a sharp improvement in India's dairy fortunes after Operation Flood's launch. 'Total milk production' had poor exponential growth before OF began (i.e. just 1.0 per cent over 1961-71) which lagged behind population exponential growth (2.3 per cent 1961-71). Numbers take the mystery out of milk shortages in the 1960s.

Agrostat/FAO/1990 shows rapid progress in India thereafter: exponential growth in total milk production of (5.2 per cent 1972-93) soaring past population exponential growth (2.1 per cent 1972-93). Thus, even if population growth had not fallen (from 2.3 per cent to 2.1 per cent), the 5.2 per cent exponential growth in total milk production would have increased per capita milk supplies. Prosperous societies usually exhibit falling fertility rates, and dairy development was probably part of this virtuous circle. Thomas Malthus would have been pleasantly surprised to have his dismal predictions on food and population refuted again.

In the milk deficit decade of the 1960s, Indian total milk production languished around 20 million Metric Tonnes. But it rallied soon after OF began and by 1993 it had more than tripled at 63m MT. In 1999 the FAO proffered estimates ranging from from 70.8 to 74m MT as it passed US production. India was winning its White Revolution.

Other noteworthy developments include a precipitous 42 per cent drop in *caput* milk excluding butter intake by Turkey from 1961 (94.2 kg.) to 1989 (55 kg.), likely due to cuts in all forms of dairy aid from all donors, including the EEC after milk quotas began in 1984.

What Agrostat data show in charts & maps

While China's small consumption increase was the murmur of a waking dragon, there is no doubt that India roused its dairy industry from the torpor of the 1960s in a lion-like rise to a leading role among world dairy producers. *No doubt?* Hardly. Although Claude Alvares' assertions that Operation Flood was a 'White Lie' (1983), concocted to build export markets for the First World, were eventually seen as hyperbole, such charges mislead readers unversed in the data. OF detractors claimed all consumption increases were due to European dairy aid, which would lead to permanent dependence. Shanti George was more even-tempered than Alvares, in her 1985 book *Operation Flood*, but following Kroese *et al.* (1979) she compared OF to a Trojan Horse. The negative publicity from George's dour attack may, if it was helpful, have goaded OF officials, Government ministers and state-controlled dairies to procure more milk from domestic farmers and cut dairy aid. Martin Doornbos and his fellow researchers also dubbed OF a failure, claiming one-third of commodities in formal cooperative processing plants was EEC dairy aid.[58]

In development literature it was trendy to express scepticism about the policies and leadership of the EEC (*aka* EC, EU), Anand, cooperatives, the National Dairy Development Board (NDDB), Operation Flood, the World Food Programme (WFP) – any actor in the White Revolution.

In retrospect these charges, made in fear that neo-colonialism, Cold War exigencies or greed would sabotage India's food security, are understandable. Fortunately, they were essentially mistaken.[59] FAO data for 1961 and 1989 show how dramatically the Indian dairy sector revived from the milk droughts of the 1960s, charting a 20 per cent rise in per capita consumption of butter & ghee and a 40 per cent rise in intake of milk excluding butter.

Such improvements are even more impressive against the country's burgeoning population growth. All this India accomplished while many other low-income countries experienced flat dairy production, and some of the countries in its comparison group, e.g. Bangladesh and Zimbabwe, languished.

The harshest criticisms of Operation Flood were made before the release of Agrostat FAO 1994 data. When the tide turned in Flood's favour, influential researchers lost interest and called it old news.

The result was that books and journals documenting the programme's success were so lacking on library shelves that, years into the new millennium, UK university students approach this author with the assumption that Flood was a boondoggle. But output and per capita consumption continue to rise.

The 11-fold rise in South Korean intake in 1961-89 (from 2.4 kg. in 1961 to 24.9 kg. in 1989) is noteworthy.

However, in absolute quantities, China's doubling of milk ex. butter intake 1961-89 (2.4 kg. to 5 kg.) invites speculation as to how far China's billion-plus people will develop taste for the so-called Western diet. The widespread appeal of pizza in global popular culture is often the first step in weakening Asian resistance to dairy products.

By 1998 European dairy experts were cooperating in dozens of Sino-EU dairy development projects there. China's potential is enormous, and milk consumption is increasing faster than some experts expected. This may be due to factors such as cognitive globalisation and the perception that milk is integral to children's nutrition and sporting prowess – as well as promotion of school milk programmes in many countries, in tandem with commercial firms such as Tetra Pak.

Data updates from FAO & OECD

After the 1984 Jha Committee mandated that processers must pay more for imports than domestic milk, moral hazard no longer dominated the system, and rural production surged unremittingly. It is no coincidence that 1984 was also the year that Europe instituted milk quotas, a form of production control that eroded the Butter Mountain and drained the Milk Lakes, for there was less use for such commodities in India. World dairy trends approached a more realistic equilibrium as the GATT process moderated production and export subsidies in the Global North.

Later data confirm claims of this book, based on Agrostat 1990 and 1995 databases, that India utilised dairy aid toward food autonomy. Fears that Operation Flood was just a shell game for European surplus disposal proved false. The FAO Secretariat now produces its *Agricultural Outlook* in collaboration with the OECD Secretariat in a format that correlates with FAO Agrostat data used above. *OECD-FAO Agricultural Outlook 2005-2014*[60] predicts [annual] World Milk Production increases of 1.9% to about 747 million tonnes by 2014, growing mainly in developing countries, Oceania and USA. (This reverses the DC/LDC balance of 1961 when developing countries produced just 18.6 per cent of milk; see **Chart 5.5**) India's status as top milk producer is secure. It has met ISO 9000 food safety standards, in exporting to countries including New Zealand and the USA, but India does not prioritise exporting due to domestic demand:

> The EU, India, the United States, Russia, Pakistan, Brazil, and China account for over two-thirds of total output. The biggest producer is the EU, while India is the world's largest single milk producing country. Producers in developing countries are expected to increase their world milk production shares, as a group, from 53 per cent to 58 per cent. The growth is expected to be strong, especially in India and China. Milk production in the OECD area… would remain relatively stable given that the majority of production is guarded by production control schemes, although milk production in Oceania and the USA, where such controls do not apply, is expected to trend higher.

Table 5.2 below draws from *OECD-FAO Outlook* Table A.24 Milk Projections to give average Production Weights (*pw*) in Million Tonnes (MT) for 1999-2003. *OECD-FAO Outlook*[61] also notes (**Table 5.3**) that about 57 per cent of milk in India is supplied by buffaloes while 'milk cow productivity growth is expected to be very high with yields growing about 3 per cent per year in the coming decade. Such growth has been the result of concerted policy action, starting with successive programmes called "Operation Flood"…'

Table 5.2.

OECD-FAO Agricultural Outlook 2005-2014 Production Weights (pw) Million Tonnes (MT) average 1999-2003		
Argentina (9.2 MT)	India (84.4 MT)	Switzerland (3.9 MT)
Australia (11.0 MT)	Japan (8.4 MT)	Turkey (9.7 MT)
Brazil (21.4 MT)	Korea, So. (2.3 MT)	United States (75.8 MT)
Canada (8.2 MT)	Mexico (9.5 MT)	Other Europe (38.4 MT)
China (13.0 MT)	New Zealand (13.8 MT)	Other Africa (24.7 MT)
EU-10 (22.0 MT)	Norway (1.5 MT)	Other Asia (63.5 MT)
EU-15 (121.6)	Russia (32.5 MT)	Other Latin Amr. (18.7 MT)
EU-25 (143.6 MT)	South Africa (2.6 MT)	World (595.4 MT)

Compiled by: B.A. Scholten (2009)

Dairy India 2007 estimates that per capita availability of milk fell from 124 grams per day in 1961 to a low of 114 grams per day in 1970; that it increased to 197 grams per day in 1995, reached 240 grams in 2005, and continues to grow quickly.[62] Drawing on FAO and other data, the *Yearbook* projects per capita availability of milk at 296 grams per day in 2010, and 340 grams per day in 2015.

Following the Agrostat data series, FAO offered FAOSTAT with much available online. Data for our comparator countries are disaggregated from total milk production into cow, buffalo, goat and sheep milk production (*c*, *b*, *g*, and *s*, respectively). **Table 5.3** below, compiled from FAOSTAT[63] shows primarily cow and buffalo milk, although goat milk and cow milk held the #2 and #5 commodity spots, respectively, on the top 20 commodity list in Bangladesh in 1995. (Several countries produce sheep, horse and other mammalian milk, although only buffalo, cow and goat milk attained the list of top 20 commodities here.)

Of course FAOSTAT data recorded in hindsight are more accurate than FAO projections before 1995. But the FAOSTAT[64] table below is also interesting for demonstrating how much food systems differ from country to country. Consider Nigeria which in 2007 still had no milk products in its top 20 agricultural commodities, while dairy was a significant part of the growing agricultural sectors of Tanzania andUganda. This was also true in Zimbabwe, although milk production plummeted, 1995-2007, amid farm policy turmoil.

On the individual level in India, where milk droughts are physically experienced, Operation Flood eased the emptiness that years of policy disarray had witnessed. It is likely that the milk famine of the 1960s was exacerbated by the economic disincentives of *sporadic* dairy aid, which was harmful until it was integrated into a monetisation programme and National Milk Grid System that promoted domestic production, procurement and marketing to urban consumers.

Table 5.3.

FAOSTAT 2007 Total Milk: Food & Agricultural commodities production/2007/sort by value [Top 20]		
	1995 MT Total	**2007 MT Total**
Bangladesh	**1,940,000.** *c* 780,000.; *g* 1,160,000.	**2,834,000.** *c* 818,000.; *g* 2,016,000.
China	nd	35,574,315
Egypt	**2,629,700.** *b* 1,358,000.; *c* 1,271,700.	**4,500,000.** *b* 2,300,000.; *c* 2,200,000.
EU	146,978,382	148,028,828
India	**62,585,000.** *b* 35,870,000.; *c* 26,715,000.	**102,100,000.** *b* 59,210,000. *c* 42,890,000.
Japan	**8,382,000.**	**8,024,000.**
Kenya	**1,985,000.**	**4,230,000.**
Korea (So.)	**1,998,445.**	**2,188,000.**
Mexico	**7,398,598.**	**10,345,982.**
Nigeria	nd	nd
Pakistan	**18,277,000.** *b* 13,984,000.; *c* 4,293,000.	**31,502,000.** *b* 20,372,000.; *c* 11,130,000.
Tanzania	**590,000.**	**850,000.**
Turkey	**9,275,310.**	**11,279,340.**
Uganda	**457,800.**	**735,000.**
USA	**70,439,000.**	**84,189,067.**
Zimbabwe	**350,000.**	**250,000.**
World	**518,960,947.** *b* 54,655,609.; *c* 464,305,338.	**653,424,715.** *b* 86,574,529.; *c* 566,850,186.
FAOSTAT 2007, Totals are cow (*c*) milk unless labeled buffalo (*b*), or goat (*g*).		

Compiled by: B.A. Scholten (2009)

The low-input/low-output cooperative Anand Pattern merits praise for multiplying production in the White Revolution., and the monetisation of European dairy aid in Operation Flood is vindicated by the evidence of positive development outcomes. Now we turn to the details of the drama in three acts.

Chapter 6

Three Phases of Flood

OF-I, OF-II, OF-III win the White Revolution

Although it is fashionable in some circles to question dairying for its alleged squandering of plants in cattle fodder, the suitability of dairy farming in many parts of the world is indisputable. To think otherwise is absurd to millions of people including vegetarians who depend on dairying for protein and other nutrients. In a variety of settings dairy animals improve people's food security by transforming plants, crop wastes and processing wastes inedible to humans into milk. India's marginal and landless farmers challenge the adage of *No free lunch* by producing what amounts to *A free glass of milk* - not to mention ghee and so on. In the summary of a 1986 report to the World Bank, Harold Alderman wrote:

> Dairy development is a major component of strategies to expand agricultural output in many developing countries. In regions which are hilly or semi-arid, a concentration on pastoralism is in keeping with the ecological resource base. In other, often more favoured regions, the proximity of urban markets provides a demand for dairy products and, hence, may encourage investment in dairying.

Set up by the Food and Agricultural Organisation of the United Nations (FAO) in 1963, the World Food Programme (WFP) judged many areas of India suitable for dairying. So, it worked from the beginning with the Government of India GOI), National Dairy Development Board (NDDB), European Economic Community (EEC, *aka* EC, EU) and other bodies to connect rural farmers with urban markets in Operation Flood, the world's biggest ever dairy development programme.

The prospect of providing income, employment and nutrition from under-utilised resources and labour was among the reasons why, by 1988, the WFP had approved dairy development projects in 30 countries, and 16 of them were already being implemented in 1987 - equal to about 8 per cent of the total value of WFP efforts. The WFP[1] admits dairy projects are among the 'most challenging' of projects because they take a long time to achieve their goals, such as improved genetics, fodder base, production and consumption, and whatever the soil, climate and social factors in a country engaged in dairy development:, 'longer-term success... depends on a variety of technical, ecological, social, economic and political factors, at both the micro and macro levels.'

India was a natural site for dairy development, wrote long-time NDDB Chairman Dr. Verghese Kurien[2], because: 'India, almost alone among non-European cultures, is a milk drinking nation. This, coupled with our large population, ensured a constant and growing demand for milk.'

Research reflects Indians' appetite for dairy foods. In an analysis of the 1987-88 National Sample Survey (NSS), T.N. Dalle and B.K. Gauguly[3] found urban elasticity of demand for milk & milk products (MMP) of 1.15. In other words, in the study city folk bought another 1.15 per cent of milk products for each additional 1 per cent increase in income. (Only well-supplied Delhi has inelasticity for MMP.) Although rural monthly per capita expenditure (PCE) is much lower (Rs158/month/rural) than urban income (Rs250/month/urban), elasticity of demand for milk & milk products is even higher (1.65) in the country. Rural dwellers spend 1.65 per cent more on milk & milk products for each 1 per cent rise in income. Although there are some regional variations in demand, Indian's generally value milk so much that even the very poor will, after meeting their fundamental cereals needs, buy a small quantity of liquid milk to whiten their morning tea or coffee. Furthermore, while Dalle & Gauguly[4] find milk demand does fall when prices rise for cereals which are the 'main expenditure item' for both urban and rural dwellers: 'prices of other commodities do not seem to be influencing the demand for milk to any significant proportion.'

But India's affinity for milk did not prevent Operation Flood from being attacked via all the factors listed by Alderman - plus vegetarian and feminist critiques. But while dairy efforts in some countries fell awry due to changing conditions (e.g. Afghanistan after the 1979 Soviet invasion) or recognition that ecological, spatial (*vis-à-vis* marketing to urban centres) or political factors left them still-born, Operation Flood prospered. OF grew in three phases (OF-I, OF-II, OF-III) from the early 1970s past its official end in 1996, when the dearth of European dairy surpluses, and preoccupation of EU officials with enlargement, monetary union and unrest in the Balkans, and the success of India's dairy cooperative movement rendered a mooted OF-IV unnecessary.

Operation Flood initially affected only about 1 per cent of the total national milk supply but had leveraged effects on infrastructure, production and consumption, as its catchment grew. It eventually enrolled about 10 million farm families in India's largest rural development project – and the world's largest dairy development programme. Like other countries in the developing world, most of India's milk remains in the traditional, unorganised sector which by its informal nature is hard to measure. In 1999 the informal sector comprised 88 to 94 per cent of India's total, depending on which FAO, World Bank, NDDB or other estimate you believed. But statistics on formal sector growth gradually crept up. A report by the International Food Policy Research Institute for the FAO[5] in 2003 calculated that of about 78 million tonnes total production in 1999-2000 'the organized sector… handled 10 to 12 per cent of all milk production or 15 per cent of the marketed surplus' while informal private milk traders handled about 88 to 90 per cent. Informal 'traditional… milk vendors/ dudhias and sweet shops [/halwais]' continued to hold about 84 per cent of sales. Commentators have stressed that Flood's biggest effect was on the vast majority of India's dairy industry which was *not* part of the formal development programme. Non-OF and informal farmers benefit economically from higher demand in urban markets, while they assimilate technical improvements fostered by Flood.

In 2009, Sharad Gupta & R.S. Khanna[6] noted that: 'Some 70 million farmers maintain a milch herd of about 105 million - 58 million cows and 47 million buffaloes, fed largely on crop residues. They account for 98 percent of all milk produced in India.'

Here we consider evidence from Agrostat/FAO/1990/1994 and other sources showing how Operation Flood sent dairying out of the doldrums. After the dismal era of 1951-69 (average annual growth: 0.7 per cent) the heavy capital investments made possible by OF contributed to impressive growth over 1971-94 (annual growth 4.7 per cent).[7] Perhaps this did not satisfy the demands of all special interest groups, but OF did set standards for dairy development that are being emulated by other countries. Although the grail of objectivity is as slippery in development research as in journalism, works by Martin Doornbos and his colleagues at the Indo-Dutch Studies on Alternative Development series have proven valuable resources for this chapter, as were observations by P.J. Atkins, John Empson, M.V. Kamath, and Shanti George, *inter alia*. Comments from OF officials and affiliated institutions (e.g. GCMMF, IRMA, NDDB) are included to highlight certain points, but this book relies more on the relatively neutral judgements of dispassionate researchers rather than, say, a point-counterpoint rendition of the polarised arguments between OF critic Claude Alvares ('White Lie') and OF head Dr. Kurien ('Black Lie'). Harold Alderman, George Mergos and Roger Slade, frequent writers and co-authors on OF contributed to one of the latest (1998) and most authoritative assessments of Operation Flood made by the World Bank -

India: The Dairy Revolution - by Wilfred Candler and Nalini Kumar. [8] However, their inclusion of this common disclaimer is slightly unsettling: 'The opinions expressed in this report do not necessarily represent the views of the World Bank or its member governments.'

This disclaimer hints that consensus on development paradigms in general, and OF in particular, has been elusive at the Bank. Statements in this report by the Operations Evaluation Department (OED) such as, 'The Bank had difficulty in recognising success' in Operation Flood, and that OF was actually 'at odds with Bank strategy' suggest the advocates of cooperativisation are engaged in a long-term war with the forces of *laissez-faire* neoliberalism. This disclaimer acknowledges that privatisation of state, or quasi-public assets such as dairy facilities (policies touted by the World Bank and IMF in the redevelopment of the former USSR and other formerly-socialist economies) can be fraught with problems. It also hints that a measure of cooperative control in agricultural sectors can maximise returns for both farmers and consumers - which is what Candler & Kumar found in India.

Meanwhile, analysis of Operation Flood as it transpired 1970~96 is valuable because, although dairy projects are unique and 'country-specific'[9] the WFP points out that they 'can be addressed by a common policy perspective.' One of the principal questions on dairy development - and of the Anand model in OF in particular - is how to discern which aspects are transferable, i.e. *replicable*, from one locale or continent to another.

Although dairy aid has become a smaller part of international food aid projects since the end of Operation Flood in 1996, insights from OF have implications for commercial development and dairy projects around the world. An indicator of India's success and expertise is that, according to Kurien, the NDDB has built a dairy plant in the Kyrgyz Republic and the NDDB board has worked with: 'dairy farmers, cooperatives and governments in a great many countries, including Uganda, Kenya, Ethiopia, Malawi, Madagascar, the Philippines, Thailand and Pakistan.'

Success? According to *Dairy India 1997*[10] per capita availability of milk, which had fallen from 1950 (132 grams/day) to 1973 (111 grams/day) rallied under OF, regaining 1950 levels in 1980 (128 grams/day) and was estimated to rise above the 200 grams/day level in 1996 (208 grams/day). Five decades after Independence, per capita availability of milk had at last risen about 57 per cent. Even more impressive, the rise of the country's dairy tides 1970~96 coincided with a population rise of around 50 per cent. Agrostat-FAO[11] shows milk production stagnated at 20.2 million tonnes annually 1961-70. After Flood began in 1970 it more than trebled to about 66 million tonnes in 1996. By 1998 India's estimated production of 70.8

million tonnes challenged the USA as top world producer and, despite drought, passed that North American dairy powerhouse around 1998.[12]

Now we will examine views supporting and opposing OF, from within and without India, and the interplay of these critiques in its evolution. India's record will be compared to a group of countries including Bangladesh, Pakistan, Turkey and Zimbabwe. Because food aid has so often been problematic, a prime goal is to draw some final judgements on the use of dairy aid in India's White Revolution.

Origins of OF

The model for the cooperative dairy structure characteristic of Operation Flood (OF) originated in 1945-46 in the Kaira district of Gujarat, roughly equidistant between Delhi and Mumbai (Bombay). Dilip R. Shah calls the coop the Anand-Kheda Milk Producers' Cooperative Union[13], but it is widely known as the Kaira District Cooperative Milk Producers' Union and by the acronym KDCPMU. The biggest coop is Amul[14] located at Anand, which by consensus became famous for 'the Anand Model', or 'Anand Pattern'. But there was to be agreement on few other aspects of this historic coop. The appropriateness of the Anand model for replication in other areas is a chronic bone of contention. P.J. Atkins notes that Gujarat already was one of India's main dairy areas, although not specialised to the extent of Cheshire in England.[15]

A.S. Patel[16] and others including Shanti George[17] note that dairy development proceeded spontaneously in Gujarat, benefiting from a rail link to Bombay built in the nineteenth century before establishment of the Anand structure, and the birth of the NDDB or OF. A geo-economic link with Bombay was a boon to Anand. As Clive Crook[18] wrote in the *Economist* about Bombay: 'Mumbai…is to Delhi as Manhattan is to Washington, DC.' Actually, it was both Anand's blessing and curse to be located just 270 miles north of Bombay, whose milk has long been partially supplied by urban cattle colonies. Kurien[19] blames British colonial policies for ensuring that milk production 'languished' at 20m tonnes in the 1960s:

> Our very best cattle were taken to the cities to meet the urban demand for milk and when they went dry they were either slaughtered or abandoned. This practice of shipping milk on the hoof was responsible for tragically eroding the genetic potential of dairy cattle in the country. A second and equally serious problem was that dairy farmers in our villages were compelled to sell milk to middle men at derisory prices simply because the Government had given these traders a monopoly of purchasing milk in return for supply to cities like Bombay.

Free marketeer Clive Crook could not put it better. Here Kurien, the *primus inter pares* of India's farmer cooperatives, attacks the legacy of price controls with the ferocity of a leader writer in *The Economist.*

Although observers roundly praised the aims of Operation Flood, Shanti George and Claude Alvares claimed OF was seldom successful at replicating the Anand model outside Gujarat. Even today a disproportionate amount of milk is procured from Gujarat. But lest critics attack Anand for geo-nepotism, Candler & Kumar explain that weighty Operation Flood investments in Gujarat paid off in efficient returns. George and Alvares condemned the single-mindedness with which OF proselytised replication of the Anand model in villages bearing little resemblance to Anand. Domestic and foreign critics complained of over-optimism - if not dissembling - in official NDDB reports.

OF detractors like George and Alvares attributed any apparent successes of OF to the advantage of Government favour, sealed by PM Nehru's public embrace of Dr. Kurien at the opening of a SMP plant for buffalo milk in 1955, continuing under PM Shastri in 1964, and on with the patronage of the Congress Party under Indira Gandhi. As Candler & Kumar's[20] evaluation for the World Bank (whose head Robert McNamara jumped on the OF bandwagon with Bank loans, 8 years after it started) notes wryly: 'Neither the visit of the Prime Minister of India nor the visit of the President of the Bank was an entirely unorchestrated event.'

In her 1985 book Shanti George claims, 'the Anand pattern propagated by the NDDB' diverged 'from the actual situation in Anand....' More recently, Candler & Kumar[21] write that the original Anand model 'clearly started from the ground up', but endeavours assisted by the World Bank such as OF-II were somewhat 'top-down', because for instance, 'target rates of growth' in membership and procurement were set from above. Although village level Dairy Coop Societies (DCSs) enjoyed popular support, Bank and OF managers were 'acutely aware' that 'rapid expansion' sometimes 'sacrificed…the Anand principles of farmer control'. So attempts were made to 'ensure democratic and accountable operations' and greater 'autonomy' for Milk Producers Unions (MPUs) and federations in management, staffing, marketing and pricing.

Although some experts claim the World Bank has *always* supported Operation Flood, it was not until 1978 that Bank head Robert McNamara offered Dr. Kurien money for the second phase of Operation Flood. Previously the Bank extended credits via the Anand-led International Development Association (IDA) to state dairy projects in Karnataka (ca. US$26.4 million), Rajasthan (US$27.7m) and Madhya Pradesh (US$16.4m).[22] But several advantages of the Anand model, such as cooperative structures and the freedom for coop managers to set milk prices free from state interference, gradually convinced the Bank that Anand was the best pattern for Indian dairy development. Like a fleet-footed politician running to the front of a moving crowd, the World Bank wanted to 'lead' the White Revolution. But haste by the Bank and the NDDB to extend the Anand pattern outside Gujarat stepped on toes. Some components of Flood are typical of top-down development programmes, in that they were imposed by officials under the auspices of the federal republic on a vast, heterogeneous country. In many cases OF's mandate to bring previously-established state dairy programmes under its aegis met unrelenting resistance. Candler & Kumar[23] found that while India's dairy cooperatives were generally profitable in the mid-1990s, state governments continued to stymie development wherever their price controls discourage production, or state regulations 'limit the ability of cooperatives to correct over-staffing.'

Although the WFP officially called OF a *project*, it utilised amounts of donated dairy product food aid comparable in scale to the surplus disposal *programmes* of the 1950s and 1960s, in international agreements usually signed at the top of the political hierarchy in the capital of Delhi. But OF had many components describable as 'bottom-up'. Harold Alderman notes that, like most forms of dairy development favoured by the World Bank, OF promoted surplus rural milk 'as if it were a cash crop'.[24] If rural production could be increased, and the logistics of transport to urban centres overcome, subsistence farmers at the bottom of economic quintiles could be integrated into the cash economy, while nutrition in urban and rural sectors was improved.

Many arguments have been marshalled against the top-down, centrally-planned, inefficient Public Sector Enterprises (PSEs)[25] that dominate almost all production employing more than 100 workers in India. By contrast, Operation Flood was a 'top-down' programme characterised by flexibility and autonomy seldom granted to managers of other industries. From its inception OF benefited from vigorous team management shared with the National Dairy Development Board. Shri Tribhuvandas K. Patel chaired the NDDB from its birth in 1946 until July, 1973 when, writes Ruth Heredia[26], 'he retired of his own accord', and began the charitable Tribhuvandas Foundation. Thereafter Kurien – often emphasising that the Anand Pattern 'does not pit man against beast' - was NDDB chairman for a quarter century until the end of 1998, when he was succeeded by his preference, NDDB managing director Amrita Patel. [27]

To understand the Anand Pattern, or Anand Model, it is important to distinguish between the parastatal NDDB, i.e. the Government entity headquartered safely away from Delhi in Anand at the insistence of Verghese Kurien, from the farmer-owned Gujarat Cooperative Milk

Marketing Federation (GCMMF) which owns the Amul dairy product brand. In practical terms the synergistic relationship between these organisations – and the fact that Kurien led both for decades – fosters the impression that they comprise what in Britain is called a QUANGO or quasi-non-government organisation. While farmer participation, indeed democracy, were ideological themes promoted by OF in the field, and Kurien *et al.* were open to feedback from village farmers, the project was led from the top by expert technocrats.

P.J. Atkins[28] described the Anand model as: 'a combination of top-down planning and bottom-up participation.' Farmers, both male and female, were active in village DCSs. But detractors complained of too little participation by small farmers in planning at the top, such as on the Indian Dairy Commission. Although Government patronage remained strong until the demise of the Congress Party in the 1990s, much OF success can still be traced to critical decisions made by Dr. Kurien, who was nationally known as the presumed successor to Tribhuvandas Patel decades before OF-I began. OF supporters claim that Kurien, who came to personify OF, resisted the overmanning, waste and limited quality that hampered government industrial champions such as steel.[29] But detractors in- and outside Government were suspicious, not to say envious of Kurien's autonomy, both in control of OF's impressive budget, and of the fact that OF was managed from Anand, far from the political infighting of Delhi. What critics call heavy-handedness, admirers deem leadership. Moreover, the failure of state milk programmes such as the subsidised urban milk scheme in Rajasthan[30], compared to steady growth in Gujarat, convinced international bankers and Delhi heavyweights alike that Anand could lead the dairy revolution nationally. Formidable problems required direction. Kurien[31] writes: 'The farmers' problems were complicated by the fact that milk would not keep beyond three hours in our climate.'

Because of the perishability of liquid drinking milk, micro- and macroeconomic efficiencies could be gained by a large-scale, top-down approach. Making and marketing milk is not like making tea kettles or selling shovels. Alden C. Manchester[32] identifies the differences between dairying and other agricultural and non-agricultural activities: 'In many way, it is unique.... The differences must be understood because they play a significant role in determining the effects of different public policies towards the dairy industry.' Compared to other activities - even growing potatoes - milk production requires specialised inputs, buildings, skilled and continuous management. Manchester also notes the difficulty of varying 'the rate of output' of cow milk, the high costs of entry or exit from dairying, and the susceptibility of dairying to sanitation problems. Although he was writing mostly about the US market, his points apply - albeit on a different scale - to milk production on the sub-continent. Manchester could just as well be describing rural India when he writes: 'Instability is inherent in milk markets. Production varies seasonally largely for biological reasons and from day to day - neither type of variation is coordinated with changes in demand.'

Compared to medium-scale manufactures of, for example, kitchen utensils or farm implements, where top-down, central management led to product stagnation due to inefficiency (e.g. the Eastbloc electrical industry described by Kazimierz Z. Poznanski[33]), some top-down strategies were useful in stimulating milk supply for India's parched cities. Milk droughts showed the inability of urban or periurban cattle colonies to supply sufficient pure milk. Such isolated enterprises, depleted by drought and disease, could not provide a stable milk supply, and their capital base was inadequate to finance processing infrastructure and hygienic transport of sufficient milk from ruralities to cities. The vulnerability of small-scale milk farmers who are not members of cooperatives is, writes Manchester, typified by a small number of processors (inviting monopolistic price-squeezes). Thus, Manchester[34] suggests the desirability of:

> Long-term commitments by producers and processors... producer groups [which are] often able to reach more favourable terms than individual producers... a public agency... as an arbitrator between buyers and sellers, providing a measure of stability which they cannot provide for themselves.

Manchester's suggestions for enhancing the welfare of poor and isolated dairy farmers of the USA in the mid-twentieth century - many of whom are again facing bankruptcy in the recession of 2009 - echo the rationale for Operation Flood in India. A crucial component of OF was top-down approval from Delhi for the NDDB and sister body the India Dairy Corporation (IDC) to control import of all gifted dairy commodities.[35] Both bodies were headed by Kurien. Before OF began in 1970, commodities were freely imported commercially or in Government programmes (generally as US or EEC surplus disposal) to increase milk supply at affordable prices to urban consumers. But this supposed free trade approach increased dependence in an era of commodity dumping. So, OF and its farmer-controlled network of dairy coops were designed to:

(1) raise the welfare of rural farmers by eliminating the control of the milk supply by village elites and petty dairy marketeers (i.e. *dudhiyas* who often doubled as moneylenders, but captured a disproportionate amount of the profits from dairying);

(2) raise production throughout the country;
(3) eliminate adulteration of milk, often with unsanitary water (even caustic soda[36] to correct the pH of soured milk), characteristic of the milk famines of the 1960s. As Acharya & Yadav[37] explain, adulteration was more rife when 'the prevailing market price of milk' was not 'remunerative';
(4) ensure the stability of milk supply to cities, *via* an interlinked National Milk Grid System (NMGS) able to meet excess demand in some markets with surplus milk drawn from others, while topping up the milk supply from buffer stocks[38] generated in India - and dairy commodities from the EEC/WFP;
(5) protect India's milk autonomy, by preparing for the donation of massive quantities of EEC dairy 'aid' with a consolidated national plan to mitigate disincentives to Indian dairy farmers, by investing profits from 'monetised' commodities into a National Milk Grid System. This NMGS could balance supply among states and reduce chances that future tsunamis of foreign commodity gifts could ruin price structures (and discourage production) around ports importing dairy 'aid'.

Objective (5) may be most important. Certainly it was controversial, because although sporadic quantities of commercial imports and dairy aid (accepted on concessionary rates or as donations) were already reaching Indian soil, critics feared granting OF authorities control of all imports was a subterfuge to permanent dependence on EEC dairy surpluses. Nevertheless, evidence shows that, on the contrary, OF was a prescient, pre-emptive initiative by Indian dairy planners to transform what they reckoned an inevitable flow (impossible to stop, given European surpluses and Indian demand) of EEC dairy aid into investment in their dairy autonomy. OF planners knew food aid had reduced the food autonomy of countries such as Nigeria, which turned from indigenous grains to American wheat. So, over the life of the programme, OF leaders astutely promoted India's independence by playing off one donor against another. Doornbos *et al.*[39] write:

> At the time of negotiations of OF-III [Operation Flood, phase III], again, NDDB officials made it clear that if the EEC were reluctant to supply additional aid, India would switch to the USA, New Zealand or Australia for continued support to its dairy strategy. Thus, it would be incorrect to argue that in the case of Operation Flood, it is primarily the EEC which has been dictating any terms of incorporation.

Like the sorcerer's apprentice, OF mastered the EEC. Although the following quotations are lengthy they are noteworthy for their evidence of the fundamental logic of OF plans - and planners. Doornbos *et al.* note:

> It has often been stressed that the basic motivation underlying Operation Flood has been precisely opposite to one that would have India surrender its autonomy in the field of dairy development in favour of an inclusion into an EEC-sponsored incorporation chain. Thus it can be argued that the programme's key objective has been to safeguard and strengthen autonomy in dairying vis-à-vis the incorporative designs of the EEC or other major dairy exporters, even if it had to be at the 'price' of the internal incorporation of India's organised dairy economy within the centralised Operation Flood framework.

Doornbos *et al.*[40] acknowledge OF planners' fear of dumping:

> The EEC, it has often been suggested by OF programme authorities, at one time had threatened to dump large quantities of surplus dairy commodities onto the Indian market. On the premise of a 'dumping threat', the safeguarding formula developed was that of an ingenious programme structure which, while accepting the EEC commodities as aid, would use them to finance the expansion of a national dairying infrastructure and keep Indian authorities firmly in control.

Put another way: *Europe offered India a lemon, and India made lemonade.* By 1970 the history of food aid was replete with instances where untimely 'donations' had benefited special interests in donor countries (by stabilising domestic prices, lowering storage costs, raising political prestige, etc.) - but harmed farmers and ultimately consumers in recipient countries by depressing farmgate prices and throwing indigenous systems into disarray (from loss of income and uncertainty over future incomes caused by superfluous food aid). Even assuming complete good will by all members of EEC negotiating teams, OF officials wisely sought to close any chinks in India's dairy armour and prevent exploitation by special interests (e.g. actors trying to corner the European milk powder market) or harm by well-meaning EEC officials who were naively unaware of the dangers posed by food 'gifts'.

An inelegant comparison serves here. Like a giant snakebite, 20 million Metric Tonnes (MT) of SMP sailing into Mumbai (Bombay) harbour could paralyse dairy structures in Gujarat, Maharashtra and beyond, so OF negotiated a plan with the EEC and WFP to 'monetise' the dairy aid. In other words, the National Milk Grid System acted as a snakebite kit flushing the entry point (or wound) around Bombay to disperse dairy commodity gifts[41] all over the sub-continent, making its price structures immune to injections of dairy aid.

Diffusion flows of milk are shown from farmers in rural villages, to procurement centres, to urban populations in **Map 6.1. [OF's] National Milk Grid 1988** and **Map 6.2. NMG 1990-91 (source: NDDB).**

In respect to a threat that the EEC might dump dairy aid on India, we can surmise such a threat need not have been made explicitly or in earnest. Why? Because, just as nature abhors a vacuum, so does international trade. (We assume that private, governmental and semi-governmental *arbitrageurs* active in dairy trade continually seek to affect world commodities markets in order to increase their profits.[42]) That is, simple recognition by special interests on either side, in Europe or in India, was enough to establish the potential for such potentially damaging dairy aid commodity shipments to be sent.

Semper paratus. For decades the EEC had produced what Shanti George[43] called 'mountainous stocks' without an 'adequate commercial outlet'.

Insufficient political will existed to institute CAP milk quotas until 1984. The destructive potential of dairy aid for Indian dairying was why George (after Kroese *et al.*, 1979) called it a Trojan Horse. But others knew these gifts could be rendered safe by monetising them into infrastructure.

Of course India faced more pressing concerns than ships full of skimmed milk powder (SMP) and butter oil (BO) steaming from Europe. Its priority in the 1960s was to end the so-called milk famine, in which the traditional, private unconsolidated supply systems, and state-assisted developments, were unable to satisfy milk demand in India's growing metro centres. Meeting demand in growing urban markets consistently over the waxing and waning of seasonal and annual supply required costly investment in modern processing centres and hygienic transport, carrying milk from producers in the hinterland to urban consumers.

See **Map 6.3. Final form of the Anand Pattern in the NMGS** below. Although rural producers would react to growing urban demand with higher production in the medium--term, Doornbos *et al.*[44] explain:

> Rather than as a strategy for increasing Indian milk production, Operation Flood has been designed as a programme for structuring the Indian milk market.... dairy aid has functioned, and still functions, as a physical input into the emerging dairy industry. As such, dairy aid provided by the WFP and the EEC has first of all served to establish the NMGS. This is one of the reasons why the programme has been dependent on commodity aid for so long.

The National Milk Grid System took years to develop. A comparison of **Map 6.1** and **Map 6.2** shows progress was still being made on the Madras-to-Calcutta (Chennai-to-Kolkata) milk transport route in the late 1980s (and continues today). It was timely that India's need for capital investments coincided with EEC dairy surpluses, as well as the political will and creativity among GOI, EEC, WFP, FAO and OF officials to seize opportunities for dairy development in a perilous scenario.

Critics who scorned the National Milk Grid System (NMGS) as stainless steel temples to neo-colonialist tied-aid did not realise how much of the equipment was actually built in India. Construction of the original four 'Mother Dairies' in Bombay (Mumbai), Calcutta (Kolkata), Delhi and Madras (Chennai) - and the later 1 million lpd Gandhinagar Dairy in Ahmedabad (see **Photos**) - reflects the meaning of milk in India's pluralistic society.

P.J. Atkins[45] argues, echoing Manchester, that as a 'valued perishable commodity' important to the nutritional and economic well-being of developing economies, 'milk is a special case' that merits capital-intensive investment: 'where the long-term benefits which accrue to society outweigh the short-term benefits.'

Milk is different from cereals - not to mention non-food commodities because: it has a constant, relatively inelastic demand. It is used daily but has to be produced on a twice-daily basis; must be processed almost immediately after production on a farm; and can be stored only for limited periods (ca. 3 hours in India) usually at high cost. Milk is a world away from coal, widgets or even wheat, which is storable for several years. Furthermore, while demand for milk is fairly inelastic (not to be confused with the high *income-elasticity* of demand for milk among the poor in India), supply is naturally elastic according to seasonal changes as well as erratic droughts, fodder shortages and disease. Harold Alderman[46] says:

> Like many field crops, milk production is seasonal but, unlike grains for example, it cannot be stored in its 'raw' form. Hence, product transformation is necessary in order to utilise flush season production effectively.

Map 6.1. National Milk Grid 1988
Courtesy of NDDB.

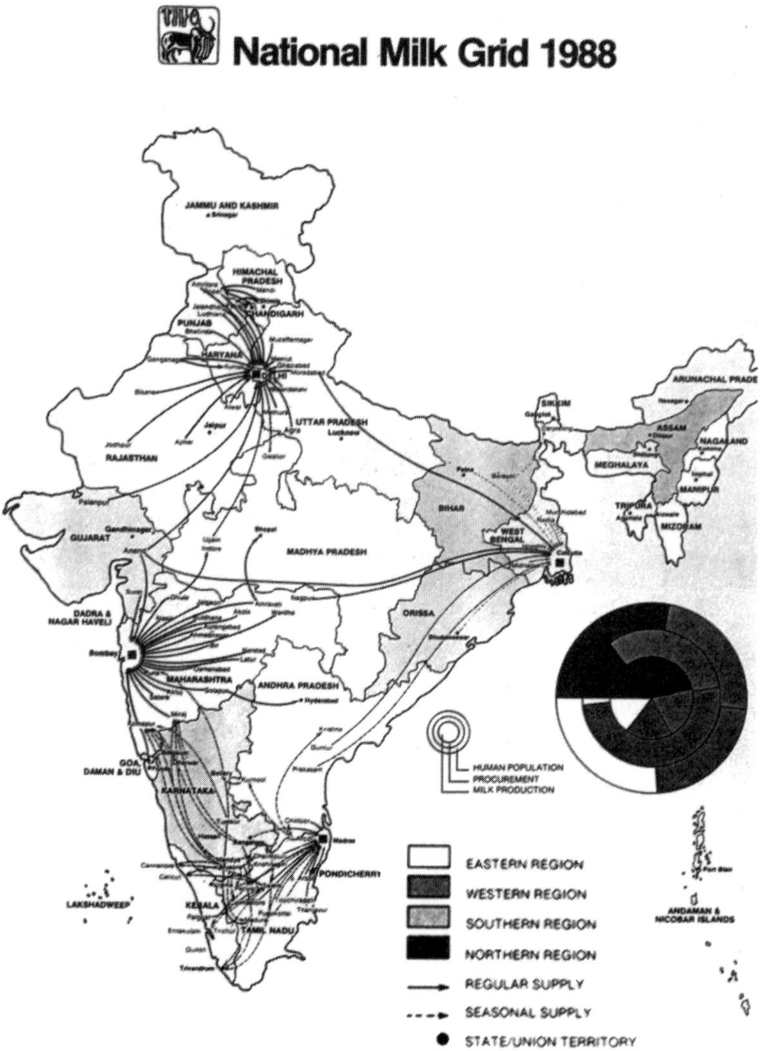

Map 6.2. National Milk Grid 1990-91
Courtesy of NDDB.

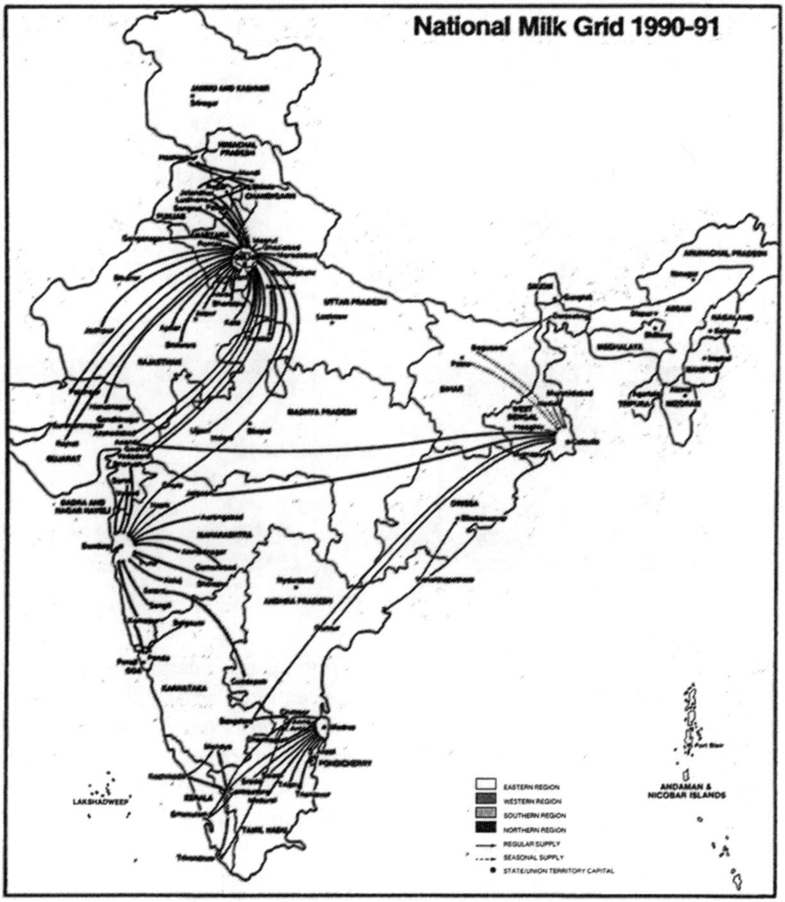

Map 6.3 Final form of the Anand Pattern in the NMGS
Courtesy NDDB.

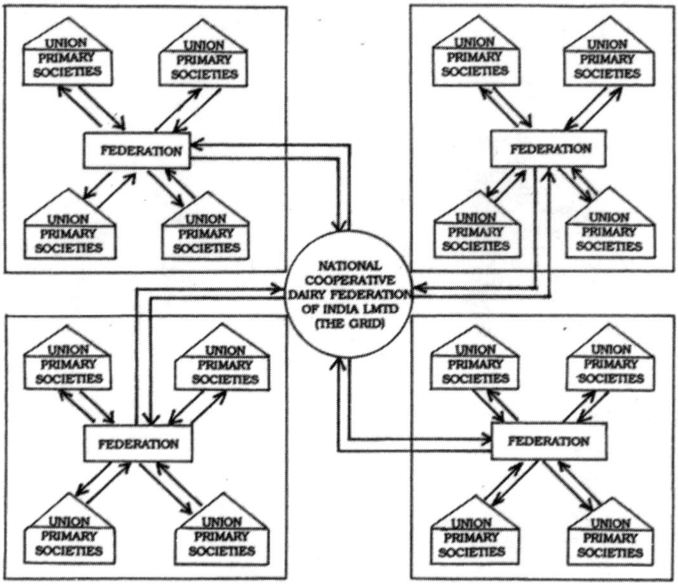

Milk production is labour-intensive, appropriate for a large rural pool of surplus labour. But streamlining supply on national scale posed logistical challenges, requiring appropriately modern processing and transport technology. Contrary to the wishful thinking of critics, such large-scale investments could not have been quickly financed by profits from 'bottom-up' dairy projects utilising only technical extension, AI, or subsidised feedstuffs. OF eventually increased such supply-side support on the village level *along with* monetising dairy aid into infrastructure.

Yes, simple inputs alone would have increased milk shipments from villages, but as supply 'trickled-up' to urban centres, too many gains would have been captured by middlemen, or spoiled in inadequate processing or transport. Prices to urban consumers would have been higher and returns to rural farmers lower. (Recall that pre-OF milk prices were above EEC/US levels, but the FAO[47] reports the 1998 litre price in India (15-20 cents/ kg.) was far below UK or US prices (31-35 cents/litre).

Table 6.1.

Agrostat/FAO data show milk production rises in Operation Flood				
x-million MT	1970	1974	1991	1996*
India	20.8	24.5	58.4	68*
France	22.8	24.6	26.4	NA
Germany	28.2	28.6	29.1	NA
USA	53.1	52.4	67.3	70*
USSR	83.0	91.8	101.3	36*

Agrostat/1994/FAO/livestock/milk production & 1998 Dairy Outlook*

As domestic milk prices lagged behind inflation, it may be more accurate to call OF and its National Milk Grid System (NMGS) a 'flood-up' rather than 'trickle-up' programme. It is unimaginable that 'bottom-up' efforts could have thrust India into what John Empson[48] calls 'the dairy big leagues' as quickly as did OF. Nor is it likely that, without investment in convenient marketing technology such as vending machines[49] and Tetra Pak containers for marketing in urban centres, such reliable urban demand could have been generated. Secure urban outlets for rural milk production gradually increased rural income security as OF (weaning itself from dairy aid) increased reliance on domestic milk. Empson notes that in 1974 India: 'then ranked with France or Germany, the two largest European producers but trailed well behind the USSR and the USA… With a population at that time of… 15 per cent of the world total, India had barely 5 per cent of the world's milk production.'

What a difference a decade or two makes. Empson writes that with a population of 845 million in 1990-91, India's share of world population had increased from 15 per cent to 16 per cent after 1974, but its milk share *had more than doubled to 11 per cent* (121.3 billion pounds/ca. 55b kg.), outstripping the *combined* production of France and Germany, and threatening the number two status of the USA, as well as the putative leading position of the soon-to-be ex-USSR. In two decades India's per capita availability of milk rose from 90.2 pounds a year (41 kg.) to 143 pounds (65 kg.) annually, according to Empson, and with a planned 172 billion pounds by the year 2000, India was set to dislodge the status of the USA and USSR as the world's two leading producers. In fact, as mentioned above, India may have bypassed the USA and ex-USSR into preeminence with 156 billion pounds (78 million US short tons or 70.8m Metric Tonnes) in 1998 (see also data in Chapter 5). This was accomplished to a cadence of criticism within and without India. On the macroeconomic level, detractors scorned dairy aid in OF as a sophisticated form of neo-colonialism.

OF supporters maintained that on the macroeconomic level India was gradually cutting commodity imports (aid) while raising indigenous production. Harold Alderman[50] observes:

> The magnitude of this aid raises the usual controversial questions of dependency and disincentives to domestic producers. However, this aid is also presented as an example of how to creatively use commodity aid to promote agricultural development.

On the microeconomic level, Shanti George criticised, with some reason, importation of Northern European breeds to tropical India, and of high-tech processing equipment to an economy with a labour surplus. OF supporters argue that, on the microeconomic level, India settled for a middle way, between inefficient low-tech and expensive, insupportable high-tech. In infrastructure, OF utilised the intermediate technology of efficiently-insulated train cars, instead of costlier refrigeration cars used in the USA and Europe, to transport pasteurised milk to urban centres. This saved costs and functioned well enough for its purposes.

Despite criticism by Claude Alvares and Shanti George over OF's payments to a Swedish firm for setting up a Tetra Pak laminated paper plant, the tetrahedron-shaped milk cartons worked well in coin-operated dispensing machines, and Kurien claimed they used 20 per cent less paper than brick-shaped designs.[51] When evidence for independence from dairy aid, or raised milk consumption or production wore thin, apologists for OF maintained that profits from higher-tech processing plants funded construction of a National Milk Grid System (NMGS)[52], which could stimulate economies of scale in transport infrastructure, which in turn could stimulate rural milk production increases, in a virtuous circle resulting in better nutrition and economic vitality in villages as well as urban centres. As for Flood's early over-emphasis on cross-breeding of zebu (non-descript) cattle with Euro-cattle, it can be said that the naiveté of some planners eventually gave way to recognition that indigenous buffalo have a greater role to play than cross-bred cows in Indian milk production. Over time, progress has been made in cross-breeding northern breeds with zebu cattle. The simplified breakdown above is offered to reprise the OF debate, which corresponded too little with reality.

OF is one example of a 'top-down' dairy marketing structure that in some respects is transferable between differing geographical circumstances. In many respects, OF resembles Britain's Milk Marketing Board, established in England, Wales, Scotland in 1933-34, and in Northern Ireland in 1955.[53] OF also resonates with the aims of the cooperatives which followed the MMB, although UK coop performance since deregulation has been problematic, partly due, in my opinion, to weakening by the Government.[54]

The goals of OF, including coop control of the cold chain from farmer to factory and routine pasteurisation[55], scarcely differ from those of the MMB, which were to improve regular supply to the cities, improve hygiene by policing adulteration, to fight endemic mammalian diseases including tuberculosis[56], and to improve the welfare of farm families formerly at the mercy of *laissez-faire* price-cutting by commercial processors.

The cooperative aspect of OF also parallels dairy coops in the USA, which processed 86% of commercially produced milk in 2002.[57] The biggest coop in the Pacific Northwest is Darigold, which grew as a regional farmer-owned coop after 1918.[58 59]

Many friends and relatives in my extended family have prospered as members of the Darigold cooperative, which augments the generally pro-coop stance of this book. To varying extents – often linked to the strength of farmer participation - organisations such as the MMB in Britain, Darigold in the USA, and OF in India have achieved similar goals including improvements in consumer welfare, farmer welfare, milk hygiene, milk demand, milk supply and reliability of supply via better infrastructure.

Organisation of food aid in India

In the decades following independence, India was a proving ground for three forms of food aid:

(1) Emergency food aid: provided on bilateral, multilateral and NGO bases in emergencies such as the famine in Rajasthan in 1968. Since then, India has admirably improved its 'self-help' abilities. The USA contributed 400,000 tonnes of maize for emergency poultry feed in the historic drought of 1987, but Delhi's actions, using stored food stocks, better distribution and Calamity Relief Funds, demonstrated India's improved response to food emergencies in regions.60
(2) Programme food aid: phased out by 1978. Before then, India absorbed nearly 60 million tonnes of bilateral programme food aid from the USA and Canada, in the years 1956-76, most of which was wheat and cereals, worth $4.8 billion in 1993 prices.61 When the US Government returned Rs16.8 billion in payments for concessionary food grain sales to the Indian Government after a 1974 agreement, some of the repatriated funds were reinvested in animal husbandry and dairy development, as well as irrigation, soil conservation and other projects benefiting agriculture in general. In the period 1968/69 to 1976/77, Canada provided India with about $361 million (1993 prices) of programme food, comprising about three-quarters cereals, nearly one-quarter in rapeseeds and oil, and the rest in skimmed milk powder.
(3) Project food aid: aimed at income transfer to the poor, scheduled castes, tribes, rural poor, women and pre-school children, school lunches, and food-for-work (FFW) projects, etc. India utilised both

domestic food and donations from WFP and other donors for FFW projects in a tradition of such schemes, notably MEGS – the Maharashtra Employment Guarantee Scheme begun 1972. Other major FFW projects were initiated in 1977, 1980, 1983 and 1989.

Project food aid entirely replaced programme aid in which wheat and rice were chiefly provided in India after 1978. In some respects, this was recognition of: economic progress made by the recipient country; the benefits to both recipients and donors of food aid, and the mutual respect required in such relationships[62]; and evidence that properly targeted project food aid posed fewer disincentives to Indian farmers, while offering potential rises in output and welfare rises in Indian dairying. Some observers believe Food-For-Work (FFW) projects, such as in Maharashtra, should be continued to augment 'entitlements' to food, while education and training prepare the next generation for work in the cash economy.

Food aid practitioners including John Shaw and Edward Clay admit it is difficult to distinguish between *programme aid* and *project aid*[63], but say that *programme aid* is always donated on a bilateral government-to-government relationship (offering balance-of-payments support, etc.), while *project aid* effects income transfers to the poor if it is carefully administered by multilateral organisations such as the WFP. Bilateral transfers remain predominant, but multilateral aid (*via* the WFP for development projects or emergency relief from war or natural disasters) is increasingly important. In 1992 the WFP channelled ca. US$3 billion in international aid to over 270 projects which over 3-to-5 years would assist 52 million people. Also in 1992, the WFP helped 26 million people (including 14m refugees) with relief food.

Such appropriately-targeted project aid is probably less vulnerable than mass programme food aid to illegal sales and other corruption. Shaw & Clay[64] note the new trends: 'By 1992, vegetable oil and dairy aid to India comprised over 50 per cent of food aid in terms of value - a remarkable change from the surplus disposal flows of 1950-70, when grain dominated aid flows.'

After a huge spike in mostly bilateral food aid to the Eastbloc after the fall of the Berlin Wall in 1989, world deliveries swung from a record in 1993 (16.8 million tonnes) back to normal in 1996 (7.5 million MT). The logical prioritisation of aid to less-developed countries in Sub-Saharan Africa reasserted itself as the multilateral portion of global deliveries rose to 35 per cent - of which 98 per cent was channelled by the WFP. Food aid to South and East Asia also declined.[65]

The WFP had refined project aid in India. By the 1970s, there was consensus in the aid community that the effectiveness of food and dairy aid could be multiplied if combined with technical expertise, and cash or loans when appropriate. Some FFW schemes evolved to offer cash payment as an alternative to commodity staples.

Clay & Shaw[66] note that in the 'closed monetization system' distinctive to WFP's project food aid to India, workers receive their full wages in cash, then have the option to buy family rations of cereals, butter oil, vegetable oil and pulses in fair-price shops. A family of 5-to-6 people can be fed on about 50 per cent of the wages. WFP ration prices are pegged about 40-50 per cent of local market prices.

But pricing food aid commodities lower than local produce sends up a red flag: Is it a disincentive to local farmers?

No, Clay & Shaw seem to imply. Such fair price shops have 'led to additional demand for locally produced food.' How? They claim investment of fair price shop sales, managed by GOI, State and WFP officials, results in additional employment and procurement of local food and goods. Computerised monitoring (presumably of prevailing market prices, etc.) supported by USAID, UNICEF and the Canadian International Development and Research Centre tries to ensure that the aggregate local economic effect is positive, and in particular, not discouraging local farm production. But how do fair price shops compare to OF urban milk sales? Monetised dairy aid sales were open to anyone lucky enough to afford them, while fair price shops are generally restricted to the poor. Critics such as Clive Crook complain too many middle-class people inveigle eligibility for such food aid schemes. Crook is just one of decades of *Economist* writers deriding economically prosperous, politically-well-organised middle-class people who lobby for 'pork barrel' benefits intended for the poor.

Likewise, in Britain's debate on student university tuition fees the *Economist* argument in favour of fees runs: *Why should a Glasgow bus driver pay taxes to send the daughter of a Knightsbridge millionaire to Oxbridge?* Translated to India, many argue: *Why must a poor person from the scheduled castes queue in fair price shops with the spouse of a university professor?* Those supporting complete economic liberalisation and deregulation saw the pre-1991 Gordion Knot of India's poverty programmes so fraught with loopholes benefiting the rich, that they reckoned the poor would be better off if the whole complex were cut asunder.

Table 6.2.

Agrostat FAO: India: commodity composition of non-cereal food aid: 1977-88 (x Thousand MT)				
Year	Dried skim milk (SMP)	Other dairy products[a/]	Vegetable oil	Butter oil (BO)
1977	26.6	4.2	70.2	14.0
1978	43.2	5.6	96.1	11.1
1979	41.7	5.2	77.6	16.8
1980	28.1	4.8	57.5	23.6
1981	72.7	6.8	54.7	23.6
1982	36.4	2.9	37.7	8.2
1983	13.1	9.0	52.0	1.4
1984	69.8	12.7	69.6	27.5
1985	10.2	10.3	44.3	4.2
1986	4.1	11.0	100.0	3.8
1987 drought...	27.2	15.9	57.8	6.4
1988	20.2	15.3	111.4	13.9
a/ Includes dairy component of blended foods (Table source: Shaw & Clay 1993: 62-65)				

As eradication of all such programmes is politically unlikely, and undoubtedly harmful to many needy people, critics must content themselves with two positive outcomes from fair price shop sales: savings to any shopper, rich or poor, releases additional cash for purchases of other food or non-food items, and proper investment of fair-price profits improves existing infrastructure, leading to more aggregate output - just as sales of OF dairy commodities built the National Milk Grid System.

Like programme aid, targeted project aid also can mitigate government macroeconomic fiscal and balance-of-payments problems, such as currency devaluations, World Bank-mandated SAPs, or price rises in oil or other necessary imports, by displacing commercial imports, while allowing more investment in domestic development.[67] This describes precisely the rationales for Operation Flood. After partial success in the Green Revolution in the 1960s, the Indian Government and EEC donors turned to the White Revolution.

Coincidentally in 1968, Europe's dairy topography was marked by 306,000 MT in the Butter Mountain and Milk Lake, while avalanches of skim milk powder gorged calves on protein. Thus was born what Ruth Heredia[68] calls the 'Billion-Litre Idea' to monetise these surpluses in India, funding infrastructure to integrate rural producers with urban consumers: Dr. Adekke Boerma, Director-General of the FAO, and Dr. Kurien collaborated, 1968-69, to win FAO/WFP approval of Kurien's revolutionary plan to 'convert aid into trade'. Let us now synopsise the three ambitious phases of Flood, commencing in 1970 when Indian dairy prices[69] were substantially above world levels, and ending in 1996, as they approached world levels and were already lower than in the USA or Europe.

Because OF and literature on it evolved over time, various sources assign slightly different time periods to its three phases. A thumbnail sketch would show, simply, that: inaugurated in 1970, OF-I was characterised by the opportunity to 'monetise' EEC commodities via the WFP and reinvest the proceeds in four metropolitan dairies, and extend the 'Anand Pattern' in cooperatives in 10 states; in OF-II dairy commodity aid was bolstered by World Bank loans to unite additional urban consumers and rural farmers (often producing just 1-2 litres a day) from as far apart as 2000 km via a road & rail tanker National Milk Grid System; and OF-III was basically an extension of preceding phases, coupled with a nationwide membership drive eventually signing 10m farmers, as OF officials weaned India of dairy aid and achieved a remarkable level of dairy autonomy by its termination in 1996. Institutions dated phases of Operation Flood according to their own participation. For example World Bank[70] documents refer to its 'fourth dairy project [which] was an integral part of OF-II'. This book adopts familiar dating used in NDDB literature after termination of the third phase in late 1996.

OF-I (1970-81): a top-down milk grid over India

Monetisation of WFP dairy aid began in Operation Flood-Phase I in July, 1970.[71] According to a 1976 WFP[72] report the objectives of OF-I were to:

(1) make milk available at stable, reasonable prices to urban consumers, including vulnerable groups such as pre-schoolers and mothers.
(2) let coops respond to consumer preferences so farmers earn a greater share of retail price.
(3) raise rural dairy productivity with the aims of achieving national dairy self-sufficiency while raising incomes of marginal and landless farmers.
(4) remove cattle from the cities.
(5) 'establish a broad basis for accelerated development of the national dairy industry in the project period as well as after.'

Objective 5 referred to the most controversial 'top-down' component of Phase I, establishing a template of what would be the National Milk Grid System (NMGS). In a diamond-shaped grid, four geographically disparate metropolitan nodes, Bombay (Mumbai), Calcutta (Kolkata), Delhi and Madras (Chennai), were chosen so that when they were linked, logistics would be as efficient as possible in balancing supply in surplus and deficit regions. Bottom-up components were initially more productive in bringing Anand's success to areas likely to replicate it. NDDB[73] literature recalls: 'Producers' cooperatives were a central plank of the project [OF-I], which sought to link dairy development with milk marketing.'

They reflected the knowledge that - as PM Shastri remarked to his host Dr. Kurien in a 1964 visit - although Anand could boast neither the best cattle nor land, coop farmers thrived because they had a ready market in Bombay. The NDDB[74] designed OF-I to: 'link the four metropolitan dairies with their logical hinterland milksheds in 10 states. OF-I (1970-81), the first attempt to replicate Anand Pattern outside Gujarat - replicated the pattern up to union tier in India's 18 best rural milksheds.'

OF Phase-I established or improved forward- and backward-linkages among these 18 'logical hinterland milksheds' and the four biggest metro centres of Bombay, Calcutta, Delhi and Madras. Objective 2 (above) alludes to commercialisation strategies in the Amul vision of creative marketing, serving both farmers and consumers and, distasteful as it was to some socialists wary of consumer culture, opening the door to advertising, modern vending machines and Tetra Pak milk cartons. At the 'union tier' level in the hinterland was a Milk Producer's Union (MPU) or regional cooperative society coordinating milk transport, 24-hour veterinary services, etc. P.J. Atkins[75] writes that the grid; 'ensures the balancing of supply and demand across the boundaries of metropolitan milksheds by transferring milk from areas of surplus to areas of deficit.'

John Empson[76] notes that OF-I began with skim milk powder (SMP) and butter oil (BO) commodities from the WFP. Doornbos *et al.*[77] cite a 1977 FAO report by M. Halse tracing OF-I origins directly to the EEC, and explaining that OF-I was proposed by the NDDB in 1968 when it realised that: '20,000 tonnes of table butter were to be presented (by the EEC) free to India...enough to wreck the Anand pattern cooperatives' market plan for some years to come.' *The Trojan Horse was at the gates!* According to Doornbos *et al.*, the GOI accepted the NDDB's proposal of OF-I for reasons including balance-of-payments advantages when dairy aid displaced commercial imports; the possibility 'to increase the meagre dairy development budget several fold and to give a big push for dairy development'; and because the GOI favoured replication in India of Anand-type coops, and thus Anand control of these EEC commodities dovetailed with official policy.

As it unfolded, this was a dramatic instance of leaders in a recipient country exerting pro-active control of forthcoming dairy aid in order to minimise disincentives to their own farmers, along with destruction of their organisational goals in linked markets. It was important to its success that the NDDB (founded in 1965 by Tribhuvandas and his assistant Kurien[78]) and the Indian Dairy Commission enjoyed strong patronage from the GOI - which had favoured the Amul/Anand model since the visit there by Prime Minister Shastri in 1964. PM Indira Gandhi, who succeeded Shastri in 1966, put more emphasis than her father PM Nehru had on Green and White Revolutions, to cut dependence on aid.

There were other reasons why the GOI wished to spur dairy development. Not least was hygiene (Objective 4). By vertically integrating and eliminating time delays in the 'cold chain' between rural producer and city consumer, OF was designed to avoid spoilage and, not least, eliminate the middleman - the local milk trader who stereotypically paid producers a pittance, then adulterated the milk with water (or worse) before selling it to a distributor. Shanti George[79] plays devil's advocate in her often-amusing 1985 critique, defending 'the petty dairy marketeer' as a likeable 'villain' whose unsung virtues included moneylending to housewives in a cash pinch. It is true the middleman is not all bad, but the Anand pattern indisputably raised national standards for milk sanitation. And colourful as *dudhiyas* were and continue to be in India's large (+/-80 per cent) informal milk sector, producers probably have as much affection for the village coop clerk who pays cash for their milk everyday - plus a yearly bonus.

A sub-component of OF-I was a plan (Objective 4) to transport cattle from urban milk colonies to rural areas. Theoretically, this would enhance the rural bovine gene pool, fuel supply and crops fertilisation, while cutting urban pollution. This proved impractical. In the first instance, cattle dung was recycled as domestic fuel even in urban areas. And the existence of many old or dry cows lolling about the streets of metropoles shows the dearth of funds to repatriate cows to ruralities.

OF-I was initially approved for five years by the WFP in 1969, but 'delays in the expansion of existing dairies, followed by the world crisis in dairy commodities which severely curtailed WFP's shipments to the projects'[80], including laggard shipments by the EEC, slowed implementation (and gave Dr. Kurien opportunity to scold aid donors on the hypocrisy of donating rancid milk powder.) Thus, instead of ending around 1975, OF-I was extended another 6 years. Besides delays in dairy aid imports and replication of the Anand pattern in the milksheds around Bombay, Calcutta, Delhi and Madras, a more positive reason to extend OF-I was recognition by the NDDB and GOI of the uses for EEC dairy aid, and that monetised aid really *could* bring greater economies of scale to Indian dairying. In any event, OF-I was extended until 1981.

Problems during OF-I:

Doornbos *et al.* as well as Shanti George discern a bias to Gujarat, which already enjoyed extensive cooperative infrastructure in five of its districts before OF-I formally began. It is true that of a total of Rs 1248 million OF-I funds disbursed, Gujarat absorbed 30 per cent of OF-I funds - about five-times that allotted to less developed Bihar and Rajasthan. Years later, following OF-III, Candler & Kumar[81] (1998) identified Gujarat investment as 36 per cent above the national average per kilogram of milk produced (compared to 24 per cent underinvestment in Maharashtra) but praised Anand for plant efficiency: 'It appears that on efficiency grounds Gujarat was not overbuilt.' NDDB authorities hotly denied that Gujarat accounted for an unreasonable share of funds, partly on the grounds that expansion there was already self-sustaining. But it can be imagined that the existence of additional funds making possible world-class facilities would have encouraged their construction in order to assist in R & D for processing, marketing, training at the Vidya Dairy, etc. It would be odd not to expect Anand to ensure whatever success was within its grasp by developing the 'promising areas'[82] of Gujarat. Purported bias and in the implementation of OF-I can also be explained by failings of a more prosaic, political nature. M.V. Kamath, a journalist-turned chronicler of OF and its director Dr. Kurien, cites chronic corruption at Patna in Bihar (which was to supply Calcutta), suggesting that project authorities were prudent when holding the purse strings tight.[83]

Doornbos *et al.*[84] cite a 1978 GOI report blaming: (1) underestimates of the 'manpower, time and money needed' to help producers set up Anand-style coops, as well as political delays by state governments such as Karnataka and Kerala[85] resistant to the Anand model; (2) the new coops modelled on Anand were left 'in the hands of local bureaucrats, while putting the responsibility for their performance on the project authority' - interests that did not, unfortunately, always coincide; (3) underestimates of the 'capability' and political will of public dairy corporations to properly run their dairies.[86] Over the years it became obvious that, except at Delhi, the dairies were built without due regard for the complex, intranational requirements of the national milk grid. Additionally, too many dairy managers (e.g. in Bihar) remunerated indigenous farmers insufficiently (depressing indigenous output) and then substituted too much imported SMP and BO, further depressing indigenous prices. This was a cardinal misuse of dairy aid, of the type John W. Mellor warned of, and it was later corrected after a rebuke in the 1984 Jha Committee Report.

The organisational competence of the NDDB, and OF authorities such as Dr. Kurien (who, for the first time in a FAO/WFP proposal, was charged with personal responsibility for success of OF-I), was bitterly questioned by Claude Alvares[87] and Shanti George. Doornbos *et al.* note that although the NDDB Annual Report 1980-81 claimed 10,423 Anand pattern societies were formed during OF-I, nearly half of these, tied to districts in Kaira, Baroda, Mehsana, Sabarkantha and Banaskantha, were actually formed *before* OF-I began.[88] Apparently, claims of early membership were inflated.

In hindsight, it is easy to criticise bureaucrats, politicians and plant managers for poor decisions and foot-dragging in the implementation of OF-I. But in the context of their times, subject to the whip-saw of inconsistent government policy, their actions appear no more culpable than the sporadic performance of rich countries, and the WFP, in deliveries of promised commodities. It is worth recalling that OF-I was implemented barely two decades after independence, while the Cold War blew political priorities in unpredictable fashion. In decades beset by civil war (Pakistan-Bangladesh), a border war (with China), and drought, it was not clear to everyone across India that a handful of technocrats and cooperative managers in Anand saw the country's dairy future clearly. Ruth Heredia[89] notes the founding of Gujarat's Kaira Coop was preceded by milk coops in Madras, Allahabad and Lucknow. Tribhuvandas freely acknowledged learning from them, and Kaira/Amul/Anand's overall superiority was earned nationally only after years of labour.

Not everything went to plan in OF-I. The plan to transfer city-kept cattle to the country was according to Doornbos *et al.*, a non-starter, due to transport shortages and a reluctance of urban cowhands to relocate, which was eventually overcome when procurement prices rose for rural producers. Embarrassingly, plans to extend milk programmes to pre-school children in 20 cities were finally launched in fewer than 10 cities, and continued only in Delhi and Calcutta.[90] Dr. Kurien disavowed responsibility for idealistic schemes that politicians pinned on the coat-tails of Operation Flood which - as Candler & Kumar's[91] 1998 World Bank report aptly noted - was a dairy project concerned less with 'remedying a production shortage' than 'providing a market for existing producers.'

The Mother Dairies, i.e. the large urban processing plants in the four metro centres of Bombay, Calcutta, Delhi and Madras (where 3 per cent of India's population consumed 6 per cent of the milk[92]) were castigated by Shanti George as white elephants of wasteful technology. Doornbos *et al.* agree, commenting that after the total capacity of the Mother Dairies was tripled from 100,000 to 300,000 litres per day during OF-I, their throughput was often far below optimal. In identifying anomalies and failures in the design and implementation of Operation Flood, Doornbos *et al.* (1990) give the impression they regard much of it as a boondoggle, but do not seem to quibble with the need for capital investments in a national milk grid *per se*. Doornbos *et al.* seem to leave it for history to judge - which it did, positively: the 1970-96 trebling of Indian milk production indicates the trebling of Mother Dairy capacity was prescient. In their 1998 report for the World Bank, Candler & Kumar acknowledge the 'important and critical strand' of two books, by Doornbos and Nair[93] (1990), and by Doornbos and others[94] (1990) at the Indo-Dutch Program on Alternatives on

Development (IDPAD) to the literature which, however: 'while critical of Operation Flood, offer few alternative policy prescriptions.' In emails in early 2009, Professor Doornbos mentioned that he was being given an opportunity by the Institute of Social Studies to comment on some of his research team's judgements in hindsight. Some of those observations are below, and others will surely see print.

Under-utilised capacity (partly due to logistical bottlenecks and low indigenous production - but largely due to improper pricing) promoted dependence of urban dairies on imported SMP and BO in production of recombined milk. Dairy aid was estimated to comprise 22 per cent of throughput around 1970, but Doornbos, van Stuijvenberg & Terhal claimed that dependence on dairy aid rose to ca. 36 per cent in 1981-82.[95] P.J. Atkins responded that their figure was misleading in the light of later data, which showed that dairy aid represented just 17.7 per cent of throughput between 1982/83 and 1983/84, and that it was predicted to fall to 3 per cent around 1990.[96] Nevertheless, some figures on processing throughput in the mid-1980s appeared as harbingers of permanent dependence on EEC dairy aid. The astounding *amounts* diverted from the EEC's milk powder and butter surplus mountains (about 127,000 MT of SMP and ca. 36,000 MT of BO) during OF-I (1970-81) hinted thraldom to Europe. On the other hand, according to M. Jul[97], supporters claimed:

> making milk available cheaply to urban consumers, Operation Flood has made milk consumption feasible for those who do not belong to the highest income groups… Some also claim that the price of milk has fallen relative to the price of most other food items and hence, milk is more accessible to lower income groups…

Besides the supply and sanitation improvements welcomed by middle-class and poorer urban consumers, other statistics reflected organisational progress in OF. Supporters lauded increased stability in milk flows to urban markets where rising demand increased income security for farmers in milksheds supplying those cities. A World Bank study by George Mergos & Roger Slade[98] in Madhya Pradesh found an 'increase in milk output attributable to' Flood was '17.4 per cent over five years'. The Indian Institute of Public Opinion (Delhi) found a 24.6 per cent yield rise in 17 OF-I milksheds over a 7-year period. Other studies found higher productivity-per-animal owned by coop members, versus non-coop farmers - but no sooner were such studies published than OF detractors sought to discredit them. Nevertheless, Doornbos *et al.*[99] conclude that rural farmers probably did gain from the improved supply system and note that the:

'indigenous procurement of milk rose from 70,000 litres per day (lpd) in 1970 to 150,000 lpd in 1981-82.'

M.V. Kamath[100] relates that OF-I was 'originally...scheduled to be over by 1975' but by the time it was completed on March 31, 1981, 'it had dragged on for another five years, to everyone's discomfiture.' Fortunately, progress was made in integrating metropoles with their 18 logical milksheds and, except for Calcutta, the Mother Dairies had won 'commanding shares' of their liquid milk markets, led by Bombay (62 per cent), Delhi (57 per cent) and Madras (45 per cent). If urban processors could ever cut EEC aid, the Flood development plan might dampen the ire of its detractors.

OF-II (1981-85): consolidation, a membership drive - democracy?

Built on the foundation of OF-I (and previous assistance by the World Bank to dairy programmes in Karnataka, Madhya Pradesh and Rajasthan), Phase II commenced Bank funding of the NDDB's drive to national consolidation, coupled with a reemphasis on democratic 'Anand pattern' principles. But Shanti George was not impressed, noting that OF-II was planned, 'without significant policy change in the basic approach' to India's problems'. At any rate, the objectives[101] of OF-II were to:

(1) enlist 10 million farmer families in a self-sustaining dairy industry by mid-1985.
(2) raise a National Milch Herd of 14m cross-bred cows & upgraded buffaloes in the 1980s.
(3) build National Milk Grid System (NMGS) linking rural farmers to 150m urban consumers.
(4) develop national dairy support: e.g. veterinary services, artificial insemination (AI); vaccines, larger dairy processing and conservation systems of domestic manufacture; provision of managerial and technical training for rural dairy plants; supply butter oil at reasonable prices for cooking, and 'extruded foods' for infants; and develop a Management Information System (MIS) for decision makers throughout the NMGS.
(5) raise the proportion of milk and milk products in a 'stable, nutritionally adequate national diet' estimated at 180 grams per capita daily.

In its efforts to heed PM Shastri's call in the 1960s to 'transplant the spirit of Anand in many other places'[102] Anand faced abundant bureaucratic resistance. Managers of previously established state and GOI dairy projects could be as compliant with Anand *dicta* as bullocks with their hooves dug into the soil. Naturally, NDDB/OF authorities sought to consolidate national control, as they expanded from 18 to 136 milksheds linked to ca. 290 urban markets[103] and developed coop cluster federations linked to the four Mother Dairies. Improving accountability at the federation level would curb corruption (which the NDDB claimed was rife in state programmes) and protect the virtue of Flood, like that of Caesar's wife. So the NDDB recommended to Delhi that coop cluster federations, rather than bureaucrats in public or state dairy corporations, become implementing agencies at state level, and that some dairy aid be allocated to local feeder-balancing dairies tied to local towns. The state federations were expected to guide formation of milkshed unions, ensuring they got off to a democratic start by holding early elections to union and federation boards. Based on the principle of one (wo)man, one vote, these reforms genuinely strengthened democratic participation by farmer-members. Bye-laws included mandatory retirement of one-third of board members annually, as well as quarterly audits and limits on society participation in loan schemes.[104] These safeguards did not always win the ardour of entrenched politicians.

Writer P. Sainath[105] writes in *Everybody Loves a Good Drought* that drought is 'among the more serious problems' faced by a country where, he adds: 'Drought relief, almost equally beyond question, is rural India's biggest growth industry.' Sainath's wit aside, the OF-II package was intelligently designed to stabilise milk supply over drought or flush and lean months. It also conveniently wrested control from uncooperative bureaucrats. Meanwhile, Anand lobbied Delhi to promote the IDC/NDDB/OF nexus. Although Tribhuvandas took pains to maintain the NDDB's political neutrality (e.g. banning the use of NDDB vehicles in political campaigns), the Congress Party was often forthcoming. It did no harm when Indira Gandhi, the Congress Party Prime Minister first elected in 1966, was re-elected in 1980. Dr. Kurien, (a crocodile who swims in milk) never forgets those who have mentored Operation Flood. On his office wall hung an autographed photo mural of Mrs. Gandhi speaking at a dairy conference. Kurien was careful that, before meeting the Janata coalition leader who defeated Mrs. Gandhi in the 1977 after the 1975-77 'Emergency', he first paid a courtesy call on Mrs. Gandhi.

Reinforcement of Anand's leadership spurred completion of the National Milk Grid System (NMGS). In Gujarat, the western region, and other favoured areas, logistical efficiencies raised rural dairy incomes. (Meanwhile, critics assailed OF for supposedly robbing the rural poor of milk shipped to relieve 'milk droughts' in the metropoles.) Increased farmer participation in coop decision-making decreased disincentives apparent in OF-I, when profit-minded processors relied too much on cheap dairy aid, in a vicious circle that discouraged indigenous production. OF critics were difficult to please. Raymond Crotty[106] wrote that at least in some instances:

'the sale of reconstituted EEC milk enables the Indian Dairy Corporation to pay a higher price than it would otherwise for milk in the village.'

At this Alderman *et al.*[107] chortled that Crotty's view was at least 'more consistent than [Shanti] George's view that Operation Flood does not raise real producer prices yet it induces producers to increase the supply of milk to the market.' Nor were critics placated by reforms in OF-II. They saw them mainly as subterfuges to further consolidate OF control of what was becoming the Third World's largest, most expensive dairy development scheme. Doornbos *et al.*[108] wrote: 'Compared to OF-I, OF-II was planned as a much more ambitious undertaking.'

The initial ambitious proposal for 1979~85, a US$200 million credit from the International Development Agency (IDA) was trimmed by the World Bank to US$150m. The Bank also trimmed projections of dairy aid to be donated by the EEC. The original budget outlay was to be Rs 4855 million, with 36 per cent derived from a World Bank loan offered to Dr. Kurien in 1978 by Robert McNamara (*via* IDA on concessionary terms), 15 per cent from repayments of OF-I loans, and the largest portion, 49 per cent, to come from sales of recombined SMP and BO. Doornbos notes a 'striking' difference between initial 'projections' and 'the real resource flows' that OF eventually controlled, and identifies two reasons for this: EEC dairy commodities were sold at *higher* prices than originally planned, and EEC dairy aid was expanded beyond expectations through 'large *ad hoc* gifts.'[109] Originally, 186 thousand MT of SMP and 76 thousand MT of BO were planned in OF-II (ca. 50 per cent mote than OF-I). But *ad hoc* EEC gifts amounted to an additional 41 thousand MT of SMP and over six thousand MT of butter from EEC storage, in OF-II (ca. 1978-87). This dairy avalanche totalled OF-II dairy aid of ca. 227 thousand MT of SMP and ca. 82 thousand MT of BO and butter - about 80 per cent more milk powder and roughly twice the butter commodities received by OF-I. Whereas most OF-I commodities were received only by the four biggest metropolitan dairies (and a few feeder balancing plants), additional *ad hoc* EEC donations in OF-II made possible the channelling (from buffer stocks) of commodities to many rural dairies which, heretofore had received none. Predictably, critics complained that too much went to the state of Gujarat, and particularly, as much as 8 per cent of SMP to the original Amul coop. The Indian minister of agriculture denied favouritism, claiming that: 'Amul received about 3.8 per cent of SMP and 4.6 per cent of BO donated under OF-I, and about 2.6 per cent of SMP and 1.6 per cent of BO donated under OF-II (till 31st March 1983).'

However, even if Amul/Anand received only its fair share of *commodities*, Doornbos *et al.* point in the same passage to evidence of *financial* favouritism to Amul in both OF-I and OF-II: out of a total estimated value of capital assets of Rs 130.7 million in 1983, the Amul coop accounted for Rs 31 million in grants and 53.4 million in assets. Had funds been embezzled, such statistics might rankle but, on the contrary, evidence abounds that funds were invested in productive infrastructure. Nevertheless, as Gujarat begat the 'Anand model', and Anand was the headquarters of OF leaders Kurien and Tribhuvandas, it was unsurprising when allocations to Gujarat were attacked by Claude Alvares and other detractors. According to Doornbos *et al.*[110] OF-II was planned not only to establish feeder balancing dairies, to raise milk supply to as many as 147 cities with populations over 100 thousand, but also to spread the Anand model geographically by enrolling 10 million more families. P.J. Atkins[111] says: 'In summary this was the diffusion and mass adoption phase of the "package" offered by OF.'

To support this extension of Anand style coops around the country, OF managers also put in motion plans to improve input services such as artificial insemination (AI) and - more controversially - to establish a National Milch Herd (Objective 2) of 10-15 million animals, in order to double production. OF-II planning was more explicit than that of OF-I and, perhaps to mitigate fears that European breeds would totally replace indigenous buffaloes[112], plans called for the 7-10 million cross-bred cows in the National Milch Herd to be supplemented by 'improved buffaloes'. Integrating buffaloes into the NMGS (which now had the technology to make powder from surplus milk in flush months, for use in lean months), was according to M.V. Kamath, made possible by a decision made by Kurien around 1953.

It was a decision so far-reaching that we have referred to it in previous chapters: Over UNICEF's recommendation to buy Dutch-made Volme equipment (which scorched buffalo milk) for a new powder-making plant, Kurien insisted on a Danish-made Niro Atomizer. The result was the first plant in India (if not the world) to make SMP from high-fat buffalo milk. Kurien's insistence on the buffalo-friendly system is a landmark case of a recipient rejecting inappropriate aid and insisting on technology appropriate to indigenous production. Kurien's rejection of UNICEF's short-sighted advice thus lessened dependence on European cows.[113] M.V. Kamath claims OF developed SMP from buffalo milk despite dissembling by a powder expert from New Zealand, whose country stood to lose export sales if OF succeeded. Kamath records Kurien's reaction: 'Then only I realised how the advice of Technical Experts is coloured by the economic interests of their respective countries.' Anand had forged ahead in the late-1950s and '60s, first in manufacturing condensed milk after a Nestlé official (to his later dismay) unwisely said it was too delicate to be made by 'natives', and later, baby food from buffalo milk against the advice of Glaxo. Thence,

Kurien called success in baby food as 'doing a Nestlé on Glaxo', claiming he had 'beaten the multinationals at their own game'.

The Economist[114] recognised how effectively the Anand-led cooperatives fought off foreign multinationals in a 2008 article. Certainly Kurien fought the White Revolution with much zeal. Whether or not it explains the tonnes of print criticism thrown at Anand for turning rural milk into baby food, ice cream and other value-added products affordable only by middle or upper class citizens is another matter. Fault-finders forget that a market for such products *already existed*, and Amul brand's erosion of multinationals' market share saved foreign exchange for the GOI.

The NDDB gratefully employed bilateral and multilateral aid which, because it was used so productively, was usually available. Cattle feed concentrate plants, planned to use processing wastes unsuitable for human foodstuffs, were prioritised under OF-II, after the model of the Kaira Union plant built with FAO and Oxfam help. This is a key example of how the low-input/low-output Anand pattern was designed for environmental sustainability, and to avoid rivalry between humans and animals for food. Reemphasis on input services, i.e. extension and training for farmers, and research on cattle breeding, feeding and health was augmented by a British-assisted vaccine plant for foot-and-mouth-disease (FMD) which critics claimed European strains were prone to. Denmark's DANIDA helped set up the NDDB's training and animal disease diagnostic laboratory at Anand, and the Swiss Government helped found the Institute of Rural Management in Anand (IRMA). During OF-II (responding to a paradigm shift among development theorists from 'basic needs' toward integrating rural sectors into national economies) extravagant claims were made, generally by non-NDDB sources, of OF's ability to reduce poverty in remote areas, even though Doornbos *et al.*[115] concede: 'The plans for Operation Flood II and III do not mention this urgent priority.'

In *Wheels of Fire*[116], a 1983 BBC-TV documentary on Operation Flood, Kurien took pains to say that, while dairy development happens to be an effective means to attack poverty, it is not the only means and must not be thought so. While not resisting the supposition that dairying can ease social problems, OF officials resolutely reiterated the principle that it was a dairy development programme, not a social programme. This attitude is expressed in NDDB policy to District Cooperative Societies (DCSs). Thus, if, as A.K. Sharma[117] found in 1995, ca. 25 per cent of the 10,000 milk societies in Uttar Pradesh were 'defunct and not working', the NDDB would target them for additional investment or closure. Candler & Kumar[118] commended the NDDB's:

> remarkably hard-headed and commercial attitude to the supplying DCSs. If a DCS cannot supply sufficient milk to cover the variable costs of collection, then after appropriate discussion, the MPU [Milk Producers Union] withdraws its collection service.

It goes without saying that not taking a hard-headed and commercial approach in OF budgeting would have been foolish. By attention to 'bottom line' profitability, OF could reinvest reasonable amounts of monetised funds from recombination of EEC dairy aid with local milk not just to finance shiny new Mother Dairies in metropoles, but more importantly to prime the pump for milk flows to the cities from poor rural farmers (remunerated at the best farmgate prices in a century). Anand officials knew it is cruel to be too kind. Supporting unremunerative DCSs would detract from anti-poverty effects of better-placed DCSs, and sacrifice the overall profitability of the national system.

Another flash point of the OF debate was milk consumption in rural villages where, claimed critics, women and children sacrificed milk consumption when the lactic cash crop was capturedby middle class, urban consumers.[119] OF had been planned to be 'neutral' regarding the welfare of so-called vulnerable groups, and an entire sub-topic of research developed on these questions. Martin Doornbos and Manoshi Mitra question the effect on women and vulnerable groups of the flow of rural milk to cities[120] but acknowledge that milk payments can be transformed into larger amounts of protein-rich legumes, pulses, etc. In light of this, Kurien[121] tartly comments that it makes as much sense 'for the poorest people to buy *caviar* as milk' instead of legumes and pulses. But writing from another vantage point, Miriam Sharma and Urmila Vanjani[122] used the pejorative phrase 'nutritional apartheid' for situations where: 'neither the rural areas in general, nor women specifically, are likely to benefit from increased milk production in terms of consumption.'

Although the phrase nutritional apartheid seems hyperbole, Sharma & Vanjani[123] may be on firmer ground criticising 'internal colonialism' in OF which, they claim, reinforces negative stereotypes in Indian gender relations: 'the modern dairy system represented by the male-controlled processing and marketing centres in the city depend upon the cheap labour-intensive work of females operating in the rural sector.'

Sharma & Vanjani's resentment of male hegemony over most new high-tech jobs offered by OF is understandable. Women's status may have suffered in some villages where OF divested women of their traditional responsibility for processing milk into ghee - turning some skilled cottage processors into glorified cowherds, while their male counterparts learned the intricacies of vacuum pumps in gleaming dairy temples of stainless steel.

Defenders of Operation Flood would respond that the programme was designed to be gender-neutral. Writing ca. five years later (1998) Candler & Kumar[124] seem to mourn the loss of village ghee-making little, emphasising instead the income from coop milk sales controlled by women, the increasing importance of Women's Dairy Coop Societies (6000 WDCSs with 300,000 members in 1998), NDDB encouragement of women to visit factories and study animal husbandry, and ample evidence that coop dairying is seen by many (or most) villagers as greatly increasing the likelihood that *girls* as well as boys attend school. Candler & Kumar conclude OF: 'provides an example of a programme redesign to address gender issues.'

OF officials steadfastly maintained their primary responsibility was raising milk production and consumption, not social engineering for all issues. The enduring effects of shifting ghee manufacture from some villages to local processors were exaggerated. As Shagufta Jamal found in her socio-economic study of ghee-making, it is generally households of a higher socio-economic status, usually with more land, that had enough surplus milk to make ghee or khoa.[125] Ideally, women can turn profits from coop milk into remunerative activities with high status, perhaps by purchasing a sewing machine for cottage textile making. One example is Gujarat, with its rich history of fine textile making. This heritage has been extended to poor women by the Tribhuvandas Foundation.

Judged by so many competing criteria, was OF-II less controversial than OF-I? No. OF-I likely enjoyed a 'honeymoon period' that was a sweet memory by 1985. Although gift dairy imports accounted for only about 1 per cent of Indian milk production[126] the physical quantities were immense, and the status of OF as the world's largest dairy development programme made it a magnet for critical study by academics and the popular press. Because concrete data were scarce, pundits had rein to cast OF according to their ideological expectations. Doornbos *et al.*[127] said the 'lack of adequate statistics' on some production and consumption trends made it necessary to judge OF-II 'indirectly'. Assessing an array of reports on OF-II by NDDB/OF, federal Government (GOI), the EC Commission and the EC Court of Auditors, Doornbos *et al.* found the latter report by the EC Auditors far more critical than the others and inferred that stagnancy in net Indian dairy production and consumption lay behind 'discontinuities' in statistics. Doornbos *et al.* assessed 'three main dimensions':

(1) Total number of milksheds covered, dairy cooperative societies established, total number of members of these societies, and total milk procurement.

(2) Milk procurement at the village level and farmers' participation, regionally desegregated.
(3) Coverage and quality of input services.

Briefly, they found dimension (1) 'was successful' but warned that 'a word of caution' was necessary, because of 'discontinuities' in (2) specifically, that dairy 'programmes in Karnataka, Madhya Pradesh and Rajasthan' were blithely included in statistics as OF-II parastatals, even though they were financed by the IDA (and World Bank) on a different basis. Doornbos *et al.* also noted that OF described its dismantling of existing dairy corporations (traditional fiefs of the states) 'in terms of democratisation and farmer control', although its actions 'had more to do' with incorporating them into the 'centralised IDC/NDDB controlled structure' behind OF. As for dimension (3) Doornbos *et al.*[128] concluded in reference to the Jha Committee Report that the increase of input services for animal health, breeding and feeding was below expectations, mostly because of slow disbursal of funds, and that regions outside Gujarat required expansion of inputs to increase performance; they[129] concluded that OF-II had: 'not caused a substantial intensification of milk production. The increase in procurement is basically due to the progressive extension of the catchment area rather than to any increased productivity per society or member.'

But the NDDB rejected calls for more emphasis on 'bottom-up' inputs and services, claiming rightly that earlier success at Amul proved an 'assured market' and a 'fair price' were sufficient incentives for coops to progress on a loan, not grant, basis. In contemporary business jargon, Operation Flood invested in future success by a Machiavellian seizure of market share - while temporarily ignoring bottom line profitability, and unit productivity. OF authorities refused to ignore the big picture, i.e. the 'top-down' importance of bringing millions of farmer families from additional areas onto cooperative rosters.

Institution building was augmented by physical capital in the National Milk Grid System (NMGS). Cynics expecting funds to be wasted on imported freon-based refrigeration systems were disappointed. Kamath[130] reported over 90 per cent of equipment was procured domestically from a growing roster of firms - virtually everything except some 'packaging…aseptic processing and ice cream' machinery and the largest homogenisers used in 1 million lpd dairies. Flood's sub-continental-sized road and rail tanker system relied mainly on cheaper, efficient insulation rather than expensive refrigeration. P.C. Bardhan[131] of the NDDB claimed the technology in dairy coops was 'efficient' but not 'labour-displacing' - experience showed coop societies collecting as little as '100 litres of milk a day are viable'.

Price reform follows the Jha Committee Report
Although it judged OF 'successful', the 1984 Jha Committee Report[132] slapped the wrists of OF authorities for: 'lack of attention for production increase and input services, *too low producer prices* and over-investment in physical capital. [Italics by author]'

Compliance by OF and state officials to the sub-text of this superficially mild rebuke on pricing by the Jha Committee was crucial to the eventual success of Flood. This is because artificially-low urban sales prices, and discouraging producer prices noted above, were the most detrimental parameters dogging the early phases of OF. However, it must be noted that they were – irritatingly - beyond the control of OF authorities in Anand. Evidence of counter-productive pricing (depressing Indian domestic prices as much as 10 per cent) was found by Michael Lipton at the Centre for European Studies in Brussels.[133] It is important to note that urban prices which were pleasingly 'fair' to consumers, but problematic for the budgets of urban processors (trying to procure sufficient domestic milk), resulted from GOI- or state-imposed price controls. Invoked to protect the poor, they too often had the effect of discouraging milk production. According to P.J. Atkins[134] the Jha Committee Report held that 'combined low urban retail prices and rural farmgate prices' set by state politicians in cities like Calcutta and New Delhi: 'offend against the principle of social justice' and are counter-productive because they have a disincentive effect upon production.

Tellingly, this situation recalled the Government price regime setting what Dr. Kurien[135] called 'derisory' prices paid farmers for milk they had to sell to Polson's[136] dairy, holder of the monopoly to supply Bombay before Kaira farmers and traders took the advice of Sardar Patel to strike and, led by Tribhuvandas, form their own cooperative in 1946. Fortunately, Delhi agreed with Anand that the Jha Committee Report was exactly right in prescribing higher farmgate prices for India's milk producers. But the two-edged sword of dairy aid had to be controlled: It is no exaggeration to say that if the price of EEC dairy commodities, set by IDC/NDDB/OF authorities on SMP and BO sold to the Mother Dairies, had not been *set to make the procurement of milk from indigenous Indian farmers relatively cheaper*, dependence on dairy aid might have continued indefinitely. If this had been the case, Claude Alvares might rightly have scorned India's White Revolution as a 'White Lie.' Fortunately, pricing policies *were* corrected to stimulate production, and national dairy autonomy was strengthened.

One OF-II goal was a doubling of milch animal yield by 1978-86, but Doornbos *et al.* found little progress. Perhaps the targets were set too high - a laudable trait in practitioners, but an invitation to criticism by social researchers such as themselves, as Doornbos *et al.* generously acknowledge.[137] With hindsight, attempting to double milk yield in just eight years might have compromised a nutritional tenet of the Anand pattern, not to pit man against beast. In the long-running furore over Flood including the export of oilseeds (see below) in *Economic & Political Weekly* and other media in the 1980s, critics accused OF supporters of grandiose claims.

Quiet confidence was more Kurien's style than hyperbole, but he responded sharply to Claude Alvares'[138] portrayal of Flood as a 'White Lie' in the *Illustrated Weekly* with a rejoinder titled 'Black Lie'.[139] Yet, despite the worst fears of their detractors, OF authorities were not just increasing their control of machinery, property, Government budgets and membership lists - they also were widening their control of the supply of the nation's *milk*. As P.J. Atkins[140] notes: 'By late 1988...procurement was running at an annual average of 8 million litres per day. This represents a fifteen-fold increase in milk supply to OF since 1970.'

Although increases in procurement by OF-related cooperatives might mask dormancy in *net* national milk production according to sceptics, OF authorities retained support in Delhi. Despite its missed target of doubling production, and exaggerated claims on extending the Anand model, the Government still bet that after a period of consolidation and infrastructure building, its investment in OF would pay off. Meanwhile, OF authorities released optimistic reports on dairy performance. **Table 13** *India's positive trends coincide with the Operation Flood era*, compiled from Agrostat/FAO/1994 data, supports these optimistic reports: compared to Bangladesh and Pakistan, India's production and consumption of the (FAO-designated) dairy food groups 'butter & ghee' and 'milk excluding butter' increased remarkably following the advent of OF-I in 1970.

But ongoing imports of EEC powder and oil inflamed the debate. Indians had suffered dashed expectations before, in industries such as steel, and in some unintended consequences of the Green Revolution. But what led critics including some farmers, opposition politicians, religious zealots and nationalists of all stripes to suspect irregular, even criminal activities in Operation Flood was their perception of a smoking gun in the continuation of aid imports longer than expected. The outcry against OF grew, not just in India, but also in Europe - especially from Left-wing elements in the European Parliament and scholars centred in The Hague. Critics doubted the ability of Brussels to dissipate its Milk Lake and Butter Mountain even after the imposition of EEC milk quotas in April 1984. They also doubted a consensus of political will by the EC to cut dairy aid. Until 1974, surplus disposal was impetus for EEC dairy aid, but thereafter it became a formal instrument of foreign policy - just as food aid had been used by the USA.

As Doornbos *et al.*[141] saw it: 'In sum, by giving support to Operation Flood-II the EEC could gain a lot.'

OF was perfect to achieve these EEC goals. The Commission could gain prestige in the First World by (emulating the US role as a provider of cereals aid) utilising its dairy surplus in development (not to mention raising the status of the Commission vis-à-vis European national governments - no small consideration to EEC leaders like Commissioner Jacques Delors). Success in OF would buoy Europe's image in the Third World and serve as a model for future projects. And diverting embarrassing milk surpluses to India would dampen criticism of the CAP in Europe. The Dutch School also notes that for the limited personnel in the EEC's aid bureaucracy, channelling huge amounts of aid to one country such as India, which had demonstrated its ability to process it, was far easier and cheaper than dividing stocks among several smaller recipients. Another appeal of giving aid to India was that it was a leading non-ACP country, and the EEC had, until OF, been castigated for ignoring non-ACP countries.

Practical considerations are seldom ignored by policy makers for long.[142] In the wake of the two world recessions induced by OPEC oil embargoes (originating ca. 1973 and ca. 1980), the non-oil producing nations of Europe sought export markets for farm products to ease trade deficits. Alarmingly, the European Commission and the Dutch Dairy Board[143] stated that building recombination milk plants in LDCs stimulated future commercial markets, and that increasing LDC demand could solve the EC milk surplus. Such bald statements bolstered Shanti George's comparison of European dairy aid to a Trojan Horse designed to lull India into dairy dependence.[144] Opponents of Flood might be forgiven utter disbelief that Europe's lactic largess was meant only to help India's farmers. Plans expected OF-II to begin with 15 per cent use of imported commodities in urban dairies until mid-1982, after which a surge of domestic production would let dairy aid imports shrink to 2 per cent in 1985.[145] So when OF authorities asked the WFP and the EC for *even larger amounts* of commodity and financial aid than used in OF-I for a planned OF-III, they met a swarm of accusers. According to Doornbos *et al.*:[146]

> The question which arises in this context is: how indispensable are these donations to sustain the programme? This question has become one of the focal points in the debate on Operation Flood ever since the proclaimed target to reach self-sufficiency was not reached by the end of 1985.

Rancour aside, OF-II counted advances. Capital from monetising WFP/EEC commodities and the World Bank loan speeded growth: by late

1985 Operation Flood authorities claimed a 'self-sustaining system of 43,000 village cooperatives covering 4.25 million milk producers.'[147] True, membership was barely half of the 10m initially targeted in OF-II, but the roster still marked a phenomenal increase in the coop portion of the formal milk sector. Compared to previous coop, state or private dairy efforts, the Anand pattern was markedly more beneficial to farmers and consumers because, according to Tushaar Shah *et al.*[148], OF not only organised farmers' coops but 'built strong allegiance' by incorporating 'modernisation and commercialisation.' While dilettantes argued the morality of producing baby food and ice cream, cooperative farmers shared Kurien's pride that their high-value-added Amul products, marketed by the Gujarat Cooperative Milk Marketing Federation, outsold Glaxo and Nestlé - whether or not their own families could afford them.

OF-III (1985-96): more dairy aid; more debate; ultimate success.

Phase-III was basically an extension of OF-II to achieve unfulfilled goals, consolidate initiatives already begun and, wrote P.J. Atkins[149], extend the cooperative sector: 'to 70,000 dairy societies, with 15 million milk animals. By 1994 it is hoped to cover 176 milksheds and to supply 13 million litres per day to about 450 towns and cities.'

John Empson[150] noted that with renewed emphasis on animal health and extension services, improving cross-breds through AI, and raising cattle feed production to 11.9 billion pounds annually, OF-III was: 'spearheading the way towards the national target for the year 2000 of production of 172.0 billion pounds [ca. 78 million MT].'

Agrostat FAO 1994 shows Indian milk production in OF-III rose from 46.7 million Metric Tonnes in 1987, to 63.2m MT in 1993. More recent FAO Dairy Outlook Reports estimate 1998 production at around 74m MT, despite drought in some regions. Thus the target alluded to by Empson for the year 2000 was in sight. The chances of this were better if existing cattle were better fed, for it has been documented by innumerable observers including Harold Alderman[151] that feed is the single biggest factor in boosting milk yield. To be fair to pessimists circa 1985, much of the favourable data in **Table 6.2** were then unavailable.

As mentioned above, there was agitation when OF and EEC officials actually *increased* the commodity and financial commitments in OF-III. This followed failure to disburse large sums held in OF accounts towards rural dairy development, or to phase out EEC food aid by the original deadline of 1985. Adding to the fracas was the revelation that the USA - anxious to divest itself of surplus stocks resulting from price supports and a strong dollar - subsidised a massive sale of 56,510 tonnes of SMP to India in 1984.[152] In the 1980s many doubters joined critics warning the stage was set for permanent dairy aid dependence. In explaining the continued reliance of OF on external dairy aid, Doornbos *et al.*[153] point to the fact that, behind the confusing claims of special interests claiming orientation of Operation Flood for the benefit of rural development, women and children, lower castes, tribals and others, OF was *not* designed with such specific 'bottom-up' goals in mind: 'OF has been designed as a programme for structuring the Indian milk market in a specific way.' Additionally, they explain that as a major source of finance for the National Milk Grid System (NMGS) and physical food stocks, dairy aid provided by the WFP and the EEC: 'served to stabilise the NMGS. This is one of the reasons why the programme has been dependent on Community aid for such a long time.'

Doornbos *et al.* add that the bulk of funds in OF control were 'directed towards building this marketing infrastructure.'[154] In brief, OF tried to raise national dairy productivity by constructing more efficient links between rural producers and urban markets **(Maps 6.1, 6.2 and 6.3)**. The gamble was that although disbursals were temporarily low to input services for feeding, breeding and (despite imprecations of Claude Alvares) crossbreds, improved national infrastructure (NMGS) would soon start repaying its investment. Then would be the time to spend more on inputs. Flood's emphasis on 'providing a reliable market' was supported by World Bank experience in Pakistan, Sri Lanka, Turkey, Zambia and Zimbabwe where - say Candler & Kumar[155] - results were mixed, but showed 'only in Turkey' was a focus on 'remedying a production shortage' with 'genetically-superior' breeding stock 'unambiguously successful'. Marketing is key. At the end of OF-Phase-III, the IDC was dissolved and NDDB authorities in Anand transferred title of NMGS infrastructure to local coops. When asked why Anand ceded control, Dr. Kurien explained divestment was planned from inception of the programme and that the NDDB was never interested in 'building an empire'.

More discussion of the NMGS

Candler & Kumar[156] reiterate that Operation Flood was 'Primarily... a marketing project' and 'only incidentally a production project.' Prior to involvement in OF, perhaps the most important lesson learned by the World Bank was: 'demonstrated in Zambia that provision of a market can be enough to stimulate production.'

This goes far in explaining the NDDB's drive to invest in the capital-heavy, much-maligned National Milk Grid System (NMGS). Like other huge marketing initiatives, OF had to aim at multiple demand-supply targets moving at different rates.[157] As predicted, the incentive of larger, stable markets and fairer prices, after compliance with the 1984 Jha Committee Report admonishment on pricing did stimulate greater supply from some milksheds. With the prospect of long-term markets for their surplus milk, many producers responded rationally to higher farmgate prices and invested in dairying by taking a loan to buy a cow or buffalo. Meanwhile, demand among urban consumers rose, not just in tandem with their rising incomes, but as they grew accustomed to availability of liquid milk and Amul products. Pressure increased on the new National Milk Grid System (NMGS) and Mother Dairies. But as the Jha-induced reforms took hold, it gradually became easier to balance rural supply with urban demand - while reducing dependence on aid.

It is worth remembering that the GOI valued the balance-of-payments support offered by dairy aid. Furthermore, and perhaps the chief point, it was apparent to anyone who understood the transport problems of India, including immense distances, the formidable climatic problems posed by summer heat affecting hygiene and preservation, and monsoons frequently washing out roads, that completion of the NMGS was a crucial piece of infrastructure, which more than AI or cattle concentrates unified India's dairy industry and put it on the path to modernity. Nor should be forgotten the prophylactic attribute of the NMGS, i.e. the ability to diffuse any future dumped commodities nationally before they permanently damaged the dairy economy of any one region of India.

Summary on Doornbos & Colleagues

Although Martin Doornbos *et al.* are not quite so keen as OF officials on the National Milk Grid System (NMGS) in particular, or the Anand-led programme as a whole, the reader is left with the impression of a barely suppressed conflict between their professional obligations as researchers, and some underlying enthusiasm for Operation Flood. Doornbos *et al.*, who at times characterise OF as a failure, admit that the 'position as social researcher' forces them to 'criticise the practitioner for unrealistic planning, or for defective implementation.'[158] Reluctantly, surmises the reader. Indicating the jury was still out on OF, Doornbos[159] *et al.* end their 1990 analysis of the use of EEC dairy aid thus: 'The present discussion as to why India has been dependent on EEC aid for such a long time cannot be extended beyond 1985 due to lack of exact information.'

Any contemporary study of Operation Flood should include the wide-ranging work of Doornbos *et al.*, but the dearth of data in 1990 that stymied their judgement on OF is past. Later data support NDDB claims, and should dispel the doubts of the Dutch School. Signs in the early 1990s that the NMGS was paying off in accelerated production rises were confirmed in the late 1990s. But two decades ago Doornbos[160] *et al.* summed up the ironies of Operation Flood neatly:

> [I]s it feasible that European dairy surplus can be donated to raise funds to stimulate milk production in India, while at the same time India sells commercial exports of oil seeds to feed Dutch and other European cows - even though oil seeds, a traditional ingredient of the Indian fodder mix, are not in surplus? From 1960 to 1979, dependence on EEC produced cattle grains declined, compared to tapioca and especially oil cake imported from India. From 169,000 tonnes of oil cake imported to the EEC in 1969, this amount had risen to 929,000 tonnes in 1982 - 'an amount far more than necessary to produce the quantity of milk that could be derived from the recombination of EEC donated dairy commodities to India in that year (van Ree [1984]).

The short answer to the question set by Doornbos *et al.* in the paragraphs above is that India needed a streamlined marketing system linking rural milch producers with urban consumers more that it needed indigenous oil seeds - thus the 'swap' of EEC SMP and BO for Indian oil seeds was a fair trade. Moreover, the NDDB was already developing the domestic oilseeds industry (see below.) An educated guess presumes that Brussels' imposition of the 1984 EEC milk quotas reduced demand for inputs such as Indian oil cake. But it is easy to understand that observers were alarmed by paradoxical trade flows prior to 1984 - particularly those cleaving to the autarkic tenets of 'self-sufficiency' which successful agricultural liberalisation in China had already revealed as outdated.

Although such fears were often misplaced, it is likely that critiques such as those of Doornbos and colleagues from IDPAD[161] helped ensure that massive shipments of European (EU/EC/EEC) dairy product aid to India did eventually cease. Without a gadfly, public policy can go awry.

Conclusions on Shanti George's benchmark critique

In the first and one of the most important book-length critiques of the White Revolution, Shanti George analysed OF policy decisions in the context of India, unlike the 'yellow journalism' of those gadflies who focused on the personalities of the combatants. As 'prosecuting attorney' George[162] entreats the reader to play 'judge' while she:

> aims to demonstrate that ...Operation Flood will not put an end to the shortages and imbalances of the country's milk sector but will exacerbate them, and worse - will damage or strain other areas of the Indian economy.

Table 6.3.

India's positive trends coincide with the Operation Flood era of 1970-1996				
MILK Total Prod'n Exp.Growth	BANGLADESH	INDIA	PAKISTAN	WORLD
ProdExGr 1961-93	1.8%	**4.1%**	3.1%	1.6%
ProdExGr 1961-71	1.5%	1.0%	2.3%	1.7%
ProdExGr 1972-93	1.9%	**5.2%**	3.9%	1.4%
ProdExGr 1980-91	3.4%	**5.4%**	5.4%	1.4%
MILKexBUTTER P'cap ConEx Gr.	BANGLADESH	INDIA	PAKISTAN	WORLD
P'capConsumptn Exp'lGr 1961-92	0.4%	1.9%	0.1%	0.2%
ConsExGr 1961-71	-0.8% negative	-1.2% neg	-0.4% neg	-0.4% neg
ConsExGr 1972-92	0.6%	**3.1%**	0.7%	0.4%
ConsExGr 1980-91	1.8%	**3.4%**	1.7%	0.2%
BUTTER&GHEE Prod'n Exp'l Growth	BANGLADESH	INDIA	PAKISTAN	WORLD
ProdExGr 1961-93	1.2%	3.1%	3.2%	1.2%
ProdExGr 1961-71	1.8%	0.1% poor	2.2%	0.9%
ProdExGr 1972-93	0.6%	**4.2%**	4.2%	0.9%
ProdExGr 1980-91	-0.8% neg	**4.1%**	5.7%	0.7%
BUTTER & GHEE P'capita Cnspt'n	BANGLADESH	INDIA	PAKISTAN	WORLD
P'capConsumptnEx -p'l Growth 1961-92	-2.4% negative	0.7%	0.2%	-1.1% neg
ConsExGr 1961-71	-0.0% poor	-1.7% poor	-0.6% neg	-1.2% neg
ConsExGr 1972-92	-4.6% worse	1.9% better	0.7%	-1.1% neg
ConsExGr 1980-91	-8.1% worrying	**2.0%** good	2.0%	-1.1% neg
INCOME (Y) GNP per capita*	BANGLADESH*	INDIA*	PAKISTAN*	CHINA*/ lo-inc-ec's*
US Dollars in 1991	$220	$330	$400	China $370 LIE:s $350 *w*
1980-91 ave. annual growth rate*	1.9% per capita GNP	**3.2%**	3.2% US aid Afghan War?	China 7.8% LIEs:3.9%*w*
ILLITERACY in 1990 (ADULTS)	78% female 65% total	66% female 52% total	79% female 65% total	China 38%*f*, 27%*t*
POPULATION	BANGLADESH	INDIA	PAKISTAN	WORLD
PopExpGr 1961-93	2.7%	2.2%	2.9%	1.9%
PopExpGr 1961-71	2.7%	2.3%	2.8%	2.1%
PopExpGr 1972-93	2.7%	**2.1%**	3.1%	1.8%
PopExpGr 1980-91	2.5%	**2.1%**	3.3%	1.8 %

Compiled by BAS. *Source*: Agrostat FAO, except **WB World Development Report 1993*: 238.

From data available in the *fin de siècle* 1990s, *India's White Revolution* has sought to show that while OF has not satisfied the desire for milk of many Indians with low purchasing power, it has satisfied *effective economic demand*, and the country's milk 'shortages and imbalances' have been greatly ameliorated since the 1960s' era of milk droughts. George also defends previously existing indigenous dairy production and marketing structures (e.g. in Karnataka, Madhya Pradesh and Rajasthan), scoring points with observations that OF can hardly take credit for gains made by bodies extant *before* their merger into OF. George follows up with assertions that, because Flood never oversaw more than 10% of the country's milk, improvements to India's dairy fortunes cannot be ascribed to it. But the magnitude of India's dairy surge since 1970, compared to the doldrums preceding it, renders that notion unlikely. And George's warnings that OF would 'exacerbate' problems through misuse of EEC aid, or become permanently dependent on them, have fortunately been proven wrong.

Yet if the measure of people and organisations is the strength of their critics, Verghese Kurien and the NDDB might rejoice, for Shanti George's Cassandra-like analysis, if flawed, is one of honest, almost heroic proportions. She mounted an attack on OF primarily because EEC commodity aid shipments could be a Trojan Horse endangering Indian social culture, agriculture and agri-economic self-sufficiency. Today these fears are subsumed in the debates on globalisation and food sovereignty. Just as Andræ & Beckmann[163] warned that *The Wheat Trap*, set by MNCs to coopt Nigeria's food systems, showed that agri-economic neo-colonialism remained a threat to the Third World, Shanti George was joined by Susan George and a host of observers warning that Operation Flood would similarly trap India.

George entertains all of the doubts aired by Doornbos *et al.* - and more. At times her attack is overweening, even contradictory, as Doornbos saw in her comments on prices paid milch farmers, above. In her preface, George properly admonishes us, who like herself might be 'fuelled by...sandwiches of Amul butter and cheese' not to forget the Indian children whose lactic needs are unfulfilled. But George's 'major argument' has been refuted. Betraying an Achilles heel of Fabian socialist guilt and pessimism, doubting that all boats can rise on a tide of milk, George as 'prosecutor' describes Flood as a 'weapon' designed to defend 'dairy planners, dairy scientists, foreign advisors' and even herself 'ensconced in the minor bastion of affluence' - all villains wielding 'daggers' under 'a cloak of concern for the masses.' In time these melodramatic insults faded, and George mended bridges with Anand by prefacing her 1994 book *A Matter of People: Cooperative Dairying in India and Zimbabwe* with a quote by Kurien: 'We are not here to develop cows - but to develop people.'

Yet, a careful reading of *Operation Flood* reveals subtleties. George argues (citing Harris 1974: 29) that just because Indian dairying can stand improvement does not entail a need for Western technology. Of course NDDB-OF officials shared her disdain for imports *if* Indian goods would suffice. But the point is well taken, if only because of the naiveté of some planners who believed European genetic stock could boost Indian production overnight - without first determining how these supercows would be fed, or kept from expiring in the heat. If one lists the policy improvements and reversals on breeding and feeding eventually made by the NDDB in OF, several items find reference in her work. The most prescient aspects of George's[164] critique are found in these words:

> The choice of alternatives is currently and inaccurately described as between tradition and modernity, rather than between indigenous and imported systems…implying as it does that the indigenous cannot change or respond to new circumstances and that the imported alone has present day relevance.

The truth of these words reverberates when one considers that today they could be applied equally to environmental, food safety and animal welfare issues in rich countries. Much of George's over-pessimism is understandable because: at the time it was written, statistics showing aggregate improvements in India's dairy performance were unavailable or in dispute. Chiefly, EEC dairy aid to OF was *increasing* in 1985, after it was scheduled to be phased out. Suspicion of continued aid flows was rational. Corollary evidence suggested India might be seduced by food aid. Writing two years before George's book, Anne M. Thomson[165] observed: 'Attempts to increase food prices significantly have, in the past few years, led to riots. Cheap bread is now regarded as a basic human right in Egypt.

Just as cereals aid priced Egyptian wheat farmers out of the domestic market and made the Egyptian Government dependent on food aid (and perhaps vulnerable to donor-influence on policy), Shanti George feared EEC dairy aid would similarly forestall India's dairy self-sufficiency, and subject Delhi to foreign policy blackmail. In truth, the OF saga could have turned out this badly, if Anand had not in the 1960s planned survival tactics to thwart anticipated dumping of EEC dairy commodities aid. But George's[166] book asserts that OF should not have invited EEC dairy aid, and not insisted on replication of the Anand model in all parts of India:

> A study of the literature on India's agricultural economy, on rural India and on Indian dairy policy has convinced me that present trends should be reversed if we are to benefit from a dairy policy that recognises the authentic roots and nature of India's dairy problems…. Such a policy would…build on what already exists, rather than to tear down indigenous structures to be replaced with imports of dubious relevance.

George had reason to reject wholesale replication of the 'Anand model' if displacing previous workable structures resulted in a long-term diseconomy to the public. But the cost of altering organisational composition must be weighed against economies-of-scale expected by incorporation into the National Milk Grid System (NMGS), in which the Anand pattern reached its final organisational evolution in the National Cooperative Dairy Federation Ltd.[167] George was, rejecting cookie-cutter replication of the 'Anand pattern' wherever capital investment exceeded probable returns. But Anand shared her concern: Tushaar Shah *et al.*[168] note that NDDB sister body, the Institute of Rural Management Anand (IRMA), was alarmed when its capital-intensive Anand-pattern Jalgaon Cooperative Union remained unprofitable - while a smaller coop, Yelgud, prospered without an accompanying processing plant.

But as to George's first point on EEC dairy aid, we have already seen evidence from sources including Doornbos *et al.* (1990) that, like it or not, massive quantities of EEC dairy surpluses were *inevitably* headed for Bombay, and the wisest policy response was made by Indian coop leaders who negotiated WFP 618 - the World Food Programme project designed to monetise EEC 'aid' to enhance Indian dairy autonomy - better known as Operation Flood. George's book is nevertheless helpful in highlighting some extravagant claims made for OF. As B.S. Baviskar observed when the IMF and World Bank were swept up by fervour for 'integrated rural development', OF 'cashed in' by suggesting that benefits could accrue to the rural poor from extension of the NMGS.[169] Although this book agrees this was true in the long-term, such claims were remote in the short-term, as the NMGS was designed to stabilise the national milk marketing system, and many rural farmers probably were oblivious to its construction. Disingenuous claims (whether or not made by Anand) invited embarrassing accusations when unmet. In response, the NDDB claimed the NMGS would stabilise and increase India's milk flow.

When George defends petty dairy marketeers, vilified by OF planners for price-gouging and milk adulteration, the reader wonders if George's defence is not just a reflex against all facets of the OF programme.[170] George finds instances where these small traders, or dudhias, perform valuable services, such as giving credit to housewives.

These examples recall Hernando de Soto's[171] defence of the social roles of 'informals' or 'black marketeers' in Peru. However, the higher income benefits of cooperative dairying for marginal farmers and safer milk for consumers outweigh the mooted credit utility of petty milk marketeers.

Minority, gender & poverty effects of OF

Some of Shanti George's other criticisms of OF are perhaps more illuminating. She disputes claims by OF advocates including researchers Somjee & Somjee (1978)[172] that 'Anand... is a powerful weapon against caste' when 'Brahmans mingle with Harijans' in milk queues. Images of these multiethnic milk qeues were powerful propaganda for Anand. George[173] says: 'Unfortunately there is more to life in rural India than standing in these queues. We are informed that such mingling has not weakened caste barriers in other arenas of interaction...and that the mingling itself is largely symbolic.'

George also charges that the Patidar caste, which dominates dairying in Anand and the state of Gujarat, extends solidarity to equivalent groups in Tamil Nadu and Maharashtra, perhaps not always to the benefit of disadvantaged groups. Undoubtedly there existed instances where this was, true. But in defence of Anand, it should come as no surprise that caste barriers which grew over centuries have not been eradicated by OF since 1970. But who can doubt that 'mingling' in milk queues is not a first step toward social and economic integration? More importantly, it bears repeating that OF was *not* designed as a cure-all for India's social ills, but as a structural reorganisation of national milk markets.[174]

Idealists court disappointment. In a study in South Gujarat, not far from OF headquarters at Anand, Franco & Chand found that while there seemed to be no general bias against tribals entering dairying, 'a final reckoning' as to the question of whether 'OF is in itself a beneficial development for the tribals?' was 'in the negative.' (Nevertheless, it stands to reason that after NMGS raised national dairy efficiency, in tandem with expanding markets in the cities, social groups, e.g. women, tribals, rural small-holders, would gradually come to benefit therefrom.) Franco & Chand blamed the preoccupation of 'OF on processing and marketing', making it less mindful of extension work needed on the feeding and breeding of cattle, etc., than optimal.[175]

Failure of OF to disburse funds on extension activities was scrutinised by the GOI and EC as we have discussed, but little outright corruption was found in the coop movement. Prudent reluctance to fund unpromising projects kept the purse strings tight and, as some auditors inferred correctly, rivalry between state governments and Anand lay behind many delays in extending inputs and services to farmers. It is worth considering that Anand may have been playing for time, withholding funds, while enthusiasm waned for the ill-conceived sub-components of Operation Flood (e.g. over-reliance on European cows and neglect of Indian buffaloes in the National Milch Herd) which Shanti George was the first to condemn.

But if tribals in the vicinity of Anand got insufficient attention it is unlikely that minorities in states outside Gujarat received more in the early phases of OF. (Note: Minorities reportedly were receiving significant gains from OF by the late-1990s.) John Empson gives evidence that a large proportion of the progress (and investment) made in OF was in the western state of Gujarat. John Empson[176] notes that:

> Regionally, production varies considerably. The main production area is the northern region, with about 45 per cent of the total, centred on Delhi; followed by the western and central regions (21 per cent) based on Bombay; and the southern region (21 per cent) based on Madras.

Like other well-managed enterprises, OF sought first to build the profitability of its core, its home base in Gujarat, and to avoid over-extension while preparing for future expansion. Analogous to public infrastructure such as paved roads, NMGS infrastructure in OF-II and OF-III (e.g. processing plants, storage facilities for pooled buffer stocks, and insulated road and rail tankers[177]) did not *directly* benefit many rural farmers as much as did feeding inputs (e.g. cattle cake pellets, and molasses urea molasses blocks[178] which increase bovines' ability to convert straw and other crop wastes into energy - and milk) or veterinary and breeding services such as AI or ET. But by raising the long-term efficiency of the national system on top, the NDDB primed the pump for increased production at the bottom of the supply chain, when inputs and services eventually came on line to rural farmers. This was not a spurious goal. Sporadic 'milk holidays' (after heavy rainfall, when production outran processor's ability to cope with supply), extending into the early phases of OF typically discouraged poor farmers' readiness to invest in dairying.

George joins researchers including Sharma & Vanjani (see below) who question the benefit of OF when cross-bred cows, bought on loans through OF programmes, add to the already onerous workload of women and children responsible for feeding and milking the animals. However, citing a World Bank study in Karnataka, Candler & Kumar[179] found that women who otherwise would seek income outside the home (entailing the removal from school of older daughters, to care for any infants) preferred the opportunity to pursue coop dairying. But Shanti George is on firmer ground questioning other gender implications of modern OF technology. George points out that in the past women made ghee at home, and controlled the income from its sale. Although the lost income for ghee might be compensated by income received from exchange in the village milk queues, OF modernisations resulted in a net loss of women's status when only men were employed in new high-tech infrastructure.[180] Candler

& Kumar[181] agree that while 'Nominally gender-neutral' this initially resulted in 'male-dominated management committees' at the village (DCS) and union (MPU) level, but female influence has since grown. Kurien[182] claims women are increasingly 'empowered' in milk societies and: 'several thousand… include only women members, leaders and employees.'

Women members increased from 66,000 in 1984-85 to about 1.7 million in 1995-96.[183] But feminists feared OF would skew dairy development toward male dominance. This is a global criticism of the mechanisation of agriculture over the last century.[184] Nowadays more development practitioners are aware that some plans are less 'gender-neutral' than others, and try to avoid the 'internal colonialism' in gender roles that Sharma & Vanjani identified in OF.[185]

For example the UK/Africa-based NGO Riders for Health (www.riders.org) which is contracted to provide transport for public health workers in countries such as the Gambia, Lesotho, Nigeria, and Zimbabwe, routinely trains women as motorcycle riders.[186] This is not just because women constitute the bulk of nurse-practitioners riding from clinics to villages, but also so that women along with the men, (who comprise most of the mechanics in the 'zero-breakdowns' programme) benefit from the knowledge and status accompanying new technology.[187]

In like spirit Shanti George calls for gender-neutral policies in Flood. Perhaps this is one reason Kurien was succeeded as NDDB Chair by a woman, Dr. Amrita Patel, in late 1998.

There are dangers in the modernisation of India's agriculture, but also benefits. For instance, despite persuasive criticism of the controversial Narmada Dam, extension of irrigation in appropriate places could result in more fodder for dairying. Echoing the warnings of Susan George and Shanti George about rich country cooptation of LDC farming, Ben Fine *et al.* (1995) might term Monsanto or Novartis' supply of Green and White Revolution inputs 'appropriationism', i.e. of dubious benefit to farmers in the field. On the other hand, while there is yet scant evidence of direct harm to humans from genetically-modified (GM) foods such as soybeans developed by MNCs, observers including David R. Harvey[188] suspect GM strains could in some instances harm the environment and traditional gene plasm. Meanwhile, the public questions how GM seeds will feed the world.

Final discussion of breeding & feeding

Some of Shanti George's contentions were eventually proven correct. Agricultural planners had pursued an ephemeral dream of a 'single-species dairy economy' with either cattle (cows) yielding rich milk as well as bullocks for traction - or a buffalo that besides rich milk could produce 'male buffalo to match the performance of the bullock'. George[189] scorned over-reliance on cross-bred cows to improve milk yield by geneticists ignorant of the multiple uses of cattle in India (traction, fuel, fertiliser), who proposed replacing '70 million buffaloes and zebu cows' with 12-25m cross-breds, while ignoring the 'poor man's milch animal[s]' goats and sheep. Although some success has been reported with cross-bred cows in recent years, Clay & Stokke[190] commented on early efforts that: 'The considerable research and extension effort to increase milk yields through cross-bred animals has been a failure.'

George rightly challenged policy makers for ignoring the buffalo's role as 'India's premier milch animal', its aptitude for rice-growing, and birthing of more female calves per lifetime than cattle - but also misconstruing the role of Indian cows/cattle as breeders of bullocks and only secondarily for milk. Planners missed the point, made by V. M. Rao[191], that while annual milk yield of US and European cows was 20-times that of Indian cows (157 kg.) and 7- times that of Indian buffalo (504 kg.): 'two-thirds of the power requirements of Indian villages are met by 80m work animals.'

Furthermore, as George notes, although Indian cows and buffalo are poor producers compared to the vaunted Friesians of the North, their upkeep (fed on straw and crop wastes) is minimal. In time Western advisors agreed that for milk production: purebred European cows were unsuitable for India; Indo-Euro half breeds might be suitable in some regions; but indigenous buffaloes may be best for India.

P.J. Atkins[192] also warned that Indian buffalo should not be overlooked in a rush to incorporate gene plasm from Europe:

> The most worrying aspect of the dependence argument is the increased use of exotic gene material to upgrade the yields of nondescript Indian cattle. There are disturbing echoes of the green revolution here. One feels instinctively that the development of the buffalo, a hardier native and a cheaper alternative, must be a better bet.

Buffalo qualities run deeper than their amiable mien. They are intrinsic to environmental sustainability in many parts of South Asia. B.N. Mathur[193] states that, '[in] hot and humid regions of Asia, the riverine buffalo contributes more than the cow towards milk production because of its ability to thrive under adverse environments'. Not only are buffalo resistant to pests that fell fragile imported cows, but according to Mathur, 'the ecological role' of buffalo where fodder is scarce 'is paramount as a bioconverter of course feeds'. Interestingly, Mathur also cites nutritional and immunological evidence suggesting lactoferrin in buffalo milk imparts disease resistance to human consumers. (Buffalo milk averages 3.4 μg/ml lactoferrin compared to just 0.4 μg/ml in cow milk.) Acting as an 'iron scavenger', lactoferrin may rob invading parasites of their iron, killing pathogens, and after 'iron bound to the lactoferrin' is absorbed by the human liver and spleen, assist haemoglobin formation in bone marrow - suggesting a role for buffalo milk in treatment of leukaemia. Lactoferrin-rich buffalo milk may also be better than cow milk for preventing viral and enteric diseases in bottle-fed infants. Also, writes Mathur, a low-lactose infant formula could help babies suffering 'lactose-intolerance/diarrhoea'. Buffalo milk is the base for traditional Indian sweets such as *khoa* and *paneer*, and the NDDB has long prized the 'superior whitening property' in coffee and tea of buffalo milk, which increases its value as a powder export. During OF-III, coop plants in India, home to 65 per cent of the world's buffalo, began exporting large quantities of buffalo milk-based cheese for pizza and other high-value-added products abroad.

Amul was buffalo-friendly. The debate on incorporation of European cows into the National Milch Herd amounted to little more than a bywater next to the stream of policy decisions flowing from the NDDB. But Anand's recognition of the superior disease-resistance of indigenous buffalo illustrated the amenability of Operation Flood planners to sensible advice from whatever source, be it coop farmer or Shanti George. Improved inputs, including concentrated cattle cake and molasses urea blocks, help a mix of cows and buffaloes - which P.J. Atkins[194] notes 'have different seasonal yield patterns' - balance seasonal milk supply in India.

John Empson[195] notes that in 1990 'just over half' (55 per cent) of India's milk was produced by buffalo (63.9 billion pounds compared to 52.9b for cows). Although they comprise just 40 per cent of milch animals, buffalo produce over half of India's milk.) After expectations for a miraculous transformation of the National Milch Herd by Euro-breeds had been dashed, the future role of buffalo was secure. However, portrayals of all efforts at cross-breeding as fruitless are wrong. P.C. Bardhan[196] said in 1989 that 8 per cent of milch animals held by Operation Flood members were cross-breds (*aka* hybrids) compared to just 5.5 per cent nation-wide. But a study probably conducted somewhat later, in 1138 villages and 13,682 milch animal households (MAH) by S. Bhide & S.K. Chaudhari[197] of the National Council of Applied Economic Research (NCAER) for the NDDB found crossbreds accounted for 14.5 per cent of dairy cattle. The trend was up. Empson expects crossing European breeds with zebu (e.g. Brahman), and other indigenous cattle (e.g. desi) to raise production, supported by more concentrates. (Feeding is often a greater production factor than breeding.) By 1990 about 331 million pounds (ca. 150,000 MT) of Amul feed concentrates were produced annually. As India improves its fodder base, including oilseeds, voracious but finicky cross-breds will play an important role in the liquid milk market. Prospects are good. According to John W. Mellor[198]: 'There is every indication that India's agricultural and marketing systems could respond to ...an increase in demand.' Mellor's assertion, made in the 1970s, came true in the 1990s. In what K.N. Ninan calls 'a dramatic turnaround', Indian oilseeds production rose 6 per cent a year, comfortably ahead of demand rising at 4 per cent a year.'[199] In a 1989 review of Ninan's book, *Oilseeds: Is Higher Price the Answer?*, Ashok Gulati notes the GOI assigned the NDDB to 'restructure the edible oil economy' on the Anand pattern[200] Kurien later told me that he did not relish taking up this major challenge.[201] Perhaps the challenge is a measure of Delhi's regard for Anand's achievements. In oil, as in milk, NDDB[202] documents show reliance on realistic pricing[203] not just technology:

> Launched in 1979 the oilseed growers' cooperative project now links nearly 0.92 million farmer members in eight States in over 6000 oilseeds growers' cooperatives. Dr. Kurien took the entrenched oil lobby head on when NDDB was appointed as the Market Intervention Agency for edible oils in 1989.

The *Dhara* brand was established to rid the market of adulterated oil - and return more profits to oilseeds producers by breaking 'the stranglehold' of middlemen in the supply chain. Tamper-proof Tetra Paks, earlier used exclusively for milk and fruit juice, not only reduced adulteration but also helped market edible rapeseed and groundnut oil as a 'branded consumer product' instead of a 'traded commodity.' Such brands could improve consumer trust as well as safety. Kurien[204] was grateful that, similar to the use of EEC dairy aid in OF: 'The Governments of Canada and the United States, through their cooperatives, have donated edible oil which we have used for this purpose.'

Dhara became 'market leader' and the housewives' choice in less than five years, but the 1990s brought more competition. Janairus Banaji[205] detailed how the post-Gulf War liberalisation of India's economy brought billions of rupees of investment by MNCs into the oilseeds industry. For instance, ITC, an affiliate of BAT diversifying from tobacco into food production, built one of India's largest processing plants for rapeseed and mustard at Alwar in Rajasthan. Glaxo, Nestlé and Zeneca also invested in agriculture, but it is uncertain if this will add to dairy inputs. Meanwhile, the NDDB has made nutritional breakthroughs, e.g. urea molasses mineral block (UMMB)[206] licks to improve bio-conversion of straw.

A welcome by-product of the Green Revolution was large amounts of roughages and straw, the main fodder for cattle of marginal and landless farmers, the bulk of today's 11 million coop members.

1991: Levelling the field?

Controversy continues on the fairness of post-1991 economic 'reforms' designed to level the playing field for private firms *vis-à-vis* cooperatives. The GATT process was already prying India's markets open to more foreign and private investment, and the balance-of-payments crisis after the Gulf War petroleum crisis included the dairy sector in a spate of liberalisations. In their 1998 World Bank study Candler & Kumar[207] note:

> Before the New Economic Policy (NEP) was announced in the 1992-93 budget…. First, NDDB had a monopoly on the importation of dairy products. Second, construction of new processing capacity was subject to industrial licensing.

Not unlike the US dot.com bubble that deflated in the year 2000, India's NEP resulted in irrational exuberance by private sector investors who rushed into Haryana, the Punjab and elsewhere to challenge the NDDB which in 1988/89 handled 61.33 per cent of milk in the organised sector (compared to 58.77 per cent in 1994/95). Nationally, private investors added ca. 1 million litres per day (lpd), which the Bank concluded led to 'excessive' overcapacity financed by 'subsidies far in excess of anything offered in the Flood period.' Cooperative officials accused multinationals (MNCs) and entrepreneurs of 'poaching' milk suppliers and selling adulterated milk. In turn, entrepreneurs accused coops of unfair protection. But even if past coop regulation unnecessarily restricted private enterprise, deregulation went too far. It made India vulnerable to financial shakedowns that William Greider (among critics including, occasionally, even free trade partisan Jagdish Bhagwati) blames MNCs for inflicting on nations worldwide. An example from the world of cars illustrates what happened in the world of cows. In the neoliberal era of *laissez-faire* capital flows it was commonplace when, in 1998-99, BMW threatened to move its Rover auto factory from England to Hungary, unless the British Government granted hundreds of millions in tax concessions. Likewise, the NDDB complained that private investors played one Indian locality against another to milk public coffers. Candler & Kumar report that in the Punjab, where private dairy activity 'both before and after the NEP' was highest, private investors got 'incentives' including state sales tax cuts from 8.8 per cent to 4.4 per cent for seven years; exemptions from 20 per cent surcharges on power consumption; a seven-year income tax holiday - and were able to offer 'assets and good will' toward their 51 per cent stake, while states generally offered *cash* for the public's minority 49 per cent equity in such joint ventures. National debate on joint ventures continues today, inviting fears of a White Counter-Revolution by Scholten & Basu in 2009.[208] Some early excesses were redressed in the 1992 Milk & Milk Products Order (MMPO)[209] requiring licensing of plants processing over 50,000 lpd. But Candler & Kumar's World Bank report notes: 'today, the "playing field", in Punjab at least, is heavily tilted in favour of the private corporate sector, which can only lead to serious misallocation of resources.

Of course the GOI's 1991 liberalisations contained desirable elements, correcting inefficiencies of India's phlegmatic 'licensing regime' scorned by Clive Crook. But deregulation of India's dairy industry too often amounted to looting of the public purse by private interests, carried out under the otherwise laudable banner of free trade. Yet, after initial alarm, it was clear the NDDB kept the loyalty of its 10 million members by paying more for their milk (up to 30 per cent more than paid by non-coop vendors) - and ploughing some profits back into village roads, wells, bio-gas projects and schools. But just as the triumph of Reagan-Thatcher neoliberalism demanded soul-searching by central-planners worldwide, the NEP's free market liberalisations obliged a thorough appraisal of the policies and implementation of Operation Flood under the parastatals of the NDDB and IDC which, 1970~90s, controlled dairy imports into the country.

In a crucial section of their 1998 report Candler & Kumar[210] cite data showing 1951-69 milk production (lagging behind population growth) rose just 0.7 per cent annually. At this rate (based on 20.74 million MT 1969-70) production in 1994-95 would have been a lamentable 24.8m MT instead of the 63.3m MT which flooded India. *But was OF the* optimum *solution to the dairy crisis of the 1960s?* Candler & Kumar posit 'three without-Flood scenarios' or 'counterfactuals' and find in OF's favour:

(1) 'Trade': Candler & Kumar (page 43) expect the 40m MT shortfall would have been met by recombined milk from imported commodities, sold at a price (Rs 8/litre) entailing a GOI subsidy of Rs 20.4 billion. The result is neutral for urban consumers, but farmers are $10.4 billion (Rs 302b) poorer in lost income.

(2) 'Autarky with Perfectly Inelastic Short-run Supply': Autarky in this scenario would have banned imports, resulting in higher prices (Rs 18.7/litre) which stimulated no production increase but, due to population rise, decreased per capita consumption. Farmers would earn nearly as much as with-Flood, but consumers would suffer.

(3) 'Autarky with Unit Elasticity Short-run Supply': Producer (farmer) surplus falls US$480 billion (Rs 14b) in this scenario.

Even when they grapple with questions of how much progress is directly attributable to OF, the personalities of NDDB leaders, or how events might have gone without-Flood, Candler & Kumar[211] imply approval:

> it appears that Operation Flood yielded large gains as compared to the three alternative policy scenarios examined. Translated into 1996 dollars, the calculated benefits in one year greatly exceed the total cost of Operation Flood (US$2.7 billion)… There is little reason to believe that alternative policy options would have yielded better results for producers and consumers than were achieved under Operation Flood.

Prognosis for coop dairying

Because most milk in large, diverse developing countries such as Brazil and India does not pass through formal channels, statistics are sketchier than in rich countries. However, India's growing formal sector - probably 11-15 per cent in the 1990s - provides relatively reliable estimates on feed production, milk production and consumption. Forecasts by experts that output might soar to 78 million Metric Tonnes in 1998 were more optimistic than the more conservative FAO (Rome) Dairy Outlook forecast of 74m MT (see data in Chapter 5). Seasoned observers[212] said in late 1998 that while FAO/World Bank estimates were somewhat higher than their own, most figures including those based on 1991 census data converged on a central figure for 1997-98 of 70.8m MT.

The backdrop was a yearly rise in world milk production of slightly more than 1 per cent: 1996 (539m MT); 1997 (547m MT) and 1998 (555m MT). The USA, with a mature dairy market, and India, with market expansion limited only by drought and consumer purchasing power, were in a dead heat for status as top world producer.

Exactly *when* India vaulted past the USA into top spot was debatable. However, since national output apparently held even at ca. 70.8m MT in 1998 despite regional drought, the outlook was positive. Much depends on climate. Severe drought (e.g. 1987-88[213]), perhaps spawned by global warming, slowed Indian dairy progress but not stop it in its tracks. Impressive distribution response by Delhi to the 1987-88 food emergency, and ever wider availability of feedstuffs to coop farmers enhanced India's dairy autonomy.

V.P. Gandhi & G. Mani[214] note that the 1987-88 National Sample Survey (NSS), the first to provide 'quantity as well as value data', showed that (from 1970-71 to 1989-90), even in rural groups expenditure on food fell from 73.6 to 64.3 per cent, and spending on cereals fell from 54.4 to just 37.5 per cent; in both rural and urban groups spending on livestock products such as meat, fish and eggs lag far behind milk, and as income grows, so does spending on milk.

Thus, as industry and service sectors continue national expansion - with a concomitant shrinking of the non-dairy farm sector - urban *and* rural demand supported extension of the National Milk Grid System to more remote villages where dairying is viable. In turn this would raise incomes of additional rural producers, bring them into the cash economy, and stimulate ancillary rural employment in education, textiles and manufacturing.

The NDDB claims its national goal of 10 million members, originally set in OF-II (1981-85) was finally met in OF-II (1985-96). This may be accurate. Candler & Kumar[215] say coop membership entails prestige (Karnataka coops listed people holding no cattle, but who valued membership), and double voting membership of spouses is sometimes allowed in village societies (DCSs). Thus as many as 10.1m members from ca. 9.3m households may be on NDDB rosters. Candler & Kumar[216] found MPUs were collecting from only 55,000 of 72,700 existing DCSs in June, 1996, meaning nearly 25 per cent of village societies were 'non-functional'.

This gives pause for thought, but reasons for it are not necessarily negative. Their World Bank evaluation offered these explanations: (1) 'Active price competition'. Candler & Kumar note that in peri-urban areas informal milk traders sometimes pay more for milk - but adulteration is endemic. (Prosperous localities seem ripe for this.) (2) 'Changed needs of milk producers'. One NDDB pouring site might be too little in growing villages. (3) 'Village politics'. As Shanti George (1985) implied, caste or other discrimination can doom a DCS. (4) 'Dishonesty'. Despite 'sophisticated... checks and balances' embezzlement occurs. (5) 'Higher income'. Introduction of soyabeans led to DCS closures in Madhya Pradesh. Soybeans give higher incomes 'but fewer by-products' fit for cattle than the cotton & groundnuts grown before.

None of these points is unexpected, and some are normal responses to changing economic situations, competition from the private sector and official policy. Several sources report that cooperative membership lists were audited to eliminate non-functional societies or members but after cuts national membership again passed 10 million producers, and was reported at about 13m in 2009.

Operation Flood met John Mellor's Rx for food aid

Sceptics rightly warned EEC dairy aid could snare India in dependence like *The Wheat Trap* (Andræ & Beckmann, 1985) caught Nigeria. But Operation Flood proved not to be the Trojan Horse of the caveats of Shanti George. When asked why dairy aid worked in India when food aid was often disastrous elsewhere, Verghese Kurien[217] answered:

> [It] was the first time aid was put in the hands of someone answerable to farmers.

John W. Mellor expresses the same insight into the inter-relationship between dairy product trade and aid in a different way. Wherever food aid programmes were unsuccessful one or more of the conditions Mellor outlined for success were probably violated. Like a doctor ordering a patient to obey *all* instructions until treatment is complete, Mellor[218] prescribes food aid but cautions, 'three demands must be met by the food donor and two by the food aid recipient':

> (1) Donor must 'provide reliable amounts': The EEC passed this test with flying colours, maintaining shipments of SMP and BO, even when opponents in the European Parliament, and a swathe of public opinion, made it politically uncomfortable to do so.219
> (2) Donor must 'provide large amounts' raising the net supplies of food in the recipient country: By all accounts, dairy aid to Operation Flood was massive, more than meeting Mellor's demand that aid must boost the net assets in a recipient country.
> (3) Donor must 'recognise the conditions of effective food aid', meaning that effectiveness of food aid can be magnified by linked aid in cash and/or technical assistance.

Some early technical advice from rich countries was unrealistic for over-reliance on Holstein-Friesian genetics (in what S.N. Mishra[220] called the 'sub-Himalayan grasslands to tropical rain forests' of India), and deceptive (when foreign countries and MNCs tried to dissuade Amul from making powder or baby food from buffalo milk in the 1950s). As for cash, the World Bank's International Development Association (IDA) and other lenders augmented EEC dairy product aid with large soft loans[221] - investments the Bank admitted in the late-1990s paid off many times over. Along with receipts from recombining SMP and BO with domestic milk in metropoles, these cash loans financed the National Milk Grid System linking Bombay, Calcutta, Delhi, and Madras - stabilising milk supply nationally - and building urban markets for greater sales from rural areas.

Recipients, according to Mellor, must:

(1) Recipient must 'give priority to agricultural development…to minimise the disincentive effects of food aid'. Here is where India's dairy leadership excelled. As detailed previously, Doornbos *et al.* noted that in the late 1960s Dr. Kurien and the NDDB preempted a threat to national dairy autonomy by winning GOI approval of a programme they designed to sell an imminent flow of dairy commodities from the EEC in a monetisation

scheme to fund infrastructure, rather than allow it to act as the sort of disincentive (wrecking domestic price structures) to indigenous farmers that Mellor warned of. M.V. Kamath presents persuasive hearsay evidence of this threat to make India permanently dependent on European surpluses. Although proof of a 'smoking gun' (establishing a Euro-conspiracy to subvert Indian dairy self-sufficiency) is circumstantial, it has been documented that some EEC leaders pondered the possibility that EEC dairy commodities could flow to India ad infinitum. Thus, it was prudent of Indian planners to construct the National Milk Grid System, so that the economic effects of drought in one region (or a surfeit of dairy 'aid' in another) could be stabilised over a wider geographical space.

(2) Recipient must 'pursue policies that spread capital supplies as evenly as possible over the labour force': In this respect, OF disappointed some observers, but time may have proved them wrong.

Claims made in the late 1980s that OF could benefit marginal, landless farmers and even widows were rubbished by critics (despite disclaimers by Kurien and NDDB officials that dairying - not rural development *per se* - was OF's mission). Reporting on OF-II and prospects for OF-III, Wilfried Telkämper[222] told the European Parliament that: 'The infrastructures introduced under Operation Flood will primarily benefit medium-sized and large agricultural holdings.'

But in a twist to the tale, late-1990s' statistics repeatedly show that poor small, landless and marginal (even widowed) producers account for 50-75 per cent of coop members. Bhide & Chaudhari[223] found over '60 per cent of milk in OF areas' was produced by 'small/ marginal and landless' farmers with 1-2 animals producing as little as a litre a day. The remarkable persistence of marginal producers in India's White Revolution is tied to the design of Operation Flood to be a low-input/low-output system that treats milk production as *ancillary* to crops production, while making it possible for small farmers or landless farm workers to earn additional income via the structure of village coops.

Mellor's demand that recipients *'pursue policies that spread capital supplies as evenly as possible over the labour force'* is technically met if it is true that OF benefited as many of India's rural poor *as possible.* Meanwhile, although Mellor's demands upon donors and recipients were generally met, rural poverty remains widespread. As critics claimed a bottom-up approach (emphasising inputs to individual farmers) would raise Indian dairy output faster, Wilfried Telkämper[224] told the EC Parliament: 'The new dairy infrastructures require a capital investment which this programme aims to provide. The capital needed for breeding cattle and fodder cannot be raised by landless peasants and small landholders.' Fortunately, monetisation of EEC aid and proper pricing did the trick.

The EC Court of Auditors[225] found that by the mid-1980s, EEC dairy aid had helped ease milk rationing. 'Solvent demand', i.e. demand for milk 'by persons who can afford to pay' was met - one of the original goals of supplying dairy aid. They noted: 'The truth is that, due to the agronomical, climatic and demographic conditions of India, it was - and is - not possible for milk to be anything but expensive.' It was becoming obvious that more of India's citizens could eventually benefit from investments in processing and marketing facilities, made possible by continued sales of EEC donations. The EC Court of Auditors (page 14) concluded:

> It is only because Community aid provided Flood... with a considerable amount of finance for the implementation of its investment programme, that the Indian authorities have recently expressed the desire for this aid to continue.

In the years after the Jha Committee Report's mandate that processors must pay more for EEC commodities than for milk from indigenous farmers, data increasingly showed production and consumption gains. NMGS infrastructure, originally financed by dairy aid, was bolstered by investments largely funded by coop milk receipts.

A gleaming example is the 1 million lpd Gandhinagar Mother Dairy commissioned in Ahmedabad in 1994. In a tour of the facility in 1998, the plant manager boasted to the author of ISO 9000 compliance and best practices in the spirit of *kaizen*, or continual improvement in manufacturing, developed by Japanese manufacturers such as Toyota. Since then, Gandhinagar has added additional capacity, and its role in the dairy revolution continues (see **Photos**).

The Summing Up

As population growth ebbed and dairy markets matured in rich countries in the 1970s, EEC dairy aid streamed into an India beset by milk rationing after a decade of stagnant production. In parallel with arguments from Clive Crook, Jeffrey Sachs, Verghese Kurien and others, it is obvious that urban milk droughts resulted more from *economic* problems (i.e. market failure resulted from bad pricing policies) than *technical* problems in processing at the top or production at the bottom.

After all, many technical snags had been surmounted in Indian dairy 'firsts' (e.g. processing buffalo milk) since the 1950s. But restrictive price control regimes, abetted by well-meaning but inefficient labour laws that effectively promoted overmanning and sacrificed productivity, and flawed pre-1970 food aid programmes that did more to advance the careers of politicians than incomes of farmers, skewed the nation's milk supply, making market failure and milk droughts inevitable.

From 1970-1996, Operation Flood improved urban, peri-urban and rural nutrition, and raised reliable incomes for 10 million farmer families. In their OED evaluation for the World Bank, Candler & Kumar[226]reported: 'By raising incomes, an apparently simple single-commodity project can have multiple beneficial effects: including nutrition, education (especially of girls), and job-creation.' By concentrating on hard cash, paid daily, with a bonus paid to farmers at the end of the year, Flood stimulated more concrete benefits than earlier development paradigms focusing on 'basic needs', making it perhaps the most important case study in 50 years of post-independence development. Candler & Kumar relate the phenomenal increase in coop farmer payments from Rs 2.1 billion in 1972 to Rs 34.0 billion in 1995 (constant 1995 Rupees). Even more positive is their observation of 'two key points':

> First that dairying is shifting, in a few cases, from a sideline activity to a serious economic enterprise and in some cases even becoming the main source of farm income. Second, dairying was particularly valued because of the reliability and regularity of payments.

This reflects marketing and logistics achievements in Operation Flood. But the continuing role of small, marginal, landless and even widowed farmers in the White Revolution is of greater importance. As late as 2005 Amul[227] estimated that: 'A majority of milk producers have one or two milch animals, and these small producers account for some 70 per cent of the milk production. On average, 22.5 percent of the income of rural households is contributed by milk.'

A Punjab Agricultural University study of two milksheds found, after factoring costs of capital, labour and land, impressive net profits of 33 per cent, or Rs 3.06 per litre of milk net return on average gross farmgate payments of Rs 9.30 per litre. Regular dairy income makes families, whose cash income once depended entirely on unreliable seasonal labour on larger farms, more eligible for credit from private banks or government schemes (Note: Coop societies and unions are prohibited from extending credit). This is a milestone in a household's economic progress, but two caveats must be made: first, even free-trade champion the *Economist* admitted - agreeing for once with Susan George - that in the 1997-98 recession the world's poorest people got poorer. This was an admission it was honest enough to repeat in the world economic meltdown beginning 2006, and marked by food riots in dozens of countries. Food demand by the growing middle classes of China and India, and biofuel programmes in rich countries, returned millions more people to food poverty. While much blame for moribund development goes to national neglect, civil war and diaspora, some diseconomies from economic globalisation were also acknowledged. The need for debt relief became apparent even to the G-7 (later G8) group of richest countries, which began negotiating with Third World countries on a case-by-case basis.

Second, despite achievements in Operation Flood, P.R. Gupta noted that many rural and urban Indians survive on barely two meals a day. Glasses of milk and ghee-based sweets remain luxuries to most. Gupta[228] echoed M.S. Swaminathan, a leader of the Green Revolution and advocate of sustainable agriculture, who describes famines in India and other countries 'not famines of food' but 'famines of work'. When there are sufficient jobs, hunger fades. Swaminathan's observation is parallel to the concept of 'entitlements' coined by Nobel Prize winner Amartya Sen. In other words, hunger is more a result of political disenfranchisement from economic opportunities, *aka* entitlements, than one of food shortages. In OF, the principle that farmers should receive a fair price for their milk was honoured. A range of measures was necessary for success, symbolised by the four-hand virtuous circle logo at the entry to Kaira District Cooperative Milk Producers Union (KDCMPU; see **Photos**).

The processing plant in Anand, cattle cake and other 'bottom-up' technical extensions to farmers were insufficient alone to treble India's milk supply; also needed were integrated commitments to processors, marketeers and consumers. Thus Anand's holistic, multifaceted strategy in Operation Flood got the prices right and streamlined milk production, processing and transport by above all mastering the marketing of rural milk to growing ranks of demanding consumers in metropolitan cities at the 'top' of the supply chain. Most of OF's critics concur with the analyses of Sen and Swaminathan regarding hunger and opportunity.

To critics who opposed Anand's capital-intensive emphasis on the National Milk Grid System and marketing to urban consumers, I commend the litany of *'No entitlements = Hunger'* and *'No jobs = Hunger'* to *'No increased sales to cities = Less income and more hunger in the countryside'*.

Empirical evidence from Agrostat/FAO shows that in the OF-I through OF-III eras, 1970-1996, Indian per capita consumption of milk (ex. butter) and butter & ghee increased significantly, compared to comparator countries like Bangladesh. There is a strong correlation between the achievements of Operation Flood with India's dairy success in the private and informal sectors. As an 'emerging economy' the share of agriculture *in toto* has shrunk (as industry and services grow) as a percentage of GDP, from 46.45 per cent of GDP in 1980-81 to about 36.82 per cent in 1994-95.[229] This makes dairy growth of 4-5 per cent per annum all the more impressive: compared to 5.63 per cent of GDP in 1980-81, dairying actually *increased* its share of a much larger national pie to 5.86 per cent in 1994-95.

Mistakes were made, lessons learned. How serious was the danger in the 1960s, that rich Europe might snare India in a lactic trap? Hard to say. But if India's cooperative leaders had not presented the FAO/WFP with a pro-active plan to monetise EEC dairy aid for investments in the country's ability to produce, process, market and distribute milk in response to the demands of lean and flush seasons, India's dairy dependence might be as ironclad as Nigeria's 'Wheat Trap'. But in 1988 OF officials[230] could claim:

> Commercial imports of dairy products ceased in 1976 except for limited imports of milk powder to overcome the severe drought of 1988. The gift imports account for less than 1% of India's milk production... all the dairy products now available in India are of Indian manufacture, without the use of any imported milk powder.

True, the exact date when all gift imports (dairy aid) to India ceased is disputed. According to Agrostat/FAO/1994, there was a marked decrease in SMP donations to India as the effects of the 1987-88 drought were mitigated. Donations from Europe (EEC/EC/EU) were down even more than from North America. However, from a low of 1740 MT of milk powder in 1990, and 3005 MT in 1991, SMP donations from the EEC to India spiked to 13,110 MT in 1992 - according to Agrostat. (European SMP donations accounted for nearly 100% of SMP received by India in 1992, with only 30 MT recorded from the Netherlands alone. Indeed, WFP donations of milk powder to India ceased after 1977, according to Agrostat/FAO/1994.[231])

Donations from other sources, e.g. the USA, the EEC, Finland and Switzerland, generally dwindled except for the unusual circumstances around the Gulf War of 1991.

Rather than a sign of dairy dependence, renewal of relatively small powder donations from the EEC in 1992 were a temporary aberration, in utilisation of monetised food aid by the Indian Government, which was restructuring its economy after an acute balance-of-payments crisis induced by oil price rises in the war. Corollary evidence for this view is that 1992 saw a doubling (compared to 1991) of 'non-cereals' food aid including large quantities of vegetable oil from North America to India, probably to alleviate Delhi's capital accounts crisis, rather than due to shortages of indigenous dairy products.

Table 6.4./Chart 6.1. EEC dairy aid to India dwindles.

	1989	1990	1991	1992
SMP	15,000	1740	3005	13,140
BO	1655	0	1000	4253
other dairy	14,048	196	94	110

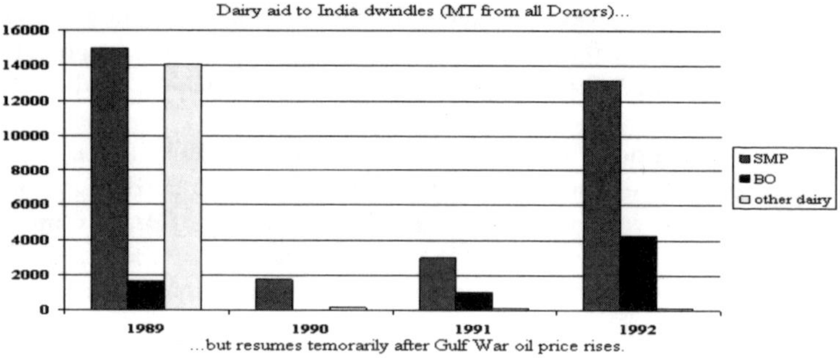

But the 1992 donations were minuscule compared to the past. Overall, it was evident that years like 1984, when India accepted *nearly 70 thousand MT of milk powder* from all donors (e.g. 50 thousand MT from the EEC), altogether more than 5-times 1992 levels, were far behind. Agrostat data showed donations of butter oil from the EEC decreased in a pattern like that of milk powder. Donations of 'other dairy products' fell similarly, distinguished only by a few hundred tonnes from Switzerland. Certainly the credibility of Operation Flood rose as EEC dairy aid ebbed, and virtually halted in the early-1990s. Like a sharp-tongued auntie, perhaps the critics of the programme deserve some credit for caustic remarks, ensuring that India weaned itself from its European wet nurse.

Global replication of the Anand Pattern?

Can other countries replicate this Flood? The answer is a *qualified yes.* Sri Lanka and several other countries have consulted with the NDDB, and Dr. Kurien once proposed a global Operation Flood. But fostering proper price structures within developing countries is a necessary prelude to economic take-off, irrespective of the use of food or dairy aid. If price controls are imposed, they should not restrict farmers' ability to meet their costs of production. Licensing laws such as Polson's monopoly which sparked the 1946 farmers' strike in Kaira District, or spurious sanitation rules must not be covers for barriers to market entry. In light of the fact that rich countries such as the United States came to dairy prominence in tandem with the cooperative movement, coops are probably poor country farmers' best organisational structure to develop domestic resources while utilising foreign assistance, whether that be technical extension or commodity gifts.

Even where dairy aid could increase food security or alleviate structural adjustment, the liberalisation of world agriculture under the GATT/WTO-1994 accords, which reduce rich country subsidies to dairy farmers and cut export subsidies, means first that stocks available for donation are depleted. Milk Lake and Butter Mountain became puddles and hillocks. (This has historic precedent: when US farm policy changed in the mid-1970s, dairy aid previously available in PL 480 dried up.) Now, like cereals stocks for food aid fell in response to GATT-1994, cuts in surplus purchases and price supports by the US Government in the 1996 Farm Bill have joined the 1984 EU milk quotas in cutting rich country stocks - and raising world dairy prices. (At least that was true until the bottom fell out of world dairy prices in 2007 – since when the EU introduced dairy subsidy exports, and the USA increased funds for the Dairy Export Incentives Programme. Such rich country backsliding on trade agreements in a world recession deepens respect for poor countries' demands for food sovereignty.) Second, the difficulty of replicating the Anand model universally in India, outside its favoured home state of Gujarat[232], reminds us that flexibility and sensitivity to local conditions are crucial to success. Furthermore, it must be said that dairy aid can be corrupted - a fact that led to cessation of it to Afghanistan - and following isolated cases of illegal sales, even threatened the reputation of OF in India. Monetised dairy product aid can, as in India, relieve recipient Government debt. But the threat is that 'aid' can be counter-productive, especially if it becomes a tool of bureaucratic empire building.

If and when surplus commodities are available as dairy aid, the record shows that *as long as proper pricing policies are followed*, sales of donated dairy aid *can* (augmented by cash and appropriate technical support) benefit recipient country farmers and consumers. But early problems in OF - before pricing changes made Indian commodities competitive with EEC aid in recombined milk sales – emphasised what is obvious: in hindsight:: food aid harms development if it prices domestic farmers out of markets. But OF worked in India (populated by 70 million milch animals) because it linked more rural farmers to urban markets. OF-like projects have been tenable in Africa[233], Sri Lanka, Pakistan, China, etc. Not to be ignored are smaller-scale (e.g. Maharashtra and Turkey) but fruitful Food-For-Work projects, or nutritional supplements to mothers and schoolchildren. However, renewal of dairy export subsidies in Europe or North America (on the pretext of producing surpluses for aid abroad) would rightly be fought as non-tariff barriers in the WTO by poorer exporters like Argentina and India.

Operation Flood taught Northern dairists that their prescriptions in breeding and feeding were not automatically suited to the South. But the economic lessons of OF transcend geographical boundaries. Put plainly: get the prices right or risk market failure. Don't hobble domestic farmers trying to supply consumers. Agrostat/FAO 1990 and 1994 computer databases demonstrated that, having more than doubled milk production and greatly raised per capita availability (during rapid population growth) Operation Flood was a success. Evidence flowed in, even from former doubters at entities including the World Bank, that the Anand principles of democratically-run cooperatives employing professional managers, marketeers and technicians not only brought order and progress to the once stagnant dairy sector, but maximised gains to farmers and consumers over other policies and, by raising farm incomes, are in turn stimulating employment and improving education (including girls), nutrition, sanitation and training essential to raising the quality of life for the majority of Indians who directly (10 to 13 million coop farmers) and indirectly (hundreds of millions of consumers) benefit from Flood.

Epilogue: On to Africa?

Did Operation Flood generate extra milk? This empirical question was debated long into the programme's existence. Soon after Flood's onset, consumption rose, but observers suspicious of EEC and GOI motives questioned whether statistics reflected the torrent of imports or a new wave of domestic production. Much of the above text has been dedicated to demonstrating that the preponderance of consumption improvements stemmed from getting economic signals right in the domestic production arena. This argument – once so hard fought – is now settled. Eventually, the World Food Programme, World Bank and other supranational institutions judged Operation Flood as one of, if not the most, successful development projects ever concluded in terms of hunger satisfied, and in the creation of ancillary opportunities arising from the marginal propensity of prospering farm families to consume health, education and other services and goods in rural communities.

Operation Flood was integral to the ongoing White Revolution. India's thirst for milk is unquenched. As the clock ticked down on the last millennium, Dr. Verghese Kurien left his chair at the NDDB to Dr. (Miss) Amrita Patel at the end of 1998. But as *Dairy Industry Newsletter*[234] noted in a 1999 interview he was, at 77, 'still around' and 'far from retired'. Kurien remained in charge of the Institute of Rural Management in Anand (IRMA), and also headed the Gujarat Coop Milk Marketing Federation, where he targeted New Zealand, Norway and Pakistan for Amul exports since: 'We have already exported Amul butter and cheese to the USA.' A few years later, Amul could boast of exporting to 40 countries. Sources close to Kurien say he never ignored unmet demand in India, but promoted exports to demonstrate that India could meet international hygiene standards, which had the knock-on effect of improving sanitation in domestic cold chains. When a multinational threatened to monopolise the Indian ice cream market several years ago, Kurien mobilised the coop's financial resources to challenge it with aggressive pricing. This marketing tactic was criticised as a waste of funds by the same critics who complained of Amul's manufacture of high-value products such as baby food. But, fearing the MNC could weaken Amul's market share in existing lines, Kurien deemed ice cream worth fighting for. The *DIN* reports:

> So Amul forced its way into the ice cream market, pricing products aggressively, and gained a 25% market share within 2 years. Amul ice cream sales this year are targeted at US $25 million, and the company have plans to increase their ice cream plants from eight to 20 in the same time.

With this renewed success, it seems the more things change, the more they stay the same. New NDDB chair Dr. Amrita Patel[235] targeted 15 million overseas Indians for Amul products available *via* the website (www.amul.com). She also lobbied the WTO to lift remaining restrictions on buffalo milk in international trade in the *Codex Alimentarius* - another instance of India acting in the spirit of free trade more than some rich nation exponents of 'free trade' which still subsidise exports.

Observers including P.J. Atkins fear the thrust of WTO accords is inimical to Third World development. Atkins cites the 1999 USA vs. EU 'banana war' as an example. The Most-Favoured-Nations pillar of GATT bans preferential treatment by Europe to imports from smallholders on St. Lucia (1993 production: 160,000 MT[236]), which were encouraged for decades from ACP countries *via* Lomé Conventions, since that entails discrimination against Honduran (1993 production: 931,000 MT) plantations dominated by US-based multinationals.

Hope remains that the banana war is the exception that proves the rule, i.e. that liberalising farm trade under GATT/WTO levels the playing field for poor food exporting countries, in the 'world is flat' parlance of *New York Times* columnist Thomas Friedman.[237] Optimistically, NDDB head Dr. Patel sees the WTO agreement as 'a clear victory both for the country and the dairy cooperatives' - since it reduces barriers to entry into world markets. She cites advantages including 'India's low-cost production' and the predominance of the buffalo which is 'an extremely efficient converter of low-quality nutrients' and producer of 'speciality products like mozzarella cheese'. Dr. Patel is determined to gird the NDDB against:

> rising international surpluses and continued support for dairy farmers and exporters in other parts of the world… India must retain and strengthen its competitive advantages.

Future WTO negotiations could further cut European dairy export subsidies, which would improve India's export competitiveness. Less predictable are outcomes on investment capital, genetically-modified organisms (GMOs) and trade-related intellectual property (TRIPs). The latter are growth sectors for arable products such as Monsanto seeds and Roundup pesticide. The same is true for technologies such as embryo transfer and cloning. (However Monsanto's GM milk-inducer, recombinant bovine growth hormone, rBGH, *aka* recombinant bovine somatotropin, or rBST branded Posilac, incurred such consumer disaffection that it was sold in 2008.) Scrutiny is needed to ensure that inappropriate technologies do not harm people, animals, the environment – or waste energy in this era of Peak Oil and Peak Food. The global meltdown that began in Thailand in 1997 long hurt Asia, Russia and Latin America. Although the buoyant US housing sector helped keep the world from depression for years after the dot.com crash and 9/11, the post-2007 economic debacle proves that cross-border flows of *unfettered* short-term capital (resisted by India, despite its post-1991 liberalisations) need reform in the WTO. The ultimate test is whether or not the purported fairness and transparency of multilateral trade improves the lives of people in developing countries.

Since Dr. Kurien welcomed Dr. Amrita Patel to the helm of the NDDB, some policy differences have risen between them on joint ventures and the roles of NDDB (state), farmer cooperative or private control of dairy procurement, processing and especially marketing.[238] In *Dairy India 2007* Kurien[239] reiterated support for farmer-controlled coops:

> '[i]t is my firm and unshakable belief that the entire value chain from procurement to marketing is the sole and exclusive domain of the farmer. The moment the farmer loses… it, being a small producer, he becomes nothing more than a contract laborer.'

This statement exudes Kurien's hostility to interference by politicians or private actors in coops. Responding to a rash of suicides of farmers bankrupted by crop failures of GM cotton, Kurien[240] articulated the benefits of cooperative dairying while rejecting the neoliberal case for special economic zones (SEZs): 'Wherever farmers have had cooperatives, there have been no cases of suicides'.

Despite differences, Kurien probably concurred with Amrita Patel[241] when, in the context of a world recession sparked by improper regulation of financial markets, India's rural sector was weathering the economic downturn relatively better than urban centres. In her chairman's speech at the 35th annual meeting in June 2009, Patel[242] said: '[The] dairy cooperative movement has always helped to provide a safety net to the most vulnerable and marginalized sections of our population, which otherwise suffers the worst consequences of any economic crises.'

This rural safety net, to which some urban unemployed banking, gem, and textile workers returned to work in thriving dairy villages is unthinkable without the efforts of dairy cooperatives since 1946, when Tribhuvandas Patel led a small milk strike in Gujarat. In future, coops can improve the resilience of more smallholders producing milk, edible oils, fruit, vegetables and salt in competition with highly-capitalised rivals.

Many publications - fewer *pro* than *con* - have evaluated the case of Operation Flood. In October 2008, Martin Doornbos, an early critic from the 'Dutch school' wrote to this author that, 'I do not rule out the possibility that our judgment today might be more positive than our conclusions at the time, but I am afraid I have not followed developments around Operation Flood for a good number of years now, so would not be able to tell.'[243] In May 2009, Dr. Doornbos added:[244]

> There is one point of information here which we had also taken up in our discussion and critique at the time. This concerns the attribution of the 'trebling' of India's dairy production to Operation Flood. In the 1980s there was not yet a 'trebling', but surely already an increase in milk production, which itself was not in dispute. Increased availability of green fodder throughout the country, as I recall, helped to account for the aggregate increases in milk production that were noted. This was true for the regions reached by Operation Flood and for the areas out of its orbit. At the time it was estimated that OF was responsible for handling less than 10% of total Indian milk production. Nonetheless, OF then claimed responsibility for 100% of India's production increases. Since then OF's own share may well have increased, though with the operation of large-scale private dairy companies and the prevalence of numerous very small-scale production units not reached by marketing routes in large parts of the country I would be surprised if OF's share of India's total milk production had now risen to anything near, let alone over 20%. But again, or still, a link is suggested between OF's marketing strategies and India's overall increase of milk production, now 'trebling'. I guess this attribution has been issued by OF authorities but think this should be taken with a grain of salt.

Dr. Doornbos' point, that India's huge informal milk sector leaves room for discussion on specific credit for increases, is valid. But this book bases its arguments for 'trebling' of milk production on FAO statistics, not claims from OF-linked institutions, and it attributes much OF success to priming the pump of the aggregate milk sector via improvements in infrastructure, agricultural extension and marketing.

A source close to Kurien says nobody denies that increased availability of green fodder, large-scale private dairy companies and numerous very small-scale production units increased production, but asks:

> What caused the 'increased availability of green fodder'? Was it not, mainly, due to Operation Flood? Feeding, including green fodder production, was a focus area under OF. What made private dairy companies and small scale production units succeed in India? Was it not due to remunerative prices that dairy farmers got, thanks to the OF emphasis on marketing? As Dr. Kurien has always said, milk production does not increase by better feeding or breeding alone, but by better marketing… OF was basically a successful marketing effort. When compared to producers of agricultural products (e.g. fruits and vegetables), milk producers have, over the years, got a better return. While OF may not have contributed to the entire production increase in milk, it has definitely caused it, to a large extent. How much of it can be attributed to OF, is always debatable.

Dr. Kurien's reaction to such repartee reportedly echoes the national motto of India: *Satyameva Jayate* (*Truth alone shall prevail*). The tide has turned in the programme's favour. In *Millions Fed*, a collection of development successes by the International Food Policy Research Institute, Operation Flood is credited with linking small farmers to urban consumers thoughout India.[245] In fact, in 2004 Kurien announced[246]:

> We have been approached by African countries such as Kenya, Uganda, Ethiopia, Mozambique and Rwanda. We have invited them to visit our facilities at Anand before finalising their plans. We are ready to help out the interested countries to develop more 'Anands'. The 'Anand pattern' will help developing countries become self reliant in dairy industry.

Operation Flood's legacy is recognised by supranational organisations. In October 2008, the World Bank announced[247] plans to replicate the Anand Pattern in Africa, and officials made a courtesy call to Dr. Kurien's private residence. President Robert Zoellick has declared that the Bank would try to replicate the low-input/low-output 'Anand pattern' in Africa. Bank Group Managing Director Ngozi Okonjo-Iweala extols the new South-South Experience Exchange Facility which can apply India's lessons in Africa. An NDDB team of specialists met with dairy counterparts in Tanzania and Uganda, which with Kenya, Malawi, Mauritius, Rwanda, South Africa, Zambia, and Zimbabwe form the Eastern and Southern African Dairy Development Association (ESADA).[248]

Domestic politicians still seek the blessing of Kurien. In February 2009, Congress Party scion Rahul Gandhi, rumoured a future Prime Minister, visited Amul dairy and IRMA before an unscheduled stop at Kurien's home for a private chat, while his entourage and local politicians waited outside. Young Gandhi saw photographs from 1955 when the first milk powder plant funded by UNICEF was inaugurated by PM Nehru and his grandmother Indira Gandhi in the company of Kurien, and also images of his father Rajiv Gandhi visiting Anand. According to long-time Kurien assistant P.A. Joseph, Rahul Gandhi told Kurien he had seen the Grameen Bank in Bangladesh for which Professor Muhammad Yunus won the Nobel Peace Prize in 2006, but what he saw at Amul was greater than that and pre-existed that institution.[249]

The subsequent election victory of the Congress Party, and the touting of Rahul Gandhi as a successor to PM Manmohan Singh, could be a favourable portent for cooperatives.

This book has highlighted neglected data showing Operation Flood to be a success. That is an understatement. Over 1970-96, Indian milk production more than trebled and per capita consumption nearly doubled to 200 grams per day as population increased about half.

Dairy India 2007[250] predicts per capita milk availability of 296 grams per day, and total production of 111 million MT in the year 2010.

India has upstaged the USA as the world's leading producer and an encore as exporter is underway. Thomas Malthus would be astonished. On balance, the actions of the EEC, the Government of India, and cooperative leaders in Anand were honourable and strikingly effective.

More work must be done in India, Africa and elsewhere. But it does not bear imagining if the White Revolution had been lost.

NOTES

Glossary

1 John Shaw & Edward Clay, *World Food Aid* (London, Heinemann, 1993), p.xi.
2 Shaw & Clay (1993), p.ix.
3 *World Development Report: From Plan to Market*, World Bank (New York, OUP, 1996), pp.188-9. Similar thresholds: low- and middle-income economies/$1090w GNP per capita; upper-middle income/$4640 and high-income economies $23,420 and world average/$4470.
4 *Webster's Ninth New Collegiate Dictionary* (1985).
5 Jagdish Bhagwati, *Protectionism* (Massachusetts, MIT Press, 1988), p.35.

Chapter 1 After the Deluge

1 M.V. Kamath, *Management Kurien-Style: The story of the White Revolution.* (Delhi, Konark, 1989), pp.166-7. Kamath also details how fine sprayers for buffalo milk powder were developed in India in the 1950s, pp.4, 94, 120.
2 Ruth Heredia, *The Amul India Story* (New Delhi, Tata McGraw-Hill, 1997), pp.54-6.
3 Personal communications. Quotes from Dr. Verghese Kurien are from interviews with the author in Anand, April 1998, unless indicated.
4 Shanti George, *Operation Flood* (Oxford, OUP, 1985), pp.23, 249, citing Kroese *et al.* (1979).
5 B.A. Scholten, 'Milk quotas help melt Europe's Butter Mountain', *Hoard's Dairyman* (10 February 1989). See also Scholten (1991) 'Trade talks threaten European farmers, too'. As late as 1991, farm subsidies consumed about 70 per cent of the EEC budget, and dairy subsidies and storage costs accounted for about 50 per cent.
6 John Empson, 'High prices stimulate Third World dairying', *Hoard's Dairyman* (10 August 1989), p.577.
7 NDDB, *Dairy Farming in India* (1998). Pamphlet from Anand. Later figures for '27 cooperative dairy milksheds...developed in 10 Indian states' are higher than figures of '18 best milksheds' in the NDDB's original OF-III proposal.
8 Heredia, *The Amul India Story* (1997), pp.109-28.
9 P.R. Gupta, *Dairy India 1997* (New Delhi, Dairy India Yearbook, 1997). Text from the yearbook and personal communications with editor Shri P.R. Gupta.
10 John Shaw & Edward Clay, *World Food Aid* (London, Heinemann, 1993), p.65.
11 Shanti George, *Operation Flood* (1985), pp.20-1.
12 NDDB, *Role of Cooperatives in Economic Development* (ca. 1998).

13 Kamath, *Management Kurien Style* (1989). Kamath and some other writers use the word 'dairists' for people in dairying.
14 Peter Singer's 1975 book is seen as a benchmark by animal welfarists.
15 Shanti George, *Operation Flood* (1985), p.158.
16 George, ibid, p.8; Scholten, MA dissertation, (Durham University, 1997) p.172.
17 George, ibid, p.14.
18 Sources: NDDB, *Operation Flood: Phase III* (September 1985). OF-III proposal from Anand. Also *Operation Flood* (1998) pamphlet.
19 NDDB, *Dairy Farming in India* (ca. 1998). This pamphlet from Anand is the base for this book's dating of OF-I, OF-II and OF-III periods.
20 Edward J. Clay & Olav Stokke, *Food Aid Reconsidered* (1991), pp.13, 16, 40.
21 NDDB (ca. 1997). The World Bank concludes OF is efficient investment.
22 NDDB (ca. 1998). *NDDB - Heralding Changes.*
23 *Economist,* Letters (15 August 1998).
24 Shaw & Clay, *World Food Aid* (1993), p.65.
25 NDDB, *Dairy Farming in India* (1998).
26 Aneja & Puri, 'India's dairy riddle unravelled', pp.3-26.
27 *Dairy India 1997*, p.14.
28 *World Outlook*, Vol. 3, No. 2 (FAO, Rome, 1998). Report obtained via FAO-Dairy-Outlook, then edited by Michael Griffin, now by Barbara Senfter.
29 Gunilla Andræ & Björn Beckmann, *The Wheat Trap The Wheat Trap: Bread and Underdevelopment in Nigeria* (Uppsala, Zed Books, 1985).

Chapter 2 Recurring Depression?

1 *Economist*, 'Is contagion a myth?' (31 October 1998), p.110.
2 Jeffrey Friedan & David Lake, *International Political Economy* (1987), pp.383-94.
3 *The European Union*, EC Parliament Publications (New York, 1995), p.4.
4 Wolfram Hanrieder & Graeme Auton, *The Foreign Policies of West Germany, France & Britain* (New Jersey, 1980), pp.105-14.
5 Personal Email from Peter Nelson, manager of an EU project in China which reprises the monetisation of dairy aid in India (8 September 1998).
6 MAFF News Release 440/98, 'UK operators will get option of receiving payment in euros - Brown' (12 November 1998). NFU Pres. Ben Gill endorsed EMU which in that year gave British farmers windfall profits.
7 *This Week*, 'Stop ignoring our military muscle' (1 August 1998), p.12.
8 *Economist*, *The World in 1997*, 'Two-faced Turkey', by Tim Hindle, p.57.
9 *Economist*, ibid, 'Asia's competing business centres', by Paul Markillie, p.112-14. Markillie claims Asia's labour costs approach EU rates.
10 *Hoard's Dairyman*, Asia trade highlighted' (10 August 1998), p.559.
11 William Greider, *One World, Ready or Not*, (New York, 1997), p.290.
12 *Economist: The World in 1997*, 'The good life after communism', p.56.
13 Jeremy Isaacs, Producer, *The Cold War* (1998). BBC TV series.
14 Kazimierz Z. Poznanski, *Technology, Competition, & the Soviet Bloc* (1987), pp.5, 54.

15 BBC Radio 2 News (Berkeley, 20 September 1998). For example, £100m meant for revitalisation of air transport was 'lost' by Russia's finance ministry.
16 James Miles, 'A difficult year for Mr. Jiang, his friends & neighbours', *The Economist: World in 1997*. Miles is a BBC correspondent.
17 *Economist*, 'Chinese traders at the door' (11 October 1997), pp.107-8.
18 *Economist*, 'Child mortality' (10 October 1998), p.154.
19 *Economist*, 'Indian farmers: power struggle' (1 November 1997), p.82.
20 Ashok Gulati 'Blinkered Vision 30/60', *India Today* (13 April 1998). Gulati questions statistics in the BJP's National Agenda for Governance (NAG).
21 *Economist*, 'That old Gandhi magic' (29 November 1997), p.87.
22 *Economist: The World in 1997*, 'The world in figures', pp.93-100.
23 Greider, *One World, Ready or Not* (1997), p.45.
24 Charles P. Kindleberger, *The World in Depression, 1929-1939* (Los Angeles, 1973), p.11. John Kenneth Galbraith called this the best book on the subject.
25 Greider, *One World, Ready or Not* (1997), p.21.
26 Eric Wolf, *Europe and the People without History* (University of California, 1982), pp.301-2.
27 Matt Ridley, *The Origins of Virtue* (Britain, 1996), pp.249, 264-5.
28 Wilfried Wesselink World Watch item in *Dairy Today* (August 1998), p.4.
29 *The Week*, 'Why has Siemens shut its Tyneside plant?' (8 August 1998), p.35.
30 *The Week*, 'Fujitsu: branch line closure', September 12, 1998, p.33.
31 Bernard Hoekman & Michel Kostecki, *The Political Economy of the World Trading System* (Oxford, 1995), p.272.
32 Greider, *One World, Ready or Not*, pp.471-3. Greider: 'In this modern secular age, many who think of themselves as rational and urbane have put their faith in this self-regulating market as piously as others put their faith in God.'
33 *Wall Street Journal*, 'Second thoughts: emerging nations are moving to stem the free flow of money', (4-5 September 1998), pp.1, 6.
34 *Economist*, 'Emerging markets', 15 August 1998, p.98.
35 *Economist*, 'Indian bonds: calling all patriots' (July 25, 1998), p.93.
36 Greider, *One World, Ready or Not* (1997), p.243.
37 Greider, ibid, p.234.
38 Greider, ibid, pp.260, 272, 273, 259-284. Greider explains the dangers of short-term capital and suggests taxing it at borders.
39 Greider, ibid, p.467.
40 Paul Krugman, 'New thinking can prevent a Great Depression', *IHT* (1 September 1998), p. 8. Among puritans obsessed with 'moral hazard', Friedrick van Hayek may have urged policies that prolonged the Depression.
41 Greider, *One World, Ready or Not*, p. 261.
42 Kindleberger, *The World in Depression* (1973), p. 64.
43 Jeffrey Sachs, 'LDC debt in the 1980s, risk and reforms', in *Crises in the Economic and Financial Structure*, ed. by Paul Wachtel. (1982).
44 Kindleberger, *The World in Depression* (1973), p.275.
45 Kindleberger, ibid, pp.242-5.

46 David Irving, *Goebbels: Mastermind of the Third Reich* (London, 1996). Irving is controversial, but this book based on Soviet archives excoriates Goebbels.
47 Gitta Sereny, *Albert Speer: His Battle with the Truth* (New York, 1995).
48 Kindleberger, *The World in Depression* (1973), pp.64, 125.

Chapter 3 Mercantilism to WTO

1 Bernard Hoekman & Michel Kostecki, *The Political Economy of the World Trading System: From GATT to WTO* (Oxford, 1995), p.235.
2 Lester Thurrow, 'America, Europe and Japan' (*Economist*, 9 November 1985), pp.21-6. Reprinted in Frieden & Lake, *International Political Economy* (1987).
3 Matt Ridley, *The Origins of Virtue* (Great Britain, 1996), pp.53-66, 230-1. Ridley suggests warfare can be a symptom of market failure.
4 Kym Anderson & Rodney Tyers, *Global Effects of Liberalizing Trade in Farm Products* (London, 1991).
5 Jagdish Bhagwati, *Protectionism* (MIT, Cambridge, 1988), p.25.
6 Edward Carr, 'Grotesque' (12 December 1992), pp.16, 1-18.
7 Paul Kennedy, *Preparing for the Twenty-First Century* (New York, 1993), p.24.
8 Kennedy, ibid, p.124.
9 Kennedy, ibid, p.125.
10 Adam Smith feared *laissez-faire* economic conditions if they produced monopolies. See *The Wealth of Nations,* Book III, Chapter IV (1776/1937), pp.388-9: 'All for ourselves and nothing for other people seems, in every age of the world, to have been the vile [evil] maxim of the masters of mankind.'
11 J.S. Nicholson, *History of the English Corn Laws* (New York, 1904), p.122.
12 Bhagwati, *Protectionism* (1988), p.24.
13 E.J. Hobsbawm, *The Age of Revolution: 1789-1848* (New York, 1962), p.359.
14 Chairman Kurien's annual report to NDDB, Amul Ltd., Website: www.amul.com (June 1998).
15 David R. Harvey, 'The US Farm Act', *Food Policy* (April 1998), pp.111-21.
16 Paul Kennedy, *The Rise and Fall of the Great Powers* (New York, 1987), pp.126-39.
17 *Economist*, 'Will the world starve?' (10 June 1995), pp.63-4.
18 Kennedy, *Preparing for the Twenty-First Century* (1993).
19 Lester R. Brown, *State of the World*: (Sydney, 1990), pp.65-7.
20 Hobsbawm, *The Age of Revolution: 1789-1848* (1962), pp.60-1.
21 Hobsbawm, ibid, p.157.
22 Horace White, in Frederick Bastiat's *Sophisms of Protection* (New York, 1888), p.ix.
23 Jean Drèze & Amartya Sen (eds), *The Political Economy of Hunger, Vol.1* (Oxford, 1990).
24 Eric R. Wolf, *Europe and the People without History* (USA, University of California Press, 1982), p.321.
25 Peter J. Atkins, unpublished PhD thesis (University of Liverpool 1977).
26 Hobsbawm, *The Age of Revolution: 1789-1848* (1962), pp.61-7.
27 Nicholson, *History of the English Corn Laws* (1904), p.157.

28 Kennedy, *Rise and Fall of Great Powers* (1987). Instructive book.
29 Paul Samuelson, *Economics: An Introductory Analysis*, 7th ed. (New York, 1967), p.649.
30 Samuelson, ibid, p.646.
31 Bhagwati, *Protectionism* (1988), p.25.
32 M.V. Kamath, *Management Kurien Style* (Delhi, 1989).
33 Hugo Young, *One of Us: A Biography of Margaret Thatcher* (London, 1989).
34 European Commission Statistics, *Economist* (26 January 1991), p.27.
35 Henry W. Erhrmann, *Politics in France* (Boston, 1983), p.29.
36 John T.S. Keeler, 'The Corporatist Dynamic of Agricultural Modernization in the Fifth Republic' (New York, 1981), p.277.
37 Keeler, ibid, pp. 225-77.
38 B.A. Scholten, 'Milk quotas help melt Europe's Butter Mountain' in *Hoard's Dairyman* (10 February 1989), pp.91, 121.
39 Scholten, 'Trade talks threaten European farmers, too', *Hoard's Dairyman* (10 October 1991), p.762.
40 Kamath, *Management Kurien-Style* (1989), p.126.
41 W.W. Rostow, *Theorists of Economic Growth from David Hume to the Present* (New York, 1990), pp.432, 428-41, 433.
42 Michael P. Todaro, *Economic Development in the Third World* (New York, 1985), p.66.
43 *India Today*, 'Blinkered vision 30/60', by Jairam Ramesh (13 April 1998), p.48.
44 J.P. Cole, *Geography of World Affairs* (Middlesex, 1979), p.174. Europe received $14.5 billion in the Marshall Plan. Contrary to myth, Germany received less than Britain, which like the USA spent much treasure in the Cold War.
45 Peter T. Bauer, *Dissent on Development* (London, 1971).
46 Rostow, *Theorists of Economic Growth* (1990), p.432.
47 Bauer, *Dissent on Development* (1971), p.164.
48 Todaro, *Economic Development in the Third World* (1985), pp.64-6.
49 Bauer, *Dissent on Development* (1971), pp.295, 306-342, 296.
50 W.W. Rostow, Book Review of P.T. Bauer, *Transaction/Society*, New York, Springer (November/December 1982), pp.88-9.
51 Although portrayed as mainstream here, Rostow was attacked by the far-Right as a figurehead of a Left-oriented political establishment dominating the USA.
52 Arturo Escobar, *Encountering Development* (Princeton Press, West Sussex 1995).
53 Todaro, *Economic Development in the Third World* (1985), pp.94-9.
54 Rostow, *Theorists of Economic Growth* (1990), p.439
55 Bauer, *Dissent on Development* (1971), pp.293-4, 297-8. Rostow and Bauer himself write that Bauer's views were influenced by the rubber industry in Malaysia and cocoa and other cash crop farming in West Africa.
56 Rostow, *Theorists of Economic Growth* (1990), p.434.
57 Todaro, *Economic Development*, pp.64-6. Todaro agrees investment is necessary but not sufficient for take-off.
58 Cole, *Geography of World Affairs* (1979), p.284.

59 Cole, ibid, pp.118, 391. India's iron and steel industry rose in Jamshedpur.
60 *Economist Book of Vital World Statistics* (1990), pp.42, 69.
61 Hobsbawm, *The Age of Revolution: 1789-1848* (1962), p.62.
62 *India Today*, 'Blinkered vision 30/60' by Jairam Ramesh, 13 April 1998, p.48.
63 Bhagwati, *Protectionism* (1988).
64 Todaro, *Economic Development in the Third World* (1985), pp.256, 258, 261.
65 Todaro, ibid, pp.409-15. Import-substitution entailed tariffs on specified imports, and subsidies for their domestically produced counterparts.
66 Martin Doornbos, Frank van Dorsten, Manoshi Mitra & Piet Terhal, *Dairy Aid and Development: India's Operation Flood*, IDPAD (London, 1990), p.15.
67 Samuelson, *Economics* (1967), p.423.
68 Hoekman & Kostecki, *The Political Economy of the World Trading System* (1995), pp.56-9.
69 Hoekman & Kostecki, ibid, *The Prisoner's Dilemma in trade policy*, p.58.
70 Bhagwati, *Protectionism* (1988), p.9.
71 Bhagwati, ibid, p.9. This quotation and paragraph above from Bhagwati.
72 Keylor, *The Twentieth Century World* (1984), p.277.
73 Hoekman & Kostecki, *The Political Economy of the World Trading System* (1995), pp.66, 202.
74 Hoekman & Kostecki, ibid, p.202. The Cairns Group include: Argentina, Australia, Brazil, Canada, Chile, Colombia, Fiji, Hungary, Indonesia, Malaysia, New Zealand, the Philippines, Thailand and Uruguay.
75 Kennedy, *Preparing for the Twenty-First Century* (1993), p.318.
76 *Economist* (22 December 1990), p.89.
77 Kennedy, *Rise and Fall of Great Powers* (1987). Robert Gilpin and William Greider support Kennedy's analysis that US military over-extension and openness to imports from Cold War clients undermined Bretton Woods.
78 Robert Gilpin, 'American Policy in the Post-Reagan Era' (1987), p.37. Paper at the Jackson School of International Studies, University of Washington.
79 *The Week*, 'Why is Airbus beating Boeing?' (12 September 1998), p.35.
80 Frances Moore Lappé & Joseph Collins, *Food First* (1982), pp.50, 176-86.
81 Keylor, *The Twentieth Century World* (1984), p.401.
82 Dan Morgan, *Merchants of Grain* (New York, 1979), pp.216, 349.
83 Agrostat/FAO/1994. Years checked: 1970, 1980, 1988, 1990 and 1993.
84 Not all US government officials knew of the impending Soviet grain deal. See Anthony Sampson, *The Sovereign State of ITT* (1974); also Dan Morgan (1979).
85 Agrostat/FAO/1994 Livestock Trade.
86 Frances M. Ufkes, 'Trade liberalisation, agro-food politics and the globalisation of agriculture', *Political Geography*, (May 1993), pp.215-31.
87 B.A. Scholten, 'Wird Bush Umwelt-Präsident?' (20 October 1990), *WWL*.
88 Andræ & Beckmann, *The Wheat Trap* (1985), p.30. They cite Clay & Pryer (1982), p.5; I. Wallerstein (1980); and P. Kilby (1965), pp.8, 19.
89 Andræ & Beckmann, ibid, p. 31. They cite USDA (1981) documents and USDA counsellor George Pope. USA expanded in Nigeria à la South Korea.

90 Andræ & Beckmann, ibid, p. 31.
91 Chapter 4 suggests India's temporary renewal of dairy imports was due to the economic crisis sparked by petroleum price rises in the Gulf War.
92 Agrostat/1994/FAO: Trade/Index/US dairy product exports/ and milk production in the computerised database.
93 *International Herald Tribune*, 'Charity finds that US food aid for Africa hurts', by Celia W. Dugger (14 August 2007).
94 Anderson & Tyers, *Global Effects of Liberalizing Trade* (1991).
95 Increased transnational trade in processed commodities among subsidiaries of MNC/TNCs may exaggerate the rise in First World market share.
96 Anderson & Tyers, *Global Effects of Liberalizing Trade* (1991), pp.12-18.
97 Anderson & Tyers, ibid, p.1.
98 *Agrostat PC* FAO/1994/Trade/Value/Economic Groups/Agricultural Products.
99 *Agrostat PC* 1994 FAO Note: In bar graph, 1961 stands for mean $US in 1961-64; 1986 stands for mean $US values 1983-86.
100 Dan Morgan, *Merchants of Grain* (New York, 1979), pp.292-4. The reputation of the USA as a reliable exporter fell when it reneged on a soybean deal with Japan in 1973. The upshot was higher prices for many commodities.
101 Hoekman & Kostecki, *The Political Economy of the World Trading System* (1995), p.206.
102 *NFU/International* 1/94, 'NFU briefing: GATT settlement in agriculture', (1994), pp.9-10. Via Martin Haworth (Part I); NFU Econ. Dept. (Part II), 5 January 1994. Its 34 pages are a practical guide to the Uruguay agreement.
103 *NFU/International* 1/94, ibid, p.10.
104 B.A. Scholten, 'Europeans may extend BST ban', *Dairy Today* (June 1993).
105 *Economist*, Editorial (17 October 1992).
106 Hoekman & Kostecki, *The Political Economy of the World Trading System* (1995), p.24.
107 Personal communication, Prof. David R. Harvey, University of Newcastle upon Tyne (UK, 1996).
108 Personal communications and interviews with officials at GCMMF, NDDB, and IRMA in Anand, (April 1998).
109 Hoekman & Kostecki, *The Political Economy of the World Trading System* (1995), p.265.
110 Hopkins, 'Developing countries in the Uruguay Round' in *World Agriculture and the GATT*, edited by William P. Avery (Boulder, 1993), pp.143-63.
111 ERS-USDA, Supplement: provisions of 1996 Farm Bill, *Agricultural Outlook*, (1996).
112 Harvey, 'The US Farm Act' (April 1998), pp.111-21. FAIR shows decoupling from the 1985 Food Security Act (FSA) through the 1990 Food, Agriculture, Conservation and Trade (FACT) Act.
113 K. Stuart & F.C. Runge, 'Agricultural policy reform in the US: an unfinished agenda', *Australian Journal of Agricultural and Resource Economics* (1997), pp.117-36.

114 B.A. Scholten, 'US Dairy 2000', *Dairy News* edition of *Farming News* [UK] (21 November 1997), pp.6-7.
115 Mark Killilea, 'A look at dairy trade winners and losers', *Hoard's Dairyman* (October 10, 1998). Killilea is a Member of the European Parliament.
116 NDDB (November 1998).
117 D.R. Harvey, 'US Farm Act' (April 1998), p.120.
118 Anderson & Tyers, *Global Effects of Liberalizing Trade*, pp.2, 63.
119 Hoekman & Kostecki, *The Political Economy of the World Trading System* (1995), p. 197. The use of cereals in biofuel in 2009 dwarfs their use in 1900, implying less food availability.
120 David R. Harvey, *et al.*, *Consultation Document: The Northern Uplands Red Meat Initiative: Summary of Situation and Outlook Report* (ca. 1998). Commissioned as part of EU help to remote regions (Objective 5b). Mike Barton of Northern Development Company (NDC), ADAS, MLC and University of Newcastle also contributed.
121 B.A. Scholten, *Consumer Risk Reflections on Organic and Local Food in Seattle, with Reference to Newcastle upon Tyne* (Durham University, 2007). Unpublished PhD thesis.
122 Hans W. Singer, *Food Aid and Structural Adjustment in SSA* (Oxford, 1991).
123 Kennedy, *Preparing for the Twenty-First Century* (1993), pp.73-81.
124 Ben Fine, Michael Heasman & Judith Wright, *Consumption in the Age of Affluence* (London, 1996), pp.47-54, 48.
125 Hoekman & Kostecki, *The Political Economy of the World Trading System* (1995), pp.144-58, 156-7.
126 Hopkins, 'Developing countries in the Uruguay Round' (1993), in W.P. Avery (1993). Hopkins cites Anderson & Tyers (1990a).
127 Hopkins, ibid.
128 Andræ & Beckmann, *The Wheat Trap* (Uppsala, 1985), p.146.
129 Hoekman & Kostecki, *The Political Economy of the World Trading System* (1995), p.89.
130 *NFU Briefing International* 1/94, pp.2, 17.
131 *NFU Briefing International*, ibid, pp.2-8. The NFU report addresses GATT/WTO issues in different order from this book, but accords with other sources. The AMS calculation is a global one made for the entirety of a country's agriculture - not sector by sector.
132 Hoekman & Kostecki, *The Political Economy of the World Trading System* (1995), p.295. AMS superseded the weaker measure of producer subsidy equivalents (PSE).
133 *NFU Briefing International* 1/94, ibid, p.8.
134 *Economist*, (1 February 1997), pp.23, 58. Powerful MNC processors like RJR Nabisco and General Mills probably have as much - or more - clout than farmers in lobbying for promotion of US food exports. Examples of ample spending include ANUGA, an international food trade fair held in seven buildings in Bonn in 1989 when US promoters occupied an entire building.

135 *NFU Briefing International* (1994), pp.4-6, 9. Another article in *The Economist* (1 February 1997), pp.23, 58, shows that the EU had already cut most CAP intervention prices (world prices in the 1986-1988 base period were low), and the EU considered the GATT tariffication agreement to be an economic victory for its still-protected farmers. Nevertheless, admission of Central & Eastern European countries to EU membership was expected to threaten remaining subsidies protecting farmers in Western Europe. A Ministry of Agriculture (MAFF) press release, (8 January 1997; 5/97, pp.1-6, p 2) 'Baldry outlines the need for CAP Reform', emphasised the pressure that incorporating former Eastbloc countries into the EU would put on the CAP. However, some researchers claimed EU enlargement did not threaten the CAP *status quo*.

136 *NFU International* (1994), p.34. Vulnerability to constraints on its ag trade was an inducement for China to join the WTO.

137 Bhagwati, *Protectionism* (1988), p.9.

138 B.A. Scholten, 'Auch in den USA Chancen für Milchquoten' in *WWL/BWL* (Stuttgart, 26 August 1989). Also *Hoard's Dairyman* (25 January 1989), and *Hoard's* (July 1990). The Reagan-Bush administration was so committed to neoliberal economics that it rejected industry pleas for supply management.

139 *Hoard's Dairyman*, 'Nasty trade dispute threatens Canada's milk markets' (25 April 1995), p.311.

140 *Economist*, 'Farm follies' (29 July 1995), p.36. Ex-Eastbloc countries desiring admission have farm sectors with ca. 27% employment, compared to EU-15's agricultural sector with ca. 6% of total employment.

141 *Dairy Today*, World Watch, reported by Wilfried Wesselink (Minnesota, August 1988), p.4. Later reports noted Denmark was so short of milk that German exporters finally broke the milk monopoly in Denmark.

142 B.A. Scholten in *Hoard's Dairyman* (10 March 1989). See also Scholten in *Dairy Today* (March 1993; March 1994).

143 *Hoard's Dairyman* (25 April 1995), p.311. US farmers in the National Milk Producers Federation claim NAFTA rules go beyond WTO rules on tariffication - thus Canada should import $1 billion more US milk annually. Deploring this classic beggar-thy-neighbour ploy *Hoard's Dairyman* urged US farmers to increase profits *via* cost-cutting and higher productivity, not overturning Canada's milk quota system.

144 If 1993 US milk production = 68,700,000 metric tonnes, multiplying that by 2204 (pounds per metric tonne) = 151 billion pounds.

145 *Hoard's Dairyman*, Washington Dairygrams (25 May 1995); 17.8 million pounds = 8900 US tonnes.

146 Drèze & Sen (eds), *The Political Economy of Hunger* (1990).

147 William Greider, *One World, Ready or Not* (New York, 1997). According to Greider, China's market is so attractive that potential trading partners could be enticed into bilateral deals violating MFN.

148 Hoekman & Kostecki, *Political Economy of the World Trading System* (1995).

149 Reuter dispatch via NFU, 'Fischler says no backing down on meat hormone' (23 January 1996). See also Kennedy's *Twenty-First Century* (1993, pp.279-82) suggesting Europe resists biotechology due to its demographics.

150 *The Week*, 'From the "failure" of free markets: a backlash begins', R. Chote (12 September 1998).

151 WTO (3 October 1998). Website: http://www.wto.org.

Chapter 4 Food & Dairy Aid

1 Verghese Kurien extolled domestic production, warning rubber manufacturers to beware 'tax holidays' granted by Delhi to foreign investors such as Bridgestone, comparing them to investments by General Foods that compromise self-reliance for edible oils (3 November 1997).

2 John Shaw & Edward Clay, *World Food Aid* (London, 1993), p.1.

3 Dan Morgan, *Merchants of Grain* (New York, 1979), pp.103-5, 13.

4 Hoover engaged US businessman Armand Hammer who relied on contacts from V.I. Lenin to Richard Nixon in his lucrative grain, fertiliser and oil deals.

5 Shaw & Clay, *World Food Aid* (1993), p.5.

6 William Greider, 'Master speculator: George Soros', *Rolling Stone* (24 December 1998), pp.133-7. See also Chapter 2.

7 Shaw & Clay, *World Food Aid* (1993), p.61.

8 Anne M. Thomson, 'Egypt: food security and food aid', *Food Policy*, Vol. 8, 3 (August 1985), pp.178-86.

9 Shaw & Clay, *World Food Aid* (1993), p.2. Commodities were sold on concessionary rates. In the 1960s the US forgave many loans if they were reinvested in India.

10 Shaw & Clay, *World Food Aid* (1993), pp.2, 11-12. Successful FFW road projects include Turkey.

11 *Food Aid Works* and *Food Aid* (1990s) Information and teaching materials from Australian International Development Assistance Bureau (AIDAB). Australia provided 50,000 tonnes of wheat annually for FFW projects in Bangladesh, funding tree planting, schools, etc.

12 M.V.Kamath, *Management Kurien Style* (Delhi, 1989), p.173. Kurien hosted PM Shastri at its dedication in 1964.

13 Ram Saran & Panos Konandreas, 'An additional resource?' in *Food Aid Reconsidered*, Clay & Stokke (eds), (London, 1991).

14 Susan George, *Ill Fares the Land* (New Jersey, 1984), p.102.

15 Agrostat/FAO/1994 estimated world population at 5.572 billion people in 1993. Over half the world's population was listed as 'low-income' comprising 3.458b persons. At the time of the World Food Summit, November 1986 at FAO Rome, world population was estimated at 5.7b.

16 'The Statistics Division History' (2006) by Edward Gillin. FAO Rome. See also FAO, '1.02 billion people hungry' (19 June 2009). The Indian Civil Service (ICS) was held in high regard.

17 Phillip C. Abbot & F. Desmond McCarthy, 'Potential welfare losses due to tied food aid', *Canadian Journal of Agricultural Economics* (*CJAE* 31 March 1983), pp.45-58, 57.
18 Kym Anderson & Rodney Tyers, *Global Effects of Liberalizing Trade in Farm Products* (London, 1991).
19 Shaw & Clay, *World Food Aid* (1993), p.ix.
20 Raymond F. Hopkins, 'Food aid and development' in *Report of the WFP* (Netherlands Seminar on Food Aid, 1993). Hopkins found surplus disposal is employed after bumper harvests in ICs, e.g.: Canada (rapeseed), Sweden (wheat), Norway (fish), Germany (egg powder), Australia and Argentina (wheat), Japan (rice) and USA (wheat, etc.).
21 Martin Doornbos, Liana Gertsch & Piet Terhal, 'Dairy aid and development: current trends and long-term implications of the Indian case' in Clay & Stokke (London, 1991), p.118.
22 A.W. DePorte, *Europe Between the Superpowers* (New Haven, 1986), p.135. DePorte cites Department of State Bulletin 16 (15 June 1947).
23 William R. Keylor, *The Twentieth Century World* (New York, 1984), p.275.
24 Charles L. Mee, Jr., *The Marshall Plan* (New York, 1984), p.261.
25 Food was a theme of all parties in the Cold War.
26 Wolfram F. Hanrieder & Graeme P. Auton, *The Foreign Policy of West Germany, France & Britain* (New Jersey, 1980), p.186.
27 Harry Truman, 'The Policy of Containment', *Public Papers of the Presidents of the United States* (1947), pp.176-80.
28 Dean Acheson, *Present at the Creation* (New York, 1969).
29 Thomas H. Etzold & John L. Gaddis, 'NSC 68' (New York, 1978), pp.383-42.
30 Shaw & Clay, *World Food Aid* (1993), p.21.
34 Title XV of the *1990 Food, Agriculture, Conversion and Trade Act.*
32 Clay & Shaw, *Poverty, Development and Food* (London, 1987), pp.187-8.
33 Hans Singer, John Wood & Tony Jennings, *Food Aid* (Oxford, 1987), pp.177-92.
33 PL 480 is the Agricultural Trade Development and Assistance Act of 1954.
34 Arturo Escobar, *Encountering Development* (Princeton Press, West Sussex 1995).
35 *Economist*, 'Down the rathole' (10 December 1994), p.101.
36 Keylor, *The Twentieth Century World* (New York, 1984), pp.276-7.
37 Charles P. Kindleberger, *The World in Depression* (Los Angeles, 1973), pp.xv, 289.
38 International Fund for Agricultural Development, *IFAD: The State of Rural Poverty* (1992), pp.5-25.
39 Shaw & Clay, *World Food Aid* (1993), p.7.
40 IFAD, *State of Rural Poverty* (1992), p.10. Alongside his speciality of food aid, Hans Singer was known for the Singer-Prebisch thesis which holds that exporters of primary commodities are at the mercy of value-added exporters.
41 Lana L. Hall, 'Evaluating effects of PL 480 wheat imports on Brazil's grain sector', *American Journal of Agricultural Economics* (*AJAE* 1980), pp.19-28.

42 Anne Thomson, 'Egypt: food security and food aid', *Food Policy* (August 1985), pp.178-86.
43 Paul Dorosh & Alberto Valdés, 'Effects of exchange rate and trade policies on agriculture in Pakistan', 84, International Food Policy Research Institute (IFPRI, 1990).
39 Ronald Soligo & Joseph Stern, 'Tariff protection, import substitution and investment efficiency', *Pakistan Development Review* (Summer 1965).

45 Greider, *One World, Ready or Not* (New York, 1997), p.199.
46 Robert Gilpin, *The Political Economy of International Relations* (Princeton, 1987a), and article in *Daedalus* (1987b).
47 IFAD, *The State of Rural Poverty*, (1992), p.11.
48 World Bank (1983).
49 IFAD (1992), p.12.
50 Jeffrey Sachs, 'Growth in Africa', *Economist* (29 June 1996), pp.25-27. Also see Sachs & Warner 'Sources of Slow Growth' (February 1996).
51 IFAD *The State of Rural Poverty* (1992), p.12.
52 Anderson & Tyers, *Global Effects of Liberalising Trade in Farm Products* (1991), pp. 2-4.
53 Sachs & Warner (1996) 'Sources of slow growth in the African economies', *Economist.*
54 *Economist Book of Vital World Statistics* (1990), pp.44-5.
55 Singer, Hans and John Wood, Tony Jennings, *Food Aid: The Challenge and the Opportunity*. (Oxford, 1987).
56 Clay & Shaw, *Poverty, Development and Food* (1987), pp.187-8.
57 Hans Singer, *Food aid & structural adjustment in SSA* (1991), pp.127, 140.
58 Edward Clay & Charlotte Benson, 'Aid for food - acquisition of commodities in developing countries for food aid in the 1980s', *Food Policy* (February 1990), pp.27-43, 39. Shipments promised by SSA countries including Zimbabwe and Mozambique were cancelled due to drought; the commitments were covered primarily by the US and EEC.
59 Shaw & Clay, *World Food Aid* (1993), p.1.
60 Susan George, *Ill Fares the Land* (1984), p.100.
61 *Economist*, 'Coffee: green as in greenbacks' (1 February 1997), p.62. See also Scholten (2007) on fair trade schemes involving Starbucks, Traidcraft, etc.
62 Greider, *One World, Ready or Not* (1997), p.185.
63 Greider, ibid, p.36.
64 Escobar, *Encountering Development* (1995).
65 Shanti George, *Operation Flood* (1985).
66 IFAD, *The State of Rural Poverty* (1992), pp.5-25.
67 Stéphane Jost, 'An introduction to the sources of data for food aid analysis with special reference to sub-Saharan Africa', Clay & Stokke (1991), pp.191-201.

GIEWS: Global Information & Early Warning System; INTERFAIS: International Food Aid Information System (WFP).

68 Bruce Scholten, 'Good for all: Riders for Health', *Cycle News* (2 July 1998).

69 FAO figures. PPP = purchasing power parity in 1997 US$.

70 FAO figures. PPP = purchasing power parity in 1997 US$.

Chapter 5 Data on India & Comparators

1 Agrostat/FAO 1990/94 lists Bangladesh on its 'least-developed ' category.

2 Martin Doornbos, Frank van Dorsten, Manoshi Mitra & Piet Terhal, *Dairy Aid and Development: India's Operation Flood* (London, 1990), p.67. In 1980 Egypt imported 7000 tonnes of SMP from the US, a trend that continued.

3 Clive Crook, 'A survey of India: time to let go' (22 February 1997), p.22. Crook draws from sources including Jeffrey Sachs, Jean Drèze and Amartya Sen, Charles Collyns of the IMF, Robert Zagha of the World Bank, and Adit Jain of the Economist Intelligence Unit (EIS) based in India.'

4 William Greider, *One World, Ready or Not* (New York, 1997), p.199.

5 Robert Gilpin, *The Political Economy of International Relations* (Princeton, 1987).

6 Jean Drèze & Amartya Sen, 'India: economic development and social opportunity'. Cited by Crook, *Economist* (22 February 1997), p.18.

7 Crook, 'A Survey of India', *Economist* (22 February 1997), p.3.

8 Crook, ibid, p.3.

9 Personal observation. Before free-market philosophies predominated, IMF staff were more likely to be called planners than economists.

10 Kazimierz Z. Poznanski, *Technology, Competition, & the Soviet Bloc in the World Market* (Berkeley, 1987).

11 Katar Singh, *Agricultural Policy in India: Need for a Fresh Look*. IRMA Working Paper No. 36 (August 1992), pp.10-11.

12 Katar Singh, ibid, pp.10-11.

13 *Economist*, 'Survey of India' (21 January 1995), p.8. Anil Jain says the firm could have done it without liberalisation, but it would have taken longer.

14 Janairus Banaji, 'Globalisation and restructuring in the Indian food industry' in *Journal of Peasant Studies* (October 1996/January 1997), pp.191-210.

15 *Economist*, 'Cotton suicides' (20 January 2007), also Vandana Shiva (2004), and Amul/GCMMF, 'Chairman's speech: 33rd annual meeting' (14 June 2007).

16 Singh, *Agricultural Policy in India* (August 1992), p.13.

17 P.C. Bansil, 'Employment potential in dairying', *Dairy India 1997*, p.118.

18 Crook, 'A survey of India', *Economist* (22 February 1997), p.22.

19 Reforms suggested by Clive Crook in the *Economist* fall generally within the free-market Chicago school of economics personified by Milton Friedman who maintained that government planning unnecessarily limited individual freedom to create wealth. Some claim that Britain's Adam Smith Institute, which informed Thatcherist economics is akin to the Chicago School. GOI policy retains more ties to Nehruvian socialism than to such laissez-faire philosophy. The economics of Harvard-educated Manmohan Singh, India's prime minister

in 2009, may be closer to the liberal instincts of John K. Galbraith than the Chicago School.

20 Pratyusha Basu, *Rural Cooperatives and Agrarian Inequalities: Local Narratives of Successful Dairy Development in Gujarat and Madhya Pradesh, India* (Ph.D. thesis, University of Iowa, 2003.) See also: Basu, *Villages, Women, and the Success of Dairy Cooperatives in India Making Place for Rural Development* (USA, Cambria, 2009). Basu notes some progress is being made with crossbreds. But it is vital to ensure that narrow commercial interests do not compromise overall sustainability. Guaging scope for foreign roles in dairy extension services is difficult because knowledge of indigenous conditions is crucial.

21 Kamath, *Management Kurien-Style* (1989). Kamath suggests Operation Flood's sins, if any, were of omission not commission.

22 Edward Clay & Olav Stokke, 'Food aid: the state of the art' in their edited book *Food Aid Reconsidered*, (1991), p.15.

23 BBC, *Wheels of Fire* (1983). Half hour film by Julian Steinhouse.

24 Bhagwati, *Protectionism* (1988), p.100. Although OF was more of a parastatal or QUANGO than a private firm, the autonomy granted its leadership allowed it to make wealth-maximising decisions denied more bureaucratic industries, including perhaps the steel industry.

25 Agrostat/FAO/1994.

26 Clive Crook, 'A Survey of India', *Economist*, (22 February 1997), pp.4, 1-26.

27 V.P. Gulati, *et al.*, *Design and Utility of a Decision Support System for Milk Cooperative Unions and Federations*. IRMA (June 1990), pp.11, 1-18.

28 Crook, 'A Survey of India', *Economist* (22 February 1997).

29 Harold Alderman *et al.*, *Cooperatives and the Commercialisation of Milk Production in India: A Literature Review*. IFPRI, 1987, p.6.

30 Martin Doornbos *et al.*, 'Dairy Aid and Development: Current Trends and Long-Term Implications of the Indian Case', in Clay & Stokke, 1991.

31 John Empson, 'India Joins the Big Leagues', *Dairy Industries International*, September 1992, pp.21-3. Empson writes that India is responsible for much of the rise in Asian milk production.

32 B.A. Scholten, 'Europe's milk quotas…' *Hoard's Dairyman*, July 1990; also Scholten (1990b) 'Pesticide und die Agrar-Umwelt Politik in den USA' [Pesticides and Agricultural Policy in the USA]', *VDI-nachrichten*: Sept. 6: 12. Original quota levels were reduced, lowering EC/EEC butter and milk powder mountains. The refusal of the neoliberal Reagan and Bush Governments to renew New Deal farm parity programmes or consider quotas, led to the shattering of meaningful price-supports for US dairying. This was in line with GATT aims but hastened the demise (ca. 7-15%) of marginal dairy farms in the USA in the 1990s which were often owned and run by single families.

33 Following Agrostat/FAO groupings, this book uses data from milk production *in toto*, and its two main sub-groups, i.e. (1) 'milk excluding butter' and (2) 'butter & ghee' to reflect various dairy performance indicators such as production quantities, exponential growth of production, and per capita intake

or consumption. Though (1) and (2) do not add up to the sum of all milk production (due to diversions such as whey and casein to other industries) these sub-groups represent principal sources of dairy intake by people.

34 INTERFAIS, *The Food Aid Monitor: 1993 Food Aid Flows*, WFP special issue, April 1994, pp.6, 1-26.

35 NDDB, *Operation Flood: a Progress Report*, ca. 1988-89, p.12.

36 Many of the dairy cattle purchased by the US government from its farmers in the 1986 herd buy-out were to be sent to China. The USA and EC/EEC were determined to cut dairy surpluses.

37 Willi Kampmann, '20 Jahre EG-Milchmarktordnung' in *Deutsche Bauern-Korrespondenz*, September 1988, pp.327-30. Dr. Kampmann of the Deutscher Bauernverband (DBV, Bonn) told me in interviews, 1989-1991, that milk quotas were imposed partly to stabilise the world price of SMP which had plummeted during years of surplus.

38 John Empson, 'India Joins the Dairy Big Leagues' in *Hoard's Dairyman*, 25 September 1993, p.692. Note: In 2009 *Hoard's* noted that US cow milk production exceeds India's, but India leads the world in combined cow and buffalo milk.

39 FAO Rome, *Dairy Outlook Report*, Vol 3/No.2, June 1998, p.3. Edited by Commodity Specialist Michael Griffin. Basic Foodstuffs Service, Commodities and Trade Division. Website: www.fao.org/waicent/ faoinfo/economic/esc/ escp/DAIRY.HTM Via email.

40 INTERFAIS, *The Food Aid Monitor: 1993 Food Aid Flows*, April 1994. WFP special issue, pp.9, 1-11.

41 INTERFAIS, *The Food Aid Monitor: 1995 Food Aid Flows*. WFP special issue, April 1996, pp.4, 1-61.

42 INTERFAIS, ibid, p.2.

43 FAO Rome, 'Brazil: Changes in Import regulations', *Dairy Outlook Report*, June 1998, p.7.

44 *Economist*, 'Winds of fortune on South-East Asia's farms', April 3, 1999, pp. 67-8. A surge in rice (58%) and prawn (35%) exports softened the crash of 1997, but urban-to-rural migration from Bangkok rose. Japanese & World Bank loans in 1999 will help finance three-quarters of a 5.9b bhat agricultural allocation to irrigation - important to combat current (cyclical) drought. The FAO estimated 70% of S-E Asians are employed in agriculture (year 2000): Thailand 57%; Indonesia 47%; Philippines 40%; Malaysia 20%.

45 FAO, *The Milk Report*, edited by Michael Griffin, February 1999. 'Peru: Pasture bred heifers preferred for milk production' by T. Bernet, Peru, p.10.

46 FAO, ibid, p.2.

47 Some Pacific islands developed 'cargo cults' after World War II. The spread of US military supplies such as milk powder, and later infant breast milk replacer, are changing diets on the Pacific Rim. What George Ritzer (2000) dubbed McDonaldization and the popularity of mozzarella-topped pizzas are increasing dairy consumption in a world population that is already half-urban.

48 FAO, 'Fun milk & coffee drinks in Japan', Dairy-Outlook-Link, 31 March 1999.

49 *Hoard's Dairyman*, 'A look at dairy trade winners and losers' by MEP Mark Killilea, 10 October 1998. Killilea claims the Cairns Group 'accounts for one-third of world farm exports.'

50 Dairy Farmers of Canada, *WTO Panel Outcome Summary* in FAO Dairy-Outlook-Link, 1 April 1999.

51 *Dairy India 1997* Glossary, pp.471, 476. Also emails from P.R. Gupta in 1998.

52 Ben Fine, Michael Heasman & Judith Wright, *Consumption in the Age of Affluence: the World of Food*, 1996.

53 Shanti George, *A Matter of People: Cooperative Dairying in India and Zimbabwe*, 1994, pp.511-12, 516,-17. George writes that Zimbabwe's dairy development is less rigid than India's which strictly adhered to the Kheda or Anand pattern. She found Zimbabwe's programme (DDP) 'encountered many of the same problems that Anand did' in trying to extend benefits to the very poor. George concluded that, as in India's OF, in Zimbabwe's DDP, 'The benefits of dairy development have generally been proportionate to the resource bases of rural households, since cattle ownership characterises the more affluent.' Nevertheless, George found that in the Chikwaka area, '...the local sales of milk have increased dairy consumption among some of the poor' and the 'milk centre and its activities' improved community morale at least in proportion to their nutritional contribution.

54 Shaw & Clay (*World Food Aid*, 1993, pp.41-3) write that food aid with non-cereals aid of mostly 'edible oils, with small quantities of dairy commodities' was 'crucial' in the first decade of Bangladesh independence.

55 Some Pakistani businessmen claim martial law imposed by PM Zia boosted economic growth, but their opponents ascribe growth to US aid in the war.

56 FAO (25 March 1999) 'Butter and heart disease ' contributed by Peter Brumby (NZ) on Dairy-Outlook-Link, via email. Similarly, the cause of some stomach ulcers has been determined as infection- not diet-based.

57 The fact that Zimbabwe's figure for milk ex. butter is the same as for butter & ghee engenders speculation that, as Agrostat/FAO literature acknowledges, the difficult decades experienced by Zimbabwe have not facilitated data gathering. Thus, the figure for Zimbabwe may a 'guesstimate'.

58 Doornbos, van Stuijvenberg & Terhal, 'Operation Flood: impacts and issues', *Food Policy*, November, 1987, pp.376-83.

59 P.J. Atkins, 'Rejoinder: India's dairy development and Operation Flood', *Food Policy*, August, 1988, pp.305-12.

60 *OECD-FAO Agricultural Outlook 2005-2014*, pp.86, 90, 83-91, (2005).

61 *OECD-FAO*, ibid, p.90.

62 *Dairy India 2007* 'Milk production and availability', by R.S. Khanna, p.34a.

63 FAOSTAT 2007 Food & Agricultural commodities production/2007/sort by value [Top Production]: http://faostat.fao.org/site/339/default.aspx, accessed November 14, 2009. Disaggregating buffalo from cow milk allows the USA to retain status as the top world producer of cow milk.

64 FAOSTAT 2007, ibid. If goat, horse, sheep or other mammalian milk is not among top 20 commodities, it is not seen on this table.

Chapter 6 Three Phases of Flood

1 World Food Programme 25th Session, 'Food aid & dairy development' (21 April 1988), pp.1-16.

2 Verghese Kurien, 'Milk, milk everywhere', *The Hindu Survey of Agriculture* (1999), pp.129-131.

3 T.N. Dalle & B.K. Gauguly, 'An analysis of consumer expenditure pattern in Indian states with special reference to milk and milk products'. Draft for SPS, NDBB (Anand, May 1997), pp.2-3, 9.

4 Dalle & Gauguly, 'An analysis' (1997), pp.11-2.

5 IFPRI-FAO, 'Policy, Technical, and Environmental Determinants and Implications of the Scaling-Up of Livestock Production in Four Fast-Growing Developing Countries', (24 July 2003). Quotes are from section 2.2.3.

6 Sharad Gupta & R.S. Khanna, 'India's unique place in world dairying', *Yearbook of the International Dairy Industry 2009*, published in Germany.

7 Wilfred Candler & Nalini Kumar, *India: The Dairy Revolution: The Impact of Dairy Development in India and the World Bank's Contribution* (Washington, DC, World Bank, 1998), pp.33, 33-38. These statistics (Table 6.1) derived from Aneja 1994, NDDB and *Dairy India 1997*. The authors are assisted by H. Alderman, G. Mergos, R. Slade among other distinguished researchers. This World Bank (OED) publication is an excellent starting point for study of OF.

8 Candler & Kumar, *India: The Dairy Revolution*, p.ii, 59, 55-60.

9 World Food Programme Evaluation, 'Mission Report on Operation Flood', *The Second, Detailed Report of.... India-618*, (India Dairy Corporation, 1976).

10 *Dairy India 1997 Yearbook*, p.11.

11 Agrostat/FAO/1994/Livestock Production/Geographical Groupings/India/Milk, total.

12 B.A. Scholten, 'India's winning the White Revolution: The success of India's Operation Flood will soon make it the world's top producer of milk', *Hoard's Dairyman* (10 April 1999), p.287.

13 Dilip R. Shah, *Dairy Cooperativization* (1992), p.67.

14 M.V. Kamath, *Management Kurien-Style: The Story of the White Revolution* (Delhi, Konark, 1989), pp.113-14. Kamath claims that despite conjecture, 'There was no such thing as Anand Milk Union Ltd.' Because KDCMPU was too unwieldy, a name competition produced 'Amul' - associated with the Sanskrit word *Amulya* meaning invaluable or priceless.

15 P.J. Atkins, 'Operation Flood: dairy development in India', *Geography* (1989), pp.259-62.

16 A.S. Patel, 'Cooperative Dairying and Rural Development: A Case Study of Amul' (1983), in Alderman *et al.,* (1987).

17 Shanti George, 'Cooperatives and Indian dairy policy: more Anand than pattern' in *Cooperatives in World Development* by D.W. Attwood & B.S. Baviskar (eds) (Delhi, OUP, 1983).
18 Clive Crook, 'Survey of India', *Economist* (22 February 1997), p.10.
19 Kurien, 'Milk, milk everywhere', *Hindu Survey of Agriculture* (1999), p.129.
20 Candler & Kumar, *India: The Dairy Revolution*, 1998, pp.60, 3.
21 Candler & Kumar, ibid, pp.11, 9-12. However, 'Entrenched political and bureaucratic interests were extremely reluctant to relinquish their influence…'
22 Candler & Kumar, ibid, pp.10-11.
23 Candler & Kumar, ibid, pp.63, 34.
24 Alderman, *The impact of cooperative dairy development in Karnataka*, 1986, p.iii.
25 Crook, 'A Survey of India', *Economist*, 22 February 1997: p.4. Crook cites India's well-intentioned capacity-licensing regime governing investment, production and labour as a culprit for laggard development.
26 Heredia, *The Amul India Story* (New Delhi, 1997), pp.247-48.
27 Personal interview with Kurien (Anand, 1998). Also, email from P.R. Gupta (May 1999). Before Dr. Kurien retired to an office at NDDB's sister body, the Institute of Rural Management Anand (IRMA), he said, 'I hope she succeeds me'. Dr. Miss Amrita Patel, born 1943, has also been on the board of the Federal Reserve Bank of India, alongside her role as MD at the NDDB. She is described by long-time observers as 'energetic', 'efficient' and 'hard-working' - and by at least one Indian postgraduate student as 'charismatic'.
28 P.J. Atkins, 'Rejoinder: India's dairy development and Operation Flood' in *Food Policy* (August 1988), pp.305-12.
29 Personal communication: Conversations at IFMA-Cologne exhibitions in 1989 and 1990, with an Indian bicycle manufacturer who had to travel to Germany to buy strong steel alloy fittings for bicycle frames because, 'The subsidised steel industry in India has no incentive to produce them.'
30 Candler & Kumar, *India: The Dairy Revolution* (1998), p.10.
31 Kurien, 'Milk, milk everywhere', *Hindu Survey of Agriculture* (1999), pp.129-31.
32 Alden C. Manchester, *The Public Role in the Dairy Economy* (Boulder, 1983), pp.3-8, 5.
33 Kazimierz Z. Poznanski, *Technology, Competition, & the Soviet Bloc* (Berkeley, 1987), pp.87-9.
34 Manchester, *The Public Role in the Dairy Economy* (1983), p.8.
35 Shanti George, *Operation Flood* (Delhi, 1985), pp.6-7, 158.
36 Candler & Kumar, *India: The Dairy Revolution* (1998), p.23.
37 SS. Acharya & R.K. Yadav, *Production and Marketing of Milk and Milk Products in India* (New Delhi, 1992), p.83. This study in Rajasthan found that that especially in the 'unorganised market', i.e. non-OF areas of Rajasthan: farmers did not believe the market price of milk remunerative, and many farmers believed the 'milk price received from them has no relationship with its quality and hence increase the quantity of milk (by mixing water) to get higher total return.' This illustrates the moral hazard of price controls.

38 Martin Doornbos, Frank van Dorsten, Manoshi Mitra & Piet Terhal, *Dairy Aid & Development: India's Operation Flood* (London, 1990), p.124. Doornbos *et al.* use the acronym NMGS. P.J. Atkins uses NMG.

39 Martin Doornbos *et al.*, ibid, p.301.

40 Martin Doornbos *et al.*, ibid, p.301. Kurien alluded to this threat in his response to Claude Alvares and other critics titled *Black Lie.*

41 Food aid sceptics appreciate the irony that the German word *Gift* means poison, and that Germany was the largest contributor to the Butter Mountain.

42 William Greider, *One World, Ready or Not* (New York, 1997), p.59. Greider shows arbitrage is universal.

43 Shanti George, *Operation Flood* (1985), p.6.

44 Doornbos, van Dorsten, Mitra & Terhal, *Dairy Aid & Development* (1990), pp.124, 135. Overall variation in milk procurement is about 1:1.8. March is usually the 'flush' month.

45 Atkins, 'Rejoinder: India's dairy development' (1988), *Food Policy.* Atkins resonates with Alden C. Manchester.

46 Alderman, *The impact of cooperative dairy development in Karnataka* (1986), p.iii.

47 FAO-Rome, Dairy Outlook (June 1998).

48 John Empson, 'India joins the dairy big leagues', *Hoard's Dairyman* (25 September 1993), p.692. With 55.1 billion pounds (ca. 25b kg.) at the beginning of OF, Indian production rose to 121.3 billion pounds (ca. 55b kg) in 1991. *(N.B. Webster's notes 1 US long ton = 1.016 metric tonnes; 1 US pound = 0.454 kilograms. 1 metric tonne=2.2046 US pounds.)* Therefore, 1974 India production of 55.1b pounds = 24,993 thousand MT, correlates with Agrostat FAO figures of 24,500 thousand MT in that year. FAO statistics from countries not enjoying the generally reliable record-keeping systems of India vary in accuracy.

49 *International Seminar on Dairying as an Instrument for Progress: the Indian Experience: Proceedings 1989*, pp.127-8. Published (1990) by NDDB (Anand 388 001 India) in association with International Dairy Federation (IDF), Brussels, Belgium. In a question and answer session, D. Tikku, of the Delhi Mother Dairy, said vending machines dispensed 1300-1400 litres per day.

50 Alderman, *The impact of cooperative dairy development in Karnataka* (1987), p.11.

51 Kamath, *Management Kurien Style* (1989), p.340. Tetra Pak became a political football between nationalists and free traders.

52 Doornbos, van Dorsten, Mitra & Terhal, *Dairy Aid & Development* (1990).

53 Ben Fine *et al., Consumption in the Age of Affluence* (1995), pp.262-3

54 Geoff Platt, editorial in *Dairy Innovation* (10 June 2009). 'In 1994, the UK deregulated its dairy industry and dismantled its statutory milk marketing boards. The move led to the establishment of dairy farmers' cooperatives, a relatively new idea for the UK dairy industry but one that had long since been an established "norm" in the rest of Europe.' The main coop was one called MilkMarque, but the Government forced its breakup into three entities in 2000.' Perhaps British family scale dairy farming would be more economically sustainable if MilkMarque had not been broken into more vulnerable coops.

55 Candler & Kumar, *India: The Dairy Revolution* (1998), p.52.
56 P.J. Atkins, 'Mad Cows and Englishmen', *History Today* (September 1996).
57 USDA, 'Cooperatives in the dairy industry' (2005).
58 Alden C. Manchester, *The Public Role in the Dairy Economy* (1983), p.17. Manchester writes that, 'Up until about 1880 [in the US], the competitive picture in fluid milk markets was largely one of atomistic competition. From then until World War I, large dealers dominated. Cooperatives became important in negotiating with dealers during and after the War.'
59 Darigold, Inc., 1993-94. I am grateful for publications, documents and personal communications from Douglas C. Marshall, then corporate counsel, and Roger D. Miller, sales manager. The extracts below illustrate the relationship between US foreign policy, world dairy export markets, and the GATT/WTO process. In 1993 the Darigold cooperative comprised 1400 dairy farmers, 1600 employees and projected $900m in sales in fiscal year 1992/93. Mr. Marshall wrote me (April 21, 1993 letter) that, 'Darigold is the largest US processor of skimmed milk powder (which we refer to as dry milk powder or NFDM)... Darigold exports large quantities of milk powder under the US government's DEIP (Dairy Export Incentive programme). In 1992, Darigold exported about 48 thousand tonnes (based on a given figure of 94,802,107) to countries including Kuwait, Panama, Trinidad/Ghana, Algeria, Chile, Brazil, Nigeria, Saudi Arabia, St. Lucia, Columbia, Egypt and Mexico.'

In documents I have seen originating from Darigold and USDA, no exports to India were recorded, suggesting either Indian self-sufficiency in milk powder, or hegemony of EU exporters in India's market. Shipments to Egypt, Jordan and Russia noted in Darigold documents suggest synergy between US foreign policy and export goals - in a pattern that this book traces to, at least, World War II. Marshall added that: 'DEIP sales for the fiscal year ending September 30, 1992 were 'about 250 million pounds [ca. 114 thousand MT] most of it NFDM, compared to 873 million pounds [ca. 397 thousand MT] of US NFDM production. And Darigold's powder was about 95 million pounds [ca. 43 thousand MT] of the total.' Figures in [brackets] are my estimates from US pounds to Metric Tonnes (MT).

Additionally, Marshall wrote that he believes original PL 480 provisions subsidising US dairy exports were discontinued during the 1960s: 'in response to pressure from certain allies, especially Australia and new Zealand. By 1985, that relationship had changed (especially with New Zealand), and congress was more interested in our dairy industry than theirs. The heavy EC subsidies had caused surpluses, and they had dumped their dairy products on the international market. The USA realised that we would either have to follow suit or use the GATT mechanism to remove all subsidies so that all countries could compete on unsubsidised basis. That was the Reagan Administration approach to GATT, and DEIP was put into the 1985 Farm Bill at least in part to put pressure on other countries.' I am grateful to Marshall, Miller and Darigold for their input, but they are not responsible for any errors in my analysis. As outlined in NSC-68, US farm policy has been tied to foreign policy. It can be hypothesised that US export policy became more aggressive *vis-à-vis* New Zealand, after that country banned US nuclear weapons from its ports.

60 Shaw & Clay, *World Food Aid* (1993), pp.61-69.

61 Shaw & Clay, ibid, p.59.

62 Kamath, *Management Kurien-Style* (1989), p.162. The refusal of OF's Kurien to accept 'mouldy milk powder and rancid butter oil' donations from Europe was a source of pride to his country-men - and a reminder to the EEC that wasteful CAP subsidies were the *primum movum* of double-edged food 'aid'.

63 Shaw & Clay, *World Food Aid* (1993), p.2.

64 Shaw & Clay, ibid, pp.2, 61-8.

65 WFP/Interfais, *Food Aid Monitor: 1996 Food Aid Flows* (May 1997), pp.1-3.

66 Shaw & Clay, ibid, pp.63-4, 58.

67 Shaw & Clay, ibid, pp.61-2.

68 Heredia, *The Amul India Story* (1997), p.210.

69 Candler & Kumar, *India: The Dairy Revolution* (1998), p.43.

70 Candler & Kumar, ibid, p.11.

71 Shanti George, *Operation Flood* (1985), p.9.

72 FAO, WFP Evaluation Report - OF, *The Second, Detailed Report of.... India-618*, IDC, New Delhi (1976), p.7.

73 NDDB, *Heralding Changes* (ca. 1998), p.1/15.

74 NDDB, *Operation Flood Phase III* (September 1985), p.5-6.

75 Atkins, 'Operation Flood', *Geography* (1989), pp.259-62.

76 John Empson, 'India joins the dairy big leagues', *Hoard's Dairyman* 25 September 1993), p.692. Empson agrees with Doornbos that WFP dairy aid was used in India before OF-I was proposed.

77 Doornbos, van Dorsten, Mitra & Terhal, *Dairy Aid and Development* (1990), pp.77, 77-89. Doornbos cites a 1977 FAO report by M. Halse, p.51.

78 Kamath, *Management Kurien Style* (1989), p.177. After inaugurating Anand's cattle feed plant in 1964, PM Shastri promoted the Anand model in India's Fourth Plan. Before Verghese Kurien become chair of the NDDB, he won GOI agreement that NDDB headquarters be located in Anand instead of Delhi and that he continue to be paid by cooperatives - not GOI. Kamath portrays Kurien as an ambitious manager who revolutionised Indian dairying - though he knew nothing about cows before leaving the steel industry to study mechanical engineering at Michigan State University. (Note: IDC was founded 1970 and later merged with NDDB.)

79 Shanti George, *Operation Flood* (1985), pp.209-18, 217-18.

80 Doornbos, van Dorsten, Mitra & Terhal, *Dairy Aid & Developmen* (1990), pp.82-3. Citing UN/FAO/WFP (September 1981) *Terminal Evaluation Report on Project India 618* - 'Milk Marketing and Dairy Development': p.17. Kurien's complaints rankled; WFP literature pointedly asserts that spoiled commodities were not common and in fact occurred in just one year of OF.

81 Candler & Kumar, *India: The Dairy Revolution* (1998), p.21.

82 Kurien, 'Milk, milk everywhere', *Hindu Survey of Agriculture* (1999), pp.130. Recently, Dr. Kurien referred to the original 18 milksheds as '17 promising areas' but the minutiae of history only reinforce its themes.
83 Kamath, *Management Kurien Style* (1989), pp.290-6.
84 Doornbos, van Dorsten, Mitra & Terhal, *Dairy Aid & Development* (1990), p.83. They cite a 1978 GOI report.
85 Kamath, *Management Kurien Style* (1989), pp.287, 310. Kamath, a staunch defender of. Kurien's management of OF, writes that, ironically, Kerala is Kurien's home state, 'But the milk revolution there has yet to come.' Concerning Karnataka, formerly Mysore, Kamath adds that it had no tradition of coops, but when its state dairy was subsumed under OF, it eventually prospered. One PhD thesis by a faculty member at a university in Karnataka noted that the state had initiated its own dairy plans before OF-I, and was therefore resistant to the Anand model.
86 Doornbos, van Dorsten, Mitra & Terhal, *Dairy Aid & Development* (1990).
87 Claude Alvares, 'The White Lie', *Illustrated Weekly of India* (30 October 1983). Cited by M.V. Kamath (1989), pp.337-40. A parliamentary row ensued.
88 Doornbos, van Dorsten, Mitra & Terhal, *Dairy Aid & Development* (1990), p.85.
89 Heredia, *The Amul India Story* (1997), p.45.
90 Doornbos, van Dorsten, Mitra & Terhal, *Dairy Aid & Development* (1990), p.84.
91 Candler & Kumar, *India: The Dairy Revolution* (1998), p.1.
92 Kamath, *Management Kurien Style* (1989), p.325. Speech by Kurien in 1977.
93 Martin Doornbos & K.N. Nair (eds), *Resources, Institutions and Strategies: Operation Flood and Indian Dairying* (1990). IDSDA.
94 Doornbos, van Dorsten, Mitra & Terhal, *Dairy Aid and Development* (1990).
95 Doornbos, van Stuijvenberg & Terhal, 'Operation Flood: impacts and issues' in *Food Policy* (August 1987), pp.376-83.
96 Atkins, 'Rejoinder: India's dairy development', *Food Policy* (August 1988), pp.306, 305-12.
97 M. Jul, 'Unexpected benefits from a dairy project', *Food Nutrition Bulletin*, 1(3) (May 1979), pp.15-19. Cited in Alderman (1987).
98 George Mergos & Roger Slade, *Dairy development and milk cooperatives: the effects of a dairy project in India*, World Bank, 1987. See NDDB/IDF (1990: pp.62-63).
99 Doornbos, van Dorsten, Mitra & Terhal, *Dairy Aid & Development* (1990), p.82.
100 Kamath, *Management Kurien Style* (1989), p.369.
101 Sources include NDDB, *Operation Flood Phase III* (September 1985), pp.6-17; Kamath (1989), pp.383-84; Shanti George (1985), pp.15-16; and FAO, *Terminal Evaluation Report on Project India 618 - Milk Marketing and Dairy Development* (September 1981).
102 NDDB, *Heralding Changes*, 'Operation Flood' (ca. 1998), p.1.
103 NDDB, ibid, p.4.
104 Kamath, *Management Kurien Style* (1989), p.370.
105 Palagummi Sainath, *Everybody Loves a Good Drought: Stories from India's Poorest Districts* (India, Penguin, UK, Headline, 1996), p.255.

106 Raymond Crotty, 'Operation Flood and the EEC', *Economic & Political Weekly*, 2 (April 1983), p.522.
107 Alderman, Mergos & Slade, *Dairy Development in India* (1987a & b). They cite Shanti George (1983) 'Cooperatives and Indian Dairy Policy: More Anand than Pattern' in *Cooperatives and Rural Development* by D.W. Attwood & B.S.Baviskar (eds) (1983, Delhi, OUP).
108 Doornbos, van Dorsten, Mitra & Terhal, *Dairy Aid and Development* (1990), pp.90, 78, 89-95.
109 Doornbos *et al.,* ibid, pp.89, 128-33.
110 Doornbos *et al.*, ibid, p.97.
111 Atkins, 'Operation Flood', *Geography* (1989), p.260.
112 S. Baviskar & P. Terhal, 'Internal Constraints and External Dependence' in Doornbos & Nair (eds), *Resources, Institutions and Strategies: Operation Flood and Indian Dairying,* (1990). Baviskar & Terhal cite All India Livestock Census reports for evidence that a 1965-75 trend toward buffaloes was followed by a striking 'upswing of cow milk production' from 1975-80. John Empson (1993) noted that 45% of Indian milk is consumed as liquid; the rest as ghee and sweets. For non-liquid milk, high-fat buffalo milk is superior to cow milk. Thus, today's >50% contribution by buffaloes in the national herd seems logical, even though more use is being made of cross-breds.
113 Kamath, *Management Kurien Style* (1989), pp.96, 100-1, 119, 120. India reportedly ceased commercial imports of SMP in the late 1970s.
117 *Economist*, 'The stay-at-home giants' (13 March 2008).

115 Doornbos, van Dorsten, Mitra & Terhal, *Dairy Aid and Development* (1989), p.315.
116 BBC, *Wheels of Fire* (1983). Film on OF.
117 A.K. Ashwani, 'Role of Cooperative Dairying and Its Impact on Resource-Poor Milk Producers in Uttar Pradesh' in *Indian Journal of Agricultural Economics*, Vol. 50 (July-September 1995), p.388.
118 Candler & Kumar, *India: The Dairy Revolution* (1990), pp.55-6.
119 Doornbos, van Dorsten, Mitra & Terhal, *Dairy Aid and Development* (1990), pp.91, 101-5.
120 Doornbos, Martin & Minoshi Mitra, 'Politics of International Dairy Aid' (November 1985), p.27.
121 Verghese Kurien. Interviews in Anand with author, April 1998.
122 Miriam Sharma & Urmila Vanjani, 'When More Means Less…in Rural Rajasthan', *Social Science & Medicine* (1993), pp.1377-89.
123 Sharma & Vanjani, ibid, p. 1387.
124 Candler & Kumar, *India: The Dairy Revolution* (1990), pp.50, 17, 52-3.
125 Shagufta Jamal, *Women in Dairy Development* (1991), pp.132, 169, 183. Households of higher socio-economic status are likely to hold more land producing fodder - a chief constraint on milk yield.

126 *OF: A Progress Report*, NDDB, March 1988, p.12.

127 Doornbos, van Dorsten, Mitra & Terhal, *Dairy Aid and Development* (1990), pp.97-100. These 'discontinuities' were worth pointing out. Candler & Kumar (1998) investigate such questions with the benefit of nearly a decade's more hindsight and find largely in favour of Operation Flood.

128 Doornbos *et al.,* ibid, Also, recall that the Jha Committee Report (GOI 1984) called OF, 'By any standard… a successful programme ', but recommended more grants to inputs services. Doornbos *et al.* were sceptical that regions with poor soil, years behind Gujarat in dairying, could readily adopt the Anand pattern without help on inputs. The Report of the EC Court of Auditors (1988) criticised a benign 1986 report on OF-II by the EC Commission for over-reliance on 'over-optimistic Indian documents'. The auditors said OF had 'achieved on a very piecemeal basis' any significant increase in per capita milk consumption, advantages to rural or urban poor, supply to cities or extension of the Anand model.

129 Doornbos *et al.,* ibid, p.100.

130 Kamath, *Management Kurien Style* (1989), pp.388-9.

131 NDDB/IDF, *Proceedings: International Seminar on Dairying* (1990), pp.59-61.

132 Jha Committee Report, GOI (1984), in Doornbos *et al.* (1990), pp.106-7.

133 Michael Lipton, 'Operation Flood and other EC aid to India' in M. Caliewaert, ed., *India and the EC*, Centre for European Studies (1985), pp.106-8.

134 Atkins, 'Rejoinder: India's dairy development and Operation Flood', *Food Policy* (August 1988), p.306.

135 Kurien, 'Milk, milk everywhere', *Hindu Survey of Agriculture* (1999), pp.129.

136 Heredia, *The Amul India Story* (1997), p.37. Polson's cut price was 2-2.5 to 4-5 *annas*/half litre.

137 Doornbos, van Dorsten, Mitra & Terhal, *Dairy Aid and Development* (1990), p.313.

138 Claude Alvares, 'Operation Flood: the White Lie', *Illustrated Weekly of India* (1983), pp.8-13.

139 Verghese Kurien, 'A Black Lie', *Illustrated Weekly* (1983).

140 Atkins, *Geography* (1989), p.260.

141 Doornbos, van Dorsten, Mitra & Terhal, *Dairy Aid and Development* (1990), pp.59-60, 70-71.

142 This author is unaware of any evidence that Britain supported OF from loyalty to India as a Commonwealth member, but the fact that OF-I began shortly before Britain's entry into the EEC in 1973 invites speculation.

143 *Zuivelzicht* (1979), p.346; also *Produktschap voor Zuivel* (1984). Cited by Doornbos *et al.* (1990), pp.65.

144 George, *Operation Flood* (1985), p.249. She cites Kroese *et al.* (1979).

145 Doornbos, van Dorsten, Mitra & Terhal, *Dairy Aid and Development* (1990), p.97.

146 Doornbos *et al.*, ibid, pp.110-11.

147 NDDB, *Heralding Changes*, 'Dr. Kurien - A Profile' (1998) handout, p.8.

148 *Dairy India 1997* 'Institutional Alternatives in Dairying', by Tushaar Shah, Vishwa Ballabh, B. Pratima & Jayesh Talati at IRMA, pp.45-6.
149 Atkins, 'Operation Flood', *Geography* (1989a), pp.260, 259-262. Out of 247m bovines, OF might then utilise 6%.
150 John Empson, 'India joins the dairy big leagues', *Hoard's Dairyman* (1993), p.692. 172 billion pounds = ca. 78 billion kilograms = ca. 78 million metric tonnes. Agrostat/FAO shows Indian milk production rose from 46.7 million MT in 1987 to 63.2 million MT in 1993. Production of 78 million MT then seemed likely by the year 2000.
151 Harold Alderman *et al., Dairy Development in India*, IFPRI, for the World Bank (1987). Also Doornbos *et al.* (1990) *Dairy Aid and Development*, p.54.
152 Doornbos, van Dorsten, Mitra & Terhal, *Dairy Aid and Development* (1990), p.127.
153 Doornbos *et al.*, ibid, pp.124-5.
154 Doornbos *et al.*, ibid, p.125.
155 Candler & Kumar, *India: The Dairy Revolution* (1998), p.1.
156 Candler & Kumar, ibid, p.55.
157 Doornbos, van Dorsten, Mitra & Terhal, *Dairy Aid and Development* (1990), pp.97, 111-12.
158 Doornbos *et al.*, ibid, pp.313-14. They deplore the extent to which discussion of OF has focused on the replicability of the Anand model, or pattern, to farmers outside Gujarat.
159 Doornbos *et al.*, ibid, p.135.
160 Doornbos *et al.*, ibid, pp.13, 54-55.
161 The Indo-Dutch Programme on Alternatives in Development (IDPAD) cited these stages: 1981-83, 1984-89 and 1990-93.
162 Shanti George, *Operation Flood* (1985), p.xii.
163 Gunilla Andræ & Björn Beckmann, *The Wheat Trap* (1985).
164 George, *Operation Flood* (1985), p.284.
165 Anne M. Thomson, 'Egypt: Food security and food aid', *Food Policy* (August 1983), pp.178-86, 182. Thomson notes that Egyptian food security improved with food aid, and that Cairo is now bound to a cheap food policy. This book also notes that US PL 480 shipments ceased after the '6-Day War' of 1967, and increased before and after the 1979 Egypt-Israel peace agreement. It seems likely that Egypt's status as 'one of the largest recipients of cereal food aid' from the USA influenced its foreign policy.
166 George, *Operation Flood* (1985), pp.xi-xii.
167 NDDB, 'Annex-B: The Anand Pattern in its final form (Dairy Sector) (1988).
168 *Dairy India 1997* 'Institutional alternatives in dairying' by Tushaar Shah, Vishwa Ballabh, B. Pratima & Jayesh Talati at IRMA, pp.45, 41-48.
169 B.S. Baviskar, *Economic & Political Weekly* (2 July 1983), p.219. Baviskar also edited a volume containing work by Shanti George.
170 George, *Operation Flood* (1985), pp.209-27. George's Chapter 10 is titled 'A man nobody wants but everybody needs: the petty dairy marketeer'.

171 Hernando de Soto, *The Other Path* (1989).
172 A.H. Somjee & G. Somjee, 'Cooperative dairying and the profiles of social change in India', *Economic Development and Cultural Change* (1978), pp.77-97.
173 George, *Operation Flood* (1985), pp.170-1. George cites S. Sambrani (1980) *Transforming the Rural Poor: The Big Push in Action*, IRMA.
174 Doornbos, van Dorsten, Mitra & Terhal, *Dairy Aid and Development* (1990), p.124.
175 F. Franco & P.G. Vijaya Sherry Chand, *OF and the Voluntary Sector: A Study of Tribal Cooperatives in South Gujarat.* ISI Delhi (1991), p.225.
176 John Empson, 'India Joins the dairy Big Leagues' (1993) *Hoard's Dairyman*:, p.692.
177 *OF Phase III*, NDDB (1985). This 60+ page proposal states that expanded infrastructure in the 'Project will enable the State Cooperative Federations/ unions to build up the basic and supporting infrastructures required to procure, process and market some 18.3 millions litres of milk per day.' In comparison, John Empson (*Hoard's* 1993) predicted that by the year 2000, OF processing would double to '68.4 million pounds a day.'
178 *Dairy India 1997* 'New Concepts in Feeding', A.K. Tripathi, NDDB, pp.305-8.
179 Candler & Kumar, *India: The Dairy Revolution* (1988), p.52. Citing Sampark (1997). Although they had 'no direct quantitative data', they confidently expect that 'given the high income elasticity of demand for education in India', OF has spawned significant educational gains.
180 George, *Operation Flood* (1985), pp.196-7. George cites N. Singh, D. Jain & M. Chand (1979) 'Milkmaids of Kaira District', ISS, New Delhi.
181 Candler & Kumar, *India: The Dairy Revolution* (1998), p.50.
182 Kurien, *Hindu Survey of Agriculture* (1999), p.131.
183 Candler & Kumar, *India: The Dairy Revolution* (1998), p.65.
184 I disagree. City slickers may joke about 'stout Olga, the Soviet tractor driver', but in my experience of US family farming, women and girls share mechanical chores, which enhance their incomes and status in town and country.
185 Sharma & Vanjani, 'When More Means Less (1993).
186 Riders for Health, *Reaching Out* (1996, England, www.riders.org). Established late-1980s, by 2009 RFH partners included African governments, the Clinton, Elton John, Bill & Melinda Gates, Schwab, and Skoll foundations, and Stanford University. Riders' core funding base is in the international motorcycle racing community.
187 B.A. Scholten, 'Case study of a grassroots charity/NGO: Riders for Health (RfH)', UCLAN conference papers *Africa & Globalisation: Towards the Millennium: 24-26 April 1998, Vol. 2* (1998).
188 David R. Harvey, Personal communication at Newcastle University (1999).
189 George, *Operation Flood* (1985), pp.85, 88, 90, 98-100.
190 Edward Clay & Olav Stokke, 'Food aid: the state of the art' (1991), in their edited book *Food Aid Reconsidered* (1991), p.15.

191 V. M. Rao, *Dairy Farming: Socio-economic Analysis of Milk Production* (1991), pp. 1-3. Rao's book is based on PhD research in Andhra Pradesh, drawing from Vinod & Achaya (1980), Nair & Vidyanadhan (1978), and Singh *et al.* (1970).

192 Atkins, 'Rejoinder: India's dairy development and Operation Flood' in *Food Policy* (August 1988), pp.306-7.

193 *Dairy India 1997* 'Products from Buffalo Milk' by B.N. Mathur, pp.357-60. Mathur was Head, Dairy Technology Div., Nat'l Dairy Research Inst. (NDRI), Karnal. Buffalo populations: India (65%), Pakistan (21%), China (5%), Egypt (4%) and Nepal (2%). Perhaps hot climates favour buffalo.

194 Atkins, 'The Geographical Structure of Operation Flood' (1989), p.5. Atkins writes that, 'This species asymmetry has implications for plant capacity, as does the extraordinary difference between lean and flush season procurement.' Ergo, the right cattle mix can reduce processing costs.

195 John Empson, 'India joins the dairy big leagues', *Hoard's Dairyman* (25 September 1993), p.692.

196 NDDB/IDF, *Proceedings: International Seminar on Dairying* (1990), p.64.

197 *Dairy India 1997*, 'Coop producers: their productivity & income', by Bhide & Chaudhari, p.63.

198 John W. Mellor (1976) *The New Economics of Growth*: p.48. Humans *and* animals eat oilseeds.

199 K.N. Ninan, 'Oilseeds development and policy: a review' in *Economic and Political Weekly*, India (25 March 1995), pp.A14-A27.

200 Ashok Gulati, 'Oilseeds: is higher price the answer?', *E & PW* (September 1989), pp.2007-8. Review of K.N. Ninan (1989) *Edible Oilseeds*.

201 Verghese Kurien. Interview with author at Anand (April 1998).

202 NDDB, *Heralding Changes* handout, Anand section (1998), p.10.

203 NDDB/IDF, *Proceedings: International Seminar on Dairying* (1990), p.63.

204 Verghese Kurien, *An Unfinished Dream*, 'World Food Prize: acceptance speech' (1997), p.382.

205 Janairus Banaji, 'Globalisation and restructuring in the Indian food industry', *Journal of Peasant Studies* (October 1996/January 1997), pp.191-210.

206 *Dairy India 1997*, 'New concepts in feeding', A.K. Tripathi, NDDB, pp.305-8.

207 Candler & Kumar, *India: The Dairy Revolution* (1998), p.49.

208 B.A. Scholten & Pratyusha Basu, 'White Counter-Revolution? India's dairy cooperatives in a neoliberal era'. *Human Geography* 2(1) (2009), pp.17-28.

209 *Dairy India 1997*, 'India's dairy riddle unravelled', (MMPO), p.14.

210 Candler & Kumar, *India: The Dairy Revolution* (1998), pp.41, 42-43, 33-46.

211 Candler & Kumar, ibid, p.43.

212 NCDFI-India, From 'Geeta' *via* Email. FAO Dairy-Outlook-Link (2 December 1998).

213 *OF: A Progress Report*, NDDB (1988), p.12. Dates drought as 1988, not 1987, as do other accounts.

214 Vasant P. Gandhi & Gyanendra Mani, 'Are livestock products rising in importance? A study of the growth and behaviour of their consumption in India', *Indian Journal of Agricultural Economics*, Vol. 50 (July-September 1995).
215 Candler & Kumar, *India: The Dairy Revolution* (1990), p.61.
216 Candler & Kumar, ibid, p.20.
217 Verghese Kurien, Interview with author at Anand (April, 1998).
218 John W. Mellor, in Clay & Shaw *Poverty, Development and Food* (1987), pp.187-8.
219 *Debates of the European Parliament* No 2-360/325 (22 January 1988), pp.325, 320-325. In explaining a vote accepting Mr. Telkämper's December 12, 1987 Report on EEC-India cooperation with particular reference to Operation Flood (Doc. A 2-247/87), a member (Habsburg (PPE) of the Committee on Development and Cooperation said: 'I will vote in favour of the report, but I feel very uneasy about doing so. I know something about India. We are always helping India, but public opinion is constantly stirred against us. So if we do help India I would ask that the Commission's first concern be to make it known that the Community has guaranteed that aid, so that Community aid is not used time and again to set public opinion against us.'
220 S.N. Mishra, 'India's livestock economy: a perspective on research' in *Indian Journal of Agricultural Economics*, Vol. 50 (June-September 1995), p.265.
221 *Official Journal of the European Communities*, No.C31, 'Court of Auditors of the European Communities, special report No.6/87 on food aid supplied to India 1978-1985 (Operation Flood II)', (February 1988), p.2.
222 Wilfried Telkämper, *Debates of the European Parliament* No 2-360/325 (22 January 1988), p.321.
223 *Dairy India 1997*, 'Cooperative producers: their productivity & income' by S. Bhide & S.K. Chaudhari, pp.61-6.
224 Telkämper, *Debates* (1988), p.321.
225 *Official Journal of the European Communities*, No.C31, 'Court of Auditors… special report No.6/87 on Food Aid' (February 1988), p. 14. In light of this meeting of effective demand, it is understandable that OF began switching surplus Indian milk production into 'luxury' products like sweets and baby food. OF's detractors were right to deplore continued nutritional deficits among India's poor, but overlooked the long-term food security to be gained by improvements to dairy infrastructure or domestic sales. Finance toward India's dairy investment also testifies to EEC and WFP compliance with Mellor's third demand on donors - that donors should supplement food aid with cash, when appropriate.
226 Candler & Kumar, *India: The Dairy Revolution* (1990), p.60, 48. Income figures correlate with ICR studies cited in *Dairy India 1997*.
227 Amul-GCMMF,'Achievements of the dairy cooperatives during the last 100 years' (ca. 2005).
228 Email from P.R. Gupta (8 September 1998). Citing Dr. Swaminathan, Gupta notes: 'It would also be appropriate to recognise the role of low purchasing power of the poor in third world countries that limits both the production of

foodgrains and consumption of whatever is available. The so-called self-sufficiency achieved in India and elsewhere is just a statistical deception because it is also recognised that a significant percentage of people in rural areas sleep hungry in the absence of money to buy food.'

229 *Dairy India 1997*, Table 100 'Value of output of milk & livestock as percentage of GDP, agriculture & crops, 1994-95': p.155. Permission to publish gratefully received from P.R. Gupta.

230 NDDB, *OF: A Progress Report* (March 1988), p.12.

231 Agrostat/FAO/1994/Food Aid I/By Recipient/India.

232 Doornbos, van Dorsten, Mitra & Terhal, *Dairy Aid and Development* (1990), p.135. The authors claim that after decades of Operation Flood: (1) Gujarat still dominates milk procurement and product manufacturing; the difference in liquid milk consumption between West, North and South is less pronounced than in fresh procurement or in manufacturing; (2) the North and South market a relatively larger portion of their fresh milk in liquid form; (3) more than half of (dry stuff equivalent) of milk procured is used for manufacture (66% in Gujarat) of products such as baby food.

233 B.A. Scholten, 'Comment on: "Clean milk poster paper in So. Africa" by Prinsloo' (2001), p.77, in *Report of the FAO E-mail Conference on Small-scale Milk Collection and Processing in Developing Countries* (29 May-28 July 2000): 144pp.

234 *Dairy Industry Newsletter*, Edited by Barry Wilson. 'Dr. Kurien is still around', back page (8 June 1999).

235 *Dairy Industry Newsletter*, 'NDDB's new boss tells of India's new milk targets', (June 8, 1999).

236 Agrostat/FAO/1994/Crops/North & Central America.

237 Thomas L. Friedman, *The World Is Flat* (2005).

238 Scholten & Basu, 'White Counter-Revolution? India's dairy cooperatives in a neoliberal era'. *Human Geography* 2(1), (2009), pp.17-28.

239 Verghese Kurien, 'The dairy scenario. Empower the farmer.' *Dairy India 2007*, (2007a), pp.7-8.

244 Vergese Kurien, Farmers don't commit suicides where they have cooperatives, by Ashok V. Desai. Voice of the South (23 June 2007b). Also: *Economist*, 'Cotton suicides' (20 January 2007).

241 Amrita Patel, Chairman's Speech: 35th Annual General Body (2009).

242 Patel, ibid.

243 Personal communication with Martin Doornbos (2 October 2008). Thanks to Dr. Doornbos for permission to publish his remarks.

244 Personal communication with Martin Doornbos, (13 May 2009).

245 Kenda Cunningham (2009a) 'Connecting the milk grid: smallholder dairy in India', chapter in *Millions Fed: Proven Successes in Agricultural Development.*, ed. D. J. Spielman & R. Pandya-Lorch. Washington, DC: International Food Policy

Research Institute. Also see: Cunningham (2009b) *Rural and urban linkages: Operation Flood's role in India's dairy development.* IFPRI Discussion Paper.

246 *Business Standard*, 'GCMMF to replicate Anand pattern in Africa', by Mitul Thakkar, (4 October 2004).

247 World Bank, 'Can India's Dairy Revolution be repeated in Africa?', (2008).

248 *Hindu Business Line* (2009) 'NDDB to provide support for dairy sector in Africa.' See Scholten & Basu (2009), and *Dairy Mail Africa* (December 2008) 'Eastern & Southern African Dairy Association (ESADA) News'.

249 Personal communications with Kurien assistant P.A. Joseph, (13 May 2009).

250 *Dairy India 2007*, 'Milk production and availability 1960-2015', p.34a.

BIBLIOGRAPHY

Abbot, Phillip C. & F. Desmond McCarthy (1983) 'Potential welfare Losses Due to Tied Food Aid', *Canadian Journal of Agricultural Economics*, March 31.

Acharya, S.S. & R.K. Yadav (1992) *Production and Marketing of Milk and Milk Products in India*, New Delhi: Mittal Publications.

Acheson, Dean (1969) *Present at the Creation: My Years in the State Department*, New York: Norton, reprinted 1988.

Alderman, Harold (1986) *The Impact of Cooperative Dairy Development in Karnataka*, DANIDA, IFPRI & World Bank, October, Washington, DC: World Bank.

Alderman, Harold, George Mergos & Roger Slade (1987a) *Dairy Development in India: Evolution, Debate and Evidence: A Review of the Literature*, draft, January, Washington, DC: World Bank.

Alderman, Harold, George Mergos & Roger Slade (1987b) *Cooperatives and the Commercialisation of Milk Production in India: A Literature Review*, August, Washington, DC: IFPRI.

Alvares, Claude (1983) 'The White Lie', *Illustrated Weekly of India*, (Mumbai) 30 October.

Alvares, Claude, ed. (1985) *Another Revolution Fails: An Investigation into How and Why India's Operation Flood went Off the Rails*, Ajanta Books, New Delhi.

Alvares, Claude (1986) 'Building export markets for the first world through "development": the case of Operation Flood in India', Series on Law, Social Action and Rural Poverty 1, pages 177-201 in *The International context of rural poverty in the Third World: Issues for Research and Action by Grassroots Organizations and Legal Activists.* New York Council on International Public Affairs

Anderson, Kym & Rodney Tyers (1991) *Global Effects of Liberalising Trade in Farm Products.* Trade Policy Research Centre, London: Harvester-Wheatsheaf.

Andræ, Gunilla & Björn Beckmann (1985) *The Wheat Trap: Bread and Underdevelopment in Nigeria*, Uppsala: Zed Books.

Aneja, R.P. (1994) 'Dairying in India: a success story', Asia-Pacific Association of Agricultural Research Institutions. FAO Regional Office for Asia & the Pacific. Bangkok.

Aneja, R.P. & B.P.S. Puri (1997) 'India's dairy riddle unravelled', *Dairy India 1997.*

Atkins, Peter J. (1988) 'Rejoinder: India's dairy development and Operation Flood' in *Food Policy* 13, August, pp.305-12. Also *Indian Dairyman* 40(9): pp.515-23.

Atkins, Peter J. (1989) 'Operation Flood: dairy development in India', *Geography*: pp.259-62.

Atkins, Peter J. (1989) 'The Geographical Structure of Operation Flood', text and maps prepared for the 16-21 January 1989 Anand International Seminar on Dairying.

Atkins, Peter J. & Paul Brassley (1996) 'Mad cows and Englishmen', *History Today*, 46(9), pp.14-17.

Attwood, D.W. & B.S. Baviskar (eds) (1983) *Cooperatives and Rural Development*, Delhi: OUP

Avery, William P. (ed.) (1993) *World Agriculture and the GATT*, Boulder: Lynne Rienner.

Banaji, Janairus (1996/1997) 'Globalisation and restructuring in the Indian food industry' in *Journal of Peasant Studies* 24(1&2), October/January, London: Frank Cass, pp.191-210.

Bansil, P.C. (1996) 'Employment potential in dairying' in *Dairy India 1997*: p.118.

Basu, Pratyusha (2003) *Rural Cooperatives and Agrarian Inequalities: Local Narratives of Successful Dairy Development in Gujarat and Madhya Pradesh, India*, unpublished PhD, University of Iowa.

Basu, Pratyusha (2009) *Villages, Women, and the Success of Dairy Cooperatives in India Making Place for Rural Development*, USA, Cambria.

Bastiat, Frederick (1888) *Sophisms of Protection*. New York: G.P. Putnam's Sons.

Bauer, Peter T. (1971) *Dissent on Development: Studies and Debates in Development Economics*, London: Peter Tamás.

Bauer, Peter T. (1981) *Equality, the Third World, and Economic Delusion*, Cambridge, MA: Harvard University Press.

Bauer, Peter T. (1982) Article in *Transaction/Society*, November/December: pp. 88-9.

Baviskar, S. & Piet Terhal (1990) 'Internal constraints and external dependence' in M. Doornbos & K.N.Nair (eds) (1990).

Bhagwati, Jagdish (1988) *Protectionism*, Cambridge, MA: MIT Press.

Brown, Lester R. with Erik P. Eckholm (1974) *By Bread Alone*. Overseas Development Council, New York: Praeger.

Brown, Lester R. (1990) *State of the World: World Watch Institute Annual Report on Progress towards a Sustainable Society.*, Sydney: Allen & Unwin.

Business Standard (2004) 'GCMMF to replicate Anand pattern in Africa [Kenya, Uganda, Ethiopia, Mozambique, Rwanda ask NDDB]', by Mitul

Thakkar. October 4, www.business-standard.com/india/news/ gcmmf-to-replicate-anand-pattern-in-africa/, accessed July 13, 2009.

Carr, Edward (1992) 'Grotesque: a survey of agriculture - the new Corn Laws.' *Economist,* 12 December.

Cathie, John (1982, reprinted 1986) *The Political Economy of Food Aid.* Hants, UK: Gower.

Clay, Edward J (1983) 'Is European food aid reformable?', IDS, Sussex, *Food Policy* 8(3), pp.174-77.

Clay, Edward J. & John Shaw, (eds) (1987) *Poverty, Development and Food.* Essays in honour of Hans Singer. Macmillan, London.

Clay, Edward & Charlotte Benson (1990) 'Aid for food - acquisition of commodities in developing countries for food aid in the 1980s', *Food Policy* 15(1), February, pp.27-43.

Clay, Edward & Olav Stokke, (eds) (1991) *Food Aid Reconsidered: Assessing the Impact on Third World Countries.* London: Frank Cass.

Clay, Edward J. & Olav Stokke (2000) *Food Aid and Human Security.* European Association of Development, EADI Book Series, 24. London: Frank Cass.

Cole, J.P. (1979) *Geography of World Affairs*, 5th ed., Middlesex: Pengun.

Crawshaw, Bruce (1989) 'Pre-Requisites for the use of food aid as an instrument of progress' in *International Seminar on Dairying,* NDDB (1990), pp.184-94.

Crook, Clive (1997) 'A survey of India: time to let go', *Economist,* February 22: 26 pages. Crook draws from Charles Collyns of the IMF, Robert Zagha of the World Bank, Jeffrey Sachs *et al.* of the Harvard Institute for International Development, Adit Jain of EIU in Delhi, and Jean Drèze & Amartya Sen in EIU/India.

Crotty, Raymond (1983) 'Operation Flood and the EEC', *Economic & Political Weekly*, 2 April, p.522.

Cunningham, Kenda (2009a) 'Connecting the milk grid: smallholder dairy in India', chapter in *Millions Fed: Proven Successes in Agricultural Develop-ment.,* ed. D. J. Spielman & R. Pandya-Lorch, Washington, DC: International Food Policy Research Institute.

Cunningham, Kenda (2009b) *Rural and urban linkages: Operation Flood's role in India's dairy development*, Discussion Paper, Washington, DC: IFPRI.

Dairy Mail Africa (2008) 'Eastern & Southern African Dairy Association (ESADA) News', by Peter Ngarulya, December, http://www.dairymailafrica.co.za/images/acrobat/dma_dec08/ESADA%20NEWS.pdf, accessed November 13, 2009.

Dalle, T.N. & B.K. Gauguly (May, 1997) 'An analysis of consumer expenditure pattern in Indian states with special reference to milk and milk products'. Draft, Sectoral Planning Sub Group (SPS), Anand.

David, Peter (1995) 'Back on top? A survey of American business.' *Economist*, 16 September.

DePorte, A.W. (1986) *Europe Between the Superpowers: The Enduring Balance.* New Haven, Yale.

De Soto, Hernando (1989) *The Other Path: The Invisible Revolution in the Third World*, NewYork, Harper & Row.

Doornbos,

Martin & Manoshi Mitra (1985) 'Politics of international dairy aid: international interest and the White Revolution', Institute of Social Studies (ISS), Indo-Dutch Programme on Development Alternatives (IDPAD), London, Sage.

Doornbos, Martin, Pieter van Stuijvenberg & Piet Terhal (1987) 'Operation Flood: impacts and issues' in *Food Policy* 12(4), November: pp.376-83.

Doornbos, Martin, Frank van Dorsten, Manoshi Mitra & Piet Terhal. (1990) *Dairy Aid and Development: India's Operation Flood*, (IDPAD), London, Sage.

Doornbos, Martin & K.N. Nair (eds) (1990) *Resources, Institutions and Strategies: India's Operation Flood and Indian Dairying*, London, Sage.

Doornbos, Martin & Liana Gertsch and Piet Terhal (1991) 'Dairy Aid and Development: Current Trends and Long-Term Implications of the Indian Case', in Clay & Stokke (1991) *Food Aid Reconsidered.*

Doornbos, Martin (2000) 'Revisiting the food aid debate', in Clay & Stokke, *Food Aid and Human Security*, London: Frank Cass, p.351-2.

Dorosh, Paul & Alberto Valdés (1990) 'Effects of exchange rate and trade policies on agriculture in Pakistan', Research Reports 84, International Food Policy Research Institute (IFPRI).

Drèze, Jean & Amartya Sen (eds) (1990) *The Political Economy of Hunger - Volume 1 – Entitlement and Well-Being*, Oxford: Clarendon Press.

Drèze, Jean & Amartya Sen (1998) *India: Economic Development and Social Opportunity*, USA: OUP. Cited by Clive Crook in *Economist*, 'Survey of India', 22 February 1997, p.18.

Economist Book of Vital World Statistics (1990) London: Economist Books.

Economist (1995) 'Farm follies', July 29, p.36.

Economist (1997) 'Coffee: green as in greenbacks', 1 February, p.62.

Economist (2007) 'Cotton suicides: the great unravelling', January 20.

Economist (2008) 'The stay-at-home giants', March 13.

Ehrmann, Henry W. (1983) *Politics in France*, Boston: Little Brown & Co.

Empson, John (1989) 'High prices stimulate Third World dairying', *Hoard's Dairyman*, 10 August, p.577.

Empson, John (1992) 'India Joins the Big League', *Dairy Industries International*, September, pp.21-3.

Empson, John (1993) 'India joins the dairy big leagues', *Hoard's Dairyman*, 25 September, p.692.

Engels, Friederich (1845) *The Condition of the Working Class in England.* Translated and edited by W.O. Henderson & W.H. Chaloner (1958), Stanford University Press (1990).

Erhlich, Paul L. (1968) *The Population Bomb*, New York: Ballantine Books.

Escobar, Arturo (1995) *Encountering Development: The Making and Unmaking of the Third World*, West Sussex: Princeton University Press.

Etzold, Thomas H. & John Lewis Gaddis (1978) 'NSC 68: strategic reassessment of 1950', in *Containment: Documents on American Policy and Strategy, 1945-1950.* New York: Columbia Press.

Ferguson, James (1990) *The Anti-Politics Machine: Development, Depoliticisation, and Bureaucratic Power in Lesotho*, Cambridge: Cambridge University Press.

Fine, Ben, Michael Heasman & Judith Wright (1996) *Consumption in the Age of Affluence: the World of Food*, London: Routledge.

Franco, F. & P.G. Vijaya Sherry Chand (1991) *Operation Flood and the Voluntary Sector: A Study of Tribal Cooperatives in South Gujarat*, Delhi: ISI.

Frieden, Jeffrey A. & David A. Lake (1987) *International Political Economy: Perspectives on Global Wealth and Power*, New York, St. Martin's Press, pp.385-94. See also Lester Thurrow (1985).

Gandhi, Vasant P. & Gyanendra Mani (1995) 'Are Livestock Products Rising in Importance?' in *Indian Journal of Agricultural Economics* 50, July-September.

George, Shanti (1983) 'Cooperatives and Indian Dairy Policy: More Anand than Pattern', in *Cooperatives in World Development,* D.W. Attwood & B.S. Baviskar (eds), Delhi: Oxford University Press (OUP).

George, Shanti (1985) *Operation Flood: An Appraisal of Current Indian Dairy Policy*. Delhi: OUP.

George, Shanti (1994) *A Matter of People: Cooperative Dairying in India and Zimbabwe*, Oxford: OUP.

George, Susan (1977) *How the Other Half Dies - The Real Reasons for World Hunger*, Montclair, NJ: Allenheld, Osmun & Co.

George, Susan (1984) *Ill Fares the Land*, Montclair, NJ: Allenheld, Osmun & Co.

Gilpin, Robert (1987a) *The Political Economy of International Relations.* Princeton University Press.

Gilpin, Robert (1987b) 'American policy in the post-Reagan era'. *Daedalus* 116/3, Proceedings of American Academy of Arts and Sciences, Summer, Princeton, pp. 33-7.

Greider, William (1997) *One World, Ready or Not: The Manic Logic of Global Capitalism*, New York: Simon & Schuster.

Gulati, Ashok (1989) 'Oilseeds: is higher price the answer?', *Economic & Political Weekly*, 2-9 September. Review of K.N. Ninan (1989) *Edible Oilseeds: Growth, Area Responses and Prospects in India*, New Delhi: OUP and IBH, pp.207-8.

Gulati, Ashok (1998) 'Blinkered vision 30/60', *India Today*, 13 April.

Gulati, V.P., B.M. Vyas, Shyam Laddha & Abhijit Bhattacharya (1990) *Design and Utility of a Decision Support System for Milk Cooperative Unions and Federations*, June, IRMA, Anand: pp. 11, 1-18.

Gupta, Sharad & R.S. Khanna (2009) 'India's Unique Place in World Dairying', *Yearbook of the International Dairy Industry 2009*, Germany.

Hall, Lana L. (1980) 'Evaluating effects of PL 480 wheat imports on Brazil's grain sector' in *American Journal of Agricultural Economics* 62.

Hanumiah, T.H. (1994) *Dairy Development in Mysore District: a geographical analysis*. Unpublished PhD thesis, University of Mysore.

Hanrieder, Wolfram F. & Graeme P. Auton (1980) *The Foreign Policies of West Germany, France & Britain*. Prentice-Hall, New Jersey.

Harvey, David R. (1998) 'The US Farm Act: "fair" or "foul"'. *Food Policy* 23(2), April, 111-23.

Hellinger, Stephen, Douglas Hellinger and Fred M. O'Regan (1988) *Aid for Just Development: Report on the Future of Foreign Assistance*, Development GAP, London: Lynne Rienner Publishers.

Heredia, Ruth (1999) *The Amul India Story*. New Delhi: Tata McGraw-Hill.

Hindu Business Line (2009) 'NDDB to provide support for dairy sector in Africa [including Tanzania and Uganda visited by NDDB.' Http://www.thehindubusinessline.com/2009/02/11/stories/20090211 50671600.htm, accessed March 2, 2009.

Hoard's Dairyman (1995) 'Nasty trade dispute threatens Canada's milk markets', 25 April, p.311. W.D. Hoard & Sons, Fort Atkinson, WI.

Hobsbawm, E.J. (1962) *The Age of Revolution: 1789-1848*. New York: Mentor-New American Library.

Hoekman, Bernard and Michel Kostecki (1995) *The Political Economy of the World Trading System: From GATT to WTO*, Oxford: OUP.

Hopkins, Raymond F. (1983) 'Food aid and development: evolution of regime principles and practices' in *Report of the WFP*, Netherlands Seminar on Food Aid.

Hopkins, Raymond F. (1993) 'Developing countries in the Uruguay Round: bargaining under uncertainty and inequality' in *World Agriculture and the GATT*, edited by William P. Avery.

International Herald Tribune (2007) 'Charity finds that US food aid for Africa hurts', by Celia W. Dugger, 14 August.

Irving, David (1996) *Goebbels: Mastermind of the Third Reich*. UK: St. Martins.

Jackson, Tony & T. Eade (1982) *Against the Grain: The Dilemma of Project Food Aid*, London: OUP.

Jamal, Shagufta (1994) *Women in Dairy Development*, New Delhi: Concept.

Johnson, Sue & Ben Rogaly (1997) *Microfinance*, London: Oxfam.

Jost, Stéphane (1991) 'An Introduction to the Sources of Data for Food Aid Analysis with Special Reference to SSA', in Clay & Stokke (1991).

Jul, M. (1979) 'Unexpected benefits from a dairy project', *Food Nutrition Bulletin* 1(3), May, pp.15-19.

Kamath, M.V. (1989) *Management Kurien-Style: The Story of the White Revolution.*, Delhi: Konark Publishers Pvt. Ltd.

Keeler, John T.S. (1981) 'The corporatist dynamic of agricultural modernisation in the Fifth Republic', in *The Fifth Republic at Twenty*, Wm. G. Andrews & Stanley Hoffman (eds), State University of New York Press.

Keylor, William R. (1984) *The Twentieth-Century World: An International History*, New York: OUP.

Kindleberger, Charles P. (1973) *The World in Depression, 1929-1939*. Revised ed. (1986), Los Angeles, University of California Press.

Kennedy, Paul (1987) *The Rise and Fall of the Great Powers: Economic Change and Military Conflict from 1500 to 2000*, New York: Random House.

Kennedy, Paul (1993) *Preparing for the Twenty-First Century*, New York: Random House.

Kroese, E., P. Keet & W. Kostelijk (1979) *Concept: Operation Flood: Over Produlitie van Melk*, unpublished Masters dissertation, Agricultural University of Wageningen. Cited by Shanti George (1985, p.249) warning that EEC dairy aid could be 'Trojan horses'.

Krugman, Paul (1998) 'New thinking can prevent a Great Depression', *International Herald Tribune*, 1 September, p.8.

Kurien, Verghese (1983) 'A Black Lie', in *Illustrated Weekly*, reprinted by NDDB, p.44.

Kurien, Verghese (1999) 'Milk, milk everywhere', in *The Hindu Survey of Agriculture*, pp.129-31.

Kurien, Verghese (1997) *An Unfinished Dream.* New Delhi: Tata McGraw-Hill.

Kurien, Verghese (2007a) 'The dairy scenario. Empower the farmer.' *Dairy India 2007,* 7-8. Delhi: Dairy India Yearbook.

Kurien, Verghese (2007b) 'Farmers don't commit suicides where they have cooperatives', by Ashok V. Desai. *Voice of the South*, June 23. Http://voiceofsouth.org/2007/06/22/verghese_kurien/.

Lappé, Frances Moore & Joseph Collins (1977) *Food First.* Abacus ed. (1982) London: Sphere.

Manchester, Alden C. (1983) *The Public Role in the Dairy Economy*, Boulder, CO: Westview Press.

Marchione, Thomas J. (1996) 'The right to food in the post-Cold War era' in *Food Policy*, 21(1), March, pp.83-102.

Mee, Jr., Charles L. (1984) *The Marshall Plan: The Launching of the Pax Americana*, New York: Simon & Schuster.

Meier, Gerald M., ed. (1987) *Pioneers in Development.* Second Series: Theodore W. Schultz, Gottfried Haberler, Hla Myint, Arnold C. Harberger & Celso Furtado, London: OUP, World Bank.

Mellor, John W. (1976) *The New Economics of Growth*, IFPRI, Ithaca, NY: Cornell University Press, p.48.

Mellor, John W. (1987) in Clay & Shaw (eds), *Poverty, Development and Food*, pp.187-8.

Mergos, George & Roger Slade (1987) *Dairy development and milk cooperatives: the effects of a dairy project in India*, Washington, World Bank. See NDDB/IDF (1990) *Proceedings*, pp.62-3.

Morgan, Dan (1979) *Merchants of Grain*, New York: Penguin.

Nicholson, J.S. (1904) *The History of the English Corn Laws*, New York: Charles Scribners Sons, p.122.

Ninan, K.N. (1995) 'Oilseeds development and policy: a review' in *Economic and Political Weekly*, India, 25 March, pp.A14-A27.

Patel, A.S. (1983) 'Cooperative dairying and rural development: a case study of AMUL', in Attwood, D. W. and Baviskar, B. S. (eds) (1988), *Who Shares? Cooperatives and Rural Development*, Delhi: OUP.

Platt, Geoff (2009) 'Dairy Farmers of Britain – what went wrong?' By the editor of *Dairy Innovation*, 10 June 2009. Www.foodbev.com/opinion/dairy-farmers-of-britain-what-went-wrong, accessed 5 September 2009.

Poznanski, Kazimierz Z. (1987) *Technology, Competition, & the Soviet Bloc in the World Market.* Berkeley, CA: Institute of International Studies.

Rao, V. M. (1991) *Dairy Farming: Socio-Economic Analysis of Milk Production.* New Delhi: Reliance Publishing House.

Ridley, Matt (1996) *The Origins of Virtue*, Great Britain: Viking.

Ritzer, George (2000) The *McDonaldization of Society.* Thousand Oaks, CA: Pine Forge Press.

Rostow, W.W. (1982) Book Review of P.T. Bauer, *Transaction/Society*, New York, Springer (Nov/Dec 1982).

Rostow, W.W. (1990) *Theorists of Economic Growth from David Hume to the Present*, New York: OUP.

Sachs, Jeffrey (1996) 'Growth in Africa: it can be done' *Economist*, 29 June , pp.25-7, February; from Sachs and Andrew Warner 'Sources of Slow Growth in the African Economies', Harvard Institite for Economic Development.

Said, Edward (1993) *Culture and Imperialism,* London: Knopf.

Sainath, Palagummi (1996) *Everybody Loves A Good Drought: Stories from India's Poorest Districts*, India: Penguin; UK: Headline.

Sampson, Anthony (1974) *The Sovereign State of ITT*, CN: Fawcett.

Sampson, Anthony (1981) *The Money Lenders: The People and Politics of the World Banking Crisis.* NY: Penguin Books.

Samuelson, Paul (1967) *Economics: An Introductory Analysis*, 7th ed. NY: McGraw-Hill.

Saran, Ram & Panos Konandreas (1991) 'An additional resource? A global perspective on 299 flows in relation to development assistance,' in *Food Aid Reconsidered: Assessing the Impact on Third World Countries*, Clay & Stokke (eds), London: Frank Cass.

Scholten, Bruce A. (1989) 'Milk quotas help melt Europe's Butter Mountain', *Hoard's Dairyman*, Wisconsin, USA. 10 February, pp.91, 121.

Scholten, Bruce A. (1989) 'Auch in den USA Chancen für Milchquoten' in *Württembergisches Wochenblatt für Landwirtschaft (WWL/BLW)*, 26, August, Stuttgart.

Scholten, Bruce A. (1990a) 'Europe's milk quotas…six years down the road', in *Hoard's Dairyman*, July, p.587.

Scholten, Bruce A. (1990b) 'Pesticide und die Agrar-Umwelt Politik in den USA' [Pesticides and ag policy in the USA]', *VDI-nachrichten.* Düsseldorf: Verein der Deutschen Ingenieren: 6 September, p.12.

Scholten, Bruce A. (1990c) 'Wird Bush Umwelt-Präsident', *Württembergisches Wochenblatt für Landwirtschaft WWL/BLW*, 20 October, p.8.

Scholten, Bruce A. (1991) 'Trade talks threaten European farmers, too' in *Hoard's Dairyman*, 10 October, p.762.

Scholten, Bruce A. (1993) 'Europeans may extend BST ban' *in Dairy Today, Farm Journal Publications*, June/July, Monticello, MN, Philadephia, PA.

Scholten, Bruce A. (1997) 'US dairy 2000: bye-bye this American guy', *Dairy News* (UK), 21 November, pp.6-7.

Scholten, Bruce A. (1998) 'Book review *Dairy India 1997*, *Food Policy* 23 (2), April, pp.211-12.

Scholten, Bruce A. (1998) 'Case study of a grassroots charity/NGO: Riders for Health (RfH)', in proceedings, *Africa & Globalisation: Towards the Millennium*, 24-26 April, Preston: University of Central Lancashire,.

Scholten, Bruce A. (1999) 'India's winning the White Revolution: the success of India's Operation Flood will soon make it the world's top producer of milk', *Hoard's Dairyman*, 10 April, p.287.

Scholten, Bruce A. (2007) *Consumer Risk Reflections on Organic and Local Food in Seattle, with reference to Newcastle upon Tyne*, unpublished PhD thesis, University of Durham.

Scholten, Bruce A. & Pratyusha Basu (2009) 'White Counter-Revolution? India's dairy cooperatives in a neoliberal era', *Human Geography* 2(1), pp.17-28.

Sen, Amartya (1981) *Poverty and Famines: An Essay on Entitlement and Deprivation*, Oxford: Clarendon Press.

Sereny, Gitta (1995) *Albert Speer: His Battle with the Truth*, New York: Knopf.

Shah, Dilip R. (1992) *Dairy Cooperativization: An Instrument of Social Change*, New Delhi: Rawat Publications.

Sharma, Miriam with Urmila Vanjani (1993) 'When More Means Less: Assessing the impact of dairy 'development' on the lives and health of women in rural Rajasthan (India)', *Social Science & Medicine* 37(11), Pergamon Press, pp.1377-89.

Shaw, John & Bruce Crawshaw (1989) 'Food for the urban poor', *GeoJournal*, November, London: Kluwer.

Shaw, John and Edward Clay (1993) *World Food Aid: Experiences of Recipients & Donors*, London: Heinemann.

Shaw, John & Edward Clay (1993) *World Food Aid*, London: Heinemann.

Shaw, John, Bruce Crawshaw & F. Fortier (1994) 'Using project food aid to help alleviate urban poverty - experience and issues', *GeoJournal* 34(3), London: Kluwer.

Shiva, Vandana (2004) 'The suicide economy of corporate globalisation', Countercurrents.org, Kumaranalloor PO, Kerala, India 686 016, www.countercurrents.org/glo-shiva050404.htm, accessed 1 May 2008.

Singer, Hans, John Wood & Tony Jennings (1987) *Food Aid: The Challenge and the Opportunity*, Oxford: OUP.

Singer, Hans W. (1991) *Food Aid and Structural Adjustment in Sub-Saharan Africa*, Oxford, OUP.

Singer, Peter (1975) *Animal Liberation: A New Ethics for Our Treatment of Animals*. UK: Avon.

Smith, Adam (1776) *The Wealth of Nations*. New York: Modern Library, 1937 ed. See Book III, Chapter IV on opposition to monopolies, page 388.

Stiglitz, Joseph (2002) *Globalisation & its Discontents*, London: Penguin.

Singh, Katar (August, 1992) *Agricultural Policy in India: Need for a Fresh Look*. IRMA Working Paper 36, pp.10-11.

Soligo, Ronald & Joseph Stern (1965) 'Tariff protection, import substitution and investment efficiency', *Pakistan Development Review*, summer.

Somjee, Geeta, and A.S. Somjee (1989) *Reaching Out to the Poor: the Unfinished Rural Revolution*, London: Macmillan.

Stuart, K. & F.C. Runge (1997) 'Agricultural policy reform in the United States: an unfinshed agenda', *Australian Journal of Agricultural and Resource Economics* (41)4, pp.117-36.

Tarrant, John (1985) 'Review of international food trade' *Progress In Human Geography* 9, pp.235-54.

Thomson, Anne M. (1985) 'Egypt: Food security and food aid', *Food Policy* 8(3) August, pp.178-86.

Thurrow, Lester (1985) 'America, Europe and Japan: a time to dismantle the world economy', *Economist*, pp.21-6. Reprinted in Frieden & Lake (1987).

Todaro, Michael P. (1985) *Economic Development in the Third World*, 3rd ed., New York: Longman.

Truman, Harry (1947) 'The Policy of Containment', *Public Papers of the Presidents of the U.S.*

Ufkes, Frances M. (1993) 'Trade liberalisation, agro-food politics and the globalisation of agriculture', *Political Geography* 12(3), May, pp. 215-31.

Wheat, Sue (1997) 'Banking on a better future', *Guardian*, 29 January.

Wolf, Eric (1982) *Europe and the People without History*. USA: University of California Press.

Young, Hugo (1989) *One of Us: A Biography of Margaret Thatcher*. London: Macmillan.

Other Sources

Agrostat•PC (1990) and (1994) digitised information series statistics (30+ megabytes), Food and Agriculture Organisation (FAO) of the United Nations (UN). Rome, Italy. Data bank for this book.

BBC (1983) *Wheels of Fire*: 30 minute film on OF directed by Julian Steinhouse, produced by Howard Smith. BBC Production in association with NordDeutscher Rundfunk & Danmarks Radio.

Darigold, Inc. (1993-1994) Farmers' cooperative in Washington, California, Oregon and Idaho, USA. Documents and personal communications from Douglas C. Marshall (corporate counsel) and Roger D. Miller (sales manager) based in Seattle, Washington.

Webster's Ninth New Collegiate Dictionary (1985) Springfield, Massachusetts, USA, Merriam-Webster Inc.

European Communities, Office of Official Publications

(1987) *The Effects of Milk Quotas on Community Agriculture*, Volume 1, Main Report, February, 139 pages, by Prof. Dr. Eric Tollens with Frans Gossens, Bart Minten & Jo Swinnen, Department of Agricultural Economics, University of Leuven, Belgium; for Eurostat/DG VI.

(1987-88) *European Parliament Session Documents (A2-0247/87 on 9 Dec).* Rapporteur: Wilfried Telkämper. 'Report...on behalf of the Committee on Development and EC-India cooperation particularly as regards Operation Flood'.

(1988) *Debates of the European Parliament* No 2-360/325, 22 January, pp.325, 320-25. Debate on Mr. Telkämper's 12 December 1987 report on 'EEC-India cooperation with particular reference to Operation'Flood" (Doc. A 2-247/87).

(1988) 'Court of Auditors of the European Communities, Special Report No.6/87 on Food Aid Supplied to India between 1978-1985 (Operation Flood II)', *Official Journal of the European Communities*, No.C31, February.

(1988-89) *Potential Farm Level and Dairy Sector Impact of the Use of Bovine Somatotropin (BST) in the FRG*: 28 pages, by Dr. Reiner Doluschitz, Prof. Dr. Jürgen Zeddies & Dipl.-Ing. agr. Ursula Baumbach, University of Hohenheim, Stuttgart. Pre-publication copy for the Commission.

(1992) *The Single Market in Action*, Luxembourg.

(1992) *From Single Market to European Union*, Luxembourg.

Government of Australia

(mid-1990s) *Food Aid Works* and *Food Aid.* Australian International Development Assistance Bureau (AIDAB). Published in Canberra.

Government of India, Amul, IDC, NDDB, OF & other Publications

(1984) *Report of the Evaluation Committee on OF-II* (Jha Committee Report to GOI, Ministry of Agriculture) by L.K. Jha, S.K. Rau, I.Z. Bhatty, N.N. Dastur, P. Bhattacharya & A.R. Shirali.

(1985) *Operation Flood Phase III: A Proposal*, NDDB, Anand.

(1987) *Indian Dairy Corporation 16th Report.* The Report of the committee deals with the action taken by Government on the recommendations contained in the the 11th report (8th Lok Saabha) of the Committee on Public Undertakings on IDC, which was presented to Lok Sabha on 30 April 1986.

(March, 1987~) *From a Drop to a Flood, 50-page NDDB handout, Anand.*

(1988) *Operation Flood: A Progress Report,* NDDB 14 pages, March.

(1990) *Proceedings: International Seminar on Dairying as an Instrument for Progress: the Indian Experience.* NDDB, Anand, India in association with International Dairy Federation (IDF), Brussels. Contributors include WFP policy advisor Bruce Crawshaw, pp.184-94.

(1997) *Dairy India 1997*, Editor P.R. Gupta. Sub-editor Sharad Gupta. Fifth edition (Established 1983). A-25 Priyadarshini Vihar, Delhi 110092 India. Tel: (91-11) 224 3039. Websites: www.indiaDairy.com and www.DairyIndia.com

(ca. 1998) *NDDB - Heralding Changes*; 15-page handout with sections on 'OF & Anand Pattern', 'Dr. Kurien - A Profile'; and 'Role of Cooperatives in Economic Development'.
(ca. 1998) *Dairy Farming in India, 4-page NDDB visitor handout at Anand.*
(2001) Central Statistical Organization (CSO), *National Accounts Statistics, 2000.* Delhi: Dept. of Statistics, Ministry of Planning, GoI.
(ca. 2005) 'Achievements of the dairy cooperatives during the last 100 years', Amul/GCMMF, www.amul.com/achievementsdairycoop.html.
(2007) *Economist* 2007; see also: Shiva (2004) and Amul (2008).
(2007) AMUL/GCMMF Chairman's speech [Dr. Amrita Patel], 33rd Annual General Body Meeting 14 June 2007.
(2009) Amul/GCMMF Chairman's Speech [Dr. Amrita Patel], 35th Annual General Body Meeting held 5 June 2009, www.amul.com/chairmanspeech.html.

Government of the United Kingdom

Ministry of Agriculture, Fisheries & Food (MAFF): press releases 1992-97, e.g. (1997) 'Baldry outlines need for CAP Reform', 5/97, pp.1-6, 2.

Government of the United States of America

(1954) 'Agricultural Trade Development and Assistance Act of 1954', official title of PL 480.
(1990) 'Title XV of the 1990 Food, Agriculture, Conversion and Trade Act' written by Mark Smith, Karen Ackerman and Nydia Suarez.
(2005) 'Cooperatives in the dairy industry'. United States Department of Agriculture (USDA). Cooperative, Report 1, Section 16.

International Fund for Agricultural Development

(1992) *IFAD: The State of Rural Poverty: An Inquiry into Its Causes and Consequences*, by Idriss Jazairy, Mohiuddin Alamgir & Theresa Panuccio, funded by Government of Finland, London: IT Pub.

National Farmers Union of Great Britain (NFU)

Press releases & reports:
(1994) *NFU Briefing: GATT Settlement in Agriculture*: pp 9-10 of 34. Contact: M. Haworth (Part I); Econ. Dept. (Part II). NFU/Int'l 1/94, 5 January.
(1996) *Reuters* dispatch (via NFU) 'Fischler says no backing down on meat hormone' by Peter Blackburn, 23 January. Plus press releases.

World Bank

(1993) *World Development Report: Investing in Health*, Oxford: Oxford University Press (OUP).

(1996) *World Development Report: From Plan to Market*, New York: OUP.

(1998) Wilfred Candler & Nalini Kumar (June, 1998) *India: The Dairy Revolution: The Impact of Dairy Development in India and the World Bank's Contribution.* A World Bank Operations Evaluation Study (OED). International Bank for Reconstruction & Development IBRD/WB, Washington, DC.

(2007) Deepa Narayan & Elena Glinskaya, *Ending Poverty in South Asia - Ideas That Work*, published by World Bank. The first of 12 success stories is on 'India's Milk Revolution' by Dr. Verghese Kurien.

(2008) 'Can India's dairy revolution be repeated in Africa?: new 'South-South' fund helps countries share real-life development solutions'. News & Broadcast press release, 11 October 2008: http://web.worldbank.org/WBSITE/EXTERNAL/NEWS/0,,content MDK:21936907~pagePK:34370~piPK:34424~theSitePK:4607,00.html, accessed 11 October 2008.

United Nations (UN); Food and Agricultural Organization (FAO), International Food Policy Research Institute (IFPRI), Organisation for Economic Co-operation and Development (OECD), World Food Programme (WFP).

(1951) Measures for the Economic Development of Underdeveloped Countries. UN Department of Social & Economic Affairs.

(1976) World Food Programme Evaluation Mission Report on Operation Flood, *The Second, Detailed Report of.... India-618*, New Delhi: India Dairy Corporation.

(1981) Terminal Evaluation Report on Project India 618 - 'Milk Marketing and Dairy Development', UN/FAO/WFP, September.

(1988) WFP 25th Session, Rome, 'Food aid & dairy development', 21 April, pp.1-16.

(1980s-1990s) *World Food Programme in India: A Flood of Changes.* Text and photos by Jeanette Van Acker. Additional photos by Andrew Moyse. This appears to be quintessential OF publicity.

(1993) *Evaluation of the World Food Programme: Main Report* by the Canadian International Development Agency (IDA), and foreign ministries of The Netherlands and Norway, Chr. Michelson Institute, December.

(1992-2007) *World Food Programme: Annual Review/Report* ,WFP, Rome, Italy. Received yearly. Also *The Food Aid Monitor* (WFP) incorporates International Food Aid Information System (INTERFAIS) data. Rome.

(1997) *Reaching the Hungry.* Emphasis on aid to North Korea. WFP Exec. Dir. Catherine Bertini notes the message at November 1996 World Food Summit Rome was, 'Growing more food is important, but it is just as important to ensure that people who need the food have access to it.'

(2000) *Report of the FAO E-mail Conference on Small-scale Milk Collection and Processing in Developing Countries*: 144pp. Including comments by Nancy Abeiderrahmane, pp.105-6, 110-11, 142; P.R. Gupta pp.76, 102-3, 144; Bruce Scholten, 'Comment on: 'Clean milk poster paper in So. Africa' by Prinsloo': p.77; and John Thornes: p.144.

(2002) IFPRI-FAO 'Impact of changing market forces and policies on structural change in the livestock industries of selected fast-growing developing countries, Final Research Report of Phase I - Project on Livestock Industrialization, Trade and Social-Health-Environment Impacts in Developing Countries. Annex I: Critical issues for poor people in the Indian dairy sector on the threshold of a new era'. The authors are Vijay Paul Sharma, Raj Vir Singh, Steve Staal & Christopher L. Delgado in Phase I, IFPRI-FAO project 'Livestock Industrialization, Trade and Social-Health-Environment Impacts in Developing Countries', funded by (DFID), UK, via Livestock, Environment and Development (LEAD) initiative at FAO. (June 2002). Contact IFPRI, Washington D.C. Email: C.Delgado@cgiar.org

(2003) IFPRI-FAO 'Policy, technical, and environmental determinants and implications of the scaling-up of livestock production in four fast-growing developing countries: a synthesis. Final Research Report of Phase II', by Christopher Delgado (IFPRI), Clare Narrod (FAO), Marites Tiongco (IFPRI), 24 July 2003. Project on Livestock Industrialization, Trade and Social-Health-Environment Impacts in Developing Countries. See 2.2.3 Structure of the Milk-Processing Sector: www.fao.org/wairdocs/LEAD/X6170E/x6170e00.HTM

(2005) *OECD-FAO Agricultural Outlook 2005-2014*, by their Secretariats. Http://faostat.fao.org/site/339/default.aspx, accessed November 14, 2009.

(2006) 'The statistics division history', by Edward Gillin. December 2006, Rome: www.fao.org/economic/ess/the-statistics-division-history/en/.

(2007) 'Country programmes', WFP Ex. Board, 2nd Reg. Session, Rome, 22–26 October. PDF: www.wfp.org/operations/current_operations/project_ docs/105730.pdf and www.wfp.org/eb.

(2007) FAOSTAT Food & Agricultural commodities production/2007/sort by value [Top Production]: http://faostat.fao.org/site/339/default.aspx, accessed November 14, 2009.

(2009) FAO report 'More people than ever are victims of hunger'. See also 19 June 2009 press release: '1.02 billion people hungry: one sixth of humanity undernourished, more than ever before': www.fao.org/file admin/user_upload/newsroom/docs/Press%20release%20june-en.pdf.

INDEX